The First Century

Daily Racing Form *Chronicles 100 years of Thoroughbred Racing*

by Joe Hirsch

Published by
Daily Racing Form Press
315 Hudson Street
New York, NY 10013

ISBN: 0-9648493-1-3
Library of Congress Catalog Card Number: 96-083143

Cover and text design by LCI Design
Printed in the United States of America

DRF
PRESS
A Division of Daily Racing Form, Inc.

Table Of Contents

CHAPTER I: 1894 TO 1920   Iron Horses and Iron Men   Page 1

Background of Frank Brunell and birth of *Daily Racing Form*. Development of The Jockey Club. Opening of Belmont Park. Cessation of racing in New York. Colin, Sysonby, Regret, Man o' War and Exterminator are famous horses. August Belmont II and James Keene rule the turf. Sam Hildreth and James Rowe Sr. are leading trainers. Carroll Shilling and Walter Miller, brilliant jockeys, quickly fade from view.

CHAPTER II: 1921 TO 1940   An Era of Growth   Page 33

Expansion of *Daily Racing Form* into national racing paper and purchase by Annenberg family. New tracks open include Santa Anita, Arlington, Hialeah, Hollywood Park and Del Mar. Pari-mutuel racing comes to New York. Black Gold, Zev, Gallant Fox and War Admiral are top horses. Col. E.R. Bradley and William Woodward Sr. are major personalities. Ben Jones, Max Hirsch, Jim Fitzsimmons and Hirsch Jacobs are outstanding trainers. Earl Sande, Eddie Arcaro, Don Meade and George Woolf are leading jockeys.

CHAPTER III: 1941 TO 1965   New Concepts   Page 99

J. Samuel Perlman directs modern *DRF*. Return of racing to New Jersey and formation of NYRA. Fink Case casts long shadow. John W. Hanes and Bull Hancock are leading personalities. Count Fleet, Whirlaway, Citation, Native Dancer and Kelso race to incredible triumphs. Woody Stephens, Charlie Whittingham, the Jones Boys and Horatio Luro are leading trainers. Bill Shoemaker and Bill Hartack are dominant riders.

CHAPTER IV: 1966 TO 1994   Complex Times   Page 159

Daily Racing Form sold to Ruppert Murdoch, then to K-III Communications. *DRF* undertakes massive programs of modernization, standardization and relocation. Introduction of the Breeders' Cup and opening of OTB in New York are major developments. The Phipps family, John Gaines and Ted Bassett are dominant personalities. Secretariat, Seattle Slew, Affirmed and Spectacular Bid are leading horses. H. Allen Jerkens and Wayne Lukas are prominent trainers. Angel Cordero Jr., Laffit Pincay Jr. and Chris McCarron are successful jockeys of the era.

Preface

This book was designed to celebrate the centennial of *Daily Racing Form*, first published on November 17, 1894. To underline the history of this newspaper and the developments that were key to its progress, the 100-year period between 1894 and 1994 was arbitrarily divided into four eras, each covering approximately 25 years.

As a background to the growth of *Daily Racing Form*, and as an attempt to capture the flavor of each particular era, a brief history of racing is part of each chapter. The leading horses, trainers and jockeys are sketched in photos, text and by the incomparable pen of Pierre Bellocq (Peb). Racing's dominant personalities and most significant developments are also part of the story.

There is no sport that can compare with thoroughbred racing for grandeur and sweep and tradition, and there are no people like racing people who can compare for sportsmanship, dedication and generosity of spirit. *Daily Racing Form* has been proud to play a small role for the past century as keeper of the legend and looks forward with anticipation to continued service to racing over the next hundred years.

Joe Hirsch
New York, 1996

Acknowledgements

This book was published, despite the author's sloth, through the good offices of George Bernet, of Daily Racing Form Press, who not only edited the manuscript but made a major contribution to its layout and the selection of the many photos that enhance its pages.

The author also wishes to express his gratitude to Pierre Bellocq (Peb), art director of *Daily Racing Form*, for his superb caricatures that grace the cover of the book. Our thanks, too, to award-winning photographer Michael Marten; Katherine Wilkins, *DRF*'s vice president of marketing; and Mandy Minger, *DRF*'s promotion manager, for their participation in the production of "The First Century."

Special thanks to Cathy Schenck and Doris Waren and the staff of the Keeneland Library for their generous support of research requests. In this connection, we gratefully acknowledge the following principal sources:

"A History of Thoroughbred Racing in America," by William H.P. Robertson, published by Prentice-Hall.

"The Great Ones," by Kent Hollingsworth, published by The Blood-Horse.

"Giants of the Turf," by Dan Bomar, published by The Blood-Horse.

"Big Red of Meadow Stable," by William Nack, published by Arthur Fields, Inc.

"The American Racing Manual," published by *Daily Racing Form*.

Joe Hirsch

Foreword

I t is particularly appropriate for this chronology to be authored by Joe Hirsch, racing's guardian conscience and loyal supporter, recipient of every major racing award, honored both nationally and internationally, and guiding light and benefactor of both the neophyte and those in need.

Joe has provided a comprehensive and chronological history of the past century of the thoroughbred industry, documenting in fascinating detail the critical events that impacted racing's past, the dominant personalities which influenced it, and the champion horses which fostered it.

Published by *Daily Racing Form* in commemoration of its 100 years of dedicated service as the industry's loyal and sole archivist of vital records, the book brings to life the dramatic peaks and the disillusioning valleys of the thoroughbred world of yesteryear. Divided into four historic segments, each covering nearly a quarter of a century, the book blends tradition with historical facts and personalities with accomplishments.

The entire spectrum of the racing and breeding industry will be eternally indebted to Joe Hirsch and *Daily Racing Form*, for their untiring and herculean efforts in producing such a treatise of historic proportions, which will serve as not only a reference to the past, but as a pathway to the future.

James E. Bassett III
Keeneland, 1996

Iron Horses and Iron Men

1894 to 1920

They were so different in every respect but two: They both set high standards of excellence for their work and both developed a keen interest in racing. The meeting of Frank Brunell and John Wolfe more than a century ago was happenstance. But almost everything that followed pertinent to the founding and publication of *Daily Racing Form* was the result of careful planning.

Brunell was 41 when *Daily Racing Form* made its debut in Chicago on November 17, 1894. He was born in London, England, came to the United States with his family as a boy and grew up in Cleveland. He landed a job as a copy boy with the *Plain Dealer*, learned the newspaper business from the ground up and made progress. His interest and ability were recognized, and he was appointed sports editor.

He moved to Chicago, went to work at first for the *Inter-Ocean* and later connected

The front page of Daily Racing Form's first edition, November 17, 1894.

with the *Tribune*. Advancement came rapidly, and he was named sports editor. Under his direction, the sports section of the *Tribune* flourished. Racing was one of the principal sports of the era, and Chicago was one of its centers.

Washington Park had opened in 1884 with Gen. Phil Sheridan as president. It was a magnificent plant the equal of the best in the U.S., with a mile and an eighth track. Its major race, the American Derby, had a value twice that of the Kentucky Derby, which was originated at Churchill Downs in 1875. When the World's Fair opened in Chicago in 1893, the American Derby was the richest race in the country.

Hawthorne opened in 1891 and was a great success. Track president Ed Corrigan was a Canadian who began his career driving trotters, then switched to racing thoroughbreds. His Modesty won the Kentucky Oaks

1

in 1884 and came to Chicago to win the American Derby, beating colts. Corrigan subsequently leased the facilities of the West Side Driving Park as a racetrack. He did well there, but decided to build his own plant in the Chicago suburb of Cicero. The *Chicago Tribune*, which devoted extensive coverage to the opening on May 20, estimated the size of the crowd at 6,000.

Garfield Park, on the south side of Chicago, was also in operation, as was the smaller Harlem track, while still another racecourse in Roby, Indiana, just across the state line, attracted many Chicagoans. All this activity stirred Brunell's imagination. He thought of a small newspaper, entirely devoted to racing, with stories and statistics of value to the reader. He was aware that previous attempts along similar lines had failed in New York, but he felt he might succeed.

One of his racing writers at the *Tribune* was Dan Murray. Over lunch one day at Hawthorne, Brunell posed the idea of a statistical history of a horserace. He and Murray batted ideas back and forth without reaching firm conclusions, but central to their conversation was the thought of fixed points of call as the horses circled the track. The birth of the racing chart was not far off.

In 1893, Brunell met another well-known turf journalist of the era, John Hervey, who often wrote under the name "Salvator." They became great friends, and Brunell confided to Hervey his plans for a racing newspaper. The ideas seemed to firm up as he related them to an enthusiastic Hervey, and shortly thereafter, early in 1894, Brunell resigned from the *Tribune* and began to gather and catalog his resources.

John Hervey, a prominent 19th century racing journalist who wrote under the name of Salvator, was instrumental in the birth of Daily Racing Form.

His greatest resource, it became evident with the passing of time, was a 23-year-old Ohioan who had developed an interest in and affinity for horses and racing while in his teens. John Wolfe, a native of Cincinnati, hoped to become a jockey and went to work as an exercise rider with the stable of Texan James Brown. Before he could serve out his apprenticeship, however, increasing weight forced a change of plans.

He returned to Cincinnati and began an apprenticeship as a printer. He enjoyed the work, and his aptitude moved him along. In 1890, he came to Chicago, secured work as a printer and followed the racing scene as a fan. Several years later, in 1894, as Brunell was planning the debut of *Daily Racing Form*, Wolfe heard about the proposed venture. He went to see Brunell with some ideas of his own. Brunell immediately offered him a job and he accepted.

Brunell said he would spend the next couple of months raising funds for the project. He asked Wolfe to make typographical plans and to secure what little mechanical equipment was needed. They could neither afford nor wanted expensive printing presses of their own. Rather they would "job" the newspaper at a commercial printing plant, and it was up to Wolfe to find the right printer at the right price.

Brunell and his wife, who is reported to have had excellent business judgment, leased a small office at 126 South Dearborn Street for *Daily Racing Form*'s first headquarters. Hervey, who often visited the Brunells both before and after publication, recalls the rickety flight of stairs to the office on the second floor. A small room, filled with second-hand office furniture, served as the business depart-

Dearborn Street, Chicago, as it looked when Daily Racing Form's *first office was established by Frank Brunell in 1894.*

ment, with the Brunells presiding from behind roll-top desks. The back room was partitioned hastily, one section given over to a large stone on which chases of type were locked up. The other section was devoted to the compilation of charts and the preparation of advertisements.

Wolfe located a good commercial printer, Bentley and Murray, located on Randolph Street, just north of the *Daily Racing Form* office on Dearborn. The chases were made up at *DRF* and then carried by hand through the streets to Bentley and Murray for printing. Then the copies were carried back to *DRF* for orderly distribution.

The first edition of *Daily Racing Form* was datelined November 17, 1894, a Saturday. On Friday evening, Brunell and Wolfe finished locking the chases about 10:30, preparatory to transporting the four pages to Bentley and Murray. The paper contained several news stories, a bit of racing gossip, and the first charts of a horse race ever published. The meeting in Roby, Indiana, opened that Friday, and the charts in *DRF* recounted the competitive history of that inaugural. Also included were charts from the Old Dominion track in Washington D.C., charts from tracks in New Orleans and Madison, Wisconsin, and entries from East St. Louis, New Orleans, Old Dominion and Roby.

A prominent artist of the day, Robert Livingston Dickey, designed *Daily Racing Form*'s distinctive titleplate, which for the past century has identified America's racing newspaper and is one of the most recognized logos in the country. Dickey also sketched prominent horses and racing personalities for inclusion in the paper during the early years of *DRF*. The price of the paper was 5 cents, at a time most daily papers sold for a penny. Before they walked over to the presses on Randolph Street, Wolfe stood one of the steel chases on end and Brunell cracked a bottle of champagne over it, as if at a ship's launching.

In a statement on Page 2 of the inaugural issue, Brunell set forth the principles that would guide the paper. "This newspaper will be published daily as long as it is wanted. *Daily Racing Form* is an experiment, the result of long observation and thought. It will be clean, up to the times, and as careful as possible. The quality will be increased in every way."

To place the era in perspective, John Hervey, in a column of memories for *Daily Racing Form*'s 50th anniversary edition in 1944, used Goodwin's Guide for 1894 as a statistical milestone. He found that Goodwin's listed some 8,000 races at recognized meetings, only 15 of which were worth as much as $10,000 to the winner. The Futurity was the richest event, with a value of $48,710. The Realization was worth $33,400 and the Kentucky Derby had a value to the winner of $4,020. The number of starters for the year was approximately 6,000, of which only two earned $50,000 or more. Dobbins, a 3-year-old, topped the list with $54,545.

The leading sire of the 1894 season was Sir Modred, whose get won $134,318. Purse distribution was less than $4 million.

By contrast, in 1992, approximately 70,000 races were run in the U.S. Sixteen races carried a value of $1 million or more, with the $3 million Breeders' Cup Classic the world's richest race. There were some 70,000 starters, with A.P. Indy, Horse of the Year, topping the earnings list with $2,622,560. Danzig led the stallions, his get earning $5,873,773. Purse distribution totaled more than $7 million in the U.S.

The young *Daily Racing Form* ran into many difficulties. Wolfe recalls a bitter winter night in that first year of operation with the heavy chases being carried back and forth between the *DRF* office and the printing plant on a wheeled cart. The carrier tipped over on a sidewalk and the type was "pied." One of the several young men accompanying the chases rushed to the office to report the accident.

Wolfe found a couple of pails and a coal shovel. He went to the scene of the accident, scooped up the scrambled type, and returned to the office for an all-night job of resetting. The task was completed at 7 a.m., and while delivery of the paper was delayed that day, the incident helped establish a tradition. No matter the problem, *Daily Racing Form* always has been available to the public. In later years, when distribution was nationwide to every recognized racetrack no matter the size, no one in the United States could say he ever attended the races in his lifetime without the availability of *DRF*.

Daily Racing Form continued to expand its circulation during the 1895 season, but business flagged that winter and Brunell suspended publication for four months. The paper resumed on March 26, 1896, and later that season, *Daily Racing Form* issued its first monthly chart book containing charts of all races run that month in the U.S.

It was in 1896 as well that Brunell, encouraged by public response to his racing paper, moved it from cramped quarters on Dearborn Street to 124 Fifth Avenue (later Wells Street) where *DRF* occupied an entire building, complete with printing presses. The irregular press runs that characterized the early days of the paper became a thing of the past.

As circulation increased and cash flow improved, Brunell, faithful to his promise in the first issue, saw to the upgrading of quality. Clinton Riley, a fine newspaperman and racing official, was added to the staff. Riley eventually became editor of *Daily Racing Form*, added many new features, and continued working until his death in 1935 at the age of 86.

Thomas Cromwell, a well-known Kentucky racing journalist and bloodstock agent, also joined the editorial staff and contributed to the development of the paper. Martin Nathenson, one of the nation's outstanding racing officials and journalists, was a contributing editor for many years. A reporter, Richard Brooks, joined *DRF* in 1904, and in 1914 became managing editor. He held that post until the death of Riley in 1935, was appointed to succeed Riley and served as editor until his own passing in 1942.

One year following the introduction of the first *Daily Racing Form* monthly chart book, Brunell brought out another new publication. The 1897 inaugural edition of the "American Sporting Manual" carried all available records for the previous season on boxing, billiards and racing, three of the major wagering sports of the era. In 1906, a decision was made to devote the record book exclusively to racing and to support the new approach, and it was renamed "The American Racing Manual."

The edition of ARM covering the 1906 season, issued early in 1907, consisted of 171 pages detailing the records of 188 horses, 230 owners, 140 trainers and 166 jockeys. The 1993 ARM covering the racing of 1992 has 1,115 pages plus a 700-page compendium, generated by computer, and includes a list of the winners of major stakes events plus the individual records of more than 75,000 horses, some 2,700 owners, more than 1,300 trainers and 3,000 jockeys.

The next major milestone for *DRF* was 1905, when Brunell decided to compile past performances and publish them along with the news and charts. As usual, Brunell studied the subject matter carefully before implementation. He came to the conclusion that a horse's past record was a good indication of how he would run in his next race, and he used the procedure in preparing charts as the basis of the past performances.

This was a mammoth undertaking, particularly for a newspaper in which all type was still being set by hand. A modernization program began with the purchase of five linotype machines, and when these units were joined by other new equipment, it became apparent that the Wells Street building was no longer adequate. The operation was moved to 441 Plymouth Court and, in short order, additional linotype machines were acquired and a large rotary press was installed, with appropriate stereotype equipment.

With circulation increasing, Brunell moved to improve distribution. He purchased the first of several horse-drawn delivery wagons to get *Daily Racing Form* to newsstands and tobacco shops throughout the Chicago area.

In many ways, *Daily Racing Form* blended easily with the fabric of American life in those can-do days at the turn of the century, just a handful of years after Teddy Roosevelt led his Rough Riders in the charge up San Juan Hill. As the Great White Fleet toured the major ports of the world in an extension of the Big Stick policy, *Daily Racing Form*, having battled for survival and won, expanded steadily throughout the Midwest and in the direction of New York.

It was a time of iron men and iron horses, and important events were taking place, as reported in *Daily Racing Form*, which would shape racing history in America for many years to come.

Perhaps the major development of the era was the founding in New York, in 1894, of The Jockey Club. In the formative days of racing in the U.S., tracks operated without supervision of any kind, setting their own racing dates, setting their own rules, setting their own policies. Tracks occasionally exchanged some information about repeated rules violators, but there was no formal list of offenders. If you were suspended at one track, you could move to another track and conduct your business unimpeded.

In 1866, the American Turf Congress was formed at a meeting in Cincinnati. In an effort to bring some order to a chaotic scene, executives of tracks in Louisville, Cincinnati, Nashville and Lexington gathered for an exchange of views. They agreed to work in concert on matters of common concern through a system of committees.

On February 8, 1894, The Jockey Club was incorporated. The group consisted of 50 members with management provided by seven stewards.

Another major development in American racing during the first

A well-dressed throng enjoyed summer racing at the new Belmont Park in 1905.

Sysonby won the Metropolitan Handicap, opening-day feature at Belmont.

part of the 20th century was the construction and opening of Belmont Park. The largest racetrack in the United States, it has been a national leader from the outset in influence among its peers and in the presentation of outstanding sport.

Jerome Park in Westchester County, north of New York City, named for founder Leonard Jerome, whose daughter Jenny was the mother of Sir Winston Churchill, was for many years America's premier track. It was replaced in that position in 1889 with the opening of opulent Morris Park, where every modern facility was available to members and patrons, including luxurious dining rooms, ballrooms for dancing and comfortable sleeping quarters to accommodate those who wanted to stay overnight to watch their horse train early the next morning. All the major stables were based at Morris Park.

Unfortunately, the track didn't last that long. By 1895, signs of strain were evident. One of the causes was a series of unfavorable legislative acts from Albany, the state capital, restricting the administration of the track. August Belmont 2d and James R. Keene, two of the most prominent men in racing, decided to act. They first formed a group called the Westchester Racing Association, then leased the facilities of Morris Park and conducted several race meetings there. The meetings were successful, but racing's future in Westchester seemed questionable. A decision was made to build a new track elsewhere.

In 1904, the Westchester Racing Association purchased 650 acres on both sides of the county line between Queens County and Nassau County. The new track was to be the biggest in America and named for the original August Belmont. When it opened on May 4, 1905, with a crowd reported at 40,000, August Belmont 2d was president and the principal directors included James R. Keene, Harry Payne Whitney, James P. Morgan and Thomas Hitchcock.

The Belmont racing strip measured a mile and a half in circumference and racing was conducted "The Belmont Way," or clockwise. Every other track in the country raced counter-clockwise, but the

Belmont directors wanted a touch to distinguish this grand new track. The 650-foot grandstand was spacious and comfortable and was flanked by a clubhouse with dining rooms, board rooms, a separate Turf and Field Club, and many other gracious amenities.

Highlight of the opening-day program was the Metropolitan Handicap in which the brilliant Sysonby was making his 3-year-old debut. Sysonby, one of the finest horses in American racing history, was conceding 10 pounds of actual weight and many more pounds on the scale of weights to the 4-year-old Race King. Sysonby got up in the final strides to earn a dead-heat, as the crowd roared.

Unfortunately, Belmont Park opened at a time when reform of all kinds was sweeping the country, a response to excesses,including racing. For example, that year Hawthorne, in Chicago, raced 260 days. The track at Gloucester, N.J., ran 176 days. The St. Louis track ran 364 days, and then, after a one-day break, ran another 108 days. They were cooking the goose that laid the golden egg.

Politicians, responding to anti-gambling sentiment, moved against racing. The third Monmouth Park, larger and more elaborate than its predecessors, opened in 1892 on the Jersey shore, raced again in 1893, and then was forced to close. Racing in New Jersey didn't resume until 1942. An anti-racing bill was placed before the New York legislature in 1908, and suddenly betting became illegal inthe state.Loopholes in the law permitted racing to continue on an oral wagering basis for two more years, but new legislation passed

Chicago's Hawthorne Park was a popular gathering place in 1903.

in 1910, and racing in New York was finished. Maryland saw the situation as an opportunity. Laurel was opened in 1911; Havre de Grace made its debut in 1912, and Bowie came on line in 1914. Kentucky also had racing during this period, and so did Canada.

Many of the leading American owners sent their stables to England and France, and the top jockeys went over to ride. The price of horses tumbled sharply in the U.S. Ed Corrigan, the controversial owner of Hawthorne, found himself bankrupt and was forced to sell the track to Thomas Carey and his family for $2,000 in cash. Corrigan also sold his once-powerful stable for a fraction of its value.

After an absence of three years, racing returned to New York on May 30, 1913. It had not yet been legalized, but the public wanted racing and officials generally looked the other way. When Belmont Park opened, a crowd of 35,000 was on hand, and track executives estimated another 5,000 people were turned away.

Feature of opening day was the Metropolitan Handicap, and the winner was Whisk Broom II, purchased in the U.S. as a yearling by Harry Payne Whitney and sent to England with trainer Andrew Jackson Joyner and jockey Joe Notter. Whisk Broom ran well abroad, came home, and despite his 126-pound assignment was sent off the 8-5 favorite. He received a warm reception from the public during the post parade, as did Notter, who was also returning from Europe. But Whisk Broom had a new trainer. Joyner was still in Europe, and Whitney's American trainer, James Rowe Sr., tightened the girth.

Racing far back behind a lively pace, Whisk Broom won the Metropolitan, and two weeks later at Belmont captured the Brooklyn Handicap under 130 pounds, stepping the mile and a quarter in a record 2:03 ⅖. That win made him the favorite for the Suburban Handicap, to be run a week following the Brooklyn. Handicapper Walter Vosburgh assigned Whisk Broom 135 pounds for the mile and a quarter Suburban, but the big horse was equal to the formidable task. Under pressure in the drive, he won by half a length from the well-regarded Lahore, while Kentucky Derby winner Meridian was third. The crowd roared again when the official clocker posted the time of 2:00, against the American record of 2:02 ⅘ set by Whisk Broom's sire, Broomstick.

Many prominent trainers of the day held watches on the Suburban, and the majority snapped between 2:01 and 2:03. However, the timer stuck by his guns and August Belmont stuck by his timer, so the record went into the books. Whisk Broom II became the first horse to win New York's three major handicaps, a feat that was not to be duplicated for 40 years, until Tom Fool's memorable sweep in 1953.

With its reopening, Belmont regained its position as America's premier track, and since that time, with the exception of the five-

Whisk Broom II captured the Suburban in 1913 to complete a sweep of New York's Handicap Triple Crown. Races at Belmont Park were run clockwise until 1921.

year period, 1963 to 1967, when it was completely rebuilt, it has consistently attracted the country's finest horses in every division. In 1921, Belmont authorities reversed the pattern of the sport, and from that time ran the races counter-clockwise like the rest of the American tracks.

Flamboyant times produce larger-than-life personalities, and the early days of the 20th century boasted an endless parade of men who made their mark on the turf. August Belmont 2d was among the leaders by any criterion.

Belmont was 37 when his father died, and until that time his interest in racing had been casual. August Belmont Sr. was born in Germany and came to the U.S. as a representative of the Rothschild Organization in connection with the banking panic of 1837. Belmont spoke seven languages, became a major figure in New York

Henry of Navarre (right), who became a crack in the August Belmont 2d stable, prepares for the start of the Sheepshead Bay Special on September 11, 1895. He defeated two strong rivals in Domino (left) and Rey el Santa Anita that day.

society and married the daughter of the great war hero, Commodore Matthew Perry.

As his stature grew, Belmont became interested in racing. He was named president of Jerome Park and raced a strong stable of horses with Jacob Pincus, who saddled Pierre Lorillard's Iroquois to win the Epsom Derby of 1881, and with James Rowe Sr., regarded as one of the greatest trainers in American racing history. Belmont gave his name to the first great American classic, the Belmont Stakes, inaugurated at Jerome Park in 1867 and won by Francis Morris' filly, Ruthless. A Belmont horse won the third running of the Belmont in 1869: Fenian, trained by Pincus and ridden by Clay Miller.

Belmont died in 1890, shortly after his crack 2-year-old Potomac won the Futurity Stakes, the country's richest race, at Sheepshead Bay, earning $67,675. In two major dispersal sales following death, 130 of his horses brought $640,000.

August Belmont 2d bought a number of his father's horses, including Lady Violet, an $11,000 yearling filly who won six stakes for him as 2-year-old the following season. Belmont's first racing star, however, was Hastings, purchased in 1895 for $37,000 toward the end of his promising 2-year-old campaign. In 1896, Hastings won the Belmont Stakes, and at 4 became a top handicap horse despite a ferocious temper.

Belmont purchased Henry of Navarre as a 4-year-old for $35,000 and saw him win the Suburban Handicap in his colors. However, the two best horses he bred raced to glory for other interests. One was Beldame, a daughter of Octagon foaled in 1901.

Belmont's wife died in 1898, and this loss, coupled with some turbulent business ventures, left him little time to tend to his racing activities. He leased Beldame at 2 and she had a brilliant 3-year-old season, winning 12 of 14 starts in the colors of Newton Bennington. Beldame was back in Belmont's barn at 4, but heavy weights in handicaps compromised her chances, and she won only twice that season and was retired in 1905.

A dozen years later, America became embroiled in World War I. Belmont, anxious to serve his country though he was 65, applied for a commission and was appointed a major in the Supply Service.

When he left for Washington, D.C., he indicated that the homebred yearlings were to be sold at public auction. On August 17, 1918, 21 of the Belmont youngsters were put on the block at Saratoga and averaged $2,475. One of them brought a bid of $14,000 from Joseph E. Widener. Another brought $13,600 from Frank Taylor. But the one who'll be remembered as long as men race horses, the Fair Play colt out of Mahubah, by Rock Sand, went to Sam Riddle on a bid of $5,000. His name was Man o' War.

One of August Belmont 2d's most celebrated contemporaries, and a key figure in every aspect of American racing for many years, was James R. Keene. Born in England, he came to the U.S. with his parents, who settled in Shasta, California. Keene taught school, edited a weekly newspaper, and in 1872 settled in San Francisco with his wife and two children. He began a supply business, servicing the gold and silver mines with horses and mules.

Keene eventually obtained a seat on the San Francisco stock exchange. His knowledge of mining served him well, and his original stake of $10,000 grew to be worth an estimated $6 million by 1875. The next year he left for New York by private railroad car, and in his first two years on Wall Street is believed to have made another $9

Beldame, one of the greatest racemares ever produced in America, did most of her winning for Newton Bennington.

million.

A lean, intense man with a full beard, he was 40 when he bought his first horse, a 3-year-old named Spendthrift, obtained from Kentucky breeder Daniel Swigert for $15,000. Shortly after his purchase, Spendthrift won the 1879 Belmont Stakes by five lengths.

Keene's first great horse was Domino, a foal of 1891. By Himyar out of Mannie Gray, she was the dam of six stakes winners. Domino was bred by Maj. Barak Thomas in Lexington, Kentucky, and sold at the Tattersall's ring in New York at 55th Street and Seventh Avenue. Keene's son, Foxhall, spotted Domino and bought him for $3,000 (against the sale average of $900). That fall, tested at Sheepshead Bay, Domino worked so fast that he bowed in both front tendons and thereafter raced in bandages.

The Keenes, father and son, merged their stables in 1893, and Domino raced in both their names. Ridden by the slashing Fred Taral, Domino won all nine of his starts at 2.

Domino went lame in the American Derby of 1894, was out for two months, but wound up his 3-year-old season with six victories from eight starts. He won four of eight starts as a 4-year-old for an overall record of 19 wins from 25 starts, with two seconds and a third. His earnings of $193,550 set a record that lasted 27 years, finally surpassed in 1920 by Man o' War.

In a limited career at stud, Domino sired eight stakes winners from 19 foals, a remarkable percentage. He was the victim of overfeeding at stud in Kentucky and died of spinal meningitis in July 1897. James Keene himself wrote the inscription for Domino's tombstone: "Here lies the fleetest runner the American Turf has ever known, and one of the gamest and most generous of horses."

Domino was the first of the authentic greats for Keene but by no means the last. Colin was undefeated in 15 starts and a brilliant runner, but many horsemen of the day, including Marshall Lilly, who galloped them both, thought Keene's Sysonby – beaten only once – the better horse. Commando, Maskette, Sweep, Peter Pan, Delhi, Ballot, Celt, Frizette, Cap and Bells – the quality of the horses Keene raced was truly remarkable.

Keene not only supplied the actors but helped put on the show. He was one of the first stewards of The Jockey Club after its founding in 1894 and later joined with August Belmont 2d in organizing the Westchester Racing Association, which built Belmont Park in 1904-5. When racing closed down in New York in 1910, Keene began to sell all his horses. Col. E.R. Bradley bought several, of which the cheapest, at $1,600, was Black Toney. He became the sire of two Kentucky Derby winners: Black Gold and Brokers Tip. Many other Keene horses became the foundation stock of stables and studs across the country. Everyone recognized that the name "Keene" on a horse was the equivalent of sterling on silver.

Another prominent figure on the racing scene of the times was born in Kentucky but made his fortune in California. James Ben Ali

August Belmont 2d was president of the new park named for his father.

Haggin (1821-1914) joined the Gold Rush of 1849 and became one of the wealthiest men in America. The grandson of a Turkish army officer, he studied law at Yale, practiced law in Kentucky, then headed west. A bold speculator, he and his partner, Lloyd Tevis, purchased the Ontario silver mine in Utah, which immediately began paying dividends of a million dollars a year. The partners also struck it rich with investments in the Anaconda copper mines and the Homestake gold mines.

Haggin had 45,000 acres near Sacramento in northern California and established a breeding farm on his property. His 1903 catalog listed 30 stallions, more than 550 broodmares, and enough yearlings and weanlings to bring the total to 2,000 thoroughbreds. The scope of his operation boggles the imagination. He purchased horses and breeding stock from every major racing center in the U.S. and from England, Ireland and Australia as well. When The Futurity was America's premier race, Haggin nominated 196 of his horses for the 1900 running.

One of his first good runners was Tyrant, winner of the 1885 Belmont Stakes while under the care of trainer Bill Claypool. Then came the immortal champions Firenze, one of the greatest fillies in American racing history, and Salvator, winner of 16 of 19 lifetime starts.

In 1897, Haggin returned to his native Kentucky. He purchased the 550-acre Elmendorf Farm, where Salvator and Firenze were bred, and eventually expanded it to 10,000 acres. At its height, Elmendorf had 350 mares in residence and 17 stallions were in service, including Salvator, who was not an outstanding sire. Haggin married a beautiful girl many years his junior and built a palatial mansion on the property, columned like something out of "Gone With the Wind." He dispersed most of his horses when racing wound down in New York in 1910, and he died in 1914 at the age of 93.

America's greatest horses during the period of 1894 to 1920 – and two of the greatest ever to race in this country – were Man o' War and Sysonby.

Sysonby, a foal of 1902, was bred by copper magnate Marcus Daly, who purchased the dam, Optime, in England and had her bred to Melton, winner of the 1885 Epsom Derby and Doncaster St. Leger. When Daly died in 1901, his horses in England were brought to the U.S. and auctioned at Sheepshead Bay in October. James R. Keene purchased Optime, in foal to Melton, for $6,600 and shipped her to his Castleton Farm in Lexington, Kentucky. The foal, arriving in February, was named Sysonby, after an English hunting lodge.

Smallish, lop-eared and slow as a yearling, Sysonby didn't inspire much confidence, and Keene thought he might possibly do better in England. His trainer, James Rowe Sr., however, saw some quality in Sysonby, and when Keene came to see the horses one day, Rowe brought Sysonby out in bandages and under a heavy blanket. Keene quickly agreed the colt was not in shape to travel, and so he was kept in the U.S.

Rowe's judgment, as usual, was good. Sysonby won his first start

Foxhall Keene and James R. Keene formed a formidable stable in the waning years of the 19th century.

by 10 lengths at Brighton Beach and then came back two days later to win the Brighton Junior Stakes by four lengths. He won Saratoga's Flash Stakes by six lengths, and a week later won the Saratoga Special by the same margin.

Sysonby was sent off the 3-2 favorite in the Futurity, richest race in the country, though the field of 16 was unusually strong and Sysonby would carry 127 pounds. Sysonby got off to a two-length lead but did not run away from the others as he had done before. Artful, a filly, was the winner, with Tradition edging Sysonby for second by a nose.

Two days after the Futurity, Rowe saw Sysonby's groom with a thick roll of money. After persistent questioning, the groom confessed that he'd given Sysonby a dose of salts before the race, taking the starch out of him.

Three weeks later, fully recovered and eager to do something, Sysonby won the Junior Champion Stakes by three lengths to conclude his season with five wins from six starts.

In a 3-year-old campaign that was to earn him a revered place in racing history, Sysonby won all nine of his starts. He began on opening day at the new Belmont Park with a brilliant performance, that saw him dead-heat with the 5-year-old Race King, to whom he was conceding 10 pounds. He then won the mile and a quarter Tidal Stakes by four lengths, the mile and a quarter Commonwealth

Handicap by four lengths and the 13-furlong Lawrence Realization by six lengths. He followed with easy triumphs in the mile and a quarter Iroquois Stakes and the mile and a half Brighton Derby.

In the $50,000 Great Republic Stakes at Saratoga, one of the richest races offered in that era, Sysonby was turned sideways at the start and bolted to the outside fence, losing some 75 yards according to contemporary reports. Oiseau, owned by Diamond Jim Brady, went to the lead and built a commanding margin, but Sysonby was along to wear him down and win, to the wild cheers of the large crowd, by three lengths.

Back in New York, Sysonby won the mile and a half Century Stakes, and ended the season with a four-length tally in the Champion Stakes at two miles and a quarter. He was put away for the winter, hailed as one of the most exceptional horses of his time.

The following spring, Sysonby was preparing for his 4-year-old season when Rowe noticed some blood on one ankle. There were pimples the next day and more blood. Within a week, his body covered with bleeding sores, Sysonby was in perilous condition. The leading veterinarians in the country examined him and finally agreed he had a liver condition. But he failed to respond to treatment and died on June 17, 1906, at Sheepshead Bay. A crowd estimated at 5,000 attended his funeral the next day at the track.

In a retrospective, racing historian and official Walter Vosburgh

Sysonby overcame trouble to win Saratoga's Great Republic Stakes in 1905.

termed Sysonby "a plain horse, but with an appearance of power about him. He had a massive body and sturdy limbs. He galloped with an enormous stride and must have had immense power in his heart and lungs. He appeared to be a super horse."

If Sysonby was a super horse in the opinion of the most informed handicapper of his day, Man o' War carried his talent to an even higher level. The big red son of Fair Play became one of the greatest thoroughbreds ever produced by any country, setting records for the mile, mile and an eighth, mile and three-eighths, mile and a half and mile and five-eighths.

It was noted earlier that Man o' War was sold to Sam Riddle for $5,000 at Saratoga. Riddle's trainer, Louis Feustel, inspected the Belmont yearlings before they were shipped to the Spa. Feustel came into racing via hunt meetings in Maryland and may have had a predilection for big horses.

In the spring of 1919, Feustel shipped the Riddle horses to Havre de Grace. Man o' War caught a cold, and developed a temperature of 106. But he got well almost as quickly as he took ill and went back to training inside of a week. He made his first start on June 6 at Belmont Park, and by then the news of his raw talent had circled the racetrack. He went off at 3-5 in a race down the Widener Chute under Johnny Loftus and won by six lengths, his five furlongs completed in :59. Three days later, he won the Keene Memorial Stakes at five and a half furlongs by three convincing lengths, de-

The name defined the event, as Upset shocked Man o' War and the racing world in the 1919 Sanford Memorial.

spite an off track.

Man o' War won the Youthful Stakes at Jamaica on June 21. Loftus had been working with the red colt in the mornings, schooling him to get away from the barrier a little faster. The homework paid off. Man o' War broke on top in the Youthful, led all the way, and won by two and a half lengths. Two days later he won the five-furlong Hudson Stakes at Aqueduct under 130 pounds. Despite his impost, he went off at 1-10 and won easily, while giving his closest rival 21 pounds.

Man o' War carried 130 pounds again to win the six-furlong Tremont Stakes at Aqueduct, then shipped to Saratoga and was an authoritative winner of the United States Hotel Stakes on August 2. Once more he carried 130 pounds and gave 15 pounds to Upset, whom he appeared to beat easily. The big red colt was six for six and was beginning to be hailed as something special, but his luck ran sour on August 13.

The six-furlong Sanford Memorial drew a field of seven, with Man o' War a 1-2 favorite under his now-customary 130 pounds. With starter Mars Cassidy indisposed, veteran official and former starter C.H. Pettingill was on duty. It took him a while to get the young horses organized for the Sanford, but he finally got them away. Golden Broom, the Saratoga Special winner, was first from the barrier, followed by Upset and Donnacona. Johnny Loftus, on Man o' War, saved ground along the rail.

When Golden Broom tired, Upset raced just outside the leader while Donnacona was just outside Man o' War. Loftus was ready to move with the red horse but was neatly boxed in with no place to go. With only a furlong left, Loftus, giving up hope of getting through on the inside, swung to the outside and put Man o' War to a stern drive. He was tardy. Upset, in receipt of 15 pounds from the favorite, won by half a length.

Daily Racing Form's correspondent on the scene, Neil Newman, noted the next day that Man o' War demonstrated in defeat he was a great horse. The writer criticized Loftus' judgment in placing Man o' War in a situation where he could get boxed in. It was pointed out that Man o' War stood a fierce drive gamely and answered almost every question in the affirmative.

Ten days after the Sanford, Man o' War and Upset met again in the Grand Union Hotel Stakes. Carrying 130 pounds and giving five pounds to Upset, Man o' War won nicely at 1-2. He also carried 130 pounds in the Hopeful Stakes at the Spa and drew off at the end to register by four lengths.

Two weeks after leaving Saratoga, Man o' War concluded his 2-year-old season in the Futurity at Belmont Park. Dominique and John P. Grier made the pace. Man o' War raced past them as if they were tied to a post and prevailed by two and a half lengths, John P. Grier holding on to be second. The final tally for the campaign: nine wins from 10 starts, and earnings of $83,325.

Man o' War was a standout at 2. C.C. Ridley, a well-known handicapper, assessed the 1920 crop of coming 3-year-olds for *Daily Racing Form* and topped his list with Man o' War at 136 pounds. He listed the second horse, Blazes, at 120 pounds and pegged Upset at 116.

Good as he was at 2, Man o' War was even better at 3, much better. Sent to the Riddle Farm in Berlin, Maryland, for the winter, Man o' War bloomed like a flower. Feustel put him on a scale at Saratoga and the colt weighed in at 970. Six months later he tipped the scale at 1,150 pounds. He "sticked" at 16.2 hands and girthed 72 inches. The boy had filled out into a man.

Because the Kentucky Derby came a bit early for a colt who did not race over the winter, and because the Preakness at Baltimore's Pimlico Race Course involved little traveling, Man o' War's connections opted to start his campaign near home. Another factor was the distance of the Preakness at that time: nine furlongs, against the

Trainer Louis Feustel (left) and owner Samuel D. Riddle came up with a legend in Man o' War.

Derby's 10 furlongs.

Paul Jones, at 16-1, led all the way to win the Kentucky Derby by a head over Upset, who, as part of an entry, went off as the 8-5 favorite.

With Johnny Loftus, Man o' War's regular jockey, ruled off the turf at the beginning of the season, Clarence Kummer was named to ride Big Red in the 1920 Preakness. They rushed to an early lead and remained in front the rest of the way, cruising through the stretch to register by a length and a half, with Upset second. Paul Jones, the Derby winner, didn't run.

Loftus, incidentally, was not the only rider ruled off at the time. Willie Knapp, Upset's jockey at 2, also got the heave-ho.

Traditionally, no reason was given, but the rulings fueled speculation that there might have been more to Man o' War's only defeat than was public knowledge. Loftus and Knapp turned to training soon after they were ruled off, and they were granted licenses.

Eleven days after the Preakness, Man o' War was at Belmont Park for the Withers Mile. Once again he raced on the lead, scoring by two lengths in 1:35⅖, two-fifths of a second faster than the American record set by Fairy Wand. The Withers appeared to remove all doubt, and when entries were taken for the Belmont Stakes, the name of only one other 3-year-old, Donnacona, was dropped in the box. On June 12, the 52nd Belmont was no contest.

43359 **FOURTH RACE—3-4 Mile. (Aug. 22, 1918—1:10⅖—3—115.) Seventh Running SANFORD MEMORIAL.** Guaranteed Value $5,000. 2-year-olds. Allowances. Net value to winner $3,925; second, $700; third, $300.

Index	Horses	A	Wt	PP	St	¼	½	¾	Str	Fin	Jockeys	Owners	O	H	C	P	S
43262^2	UPSET	w	115	5	1		2^h	2^1	1^h	$1\frac{1}{2}$	W Knapp	H P Whitney	10	12	8	7-5	1-3
(43262)	MAN O' WAR	w	130	6	5		4^4	$3^{1\frac{1}{2}}$	3^3	2^3	J Loftus	Glen Riddle F'm	7-10	4-5	11-20	out	—
(43321)	GOLDEN BROOM	wB	130	3	2		$1\frac{1}{2}$	1^1	$2^{1\frac{1}{2}}$	3^2	E Ambr'se	MrsWMJeffords	9-5	$2\frac{1}{2}$	$2\frac{1}{2}$	1-2	out
43311†	CAPT. ALCOCK	wB	112	4	7		7	7	6^2	$4^{1\frac{1}{2}}$	C Rob'son	J E Madden	50	200	100	30	10
43256	ARMISTICE	wB	112	2	3		5^8	5^2	$5\frac{1}{2}$	5^5	L McAtee	W R Coe	50	50	50	15	5
43218	DONNACONA	w	112	7	4		3^1	4^5	$4\frac{1}{2}$	6^1	W Kelsay	G W Loft	20	50	30	8	3
43256	THE SWIMMER	wB	115	1	6		6^3	$6^{1\frac{1}{2}}$	7	7	R Simpson	T F Henry	30	50	50	15	5

†Added starter. **Time, $23\frac{1}{5}$, $46\frac{4}{5}$, $1:11\frac{1}{5}$. Track fast.**

Winner—Ch. c, by Whisk Broom II.—Pankhurst, by Voter (trained by James Rowe; bred by Mr. Harry Payne Whitney).

Went to post at 4:10. At post 4 minutes. Start poor and slow. Won driving; second and third the same. UPSET followed the leader closely from the start, moved up with a rush in the last eighth and, taking the lead, held on gamely when challenged and just lasted long enough to withstand MAN O' WAR'S challenge. The latter began slowly, moved up steadily to the stretch turn, where he got into close quarters, then came to the outside in the final eighth and, responding gamely to punishment, was gaining in the closing strides. GOLDEN BROOM showed great speed in pacemaking, but tired when challenged. CAPT. ALCOCK began slowly and closed a big gap. ARMISTICE ran well from a poor beginning. DONNACONA ran forwardly in the early running, but was carried wide on the stretch turn and tired.

Scratched—43069 Peace Pennant, 112; 43291 Ten Can, 112.

Man o' War was involved in two of the most shocking results in modern thoroughbred racing, as these Daily Racing Form *charts show. Upset gave final testimony to his name when he stunned Man o' War in the 1919 Sanford Memorial (above). "Big Red" added to his legend with a 100-length victory in the 1920 Lawrence Realization (below).*

49857 **FOURTH RACE—1 5-8 Miles. (Sept. 6, 1919—2:47⅗—3—116.) Twenty-eighth Running LAWRENCE REALIZATION.** $5,000 Added. 3-year-olds. Net value to winner $15,040; second, $1,033.33.

Index	Horses	A	Wt	PP	St	¼	½	¾	Str	Fin	Jockeys	Owners	O	H	C	P	S
(49540)	MAN O' WAR	w	126	2	2	1^{20}	1^{20}	1^{30}	1^{50}	1^{100}	C Kummer	Glen Riddle Fm	1-100	1-100	1-100	out	—
49823^3†	HOODWINK	w	116	1	1	2	2	2	2	2	E Ambr'se	Mrs W M Jef'ds	60	80	60	out	—

†Added starter.

Time, $23\frac{3}{5}$, $47\frac{4}{5}$, 1:13, $1:38\frac{2}{5}$, $2:03\frac{3}{5}$, $2:28\frac{4}{5}$, $2:40\frac{4}{5}$ (new American record.) **Track fast.**

Winner—Ch. c, by Fair Play—Mahubah, by Rock Sand (trained by L. Feustel; bred by Mr. August Belmont).

Went to post at 3:42. At post 1 minute. Start good and slow. Won easily. MAN O' WAR set a great pace under stout restraint for the first three-quarters and was allowed to run freely to the homestretch, where he was taken under restraint. HOODWINK made no effort to keep pace with the leader.

Scratched—49126 Sea Mint, 116.

Man o' War went to the front at the outset and stayed there under a stout hold, with Donnacona following. Favored at 1-25, Man o' War drew out to lead by seven lengths on the turn, by 12 lengths at the furlong pole and by 20 lengths at the winning post. He set an American record of 2:14⅕ for the mile and three furlongs.

The Belmont can be draining, but not the way Man o' War won. Ten days later, he was at Jamaica for the Stuyvesant Handicap. He was weighted at 135 pounds, but despite this steadying package, management couldn't round up a corporal's guard to run against him. He won by eight lengths in a high gallop with Yellow Hand, the only other runner, second under 103 pounds.

Man o' War had one real challenge during his 3-year-old season, and that came in the Dwyer Stakes at Aqueduct on July 10. Man o' War and John P. Grier launched their duel early, the first half-mile in a zippy :46, a time faster than the track record. The first six furlongs in 1:09⅗ was also faster than the track record, and the two colts were about dead even. Eddie Ambrose called on John P. Grier and took command momentarily, but now Kummer asked Man o' War to run, and he regained the lead, getting the mile in a track-record 1:36. He drew clear at the end to score by a length and a half, the nine furlongs in the American-record time of 1:49⅕.

It was on to Saratoga, where Earl Sande had the mount on Man o' War in the mile and three-sixteenths Miller Stakes. Despite topweight of 131 pounds, Man o' War won easily, by six lengths. Two weeks later, on August 21, he won the Travers under Andy Schuttinger by two and a half lengths. Schuttinger was easing the big red colt through the final furlong but he still equaled the track record of 2:01⅘ for a mile and a quarter. On September 4, at Belmont Park, it was the Lawrence Realization, and only one other horse was entered against him. Man o' War won by a margin estimated at 100 lengths, the largest margin ever to appear in a *Daily Racing Form* chart. Despite the absence of competition, the winning time of 2:40⅘ for the mile and five furlongs was an American record, breaking Fitz Herbert's mark by more than four seconds.

One week later, in the Jockey Club Gold Cup, Man o' War won by 15 lengths, producing another American record of 2:28⅘ for the mile and a half. Favored at 1-100, he was headline news in every

BIG RED

By J.A. Estes

The days are long at Belmont,
Speed they never learn.
And it's many a day since Man o' War
Has looped the upper turn.

The guineas stopped their rubbing,
The rider dropped his tack
When the word went round that Man o' War
Was coming on the track.

The crowd was hoarse with cheering
At ancient Pimlico
The day he won at Preakness—
But that was long ago.

The dust is deep at Windsor,
The good old days are done,
And many a horse is forgotten,
But they still remember one.

For he was a fiery phantom
To that multitudinous throng—
Would you wait for another one like him?
Be patient: years are long.

For here was a horse among horses,
Cast in Titan's mold,
And the slant October sunlight
Gilded the living gold.

He was marked with the gods' own giving
And winged in every part;
The look of eagles was in his eye
And Hastings' wrath in his heart.

Young Equipoise had power
To rouse the crowded stand,
And there was magic in the name
Of Greentree's Twenty Grand,

And Sarazen has sprinted,
And Gallant Fox has stayed,
And Discovery has glittered
In the wake of Cavalcade…

We watch the heroes parading,
We wait, and our eyes are dim,
But we never discover another
Like him.

This poem, published long after Man o' War's career was over, and repro-
duced in part here, summarized the legend that surrounded "Big Red."

Trainer Louis Feustel smoked many a celebratory cigar during
Man o' War's epic career.

paper in America and creating fans for racing with his exploits. On September 18, he was at Havre de Grace for the Potomac Handicap. Carrying 138 pounds over a deep and tiring strip, he set a track record of 1:44⅗ for the mile and a sixteenth while conceding 30 pounds to the runner-up.

For his final start, Man o' War was sent to Kenilworth Park, near Toronto, for a meeting with the 4-year-old champion and first Triple Crown winner, Sir Barton. Sir Barton was not at his best, and Man o' War, to the tremendous applause of appreciative Canadians, won off by seven lengths, setting a track record of 2:03 for the mile and a quarter. But even on the best day he ever had, Sir Barton was going to finish second, for he was running against the "mostest hoss."

Man o' War was 11 for 11 in that glorious campaign, with five American records. He increased his record earnings to $249,465.

That fall, when seeing handicapper Walter Vosburgh at the races one afternoon, Riddle asked what weight he would assign Man o' War if he returned for another season.

"The highest I've ever assigned," Vosburgh answered promptly. Riddle thought about that for a while, concluded that Man o' War had done everything that could be expected of a horse, and made the decision to send him home. He was a good sire, producing a Triple Crown winner in War Admiral and some others of merit. There never was the slightest chance that he could get a horse as good as himself, for there was only one Man o' War.

While Man o' War and Sysonby were the greatest horses of their time, it would be unthinkable to allude to racing in the first quarter of the 20th century without at least some reference to three other remarkable performers. They are Colin, one of the few horses to remain undefeated; Exterminator, whose record of 50 wins from 100 starts is a testimonial to his consistency and durability; and Regret, the first filly to win the Kentucky Derby.

Colin, bred and owned by James R. Keene and trained by James Rowe Sr., was a foal of 1905 by the brilliant Commando out of Pastorella, the dam an English stakes-winner purchased by Keene for $10,000 out of the Marcus Daly dispersal. Colin made his first start on the straight course at Belmont Park on May 29, 1907. A field of 23

Colin, shown in 1908 with Joe Notter up, was unbeaten in 15 starts as a 2- and 3-year-old.

maidens charged down the Widener Chute, and Colin, who broke on top, won by two lengths, timed in 1:01. Two days later, Colin ran again and this time set a track record of :58, winning the National Stallion Stakes by three lengths.

Colin made his third start in a week on June 5. Carrying 125 pounds in the Eclipse Stakes, he made all the pace despite bucked shins, and was under constant pressure from Harry Payne Whitney's good colt, Beaucoup. The two colts raced the final quarter-mile as a team with Colin winning by a head. The shins would have discouraged an ordinary horse, but Colin was all about winning.

Rowe dealt with the shins and brought Colin back in three weeks to win the Great Trial Stakes at Sheepshead Bay. With each race, Colin gained the increasing respect of racing men as an exceptional animal. He won the Brighton Junior at Brighton Beach, the Saratoga Special and the Grand Union Hotel Stakes at the Spa, the Futurity and the Flatbush at Sheepshead Bay and the colt division of the Produce Stakes at Brighton Beach. Competing in the colt division of the Matron Stakes at Belmont Park, he carried 129 pounds and won by three lengths over Fair Play, Man o' War's sire, who carried 122 pounds. Walter Miller, the riding sensation of the time, was in the saddle as he had been for most of Colin's races at 2.

To conclude the season with ruffles and flourishes, Colin won his

12th race from 12 starts in the Champagne Stakes at Belmont Park, beating Stamina by six lengths and setting an American record of 1:23 for seven furlongs down the straight course. The whole country was talking about him and speculating on his 3-year-old campaign.

Colin made his 3-year-old debut on May 23, 1908, in the Withers Mile at Belmont Park and won easily by two lengths, but came out of the race lame and was declared from the Belmont Stakes the following week. Contemporary reports suggest he bowed a tendon, though there was never an official explanation, in keeping with the stable secrecy that prevailed in that era. Joe Notter replaced Miller as Colin's jockey, and, there was no explanation of this move, either.

Heavy rain fell on Belmont Park an hour before the Belmont Stakes, and following a meeting between owner Keene and trainer Rowe, Colin was announced as an added starter. The mile and three-furlong Belmont, on a muddy track against a small but formidable field, didn't seem like an ideal spot for a horse with a bowed tendon. Fog moved in just prior to the race, and between the fog and the rain, the Belmont was invisible from the stands.

No time was taken and the chart of the Belmont was abbreviated, for the horses did not come into view until they turned for home. Colin had a five-length lead. Near the finish, Notter glanced back at Fair Play and relaxed on Colin, who eased up as Fair Play came on. The crowd gasped, but Colin won by a head. Many expressed the thought that Notter went to sleep, but Notter, the coun-

Trainer James Rowe Sr. (left) and owner James R. Keene were the men behind the brilliant Colin.

try's leading money-winning jockey that season, said trainer Rowe told him to make as little use of Colin as possible in view of the injured foot and poor track conditions.

Legislation was passed which made betting on a race a crime in New York. Keene thought Colin could bring out a crowd, even if there was no betting. The colt was entered for the Tidal Stakes at Sheepshead Bay on June 20, a betless exhibition at a mile and a quarter. With the stands half full, Colin won easily by two lengths, giving him a record of 15 wins from 15 starts and earnings of $178,110.

He was through for the season.

With racing in New York just about finished due to reform legislation, Keene had Colin shipped to England to race in 1909. Sam Darling, a great English horseman, was his trainer and tried him on the Newmarket Heath one morning with Jack Snipe, one of Britain's fastest sprinters. Colin won easily, to the surprise of Darling and other work-watchers, but the effort was costly. Colin went wrong soon after and was retired to stud.

Standing first in England and then the United States, Colin was not a distinguished sire. But when it came to racing and the ability to overcome travail of all kinds, he was one of the best there ever was.

Exterminator was a horse of amazing accomplishment. He ran 13 races of a mile and three-quarters or longer and won 11 of them, including three victories in the Pimlico Cup at two miles and a quarter. He carried 130 pounds or more 35 times and won 20 times. And, of course, there were those 100 starts and 50 victories.

By McGee out of Fair Empress, by Jim Gore, Exterminator was a foal of 1915, bred by F D. Knight near Nicholasville, Kentucky. He was sold to J. Cal Milam for $1,500, at a sale in which the average price was about $930 and the top price was $9,500. He did not do well physically in the early part of his 2-year-old season and was gelded. He made his first start at Latonia, near Cincinnati, on June 30 in a six-furlong race and won by three lengths.

He won and lost races at Windsor, Ontario, and lost a race at Kenilworth Park, near Toronto, for a record of two wins in four starts. At that time, he was just another horse.

Exterminator walked quietly to the paddock when accompanied by his closest buddy, "Peanuts" the pony.

Milam met in Lexington, and Kilmer paid $9,000 in cash for Exterminator, plus two fillies worth $500 each. Exterminator worked with Sun Briar twice before the Derby. There are conflicting reports about these moves, some indicating Exterminator did fairly well and others indicating he was beaten decisively by Sun Briar both times.

There are also conflicting reports about Sun Briar's condition on the eve of the Derby. In any event, McDaniel chose not to run him and entered Exterminator, to Kilmer's reported disgust. Exterminator was 30-1 in a field of eight, got through on the inside entering the far turn, and rallied in the mud to win by a length under

He filled out during the winter and began to attract attention. One pair of eyes he caught belonged to Uncle Henry McDaniel, a fine trainer who was preparing Willis Sharpe Kilmer's champion Sun Briar for the Kentucky Derby. Sun Briar worked a mile in 1:46 at Churchill Downs about the same time Exterminator, working at the Association track in Lexington, went a mile in 1:40. When Kilmer asked McDaniel to buy a work horse for Sun Briar, the trainer remembered Exterminator's workout.

Some 10 days prior to the 1918 Kentucky Derby, Kilmer and Willie Knapp. When accepting the trophy, Kilmer had little to say.

Exterminator's form during the summer and early fall was moderate, but he began to get good with the arrival of cooler temperatures. He won a small stakes at Laurel and two at Pimlico, then closed his campaign at Latonia with victories in the Latonia Cup and the Thanksgiving Handicap. That gave him a 3-year-old record of seven wins from 15 starts, with four seconds and three thirds.

He won nine of 21 starts at 4, including the mile and three-quarter Saratoga Cup and the two and a quarter-mile Pimlico Cup. He had

Exterminator (inside) beat the doughty Grey Lag a head in the memorable 1922 Brooklyn Handicap at Aqueduct.

and sent off the solid 7-10 favorite. Rating off the early pace set by the filly Polly Ann under 103 pounds, Exterminator and Grey Lag came through the stretch as a team. They went neck and neck until Exterminator reached out and won by a head in a memorable effort.

That Brooklyn appeared to exact a toll from Exterminator. He won the Saratoga Cup that summer and several other good stakes, but the spark was gone. He raced three times as an 8-year-old in the spring of 1923, won the Philadelphia Handicap at Havre de Grace, and was sent home. The

an even better season at 5, with 10 victories from 17 starts. Exterminator set an American record of 2:56⅖ for the 14 furlongs of the Saratoga Cup, set another American record in winning the two-mile Autumn Gold Cup in 3:21⅕, and won the two miles and a quarter Ontario Jockey Club Cup under 134 pounds.

Like Old Man River, Exterminator just kept rolling. He won eight of 26 starts at 6, capturing Saratoga's Merchants and Citizens Stakes at 13 furlongs under 130 pounds, and the mile and a quarter Toronto Autumn Cup under 137. As a 7-year-old in 1922, he won 10 of 17 starts. He carried 133 pounds to win the Clark Handicap at Churchill Downs, going nine furlongs, and won the 10-furlong Kentucky Handicap at the same track under 138 pounds. For the Brooklyn Handicap at Aqueduct, he was assigned 135 pounds, while Grey Lag, the 4-year-old champion, was assigned 126

following spring, Kilmer sent Old Bones to Tijuana for the rich Coffroth Handicap. Exterminator won the prep race but finished fourth in the Coffroth. He continued to race throughout the season, in Maryland and in Canada, and won two races.

There was some thought of racing him at 10, but his retirement was announced at the end of the 1924 campaign and he concluded with 50 wins, 17 seconds and 17 thirds from 100 starts. His earnings of $252,996 placed him second on the all-time list to Zev's $313,639, and his fame, earned with honesty and perseverance, lasted through the end of the century.

Regret, bred and owned by Harry Payne Whitney and trained by James Rowe Sr., didn't race often. Her entire career consisted of 11 starts over four seasons. But she accomplished so much in that time, and with such panache, that she is a treasured highlight in the tapestry of the American turf.

Among the mares Whitney purchased from the dispersal of his father's (William Collins Whitney) estate was Daisy F. A winner of 23 races, she was by Riley, a Kentucky Derby winner, out of Modesty, an American Derby winner. Daisy F.'s first foal, by the brilliant Hamburg (winner of 16 of 21 starts), was a filly, Jersey Lightning. She won only once, but, covered by Broomstick, produced one of the greatest of American fillies: Regret, who was bred in New Jersey.

A foal of 1912, Regret began training at Brookdale Farm, five miles from the site of the present Monmouth Park. She was ready to run when Rowe sent her to Saratoga in the summer of 1914, and she started three times at the Spa. All three were stakes run in a span of two weeks, and Regret won them all.

Her first race was the Saratoga Special, and she was made co-favorite with the top colt of the year, Pebbles. Joe Notter sent Regret to the lead, and she remained there throughout the six furlongs, winning by a length. A week later, she carried 127 pounds in the Sanford Stakes on a sloppy track and again beat colts, winning by a length and a half. The following week it came up muddy for the Hopeful Stakes, and Regret was shuffled back early in the field of 11. Notter maneuvered her to the better footing in the middle of the track, and in a rousing finish she got up to score by a half over Andrew M., who was in receipt of 13 pounds from one tough filly.

WINNING HORSE, RIDER, TRAINER, OWNER

TRAINER JAMES ROWE

JOCKEY NOTTER

REGRET

HARRY PAYNE WHITNEY

Regret, pictured here in a 1915 newspaper account, was a heroine to all her connections.

Whitney and Rowe both thought Regret had done enough to establish her supremacy, and she was sent home to grow and develop. She made her first start at 3 in the Kentucky Derby, an extraordinary feat in itself. She worked well that spring at Brookdale but was off her feed after shipping to Churchill Downs.

Rowe, making his first appearance in Louisville since 1881 when he saddled Hindoo to win the Kentucky Derby, worked the filly twice at Churchill Downs at the Derby distance of a mile and a quarter. The first drill was timed in 2:14⅗. Three days before the race, she worked again and was timed in 2:08⅗. Her people still wondered if Regret was ready, but the public liked her chances and sent her off the favorite. Breaking from post 2, Notter had her on the lead in a twinkling and kept her there. When Pebbles challenged in mid-stretch she drew off and, in the words of the chart in *Daily Racing Form*, won eased up, her margin two lengths. The media, lured to Louisville by Col. Matt Winn, went wild over the filly's victory, and Winn always credited Regret with the publicity that made the Derby a national institution.

Owner-breeder Whitney was ecstatic. "I told Rowe," he said, "I didn't care if she ever won another race if she could only win the Derby."

Three months after the Derby, Regret made her only other start as a 3-year-old, in the Saranac Mile at Saratoga. Her most formidable opponent was The Finn, winner of the Belmont Stakes, the Withers and the Manhattan Handicap. Carrying 123 pounds to The Finn's 126, Regret left him for dead, leading all the way to score by a length and a half.

Regret made two starts at 4. The mile and a quarter Saratoga Handicap was her seasonal opener on July 31. She was heavily favored, and the handicapper asked her to give weight to most of the field. Regret broke on top as usual, led for the first half-mile, and then began to back up. She finished last in a race won by Stromboli, an outstanding handicap horse.

Was Regret "short" in her first defeat? Three weeks later, racing at a mile in overnight competition, she led all the way and won easily. Then, like the precious jewel she was, she was put away for another day.

As a 5-year-old in 1917, Regret opened with a sprint race at Belmont Park, going five and a half furlongs down the straight course. She won by eight lengths.

That set the stage for the Brooklyn Handicap of 1917, one of the greatest races ever run in the United States. On June 23 at Aqueduct, three Kentucky Derby winners — Regret, Old Rosebud and Omar Khayyam — ran with such handicap stars as Roamer, Stromboli, Boots and Borrow. Boots was a slight choice over the entry of Regret and the 9-year-old Borrow.

Willie Knapp, riding Borrow, chatted with Rowe before the Brooklyn. Rowe advised him that Whitney preferred to win with Regret but cautioned him to remain alert if Old Rosebud or Roamer,

Regret wore the roses in 1915, the first filly ever to win the Kentucky Derby.

the main threats, looked ready to pounce. Frank Robinson, riding Regret, sent his filly to the front at the start and she led, repulsing many challenges. But Robinson, who was the country's leading jockey the following season, began to ease Regret in the stretch as Old Rosebud surged.

Knapp, who had been riding Borrow along the rail, saw Old Rosebud challenge and remembered Rowe's caution. Borrow flew through the stretch and turned Old Rosebud away, but his momentum continued and he bested Regret by a nose on the winning post. The time for the nine furlongs of 1:49⅖ was an American record. Whitney, entering the winner's circle to accept the trophy for Borrow, had tears in his eyes.

Regret raced twice more that season, winning Belmont's Gazelle Handicap by three lengths and giving the CCA Oaks winner, Wistful, 24 pounds.

Regret made her last start at Aqueduct on September 25, and carried 127 pounds over the seven furlongs in the track-record time of 1:24⅕. She was retired and sent home. She did not produce a horse with a fraction of her quality, but she had done enough on the racetrack to earn immortality.

Two of the greatest trainers in American racing history were James Rowe Sr. (1857-1929) and Sam Hildreth (1866-1929). They dominated their era, built reputations which command respect to this day, were good friends even as they competed fiercely against each other, and died a month apart. Between them they saddled an incredible 15 winners of the Belmont Stakes, eight for Rowe and seven for Hildreth. In the 24 years from 1904 to 1928, the stables they trained led the national earnings list 15 times, nine for Rowe and six for Hildreth.

Rowe was born in Fredricksburg, Virginia. At 10, he lived in Richmond with his family, operated the newsstand at the Exchange Hotel and exercised the horses in the hotel's livery stable early each morning. It was in the latter capacity that he attracted the attention of a hotel guest, Col. David McDaniel, a prominent horseman of the time. McDaniel, admiring the lad's work ethic, offered him a job with his stable and an opportunity to ride if he learned the skills. Rowe learned, and promptly.

Four years later, in 1871, he was the country's leading jockey, and he retained his title in 1872 and 1873.

He was tall for his age, and soon his frame began to fill out, thus his riding career was relatively brief. He left McDaniel in 1874, landed a job riding horses in the P.T. Barnum circus in New York, and then returned to the racetrack as a trainer in 1876.

After a brilliant run with such horses as Luke Blackburn, Hindoo and Miss Woodford in the early 1880s, Rowe became a racing official in 1884. He returned to training in 1888, but again became an official when his patron, August Belmont, died in 1890.

Rowe, however, was a trainer at heart, and left the judges' stand

33963 FOURTH RACE—1 1-8 Miles. (June 24, 1916—1:50—3—108.) Twenty-ninth Running Brooklyn Handicap. Guaranteed Value $6,000. 3-year-olds and upward. Net value to winner $4,850; second, $700; third, $300.

Daily Racing Form's *chart of the 1917 Brooklyn Handicap illustrates why it was considered one of the greatest races ever run in America. Borrow beat stablemate Regret (one of three Kentucky Derby winners in the field) much to the sorrow of owner Harry Payne Whitney.*

again in 1900 to train for Keene.

When Rowe took over Keene's horses, Domino's best son, Commando, was coming to the races. Commando won five of six starts at 2, and his only defeat, in the Matron Stakes, was blamed by contemporary newspaper accounts to poor riding by Harry Spencer. Commando made his 3-year-old debut in the Belmont Stakes May at a mile and three furlongs at Morris Park, winning comfortably by two lengths.

Both the winning trainer and colt were extraordinary individuals. It was a feat to have Commando ready to win at 11 furlongs in his seasonal debut, and it was a feat to have Commando come back a week later to win at a mile in the Carlton Stakes at Gravesend. Thus, Commando was a heavy favorite on July 4 at Sheepshead Bay when he ran in the mile and five-furlong Lawrence Realization. After stalking the pace for the first mile, he moved to the front and looked like a certain winner until he broke down in the stretch. The Parader passed him to win by two lengths.

"We never knew how good he was," Rowe commented later in a retrospective. "Nothing could extend him."

Commando should have had a perfect record. Colin did, going 15 for 15, and when he was retired, Rowe told friends that the only epitaph he wanted on his gravestone was "He trained Colin." Rowe also trained a succession of cracks for Keene, including Sysonby, Peter Pan, Maskette, Superman, Delhi, Affliction, Hilarious, Restigouche, Dolly Spanker, Celt, Ballot and Iron Mask. In 1910, with racing banned in New York, Keene retired from the sport. He died in December 1912.

Shortly after Keene's death, Rowe went to work for sportsman Harry Payne Whitney. When racing returned to New York that spring, on May 30, 1913, it was Rowe who saddled Whitney's American-bred and English-raced Whisk Broom II to win the featured $2,500 Metropolitan Handicap, and later the Brooklyn and Suburban handicaps. Other stars Rowe trained for Whitney were Regret, Borrow, Pennant, Dominant, Bunting, Johren, John P. Grier, Upset, Wildair, Tryster, Goshawk, Thunderer, Vexatious, Prudery, Bonnie Pennant, Happy Go Lucky, Exodus, Whichone and Boojum. He was still active in racing when he died in August 1929, although his son, James Rowe Jr. was the trainer of record.

Tall, handsome and personable, Rowe was very serious about his work. One foggy spring morning, training at the Brookdale Course in New Jersey, he told Marshall Lilly, his famous exercise rider, to go a mile in 1:39. Lilly, who always wore a derby to work (in which he would conceal a half-pint of brandy), rarely missed by more than a fifth of a second but returned in 1:40 and Rowe wanted to know why. "Man came out of the fog on the far turn and walked across the track, right in front of my horse," Lilly said.

"You should have run the fool down," Rowe said.

Marshall Lilly, his trademark derby hat firmly planted on his head as he worked Colin, was one of the most famous exercise riders of the century.

"Did," said Lilly. "That's why I'm late."

Those were the days of iron men and iron horses, and one of the toughest, as well as one of the best, was Sam Hildreth. Training his own horses and those of such celebrated racing men as Ed Corrigan, Lucky Baldwin, William Collins Whitney, August Belmont and Harry Sinclair, he was so successful that he became a legend in the sport. Long after his death in September 1929, his name was synonymous with training horses.

Hildreth was born in Independence, Missouri, in 1866. His father, Vincent, was a horse trader and racing man, and Sam learned quickly. When he was just shy of his sixth birthday, he is reported to have traded a horse in a transaction that earned him more than $700. When he was a few years older, he rode for his father in quarter-horse races, competing against others of his age group, including a lad named Charles Curtis, who became vice president of the United States under Herbert Hoover. Hildreth and Curtis remained friends all their lives.

Hildreth became too heavy to ride at 17. He wanted to train horses but found it difficult to assemble a worthwhile stable. He became a blacksmith, made enough money to buy himself some horses and also learned a trade that was to help him immeasurably as a trainer. The foot is everything to the horse, and Hildreth knew feet. As he won races in the Midwest, he also became a big bettor. After a string of coups, many bookmakers refused to accept his wagers. So he employed betting commissioners, and many of his bets were placed by Frank James, who, with his brother Jesse, at one time was active in the railroad business.

One afternoon in New York, in 1898, Hildreth was approached by William Collins Whitney, who had come into the sport at 57. Whitney asked if Hildreth would train his horses. Hildreth asked when Whitney would like an answer, and Whitney said, "Now." The answer was "Yes."

One of the best he trained for Whitney was Admiration, a foal of 1896 by Kingston. As a 3-year-old filly, she opened the season with victories at Gravesend at six furlongs and at a mile and a sixteenth. Then, at Sheepshead Bay, she won at six furlongs and a mile, running not only against fillies but colts and even older horses. She became the sensation of the East, prompting a match race against another top filly, May Hempstead, winner of the Tennessee Oaks and the Tennessee Derby. May Hempstead had come east, won at a mile at Sheepshead Bay, and her people were confident.

The match, at $5,000 a side with an additional $5,000 posted by the association, was held at Sheepshead Bay on July 1, 1899. Both fillies carried 107 pounds in the one-mile event, with Nash Turner on May Hempstead and Dick Clawson on Admiration. May Hempstead dashed to the lead, but Admiration drew abreast at the half-mile pole and was half a length in front after six furlongs. Admiration proved best in the drive, winning by two lengths.

Hildreth was ruled off by The Jockey Club in 1900 – explanations were not in style in that era – so he adjourned to the Midwest again where they had their own rules. He began buying horses and continued winning races. He had a big winter in New Orleans in 1903 and purchased the handicap star of the meeting, McChesney. E.E. Smathers, a prominent trotting horse owner, switched to thoroughbred racing about the same time by buying Hildreth's entire stable and signing the trainer to a contract for $25,000 a year, a whopping sum at the time. Shortly after, Hildreth shipped the sta-

ble to Chicago, where, at the Harlem track, McChesney won the Harlem National Handicap under 127 pounds and Smathers won a bet of $100,000.

Hildreth was reinstated in 1905 and came east almost immediately. He began to put together a string of horses that won its share, and he kept upgrading. He purchased King James and Joe Madden from John Madden, and bought Fitz Herbert from Herman Brandt. Hildreth always played good music, but in 1909 his band became a symphony orchestra as he led the list of leading money-winning owners and also led the trainers in money won. In a 16-year span, from 1909 through 1924, Hildreth was the leading money-winning trainer nine times.

King James alone would have made 1909 a memorable season for Hildreth. The Plaudit colt couldn't handle Colin as a 3-year-old of 1908 but won 10 races from 12 starts as a 4-year-old and was second twice. Racing in the Los Angeles area that winter, he won the California Handicap at a mile and a quarter under 129 pounds on a heavy track in mid-February. Nine days later, he won the Speed Handicap at six furlongs under 142 pounds. Finishing behind King James in the latter event were Roseben, who won 52 of 111 career starts, and Jack Atkin, who won 56 races from 136 starts.

Joe Madden and Fitz Herbert were 3-year-olds in that glorious Hildreth campaign of 1909. Joe Madden won the Belmont Stakes and other features, while Fitz Herbert started 15 times, won 14 and finished second once.

In the meantime, racing in New York was going down the legislative tube. Hildreth was leading owner and trainer a second consecutive year in 1910, but when racing was banned in New York in 1911, he took his horses to Canada and kept on winning. At the end of the 1911 season, he sold his entire stable to piano manufacturer Charles Kohler, signed on as trainer and shipped the horses to France. Foreign horses were not permitted to compete on the flat, so Novelty, Restigouche and other stable stars were converted to jumpers. How did they do? They were trained by Sam Hildreth, who could teach a pig to fly.

Kohler died in 1913, just as racing returned to New York. and Hildreth came back to the U.S. and was immediately signed as trainer by August Belmont, chairman of The Jockey Club. Belmont had been chairman in 1900 when the Club ruled Hildreth off, but that incident never intruded upon their subsequent relationship.

Hildreth developed the outstanding handicap horse, Stromboli, for Belmont. In 1914, Stromboli won 11 races and beat Roamer, the season's leading money winner, in the Baltimore Handicap at Pimlico. Another celebrated Belmont colt trained by Hildreth was Hourless, winner of the 1917 Belmont Stakes in track-record time. Hourless was beaten by Kentucky Derby winner Omar Khayyam in the Brooklyn Derby and in the Lawrence Realization. Hildreth could understand the former loss because of the off track, which didn't suit Hourless. He couldn't, however, understand the Realization in which Hourless was trapped in a pocket in a three-horse field and jockey Jimmy Butwell dropped his whip. Despite these shenanigans, Hourless was only beaten a

August Belmont (left) and trainer Sam Hildreth formed an unlikely, but very successful, team.

nose.

The situation called for a match race, with Matt Winn as host at Laurel. On October 18, 1917, a crowd estimated at just under 20,000 jammed Laurel. When they arrived they learned that Frankie Robinson was going to ride Hourless. It had been assumed Butwell would have the mount as usual, but Hildreth sent his assistant to the jockeys' quarters, offered Robinson the ride and received an enthusiastic acceptance. Robinson was the country's leading jockey in 1916 with 178 winners, but his engagement by Hildreth in a race of such importance as the Hourless-Omar Khayyam match was unexpected.

Equally surprised was the decision by Omar Khayyam's veteran rider, Everett Haynes, to send his horse to the front at the start. Omar Khayyam came from 10th place to win the Kentucky Derby and usually won with a strong finish. But Haynes knew speed usually wins match races. Omar Khayyam was in front by two lengths after a first half-mile in :47.

Robinson waited and eventually turned Hourless loose in the upper stretch. Hourless was in front at the furlong pole and won by a bit more than a length in the track-record time of 2:02 for the mile and a quarter. The last quarter of this memorable race was accomplished in :23⅗. Owner Belmont donated the $10,200 purse to the Red Cross. Robinson won his second jockey title in 1918. He was killed in a spill at Bowie in April 1919.

August Belmont, commissioned a major, disposed of most of his horses late in 1917 and threw himself into the war effort. Hildreth purchased a son of Fair Play named Mad Hatter for $5,000 from the Belmont stable, and the colt went on to win almost $200,000, including two victories in the Jockey Club Gold

Papyrus, with English jockey Steve Donoghue up, was first on the track for the October 21, 1923, match race at Belmont Park, with Zev and American champion rider Earle Sande just behind.

Cup. Another of Hildreth's many shrewd acquisitions for his own account was Purchase, an Ormondale colt bought from George Smith. The unusually handsome Purchase beat Triple Crown winner Sir Barton in the Dwyer, beat Eternal in the Southampton Handicap and won the Saranac Handicap at Saratoga under 133 pounds. He won nine of 11 starts in that season of 1919, and Hildreth often commented that Purchase was the best horse he trained. After two successful years on his own, Hildreth formed a racing partnership with oil man Harry Sinclair.

The partnership started out by buying Inchcape for a whopping $115,000 after he broke his maiden at first asking. Inchcape then won the Tremont Stakes by seven lengths for Sinclair and Hildreth,

but broke down and was out for the rest of the year. Inchcape was bred by John Madden, who had sold Hildreth many good horses over the years. To make up for Inchcape, who raced once at 3 and broke down again, Madden sold the partners a colt named Grey Lag, who, trained by Max Hirsch, had won the Champagne. Sinclair, a multimillionaire, wanted to keep buying horses. Hildreth, not in the same league financially, sold out his half to his partner and remained on as trainer.

Grey Lag, a 3-year-old in 1921, won nine of 13 starts, including the Belmont Stakes, the Dwyer and the Empire City Derby. He also won the Knickerbocker Handicap under 135 pounds and beat older horses in the Brooklyn. Sinclair's Rancocas Farm Stable topped the list of money-winning owners, while Hildreth was the training leader in money won and races won.

The horse with whom Hildreth is most closely associated in the pages of racing history was a 2-year-old in 1922. Zev, bred by John Madden and sold to Sinclair privately, was by The Finn out of Miss Kearney. A promising juvenile, he finished in the money in 11 of his 12 starts and won the Grand Union Hotel Stakes at Saratoga, while finishing second in the Futurity and third in the Hopeful.

Freshened over the winter, Zev – named for Sinclair's attorney,

Zev became a national hero when he beat Papyrus by five lengths in their celebrated 1923 match race.

William Zeveley – commanded attention in the spring by beating older horses in the opening-day feature in New York, the Paumonok Handicap. The Preakness preceded the Kentucky Derby that year and Zev went to Pimlico, only to be kicked by another horse shortly before the start. Zev finished up the track, but ran again three days later and won a small stake.

Coming off a victory, Zev should have been one of the favorites in the Kentucky Derby, particularly with Earl Sande in the saddle. Sande had been America's leading money-winning jockey of 1921 and was gaining a reputation for winning the big races. Instead, Zev was 19-1, with the three-horse Whitney entry of Enchantment, Rialto and Picketer the choice at 23-10 in a field of 21.

Breaking from post 10, Sande put Zev on the lead and kept him there, winning by a length and a half from the 20-1 Martingale, with the favored entry finishing sixth, seventh and fifteenth. Zev then proceeded to win the Withers, the Belmont Stakes, the Queens

County Handicap and the Lawrence Realization, his reputation growing with every victory.

Officials at Belmont Park, caught up in a surge of American pride, cabled a challenge to owners of Epsom Derby winner Papyrus – Derby winner against Derby winner. To add to the attractiveness of the offer, the $100,000 pot would be divided $80,000 to the winner and $20,000 to the loser, so that no one would go home empty-handed. The challenge was accepted, and Papyrus sailed from England September 22. The most difficult aspect of the eight-day trip abroad the Aquitania was preventing fellow passengers from feeding him snacks from their dinner tables.

His arrival in New York was worthy of a film star or a princess royal. The city boasted a dozen or more newspapers in those days, and each was represented by several staffers and photographers. A police escort accompanied the horse van to Belmont Park, and trainer Basil Jarvis' traditional sang froid was severely tested.

Zev broke out with hives in the three weeks before the match but recovered nicely. Papyrus missed a few days of training with an ankle but also recovered, and two days before the race electrified the press and public with a nine-furlong work timed in 1:50⅗, one and one-fifth seconds off Man o' War's world record. The race was set for Saturday, October 20, and rain began to fall Friday night. The track was a sea of mud Saturday morning, and Andrew Jackson Joyner, the noted trainer, led a delegation of colleagues in recommending to

Jarvis that he put mud caulks on Papyrus. Jarvis thanked them for the suggestion, but said he didn't want to confuse his colt any more than necessary in strange surroundings.

Champion English jockey Steve Donoghue rode Papyrus, who went to the post a slight favorite, while Sande rode Zev as usual. When the two horses walked out onto the muddy track, a huge crowd estimated at more than 50,000 roared a welcome. Technicians, preparing for the first radio broadcast of a horse race, saw to last-minute details on the roof of the packed stands. Jarvis and Hildreth stood at trackside together, watching the race.

Papyrus sped to an early lead but Donoghue quickly took hold of him, permitting Zev to move up. Zev, racing comfortably, began to open up, while Papyrus, with his smooth English shoes, couldn't keep pace. As Zev rounded the turn into the stretch, with a quarter of a mile remaining, Jarvis tugged at Hildreth's sleeve and congratulated him. Zev won by five lengths and accomplished the mile and a half in 2:35⅖, a commentary on track conditions.

Hailed as a national hero, Zev wasn't through for the season. He won the Empire City Autumn Championship, then was shipped to Kentucky for the Latonia Championship at a mile and three-quarters. In Memorium upset Zev, winning by six lengths, setting up another match. Zev traveled to Pimlico for another victory, then adjourned to Churchill Downs for the November 17 engagement with In Memorium. In the mile and a quarter match, the 3-year-old Zev carried 126 pounds while the 4-year-old In Memorium carried 114. In Memorium led, but Sande got Zev up in the final stride with

Edward (Snapper) Garrison had a finish named for him.

a great ride to win by a nose.

That gave Zev a season record of 12 wins from 14 starts, a second, and earnings of $272,008. Hildreth's other successes brought Rancocas Farm's earnings for 1923 to a record total of $438,849. It was a clean sweep for The Team, with Sinclair the leading owner, Hildreth the leading trainer and Sande the leading jockey in the department that mattered most to all three: purses won.

Zev retired to stud, proved virtually sterile, and was returned to training as a 9-year-old. Through a series of inadvertances, he was still racing at 13 in cheap claiming company, but Sinclair learned of this, bought him back and retired him to Rancocas Farm for the rest of his life.

At the time, Sinclair's attention was commanded by a Congressional investigation into the Teapot Dome oil leases. The notorious case dragged on for several years, Sinclair was tried and acquitted on charges of conspiracy with Secretary of the Interior Albert Fall. However, he had to serve several months in prison after being found guilty of contempt of Congress for refusing to testify.

Hildreth continued to train until shortly before his death in 1929. He saddled some winners but never again had one to compare with Zev. He was mourned as one of the greatest horsemen produced in America, and to this day his name is an icon in the profession.

Where Hildreth and Rowe were titans of their era in the training of horses, there were no comparisons among the jockeys in the first 20 years of the 20th century.

Isaac Murphy was the giant in the post-Civil War period, compiling a remarkable record of 628 victories from 1,412 mounts for a career percentage of .44 that remains the standard. Born in Lexington, Kentucky, on Jan. 1, 1859, he rode from 1874 to 1890 and had three Kentucky Derby winners to his credit.

Jimmy McLaughlin, leading jockey in the U.S. for four consecutive seasons (1884-1887), gained great renown with six winners of the Belmont Stakes in the seven-year period from 1882 to 1888.

Edward (Snapper) Garrison (1868-1930) became so famous for his powerful moves through the stretch that the term "Garrison finish" became part of the language of the era. In a 15-year career from 1882 through 1897, he rode nearly 700 winners, an exceptional total for that time. In 1894 he was the world's highest-salaried jockey, receiving a $23,500 retainer for first-call services from August Belmont.

There were many outstanding riders who starred in the first two decades of the 20th century, including Johnny Loftus, who rode Sir Barton to sweep the first Triple Crown in 1919; and Joe Notter, who won important races with Ballot, Sweep, Whisk Broom II, Pennant, Celt, Borrow, Fair Play and Peter Pan. But perhaps the two most brilliant riders of the time, their careers like comets which light the skies briefly only to fade from view, were Walter Miller and Carrol Shilling.

Miller was born in New York. The son of a shoemaker, he earned a few dollars working at Sheepshead Bay and quickly became fond of racing. He was a natural athlete. He began riding at 15 in 1905,

Walter Miller (right), a riding star of the first magnitude early in this century, spent the winter of 1905-06 in San Francisco with his agent, the young James (soon to be Sunny Jim) Fitzsimmons.

and rode 176 winners that season. Dave Nicol, who led the list, rode 221 winners. Miller attracted the attention of a well-liked young horseman, Sunny Jim Fitzsimmons.

During the winter, when most stables freshened their horses, Mr. Fitzsimmons often worked as a jockey's agent to help support his family. He took Miller's book in the winter of 1905 and the pair went to San Francisco, where Miller got off to a great start. They were still there when the great earthquake hit, and Mr. Fitz told harrowing stories of he and Miller ducking for cover under tables in their hotel room as the walls came tumbling down. Fortunately, both escaped without injury.

Returning east in the spring, Miller rode more winners than usual and by the end of the 1906 season had compiled the record total of 388 winners, with an equally fantastic percentage of .28. The previous mark was held by Earl Hildebrand, who rode 297 winners in the 1904 with a percentage of .25. Miller, in his record splurge, rode five winners on one five-race program at Brighton Beach on July 28, 1906. He also rode five winners that fall at the Benning track near Washington D.C.. He was the toast of the racing world and was often seen in the company of his good friend, John McGraw, manager of the New York Giants. Miller was a crack second baseman with the Sheepshead Bay jockeys team, and McGraw occasionally invited him to work out with the Giants.

Miller had another great season in 1907, riding 334 winners and duplicating his winning percentage of .28. James Rowe Sr., one of the country's most successful trainers, engaged Miller to pilot the sensational 2-year-old, Colin, who went through the campaign undefeated in 12 starts. But in 1908 Miller's total dropped to 194 winners. As racing was being phased out in New York, Miller went to Europe, rode with mixed success, and then returned to the United States and lived quietly in New York.

He suffered a severe illness in 1945 that led to a mental breakdown, and when elected to the Hall of Fame in the National Museum of Racing in Saratoga in 1957, he was unable to comprehend the honor. He died the following year, with no one in racing aware of his passing. None of the eight New York newspapers carried an obituary.

Shilling was born in 1886 in Amarillo, Texas, grew up on a cattle ranch, and was on a horse before he could walk. If there was ever a natural rider in this country, it was Shilling. He learned about pace and some of the finer points on the racetrack, but he knew about horses long before he put on his first set of silks.

Shilling started at bush tracks in the West, and worked his way to New York, acquiring a reputation for exceptional ability at every stop. In New York he came to the attention of Sam Hildreth, who

Carrol Shilling had a brilliant riding career but died in obscurity.

engaged him to ride the sensational 2-year-old, Novelty, in 1910. Hildreth watched Shilling in action for several months and then called him the best rider he had ever seen. Hildreth threw compliments as often as he threw manhole covers, but he never tired of talking about Shilling.

"He showed every quality that a finished rider could possess," the great trainer said. "He had an uncanny ability to break a 2-year-old away from the post, a judgment of pace that made you think he had a stop-watch in his head, a seat so light that he was like a feather on a horse's back, and a knack for getting every ounce out of his mount."

From 1904 through 1912, Shilling rode 3,838 races, and won with 969 mounts, for a handsome percentage topping .25. His best year was 1911, when he rode at a winning average of 36 percent, one of the highest on record. In 1912 he rode Worth to win the Kentucky Derby, but later that season was ruled off for life because of rough riding.

His knowledge of horses and his skills led to a long series of jobs as an exercise rider and stable foreman, but he was unsuccessful in his attempts to be reinstated as a jockey. He became increasingly morose, took to drinking, and in 1948 was arrested in Maryland for vagrancy. In 1950, his body was found lying beneath a horse van parked near Belmont Park in mid-January. Apparently he had frozen to death.

An Era of Growth

1921 to 1940

In 1922, Frank Brunell, founder of *Daily Racing Form*, made a decision to sell and retire. He was 69 years old, had worked hard all his life and wanted a few years to see and enjoy the world.

Brunell considered the asking price. It had to cover the office in Chicago, an office that had been opened a few years earlier in New York on 32nd Street off Sixth Avenue, plus a smaller office in Buffalo, New York, designed to serve patrons in the Toronto area. He decided to ask $400,000.

Brunell contacted only a few people. The market was limited, and not many people could come up with $400,000 in cash. That was the kicker in the deal: It had to be cash. Among those who learned of *Daily Racing Form's* availability was Moses "Moe" Annenberg, director of circulation for the Hearst newspapers.

Noting the rise of interest in racing after World War I, Annenberg, a keen businessman, thought *Daily Racing Form* would be a good investment. He agreed to the price and told

By 1931, Moses L. Annenberg owned both The Morning Telegraph *and* Daily Racing Form.

Brunell he would give him a cashier's check, guaranteed, to cover the sale. Brunell said he didn't want a cashier's check, only cash.

On the morning of the sale, Annenberg, accompanied by his 14-year-old son, Walter, went to a bank on the corner of Eighth Avenue and 34th Street in New York where a friend was vice president. Annenberg explained that he needed $400,000 in small bills for an acquisition and the money was bundled and wrapped in newspapers.

Young Annenberg, who was to become Ambassador to the Court of St. James, owner of *Daily Racing Form*, founder of Triangle Publications, and one of the world's most celebrated philanthropists, carried the package of money as he and his father were driven to the office of *Daily Racing Form*. Moe Annenberg shook hands with Brunell, gave him the package of money, the papers were signed, and the transaction was consummated with all deliberate speed.

A master of circulation, Annenberg quickly set about increasing the readership of his newspaper. At the end of the first year of operation under new ownership, *Daily Racing Form's* profit was almost $400,000, the price Annenberg paid. In subsequent years, the newspaper was a steady money-maker, and Triangle Publications executives alluded to it as the "cash cow" of the organization.

When he bought *Daily Racing Form*, Moe Annenberg brought with him four associates from the Hearst circulation department: William Moore, Hugh Murray, Joe Bannon and William McMurray. Subsequently, Moore purchased the New York *Morning Telegraph*, a newspaper devoted to the theatre and the turf, and competed for business with *Daily Racing Form*.

The Morning Telegraph, founded in 1833, had many owners prior to the turn of the century. In 1898, when he first became active in racing, William Collins Whitney purchased *The Morning Telegraph* and enjoyed a brief role as publisher. When Whitney died in 1904, Edward Russell Thomas, owner of the fine horse Hermis, purchased the paper from the Whitney estate.

William Lewis was the editor and publisher for Thomas, who spent much of his time in Europe. One of the columns in the paper at that time was "Masterson's Views of Timely Topics," mostly about boxing, written by William Barclay Masterson. This was, of course,

The Morning Telegraph, *which became a sister publication of* Daily Racing Form *in 1931, had a glorious history of its own. Shown here is a portion of page 1 of the November 29, 1927 edition.*

Bat Masterson, once the sheriff of Ford County, Kansas, and later a peace officer with Wyatt Earp in Dodge City. Masterson's main job with *The Morning Telegraph* was bodyguard for editor-publisher Lewis. A quiet, stocky man who favored blue serge suites, Masterson had many visitors at the paper, including prizefighters Jim Jeffries, Jack Johnson, Jess Willard and Jack Dempsey. Following a heart attack, he died at his desk.

Originally located downtown on West Street, *The Morning Telegraph* moved in 1915 to the car barn on Eighth Avenue near 40th Street, across the street from the old Madison Square Garden. In 1934, it moved to West 26th Street and 10th Avenue, and its last home, beginning in 1951, was on West 52nd Street off 10th Avenue.

When Edward Russell Thomas died suddenly in 1926, *The Morning Telegraph* was operated briefly by his widow, Lucy Cotton Thomas. But she remarried and sold the paper to Roi Tolleson, a red-haired native of Georgia who loved to gamble. After a run of luck at the New York tracks, Tolleson, a printer by trade, had enough money to start his own paper with past performances called the *Daily Running Horse*. Handicapping under the name of El Rio Rey, Tolleson picked winners like grapes and long lines of players lined up at newsstands throughout New York each evening to buy his paper. When he bought *The Morning Telegraph*, he continued to pick winners, and his star shone brightly. But like most handicappers, he waned after waxing and was forced to sell the paper in 1928 to Moore.

Moore's regime at *The Morning Telegraph* was brief and rousing. He hired Hearst's star writer, Gene Fowler, and made him managing editor. Ring Lardner was hired to write three columns a week. Top reporters and sports writers were hired from the *New York Times* and *Herald-Tribune*, and a fashion editor was hired from *The New Yorker* to introduce a page of women's fashions. *The Morning Telegraph* made quite a splash for a short time but the start of the Depression in 1929 rubbed the bloom off Moore's rose, and he was glad to sell it in 1931 to Moe Annenberg. Now *The Morning Telegraph* and *Daily Racing Form* were under the same management and would remain so until *The Morning Telegraph* suspended publication on April 3, 1972.

In the period following World War I, American racing experienced the dramatic growth anticipated by Moe Annenberg. Throughout the country, tracks opened that were to become among the finest and most popular in the U.S.

The first of these was Hialeah, which opened in a suburb of Miami on January 15, 1925. Developer James Bright provided the

Hialeah's ornate Spanish architecture was a drawing card when the Florida track opened in 1925.

initial impetus, but Hialeah didn't make significant strides toward prominence until Joseph E. Widener of Philadelphia, who made his money in street transportation, took command of the track in 1930.

He transformed it into the most beautiful course in America with graceful Mediterranean architecture that remains a treat to the eye, 70 years later.

Hialeah continued its growth and international celebrity under Gene Mori of Vineland, New Jersey, owner of Garden State Park near Philadelphia, who bought Hialeah in 1954. Mori rebuilt the clubhouse, enhanced the stable area and presented superb winter racing for 18 years. A group headed by John Galbreath of Columbus, Ohio, purchased Hialeah from Mori for a reported $21 million in 1972 but ran into a period of financial uncertainty shortly thereafter, and shareholders sustained heavy losses. John Brunetti, a New Jersey developer, acting in concert with the city of Hialeah, took over the track in 1977 but lost the choice mid-winter racing dates to Gulfstream Park and experienced a steady decline.

Chicago got two major racetracks in the 1920s. Old Washington Park was dismantled in 1906 as a result of reform activity. When oral betting was declared legal in Illinois in 1924, a group headed by Tom Bourke and Robert Sweitzer began construction of a luxury racing plant at Homewood. Opened on July 3, 1926, the new Washington Park was a track with all the amenities and a long stretch that measured 1,320 feet. The track offered important purses and attracted strong competition, but was not in the best financial health. Enter an old pro, Matt Winn of Churchill Downs, who organized a syndicate in 1927 that purchased Washington Park and quickly put it on an even keel.

In the same year of 1927, H.D. (Curley) Brown opened Arlington Park in a northern suburb, Arlington Heights. An ambitious project, it included a nine-furlong training track, a figure-8 steeplechase course and a polo field. A golf course and a tennis club were other attractions. Arlington raced a brief inaugural meeting beginning Oct. 13. While business was good, shaky financial leadership put the track in peril, and a Chicago group including John D. Hertz, Otto Lehman and Charles McCulloch took over the operation in 1928.

In 1935, a Chicago developer and keen racing fan, Benjamin F. Lindheimer, took over Washington Park, made notable improvements and upgraded business. In 1940, Lindheimer was part of a syndicate which bought Arlington Park. He integrated the racing programs at both tracks and presented the best summer racing in the U.S. until his death in 1960. He was succeeded by his daughter, Marje Everett, who also presented major racing. Following a politi-

By 1933, Arlington Park was doing substantial business, as witnessed by this Fourth of July crowd.

cal scandal in the early 1970s, Arlington was purchased by the Madison Square Garden Corporation, whose chief executive, David (Sonny) Werblin, introduced the Arlington Million, the world's first million-dollar race, in 1981.

Washington Park, site of the Nashua-Swaps match race on August 31, 1955, gradually declined in popularity and was closed in 1970. A fire destroyed Arlington Park on July 31, 1985, but industrialist Richard Duchossois purchased control of the track, operated out of tents for three seasons, and built a spectacular new Arlington International for an estimated $175 million that opened in 1989.

When California passed a pari-mutuel law in 1932, Anita Baldwin proposed to build a track on the estate of her late father,

Elias (Lucky) Baldwin, in the Los Angeles suburb of Arcadia. When she abandoned the project, a group stepped into the picture, got construction under way and completed Santa Anita Park in time to open on December 25, 1934. The group was headed by San Francisco dentist Dr. Charles Strub and Los Angeles business executive Leigh Battson. Movie producer Hal Roach was first president of the track, which attracted a crowd of 25,000 for its opening.

Movie producer Hal Roach (standing) was president and San Francisco dentist Dr. Charles Strub was majority owner when Santa Anita Park opened in 1934.

Just prior to opening day, December. 25, 1934, the Arcadia, Calif., site of Santa Anita still needed some finishing touches.

Under Doc Strub's direction, Santa Anita attained steady success. He introduced a $100,000 race at the height of the Depression and the Santa Anita Handicap became one of America's great races. Equipoise was the favorite for the first running on February 23, 1935. He was opposed by such cracks as Twenty Grand, Mate, Top Row, Ladysman, Head Play, Time Supply and Faireno. None of these won. Instead, the surprise winner was the former steeplechase horse, Azucar, owned by Freddie Alger of Detroit and trained by A.G. (Lex) Wilson. Azucar won by two lengths under George Woolf, the legendary "Iceman."

Strub saw Santa Anita become the most important racetrack in the West before his death in 1958. He was succeeded as president, and later as chairman of the board, by his son, Robert. Bob Strub developed into a top racing executive and led Santa Anita to further successes until his death in 1993, from Lou Gehrig's disease. Strub was succeeded as Santa Anita's chief executive officer by Steve Keller.

Four other tracks which were to play major roles in American racing also opened in the 1930s. They were Keeneland (1936), Del Mar (1937), Hollywood Park (1938) and Gulfstream Park (1939).

When the Association track closed in 1933 after more than a century of operation, Lexington, Kentucky, headquarters of the nation's breeding industry, was left without a track. Major Louie Beard, manager of the Whitney family racing interests, called a meeting at which the Keeneland Association was founded, with Hal Price Headley as president. A tract of 150 acres was purchased from horseman John Oliver Keene along the Versailles Pike and Keeneland opened on October 15, 1936, as a nonprofit enterprise, dedicated to the best in racing with all income above expenses and capital improvements earmarked for local charities. William T. Bishop served as general manager for many years before his departure for Oaklawn Park.

Headley was succeeded by Louis Lee Haggin, who

Hal Price Headley served as first president of the Keeneland Association.

brought stature to such traditional races as the Blue Grass Stakes for 3-year-olds, the Ashland for 3-year-old fillies, the Breeders Futurity for 2-year-olds and the Spinster for fillies and mares. He was followed by Ted Bassett, at one time head of the Kentucky State Police. Under Bassett's leadership, Keeneland's facilities were expanded and upgraded extensively in the 1980s, and he hosted an official visit by Queen Elizabeth II of England. When Bassett was named to the presidency of the Breeders' Cup, he was followed at Keeneland by Bill Greeley, who had served as general manager.

Del Mar, located on the Pacific Coast just north of San Diego, opened July 3, 1937, with crooner Bing Crosby as president and actor Pat O'Brien as vice president. From the outset it was a popular resort course and, with the steady upgrading of facilities, became the Saratoga of the West. Operating under a long-term lease from the county, which owns the land, Del Mar was completely rebuilt in the early 1990s by the current management group, headed by chairman John Mabee, a prominent breeder, and president Joe Harper, one of racing's top executives and a grandson of film producer Cecil B. DeMille.

Jack and Harry Warner of the Warner Bros. film studio were the principal investors in Hollywood Park, and Jack Warner was chairman of the board when "the track of lakes and flowers" opened on June 10, 1938, in Inglewood, a suburb of Los Angeles near the airport. The original stands were destroyed by fire but the plant was quickly rebuilt and Hollywood, for many years, was the national leader in attendance and wagering.

Film producer and director Mervyn LeRoy followed Harry Warner as chief executive and served with distinction for many years, together with vice president and general manager Jimmy Stewart. Marjorie Lindheimer Everett became chief executive in the 1970s and directed extensive renovations of the stable area and the stands, while enlarging the main track from eight to nine furlongs.

Hollywood Park played host to the first Breeders' Cup in 1984 and again in 1987. After a bitter legal battle, Everett was replaced as chief executive by industrialist R.D. Hubbard.

Gulfstream Park in Hallandale, Florida, just north of Miami, opened on February 1, 1939, racing in competition with Hialeah. A crowd of 18,000 was on hand for opening day and wagered $224,000, while at Hialeah a crowd of 7,600 wagered $292,000. Jack Horning, a prominent young sportsman, headed the group which opened Gulfstream. Financial difficulties threatened the track's existence, however, and the track was closed from 1940 through 1943. It reopened in December 1944, with landscaper James Donn Sr., who took over the property after paying outstanding bills, as president. A racing enthusiast, he enjoyed operation of the track and saw it develop into a major facility, with the Florida Derby becoming an important milestone on the road to the Kentucky Derby.

After battling with Hialeah in the legislature for many years over the choice mid-winter racing dates, Gulfstream moved to the forefront in the early 1970s. The senior Donn was succeeded as president by his son, James Donn Jr., in 1961. Following the latter's death in 1978, he was followed by his son, Doug Donn. As Gulfstream prospered, Doug Donn directed the rebuilding of the entire plant on a step-by-step basis. When some family members expressed a desire in 1990 to cash in their interests, Gulfstream was sold to Bert and Diana Firestone for a reported $90,000,000, with Japan's Orient Corporation financing the purchase. When Firestone's real estate holdings came under pressure from recession in 1991, the Orient Corporation took control of the track and asked Doug Donn to remain on as president.

In addition to the opening of many major racetracks, two of the most significant developments of the time were the starting gate and the photo-finish camera. Prior to the introduction of the gate, pub-

Del Mar was star-struck from the beginning, with Pat O'Brien as vice president and Bing Crosby as president when the track opened. Bill Quigley (right) did all the hard work as general manager..

Del Mar's first customer on opening day, July 3, 1937, got a smile and a welcome from Bing Crosby.

James Donn Sr. (right) and his son James Jr., pictured here in 1972, guided Gulfstream's fortunes for four decades.

A capacity crowd watched the field parade to the post for the first race ever run at Gulfstream Park, on Feb. 1, 1939.

lic patience was tried repeatedly at tracks throughout the country where each start could take up to 15 minutes or longer. As for the camera, the endless stories of mistakes by placing judges ended abruptly when photos of the finish were posted.

As early as 1894, races were started out of a gate at Maspeth, Long Island. A gate with separate stalls was tried at Bowie in 1923. The Jarvis-Waggoner gate was in use at Lexington, Kentucky, in 1927, and the Bradley-Stewart gate was used at the Fair Grounds in New Orleans in 1928. However, the first regular use of a starting gate is considered to have begun at Hawthorne at the fall meeting of 1929, when John Bahr introduced his version of the gate.

While photo-finish cameras were in widespread use in the early 1930s, Santa Anita introduced the first camera that could print an acceptable photo for public inspection in three minutes. The new cam-

era, developed by film industry professionals, was on line when Santa Anita opened its doors on Christmas Day, 1934.

The two most prominent racing men of the era were Col. Edward Riley Bradley, who raced as the Idle Hour Stock Farm, and William Woodward Sr., chairman of The Jockey Club for 20 years and master of Belair Stud. Between them, they won the Kentucky Derby seven times from 1921 through 1939, and in every instance with a homebred. Their backgrounds were as diverse as possible, but both were gentlemen of the old school, who played by the rules and expected others to do likewise.

Col. Bradley, born in 1859 in Johnstown, Pennsylvania, had a colorful life as a young man. He worked briefly in the steel mills around Pittsburgh and then headed west to a succession of cattle towns and mining camps, where he became a faro dealer, a book-

Before the introduction of the starting gate, walk-up starts tried everyone's patience. This field is about to leave Hialeah's starting barrier in 1934.

When the starting gate came into widespread use in the early 1930s, large fields could be dispatched with a minimum of fuss and delay.

maker and casino owner. He also worked as a cowboy, gold prospector and Indian scout, if contemporary accounts can be believed.

When he left the West, he made his headquarters in the Midwest, visiting such racing centers of the era as Hot Springs, Memphis and St. Louis. He made book at the tracks, accumulated some working capital and moved on to Chicago where he bought the Del Prado Hotel. He also had an interest in casinos in Long Branch, New Jersey, and Rockaway Beach, New York. In 1895, he started the Bacchus Club, a casino in El Paso, Texas, and in 1898 opened the Beach Club in Palm Beach, Florida. It was considered the finest gambling establishment in the U.S.

The colonel was a gambler all his life and made no secret of it.

In 1934, a Senate investigating committee conducted hearings into alleged connections linking the Fair Grounds, a track Col. Bradley owned briefly in the 1920s, with certain New Orleans crime syndicates. Sen. Huey Long asked Bradley his profession.

"I'm a speculator, racehorse breeder and gambler," the colonel replied.

"What do you gamble in?" Long persisted.

"Almost anything," Col. Bradley replied, "and I always pay 100 cents on the dollar."

In the summer of 1898, while he was living in Chicago, Col. Bradley didn't feel well. His physician, Dr. Leonard St. Johns, prescribed an active outdoor life if the colonel expected to live a full threescore and ten. Shortly thereafter, Col. Bradley bought a cheap horse from the well-known trainer, Eugene Leigh. The selling plater was named Friar John. Col. Bradley came out to the track one morning to see Friar John train and liked it so much he returned the next morning.

On July 27, 1898, Friar John made his first start in Bradley's green and white colors, going a mile and a sixteenth at the Harlem track in Chicago. He won, earning a purse of $300. Bradley had found an ace he could keep: thoroughbred racing. He looked for another horse and found a gelding named Brigade whom he purchased for $500. Brigade won in Chicago in the summer of 1899 and then was shipped to Saratoga, where he won on August 18. Brigade broke down in the race but not before winning a large bet for Col. Bradley.

In 1903, the Colonel bought a gelding named Bad News, by Flying Dutchman, and in the fall of that season, Bad News gave Bradley his first stakes victory at New York's Morris Park. Bad News travelled fast and won 54 times from a career of 185 starts, most of those wins in Col. Bradley's silks. Like many gamblers, Bradley was superstitious. Because Bad News did so well by him, he would name all his horses starting with the letter B.

Three years later, he bought a 333-acre farm in Lexington, Kentucky. It was called Ash Grove. He planned to breed horses

Bad News, here with Willie Knapp aboard, was so good he inspired Col. E.R. Bradley to name all his horses starting with the letter B.

there, and Mrs. Bradley (Agnes Curry of St. Louis) renamed it Idle Hour Stock Farm. His adviser was an English veterinarian, Dr. M.M. Leach, who had settled in the Lexington area and was an authority on pedigrees.

Col. Bradley kept buying horses while racing was banned in New York and many other major centers, sending his stable to Maryland and Canada and supporting the tracks in Kentucky. A friend, William Prime, purchased 18 colts from the famed stable of James R. Keene. In 1912, Prime lost more than a million dollars in the cotton market and decided to sell the horses. Col. Bradley loaned him $20,000 and purchased four from the sale. One of the four was Black Toney, whom he acquired for $1,600. Black Toney was only moderately successful on the racetrack but became a top-flight stallion.

Cliff Hammond, who had been training the Idle Hour stable, died in 1918 and was succeeded by H.J. (Dick) Thompson. Thompson had a 2-year-old named Behave Yourself in 1920 who was not a world-beater but showed some promise, particularly at Churchill Downs. In 1921, Thompson saddled Behave Yourself to win the Kentucky Derby by a head. The runner-up, also owned by Bradley, was Black Servant, while Harry Payne Whitney's favored entry of Prudery, a filly, and Tryster finished third and fourth. The only other owner to finish one-two in the Derby at that time was Commander J.K.L. Ross, whose Sir Barton and Billy Kelly swept the 1919 Run for the Roses.

Col. Bradley and Dick Thompson had their second Kentucky Derby sweep in 1926 when Bubbling Over led all the way to win by five lengths over his stablemate, Bagenbaggage. Col. Bradley had his third Derby tally in 1932 when

Bubbling Over was jockey Albert Johnson's second Kentucky Derby success.

Colonel Edward Riley Bradley (left), shown here in 1930 with James Butler, was one of the dominant racing personalities through the '20s and '30s.

Thompson sent out Burgoo King to win by five lengths. Burgoo King was by Bubbling Over. The following year, 1933, Col. Bradley was victorious a fourth time when the maiden Brokers Tip won an infamous duel through the stretch with Head Play by a nose as Don Meade on the winner and Herb Fisher on the runner-up whipped and grabbed at each other in a never-to-be-forgotten chapter of classic racing history.

Interestingly, two of the colonel's best horses were upset in the Derby. Blue Larkspur, a Black Servant colt who won 10 of 16 starts including the Arlington Classic, was the favorite for the 1929 Derby but was sent to the post in smooth shoes, rather than the mud caulks he needed badly for the muddy track. Slipping and sliding

under Mack Garner, he finished fourth in a race won by Clyde Van Dusen. Trainer Thompson, recuperating from an appendectomy, was not present for the race and his assistant, presumably caught up in the excitement of the afternoon, forgot to request caulks from his blacksmith. Blue Larkspur wore caulks for the Belmont Stakes, also run on a sloppy track, and was the winner.

Blue Larkspur was 17-10 in his Derby. Col. Bradley's Bimelech was 2-5 in the 1940 running. Champion 2-year-old of 1939, Bimelech, the last son of Black Toney and a full brother to Black Helen, won his 3-year-old debut in the Blue Grass Stakes at Keeneland and also won the Derby Trial at Churchill Downs during Derby Week. Under Frank Smith, he took the lead in the Kentucky

Burgoo King, a son of Bubbling Over, shown with Laverne Fator up, was Col. Bradley's third Kentucky Derby winner, scoring by five lengths over Economic in the 1932 running.

The 1933 Run for the Roses went down in infamy as Don Meade on Brokers Tip (right) and Herb Fisher on Head Play engaged in hand-to-hand combat through the stretch at Churchill Downs.

Derby at the quarter-pole but couldn't hold off a strong finish by Gallahadion, who won by a length and a half. The Colonel, 80 at the time, was disappointed.

One week later, after leading all the way, Bimelech won the Preakness with Gallahadion third. He also won the Belmont Stakes, with Gallahadion fifth. The Colonel, who regarded the Kentucky Derby as special, accepted congratulations with a smile but his heart wasn't in it. He didn't miss much, but he missed the Triple Crown. Bimelech, trained by Bill Hurley following the death, in 1937, of Dick Thompson, was out of La Troienne, a modest runner in England before she was purchased by Thompson on behalf of Col. Bradley in 1930 and imported to the U.S. She became one of the most influential broodmares of the century, a veritable fountain of top-class bloodstock.

Bradley suffered a heart attack in 1940 and no longer wagered on anything, a major concession to his health. He disposed of his Hialeah stock in 1943, and two years later closed his celebrated Beach Club in Palm Beach. He also sold his 2-year-old filly champion of 1944, Busher, to film magnate Louis B. Mayer, for whom she was Horse of the Year 1945.

Col. Bradley was 87 when he died at Idle Hour in Lexington on August 15, 1946. His wife had died some years earlier, there were no children, and none of the immediate relatives was interested in continuing the stable. The executors put up everything for sale, and that fall the farm and 87 horses brought $2,681,545 from a syndicate of Ogden Phipps, Jock Whitney of Greentree Stud and Bob Kleberg of King Ranch, the three sportsmen making their selections by lot. La Troienne became the property of Greentree while carrying the dam of stakes-winning Cohoes. Nine of La Troienne's daughters foaled the dams of 41 stakes winners, including Buckpasser, Straight Deal, Affectionately, Hitting Away, The Axe II, Malicious, Priceless Gem, King of the Castle, Batter Up and But Why Not.

Bradley was very innovative. He introduced fiber skullcaps for jockeys, and rubber riding gear for cold, wet weather. The barns at his farm and at his racetracks always provided cross-ventilation and comfortable living quarters for personnel. He experimented with oats fortified by ultraviolet rays and constructed a roofless barn to expose horses to daylong sunshine in good weather.

Above all, he distinguished himself by his sportsmanship. He scrupulously avoided affixing blame following a defeat and never questioned a decision by an official. As a gambler, he knew how to win and he knew how to lose, and it was difficult to tell the outcome of a race by his demeanor. All of racing mourned his passing.

William Woodward Sr., an influential presence in American racing for many years as an owner and breeder of top-class horses and as chairman of The Jockey Club, was born on April 7, 1876, in New York City. He became acquainted with racing early on, was permit-

William Woodward Sr. cut an imposing figure in American racing as owner, breeder and chairman of The Jockey Club.

ted to accompany his father each year to see the Belmont Stakes, and enjoyed recalling the 1888 running in which Sir Dixon won by 12 lengths over the only other starter, Prince Royal.

He graduated from Groton, Harvard and Harvard Law School, and his first job in 1901 was as secretary to Joseph Choate, U.S. ambassador to England. During two years of service in London, Woodward made frequent trips to Newmarket, Ascot and Epsom, and gained a lasting fondness for English racing.

Returning to New York in 1903, he joined the staff of the Hanover National Bank, of which his uncle, James T. Woodward, was president. Woodward bought a few horses when he was back in the States. Racing was beginning to feel the effects of reform legislation, and prices were dropping on thoroughbred bloodstock. Woodward bought three mares for $50 each and a stallion named Capt. Hancock for $300. One of the mares, Charemma, to the cover of Capt. Hancock, produced Aile d'Or, Woodward's first winner. A foal of 1906, Aile d'Or became the dam of Lion d'Or, who captured the Toboggan Handicap of 1920 for Woodward's first stakes victory. Lion d'Or was by Heno, the first stallion to stand at Belair Stud after Woodward was owner.

After assuming the leadership at the Hanover Bank, Woodward spent most of his time on bank business. In 1916, however, he read of a forthcoming sale of bloodstock in Paris and cabled a friend to buy him some mares. For $5,000, the friend bought five daughters of the undefeated Ajax. However, the war prevented them from leaving the country, and they did not arrive in America until 1919. That is, four of them arrived. One mare was washed overboard and drowned in the Atlantic. La Flambee, who arrived safely, became the great-granddam of Triple Crown winner Omaha.

It was also about this time that Woodward became associated with Arthur Boyd Hancock, owner of Clairborne Farm in Kentucky and Ellerslie Farm in Virginia. Woodward eventually moved his mares to Claiborne Farm to take advantage of the many stallions in the Lexington-Paris area. For years, Belair Stud sold a portion of its yearling crop at Saratoga and access to stallions was important.

Two events turned the picture around for Belair Stud. In 1923, Woodward hired as his trainer a former jockey and jockey's agent and a one-time streetcar motorman named James Fitzsimmons, from the Sheepshead Bay area of New York. The first Belair starter saddled by "Mr. Fitz" was Beatrice, a 2-year-old filly who won at Jamaica on April 30, 1924. Fitzsimmons went on to a glorious career, developing two Triple Crown winners for Woodward (Gallant Fox in 1930, Omaha in 1935) and many other outstanding horses.

Two years later, in 1925, A.B. Hancock Sr. put together a syndicate which included Woodward, Marshall Field and R.A. Fairbairn to purchase the French stallion Sir Gallahad III for $125,000. Sir Gallahad, who left one crop in France, was moved to Claiborne Farm. His first American foals were dropped in 1927, and they in-

After sweeping the Triple Crown in 1930, Gallant Fox beat older horses in the Lawrence Realization, holding off Questionnaire by a nose.

cluded Gallant Fox.

Gallant Fox, a winner of $328,165, was a huge success as a racehorse, with 11 victories from 17 starts. He was particularly brilliant at 3, winning nine of 10 outings, including a sweep of the Triple Crown events, the Wood Memorial, the Dwyer, the Arlington Classic, the Saratoga Cup, the Lawrence Realization and the Jockey Club Gold Cup. The only race he lost that year was the Travers, when the 100-1 Jim Dandy beat him on the money in one of the greatest upsets of all time.

In all, Woodward bred more than 90 stakes winners, including Nashua, who won the 1955 Preakness and Belmont Stakes in the colors of William Woodward Jr., and then beat the Kentucky Derby winner, Swaps, in a memorable match race at Washington Park on August 31. The senior Woodward died at this home in New York City on September 26, 1953. He was 77.

Woodward bred to get classic horses, and in the 10-year period from 1930 to 1939, Fitzsimmons saddled five winners of the Belmont Stakes for him. After Gallant Fox came Faireno (1932), Omaha (1935), Granville (1936), and Johnstown (1939). It may not have been quite as spectacular as Woody Stephens' five consecutive Belmont winners during the 1980s, but it was an impressive feat.

A man of imposing stature, six feet tall with large chest, broad shoulders, a ruddy complexion, piercing blue eyes and a sweeping mustache, Woodward was the final arbiter of American racing for many years. He was elected to The Jockey Club in 1917, became chairman in 1930, and held that post until 1950. As chairman he spoke out on many occasions against England's Jersey Act, which since 1913 barred certain American bloodlines from the English Stud Book because of "impurities" in their pedigrees. These included the Fair Play line and that stallion's son, Man o' War. He had the satisfaction of seeing all such restrictions removed in 1949.

It was during his watch as chairman that Marshall Cassidy was appointed executive secretary of The Jockey Club. Cassidy, with the full support of Woodward, was the impetus behind improvements in the starting gate, the photo-finish camera, the film patrol and many other progressive developments.

Yet, Woodward called himself a Victorian, and always dressed, spoke and behaved in conservative fashion. Among Woodward's hobbies was the collection of fine sporting oils, including portraits of noted horses of the past. It was an outstanding collection and now can be seen in the Woodward Wing of the Baltimore Museum of Art.

The three outstanding horses of the period 1921 to 1940 were War Admiral, Seabiscuit and Gallant Fox. Two were Triple Crown winners, classic in pedigree and classic in performance. The other, Seabiscuit, was a remarkable animal who accomplished some re-

War Admiral delayed the start for eight minutes, but was flying at the end of the mile and a half Belmont on June 6, 1937, as he became the fourth American Triple Crown winner.

markable feats during a remarkable career.

War Admiral, the "Greatest Son of the Mostest Hoss," was owned and bred by Sam Riddle. Born in 1861, Riddle came from Glen Riddle, Pennsylvania, where his grandfather founded a textile mill. He became head of the family business as a young man but it was evident to everyone his main interest in life was horses. He rode successfully at hunt meetings in Maryland and Pennsylvania, and began racing a stable about the time World War I was getting under way in Europe.

Riddle seemed to have a good eye for a horse. In 1917, he bought Star Fancy, who was a good winner and later became the dam of the hard-hitting Crusader. In 1918, he obtained a long-legged Fair Play colt out of Mahubah for $5,000 and became known to history as the owner of Man o' War.

When Man o' War went to stud, Riddle and those close to him began buying mares. Riddle was particularly close to Walter Jeffords, whose wife was the niece of Mrs. Riddle. Jeffords acquired the unraced Bathing Girl for $4,000, in foal to Harry of Hereford, a full brother to Swynford. The resulting foal was Annette K., named for swimmer Annette Kellerman. The tiny Annette K., barely 15 hands at the withers, only raced once, but bred to Man o' War got War Glory, a good one in 1930.

Riddle bought Annette K. privately from Jeffords, bred her to Sweep and got Brushup, who was even shorter than her dam. Brushup failed to win in three starts, was bred to Man o' War, and this mating produced War Admiral. It was a unique union. War Admiral's five full sisters were not much account. One never raced. Three never placed in a race, and the fifth filly won one race as a 2-year-old.

War Admiral, a foal of May 2, 1934, was trained by George Conway. Conway had worked for Matt Byrnes when the latter had such cracks as Salvator, Firenze, Parole, Wanda and other good ones. Conway was assistant to Louis Feustel when Man o' War was in his prime, and when Feustel's successor, Gwynne Tompkins, left in 1925, Conway became head trainer.

War Admiral won at first asking on April 25 at Havre de Grace and made it two victories for two starts a month later at Belmont Park. He finished third in the National Stallion Stakes, won by Jerome Loucheim's Pompoon, the best 2-year-old that season, and was second in the subsequent Great American to Fairy Hill, a good colt who went on to capture the Santa Anita Derby at 3.

Sidelined by a a cough, War Admiral missed the entire Saratoga meeting when Maedic was the star. That colt swept five stakes, in-

Trainer George Conway led War Admiral to the winner's circle after the 1937 Belmont Stakes. Charlie Kurtsinger was the jockey.

cluding the Hopeful, the Grand Union, the Sanford, the Saratoga Sales Stakes and the Flash. War Admiral and Maedic hooked up in the Eastern Shore Handicap at Havre de Grace on September 19. In a field of 15, Charlie Kurtsinger got War Admiral away quickly, took control of the race and the Admiral was home free by five lengths. Maedic? Still running.

He may have been a bit tenuous as a young horse, but War Admiral was perfect at 3. He was a big little horse, only 15.2 hands in height but with well-developed shoulders and quarters. He also carried himself well, and many contemporary observers said they saw the look of eagles in his eyes.

He debuted on April 14 at Havre de Grace, winning at six furlongs, and then came back 10 days later to capture the Chesapeake, traditional steppingstone to the Kentucky Derby, at a mile and a sixteenth. War Admiral won the Chesapeake with a flourish, taking command at the start and winning off by six lengths. Riddle often passed the Kentucky Derby with his good 3-year-olds – he did it with Man o' War – but now the old gentleman was getting into the spirit of the game.

Favored at 8-5 by a record crowd of more than 70,000, War Admiral, with Charlie Kurtsinger up, went to the front at the start from the No. 1 post position despite having been a bit fractious at the gate. The Admiral led all the way in a field of 20, built a margin of three lengths at the furlong pole and then coasted home in front of Pompoon, scoring by almost two lengths. *Daily Racing Form's* chart says the winner was "in hand." His time of 2:03⅕ may not sound like much, but it was the second-fastest running, to Twenty Grand's 2:01⅘.

One week later in Baltimore, the locally owned Pompoon, after working smartly at Old Hilltop, was installed the second choice for the Preakness at 5-1 to War Admiral's 3-10. The Admiral again drew Post 1, got the lead on a "good" track and maintained a steady pace. Pompoon drove up at the final turn, cut the corner and dropped inside of War Admiral for the drive. Eight lengths ahead of their six opponents, War Admiral and Pompoon staged a match race to the wire, with War Admiral the winner by a head in a zippy 1:58⅖, just two-fifths off the track record for the mile and three-sixteenths. Wayne Wright, on Pompoon, used his whip repeatedly while Kurtsinger, on the Admiral, never drew his stick.

The Belmont drew a field of seven, with War Admiral favored at 9-10. He was irascible at the gate, delaying the start for eight minutes with a series of antics, frequently dragging an assistant starter with him. Finally, as they left the gate, the Admiral stumbled, grabbing the quarter of his right front foot and shearing off about an inch of hoof. Blood spurted from the wound, but War Admiral raced to the lead, opened an advantage of four lengths, and held all challenges safe to win by three lengths. His time of 2:28⅗ for the mile and a half was a track record and equaled the American record set by his sire, Man o' War, in 1920. The gritty War Admiral received a hero's ovation from the crowd, many of whom could see the blood coming from his foot.

Conway gave War Admiral more than four months to grow a new hoof, and the colt returned to competition at Laurel in late

War Admiral led the parade onto the track for the November 1, 1938 Pimlico Special, with Seabiscuit wearing the No. 2 saddlecloth.

At the finish, as this composite photo shows, Seabiscuit was first by three lengths under jockey George Woolf with War Admiral and Charlie Kurtsinger well-beaten.

October, galloping to victory at a mile and a sixteenth in allowance competition. He won smartly, with the Suburban winner, Aneroid, second. This set up War Admiral for the mile and a quarter Washington Handicap, which he won resolutely from a field of good handicap horses. Four days later, he concluded his campaign with a victory in the mile and three-sixteenths Pimlico Special, for which he was sent off at 1-20 despite topweight of 128 pounds. He made such a strong impression that Riddle received a genuine offer of $250,000, a huge sum for the time. Riddle quickly turned it down.

Seabiscuit had enjoyed a superb season as a 4-year-old of 1937, and demand raged for a match race between him and War Admiral. Belmont Park officials put together a proposal for a $100,000 duel, winner take all, to be run at a mile and quarter on Memorial Day, 1938. Shortly before the race, Seabiscuit was withdrawn and War Admiral was entered in the Queens County Handicap on June 6. Carrying 132 pounds in the mile feature, he won easily.

Three weeks later, however, he suffered his first defeat in 12 starts when he finished fourth in the Massachusetts Handicap at Suffolk Downs. Carrying 130 pounds, he turned in a dull effort and the prize went to the 3-year-old Menow, who carried 107 pounds. But he regained his form at Saratoga, winning the Wilson Mile, the Saratoga Handicap at a mile and a quarter, the Whitney Handicap at a mile and a quarter, and a fourth stakes, the Saratoga Cup at a mile and three-quarters. In each of these four appearances at the Spa, War Admiral led all the way. Nobody ever had a better summer at Saratoga, including Diamond Jim Brody and Bet-a-Million Gates.

That fall, he won the two-mile Jockey Club Gold Cup in comfortable fashion, setting up a meeting with Seabiscuit in the Pimlico Special on November 1. Trainer Tom Smith and jockey George Woolf needed an edge and employed the element of surprise. War Admiral always came out of the gate running while Seabiscuit was never known for early speed. On this occasion, however, Woolf whipped Seabiscuit to an early two-length lead, startling Kurtsinger for an instant.

War Admiral, working hard, drew even with Seabiscuit and may even have inched ahead at the half-mile pole, but Woolf had some horse left, regained command and went on to score by three lengths in a track-record 1:56⅗. War Admiral ended an outstanding season with a victory in the Rhode Island Handicap at Narragansett Park but Horse of the Year honors went to Seabiscuit.

War Admiral became America's leading sire in 1945, the year his daughter, Busher, was voted Horse of the Year. Other cracks he sired included Blue Peter, Busanda, Searching, Admiral Vee, Cold Command, Striking and Mr. Busher. Because Man o' War was who he was, there was no way War Admiral could have lived up to public expectations. But he was an extraordinarily good horse, deserving of a higher ranking in history than he is generally accorded.

Very few horses make 35 starts in their career. Seabiscuit, one of the great stars of the era, made 35 starts as a 2-year-old. Bred by the Wheatley Stable of Mrs. Henry Carnegie Phipps and trained by Sunny Jim Fitzsimmons, he started 18 times before he broke his maiden at Narragansett Park on June 22, 1935. He equalled the five-furlong track record of 1:00⅗ and four days later raced five furlongs in :59⅗ to win the Watch Hill Claiming Stakes.

Seabiscuit began the campaign in relative obscurity. He won two overnight purses in his first 10 starts, captured a claiming stakes at Saratoga by six lengths and then won a graded handicap by four lengths. Enter Charles S. Howard. Born in Georgia, Howard rode up San Juan Hill with Teddy Roosevelt during the Spanish-American War, was a professional bike racer briefly, and later opened a repair shop in San Francisco. In 1905, he started selling automobiles and selected a brand named Buick. He became the sole Buick distributor in California, and his agency was once considered the largest in the world.

Howard became one of the major land buyers on the West Coast, then focused on yachting, polo, hunting and, finally, racing. He bought some horses in 1934 and gave them to Buster Millerick. Tom Smith, known as "The Silent One," had a division of the stable at Midwestern tracks. He was racing in Detroit when Seabiscuit was transferred to his barn. It came about simply enough. Howard visited Saratoga for a round of parties and stopped by Fitzsimmons' barn one morning, looking to purchase a nice allowance horse. Mr. Fitz said he could have Seabiscuit for $7,500, and Howard shook hands on the deal.

At that point, Seabiscuit had won nine of 47 starts, and earned less than $18,500. In Howard's colors, he won 24 of 42 starts and almost $420,000. Perhaps those two Saratoga wins were an indication of better days ahead for him. In any case, when he arrived in Detroit he promptly won the Governor's Handicap and came back to score in the Hendrie Handicap. He placed in two stakes in Cincinnati, then transferred to New York where he won the Scarsdale Handicap. From the Big Apple he travelled across country by rail to San Francisco, where he won the Bay Bridge Handicap and the World's Fair Handicap. His seasonal earnings of almost $30,000, most of that sum for Howard's account, was about three times the purchase price.

A dramatic moment in 1938 at Del Mar: Seabiscuit (on rail) is all-out to hold off Ligaroti by a nose at the end of a roughly run match race that saw jockeys George Woolf and Spec Richardson both suspended.

Seabiscuit became a national star as a 4-year-old in 1937, winning 11 of 15 starts and almost $170,000, although he lost a heart-breaker by a nose to the brilliant Rosemont in the Santa Anita Handicap. Seabiscuit rebounded with a seven-length triumph in the San Juan Capistrano, and then adjourned to San Francisco for two stakes victories at Bay Meadows, in the Marchbank and Bay Meadows handicaps, before heading east for the summer.

One of Seabiscuit's finest hours came in the Brooklyn Handicap at Aqueduct. With Red Pollard in the irons, Biscuit went to the front at the start and remained there, winning by a nose from Suburban winner Aneroid, with whom he was equally weighted at 122 pounds. Seabiscuit followed this memorable performance with two record-setting appearances: winning the Butler Handicap at Empire City after a mile and a sixteenth in 1:44⅕, and capturing the Massachusetts Handicap at Suffolk Downs with nine furlongs in 1:49. The winner had 130 pounds up, another mark of quality. Seabiscuit was Horse of the Year at 5 in 1938, though he lost two heartbreakers at the start of the season in a fashion that might have compromised the psyche of some animals. Aneroid, in receipt of a dozen pounds from Biscuit, beat him a nose in the San Antonio. Then came the dramatic Santa Anita Handicap, with George Woolf replacing the injured Red

Pollard. Stagehand, a 3-year-old in receipt of 30 pounds from the Seabiscuit, hooked the favorite through the stretch and beat Seabiscuit a nose, the second straight year he lost the country's richest race by the smallest possible margin.

Later that winter, Biscuit went to Mexico to win the Caliente Handicap by seven lengths. From there he went to San Francisco and won the Bay Meadows Handicap in a record-breaking 1:49 for the nine furlongs. He was a clear and present danger again, while back in Florida, War Admiral, Horse of the Year 1937, enhanced his stature with a tally in the Widener. Everyone called for a match race, and Belmont Park offered $100,000 and the date of May 30 as a vehicle. both sides accepted, but Seabiscuit was withdrawn at a late hour.

A new proposal had the two horses meeting in the Massachusetts Handicap on June 29. Once again, War Admiral was ready, but on the afternoon of the race, Seabiscuit was scratched without explanation. He shipped to Chicago for Arlington Park's Stars and Stripes Handicap on July 4, carried topweight of 133 pounds in the rain, and was upset by War Minstrel. But after travelling on to Los Angeles, Biscuit won the first Hollywood Gold Cup in a hack canter after setting a track record of 2:03⅖ for the mile and a quarter while carrying 133 pounds. George Woolf rode.

Ligaroti, a South American import, was making a splash in West Coast racing circles about that time. Owned by the Binglin Stable of Bing Crosby and Lin Howard – the latter a son of Seabiscuit's owner, Charles Howard – Ligaroti gained popularity and the management of Del Mar put up $25,000 for a match race against Seabiscuit. To put the duel in perspective, Biscuit carried 130 pounds to Ligaroti's 115, and the primary purpose, according to contemporaries, was to ensure an appearance by Seabiscuit at the resort track near San Diego. The California Horse Racing Board prohibited wagering.

The large crowd on hand for the August 12 feature gasped when the two horses turned into the stretch side by side, after a first mile in 1:36. Then, Noel Richardson on Ligaroti grabbed Biscuit's saddle cloth. Woolf promptly rapped Richardson with his whip. Richardson reached for his opponent's bridle, and Woolf responded with another blow of his whip. As their riders battled, the two horses raced to the finish line, and at the winning post it was Seabiscuit by a nose in a record 1:49 for the nine furlongs. The stewards reviewed the incident, permitted the numbers to stand and gave both jockeys the rest of the meeting off.

In New York that fall, Seabiscuit ran in the mile and a half Manhattan Handicap and finished third while conceding gobs of weight. The race was considered a prep for the Jockey Club Gold Cup that was expected to attract both Seabiscuit and War Admiral. Once again, however, Seabiscuit's people blinked and shipped him to Maryland where he won the Havre de Grace Handicap from Menow and Esposa.

As public pressure for a match grew hourly, Pimlico's young president, Alfred Gwynne Vanderbilt, stepped into the breach. He signed the two for a winner-take-all match worth $15,000 on November 1. Seabiscuit was given a final prep in the Laurel Stakes, but Jacola, a nice 3-year-old filly in receipt of 24 pounds from Biscuit, beat him smartly, setting a mile record with her 1:37.

War Admiral, winner of 16 of his last 17 starts, was sent off a heavy favorite for the match at 1-4. Seabiscuit was 2-1 in the wagering but had the element of surprise going for him. Woolf sent Biscuit to the front out of the gate, surrendered the lead briefly leaving the half-mile pole, and then came on again to score by three lengths in track-record time for the mile and three-sixteenths.

As he turned 6, Seabiscuit was pointed for Sun Beau's earnings record, less than $40,000 away. The Santa Anita Handicap on March 4 was the prime target, and Biscuit prepped for that engagement at Santa Anita on February 15. He was upset at one mile, came out of the race lame, and was sent to a farm 125 miles north of San Francisco owned by Howard. Seabiscuit was at the farm most of the year and was bred to seven mares. He returned to the stable that fall and was kept in training to pursue the money record.

Heavy rains in California during the winter of 1940 postponed Seabiscuit's appearance four times. When he finally got to the post on February 9, he was upset at seven furlongs, and week later he was beaten off in the San Carlos Handicap. Just when it appeared he might be ready for retirement, Biscuit won the mile and a sixteenth San Antonio Handicap in track-record time, with stablemate Kayak II, winner of the Big Cap the previous year, two and a half lengths back in second place.

Charlie Howard's entry was 7-10 in the Santa Anita Handicap, and Red Pollard was back to ride Biscuit. Pollard placed his mount just off the pace, moved to the lead near the eighth pole, then accelerated to beat Kayak II by half a length in a track-record 2:01⅘ for the mile and a quarter. The victory gave Seabiscuit a record of 33 wins from 89 starts, with 15 seconds and 13 thirds, and he was the first horse to win more than $400,000. His total was $437,730.

Retired to stud that spring, he was not an outstanding sire. He got four stakes winners of ordinary quality throughout his career as a stallion. But he was never forgotten as a racehorse — one of the best handicap champions of the century.

Gallant Fox was an outstanding 3-year-old in 1930, the year he

William Woodward Sr. proudly led Gallant Fox to the winner's circle on June 7, 1930, after the colt swept the Triple Crown with Earl Sande aboard.

swept the Triple Crown. He only lost one race that season from 10 starts and set an earnings record of $308,275 that stood for 17 years. But the Fox of Belair, as he was known, was essentially a lazy individual.

"When he had competition," his trainer, Sunny Jim Fitzsimmons, often said, "he could run like the wind. But as soon as he whipped everybody and got the lead, he would slow to a walk."

That approach carried over to his training, too. Gallant Fox did not care much for morning workouts, and Fitzsimmons had to supply a lot of trial horses to give him the competition he needed to insure his fitness. When it was his time, there were always two and sometimes three horses that worked with him, breaking off in relay fashion to pace him. You couldn't fool The Fox, either. If the work horses were not in the proper spot and ready to go, he would pull himself up and the whole ploy would have to be started again. But he could run, and when a horse can run, trainers put up with all sorts of antics.

He wasn't all that appealing when he first came to Mr. Fitz at 2. He was from the first American crop of Sir Gallahad III, and no one knew what to expect. He was big, somewhat ungainly, given to daydreaming, slow from the gate; an equine version of a teenager. In his first start, on June 24, he finished third in a five-furlong maiden race at Aqueduct. Five days later in the Tremont Stakes, his performance was even more moderate and for the only time in his career he failed to bring back at least a portion of the purse.

This picture tells the story of the 1930 Travers at Saratoga, for even as the 100-1 Jim Dandy whizzed by, nearly every fan on the rail was looking up the stretch in vain for the heavily favored Gallant Fox.

51835
Aug.-16-30-Sar

FIFTH RACE—1 1-4 Miles. (Man o' War, Aug. 21, 1920—2:01⅖—3—129.) Sixty-first Running TRAVERS STAKES. $5,000 Added. 3-year-olds. Allowances. Net value to winner $27,050; second, $4,000; third, $2,000; fourth, $500.

Index	Horses	A	Wt	PP	St	½	¾	1	Str	Fin	Jockeys	Owners	O	H	C	P	S
51509	JIM DANDY	w	120	2	1	3¹½	3³	1¹½	1³	1⁸	F Baker	C Earl	50	100	100	10	out
(50339)	GALLANT FOX	wb	126	4	4	2³	2³	2ʰ	2ⁿᵏ	2⁶	E Sande	Belair St'd Sta	3-5	13-10	1-2	out—	
(51656)	WHICHONE	wb	126	3	2	1½	1ʰ	3⁸	3⁸	3³	R W'kman	H P Whitney	7-5	8-5	8-5	1-6	out
51407³	SUN FALCON	wb	117	1	3	4	4	4	4	4	F Col'letti	W S Kilmer	30	40	30	3	out

Time, :25, :49⅖, 1:13⅗, 1:42, 2:08. Track heavy.

Winner—Ch. c, by Jim Gaffney—Thunderbird, by Star Shoot (trained by J. B. McKee; bred by Mr. W. S. Dudley).

WENT TO POST—5:20. OFF AT ONCE.

Start good and fast. Won easily; second and third the same. JIM DANDY was restrained back of the early pace, moved up fast on the inside rounding the stretch turn, shook off the leaders and drew away at the end. GALLANT FOX forced the pace from the start, moved away when settled on the back stretch on the outside, was carried wide turning for home, but could not overtake the winner. WHICHONE was hustled into command at the start, displayed good speed in the going, but tired badly in the stretch and pulled up very lame. SUN FALCON was outrun from the start and had no mishaps.

Scratched—51407 Caruso, 120.

Daily Racing Form's *chart of the 1930 Travers Stakes.*

In the Flash Stakes, on the opening program at Saratoga, Caruso charged to the lead despite his 125 pounds. Sarazen II, under 130 pounds, was in pursuit. Gallant Fox was well back but beginning to get in gear. Under 112 pounds, the Fox came on with a rush and won by a length and a half from Caruso. Caruso turned the tables, however, in the United States Hotel Stakes when both colts carried level weights.

Beaten a neck by Polygamous in the Futurity Trial at Belmont Park that fall, Gallant Fox wore blinkers in the Futurity, went past Boojum to the lead in the stretch, thought the job was finished and began to slow down. Whichone and Hi-jack went past him. He was able to conclude his season on an encouraging note, however, winning the Junior Champion Mile from a small field. It was a modest accomplishment, but he seemed decent enough when asked to go a distance, and his people made plans to try him for the classics.

Owner-breeder Woodward, realizing the need for a heady rider on Gallant Fox, sought out the best. That was Earl Sande, three-time champion jockey, who had retired in 1928 and was training his own horses. He rode them occasionally, too, so he was fairly fit. Woodward made Sande an offer he couldn't refuse, and the results of his efforts were almost perfect.

Gallant Fox began his 3-year-old season in impressive fashion on April 26, winning the Wood Memorial at Jamaica by four lengths from Crack Brigade. The Preakness was the first of the Triple Crown races that year, run on Friday, May 9. Gallant Fox, the even-money favorite, got in trouble on the first turn, but his speed got him clear and he went on to score by almost a length over Crack Brigade. On May 17 at Churchill Downs (they went to the first Saturday in May in 1932) Gallant Fox was 6-5 in a field of 15. He was in close quarters early, but Sande, unruffled, guided him to the outside, and he proceeded to make up ground. He had the lead leaving the backstretch, was in front by two lengths at the furlong pole and held that margin to the wire, with the 22-1 Gallant Knight second.

Harry Payne Whitney's Whichone, who beat Gallant Fox in the Futurity, made his 3-year-old debut in the Withers Mile at Belmont on June 7, and Mr. Fitz, sizing up the threat, set the Fox down for one of his famous works. Gallant Fox drilled a mile in a sensational 1:36⅖, but despite the move, Whichone was established the 4-5 favorite in the Belmont.

Sande sent the Fox to the lead from the start and settled him down in the backstretch. When Whichone came to within a length at the head of the stretch, Sande had plenty of horse left and the Fox won by three lengths, with little wasted effort. Gallant Fox had duplicated Sir Barton's feat of 11 years earlier, and it was mentioned in

The Jones Boys at Arlington Park, circa 1953. Plain Ben (left) had by that time turned over almost all the training duties to son Jimmy.

the newspapers but not in detail.

The 1930 Travers at Saratoga is one of the most famous races in the annals of the American Turf. Gallant Fox, unbeaten that season, was the 1-2 favorite in a field of four. Jim Dandy, who had 19 starts that year without winning a race, was 100-1.

Sonny Workman, introducing an unexpected note, sent Whichone to the front at the start of the Travers. Sande asked Gallant Fox to run with Whichone, and the two battled hard in the deep mud, that only Saratoga can produce. Which one tired on the final turn, carrying The Fox wide as Jim Dandy slipped by on the rail. Jim Dandy went on to win by eight lengths, earning himself a page in racing history, and a Jim Dandy of a page at that.

Gallant Fox completed his season with a victory in the two-mile Jockey Club Gold Cup to become the first horse to earn more than $300,000 in a single season and he was retired with a record of 11 wins from 17 starts and total earnings of $328,165. He had five stakes winners from his first crop of 18 foals, including the Triple Crown winner Omaha, while his second crop included Horse of the Year Granville, and Flares, winner of the Ascot Gold Cup.

∞∞∞∞∞∞∞

Has any era of American racing – or that of any other nation – produced three trainers of the stature of Ben Jones, Jim Fitzsimmons and Max Hirsch? Among them they saddled 12 winners of the

Kentucky Derby, eight winners of the Preakness, 11 winners of the Belmont Stakes, and won Horse of the Year honors eight times. They were legends in their time, and they come down to us through the corridors of history as giants of the game.

To his contemporaries and to racing historians who prowl the byways of yesteryear, Plain Ben Jones of Parnell, Missouri, was the greatest horseman America ever produced. He is credited with six Kentucky Derby victories and has countless other statistical triumphs. But his true stature in racing is best measured by the vast respect in which he was held by those who raced against him throughout the country and by those who knew him best.

Bennie Creech was a marvelous horseman throughout the Midwest during the first half of the 20th century, and a keen observer of the racing scene. He raced in competition with Jones for years, understood the intuitive skill that he brought to bear in his work and was a fan. Creech was a hard-bitten individual and spent praise like hundred-dollar bills, but whenever the conversation turned to the art of horse-training, Creech said there was no one who could compare to the man they called B.A.

"A lot of guys can look at a horse and tell you something about him," he would say. "But Ben Jones can look right through a horse and tell you what he's made of. There's never been anyone like him."

Benjamin Allyn Jones was born on December 31, 1882, on his father's cattle ranch near Parnell. Horace Jones, Ben's father, came from Lafayette, Indiana, drove wagon trains from Omaha to Denver, was a cattle agent in Ottumwa, Iowa, and headed for Texas after the Civil War. Driving his family in a buckboard, he was passing through Missouri when a blizzard forced the Joneses to seek shelter for the night. He found it in Parnell, liked the looks of the land, and decided to remain. He bought a farm and operated a flourishing cattle business.

There was a small racetrack on the farm, and on Sunday after-noons informal racing provided entertainment for the entire community. Jones was captivated by the challenge and color of the sport, which was illegal and operated with the sufferance of the local sheriff. Under pressure from reformers, the sheriff came to close the track on one occasion, but B.A. diverted him to a nook full of moonshine and saved the day.

Ben attended the State Agricultural College of Colorado (now Colorado A&M), and studied animal husbandry and played football. After college, he worked on his father's ranch, bought a couple of horses for the county fair circuit throughout Missouri and neighboring states. His first victory came at a gyp track near Fort Worth, Texas. His father wanted him to give up the "horse foolishness" and return to the farm full time, but Jones saddled several good winners and was past the point of no return.

For the next 20 years, Jones raced at tracks throughout the Midwest, Mexico and Canada, winning races and making a name for himself.

"What I learned about training, I learned pretty much by myself," he once said. "If you didn't learn, you didn't eat. Of course, I talked with some of the old-timers, but it was pretty rough at the start. I left home fearing those other boys, but after I started to win races, they started to fear me."

A big, powerful individual, he became known as an outstanding barroom fighter, and some of his battles were legendary. On one occasion, while racing in Canada, he claimed a horse from another trainer who refused to surrender the horse and hid him. The horse was eventually found in a local garage and the stewards called the two trainers in. The man whose horse was claimed made a remark reflecting on Jones' honor, whereupon B.A. hurled himself at the man and they battled furiously on the floor, to the horror of the stewards. Finally, Jones bit the man on his head and the stewards separated them. Biting was a serious offense at the time, and Jones

Ben Jones, perhaps the greatest trainer America has ever produced, was credited with six Kentucky Derby winners and two Triple Crown winners. Whirlaway (Eddie Arcaro up) wore blinkers modified by Jones in his 1941 Triple sweep.

had to be smuggled back across the border.

On another occasion, while racing in Juarez, Mexico, Jones heard fellow trainers say that the bandit general, Pancho Villa, was on his way with his troops, seeking fresh mounts. Jones' best horse, Lemon Joe, was all black, and Villa's cavalrymen loved black horses. Jones took some mud, balled up a gob and placed it under one of Lemon Joe's hooves, and wrapped a potato sack around it like a crude bandage. When Villa's men came, they searched the barns and took all the black horses. They led Lemon Joe out of his stall, too, but as he hobbled around they quickly concluded he was unsound and left him alone. Jones won many a race with him after that and learned a lesson that was to bear fruit again another day.

He started to breed horses at Jones Stock Farm but found that a good stallion was an essential part of any program. Friends told him of a young stallion standing in a neighboring state, and he went to see for himself. He liked the appearance of Seth, a son of Adam out of Purity, by Deceiver, and took a lease with an option to buy. Bringing him back to Parnell, Jones struck gold. Seth was a prolific sire of runners, and Jones won small stakes with Captain Seth, Major Seth, Dolly Seth and other sons and daughters of his new stud horse. Captain Seth won 13 of 19 starts as a 2-year-old and was never out of the money. Jones' reputation spread throughout the Midwest.

Ben Jones was 24 when his son, Horace Jr., was born in 1906. The youngster quickly gained the nickname of Jimmy, loved working and riding the horses at the farm, became an assistant to his father during summer vacations from school and later took a few horses to bush tracks on his own with some success. He attended Northwest Missouri State College with the thought of becoming a veterinarian but the lure of the racetrack was too strong. He dropped out after two years and took some of the Jones horses to Southern tracks, saddling his first winner in New Orleans in 1926.

Jimmy called his outfit the Do-mor Stable.

Seth, remarkably successful at Jones Stock Farm, fell in the paddock in 1927, broke his neck, and was dead at 19. The Joneses sought replacements, but none proved out. Had Seth lived, they probably would have continued racing their own stables, but when the winners began coming a little slower and the nation was gripped in the Depression of the early 1930s, they expressed interest when approached by Kansas City merchant prince Herbert Woolf.

Ben Jones went to work for Woolford Farm in 1932 at a

Warren and Lucille Wright, whose Calumet Farm horses were the toast of American racing, were prominent Saratoga visitors in August of 1940.

$50,000 in wagers on the race, and was so delighted with the victory that he gave Jones an extra $5,000 in addition to his 10 percent of the $50,000 Derby purse.

Winning the Kentucky Derby made Jones a national figure, and his advocacy of winter racing, particularly for 3-year-olds pointed for the classics, commanded attention. Many leading stables accustomed to going to winter quarters for a holiday began racing at Hialeah, the Fair Grounds and Santa Anita, and Jones, more than any other individual, was responsible.

salary of $750 a month while Jimmy raced the remaining horses for a season or two and then sold the stable and mares for whatever they would bring and joined his father. Woolford Farm began winning races with daughters of the stallion Insco, including Inscoelda and Insco Lassie. There was also a promising Insco colt in the 1937 crop of homebred 2-year-olds, and Herbert Woolf named him Lawrin.

Lawrin won only three of 15 starts at 2, but finished second in six consecutive races as if knocking at the door. Jones decided to race him the winter of his 3-year-old season, brought him to Hialeah and won the Flamingo Stakes with him. Fighting Fox was the 7-5 favorite in the 64th Kentucky Derby of 1938, but the winner, under a dashing young jockey named Eddie Arcaro, was Lawrin, trained by Ben A. Jones. Woolf, a good sport, is reported to have won

Jones also revolutionized the training of horses. Before he made such a powerful impact on the racing scene, trainers pointing for important races wanted to insure their horses' fitness. They did this by working the full distance of the race at a lively clip. Jones, on the other hand, prepared his horses for major events with a six-furlong breeze at a moderate pace. As his reputation burgeoned, more and more of his colleagues, observing his methods, voted their approval by copying his style.

On an August morning in 1939, Jones, racing in Chicago for the summer, was invited to breakfast at the Drake Hotel by Warren Wright and his wife, Lucille. Heir to the Calumet Baking Powder fortune, Wright began racing thoroughbreds in 1932 and had a bit of success with trainers Bert Williams and Frank Kearns. But Wright set high standards, and a bit of success didn't interest him.

"We want to win the Kentucky Derby," Mrs. Wright, always outspoken, told Jones flatly as he drank his orange juice. By the time coffee arrived, Jones agreed to go work for Calumet Farm on September 1, with Jimmy as his assistant.

That was the start of perhaps the most successful association of trainer and owner ever recorded. The full impact of the work of the Joneses at Calumet can best be perceived from the trophies won by Calumet Farm horses from the fall of 1939 to the retirement of Jimmy Jones in 1965. This unparalleled collection included seven Kentucky Derby trophies and two Triple Crown trophies. When Mrs. Wright (later Mrs. Gene Markey) visited the farm in Lexington, Kentucky, every spring and fall, a houseman spent two weeks in advance of the visit getting the trophies out of the vault, polishing them, and setting them in a display case.

The Calumet horses were stabled in New York. The Joneses spent several weeks sorting them out and getting to know them. The first horse they ran for Calumet was a winner, and so were the next nine.

The next season, their first full year on the job, the Joneses found they appeared to have just one 2-year-old with promise, a colt with a long tail by Epsom Derby winner Blenheim II who was im-

A familiar sight in the winner's circle at Churchill Downs: The Jones Boys and Eddie Arcaro, this time with 1941 Triple Crown winner Whirlaway.

ported to the United States in 1936. Whirlaway proved a horse who required a lot of schooling, a lot of patience, a lot of training. Ben Jones, mindful of his goal as defined by Mrs. Wright at the breakfast, decided to work with Whirlaway almost exclusively, with Jimmy training the rest of the stable. During the Arlington Park meeting in the summer of 1940, Ben Jones sat for hours on his pony under a broiling sun, patiently working with Whirlaway and attempting to cool out some of the hot blood he inherited from Blenheim.

Whirlaway showed improvement. Third in the Arlington Futurity, he went to Saratoga to win the Saratoga Special and the Hopeful, while placing in finished third in the Futurity at Belmont Park and the Pimlico Futurity. He was gaining the confidence of his trainer.

Whirlaway and the stable were shipped to Miami for winter racing. Ben Jones, after viewing the situation and assessing his colt, decided not to run him in the Flamingo. Warren Wright, on the other hand, was raring to run. Jones, recalling the visit of Pancho Villa to Juarez, put a light blister on Whirlaway, wrapped the leg in bandages, and proclaimed to one and all that the colt was temporarily hors de combat.

Before departing for Kentucky, Jones estimated that Whirlaway would benefit from a short, sharp race, and entered him in a sprint at Tropical Park. Warren Wright, fishing in the Florida Keys on his yacht, was reading the Miami *Herald* at breakfast one morning when he saw his colt's name in the entries. He quickly dressed, hired a car and driver and rushed to Tropical Park, arriving shortly before post time. He told Jones in words of one syllable that Whirlaway was a distance horse and that it would be wrong to run him in a sprint. Jones, never a diplomat, replied in words of one syllable that he was training the horse, and that as long as he was, the horse would run. Jimmy Jones, watching the two rugged individualists get red in the face, wondered if either would have a heart attack before the Joneses were fired.

Wright, furious but silent, plopped into his box seat. Whirlaway came out on the track looking a picture, trailed badly as usual during the early part of the race, and then finished like an express train to get up in the last jump. Soon many of Wright's friends dropped by the box to congratulate him and slowly the frostiness wore off. He turned to B.A., shook his hand, and said he would never again try to interfere in the training of the horses.

Whirlaway, benefitting from that sprint, finished second in the Blue Grass at Keeneland despite pursuing an erratic course. He was an erratic second again in the Derby Trial on the Tuesday of Derby Week. B.A. knew that a change of equipment was in order, but not many horsemen would risk a change on the eve of a Kentucky Derby for which their horse was favored. Jones' confidence in his own judgment resulted in a one-eyed blinker for Whirlaway, the cup on the outside so that the colt's vision to the outside would be blocked. This would have the effect of keeping him from bearing out and would force him to rely more on the rider, giving the rider more control.

The day before the Derby, Whirlaway opened up through the stretch with his new blinkers on. To test their efficacy – and perhaps to convince jockey Eddie Arcaro that the problem was solved –

Jones put himself at risk. Mounted on his pony and wearing his customary work clothes of an old suit, sport shirt buttoned at the neck, and stockman's Stetson, he positioned himself 10 feet off the inner rail and directed Arcaro to bring Whirlaway between himself and the rail as he finished his blowout.

"I had some doubts," Arcaro was to comment later, "but if that old man was game enough to sit there and risk me running him over, I was game enough to go through that narrow opening. Whirlaway handled perfectly, and I felt we had a great shot in the Derby."

King Ranch's Dispose set the pace in the 67th Kentucky Derby on May 3, 1941, prompted by the second choice, Charles S. Howard's Porter's Cap, with the 29-10 favorite, Whirlaway, eighth in a field of 11 during the early stages. The Calumet colt began to move leaving the half-mile pole, raced between horses entering the stretch and, long tail waving behind him, took command at the three-sixteenths pole and opened up on his pursuers. His margin of three lengths increased to four and then five, and as the large crowd roared its approval, he kept pouring it on. He won by eight lengths, a record margin, and set a track record of 2:01⅖ for the mile and a quarter.

On the victory stand in the winner's circle, Jones was embraced by the Warren Wrights. Less than two years from the date of their Chicago breakfast, when they told him they wanted to win America's premier race, Jones had delivered as promised.

One week later, in the 66th Preakness at Pimlico, Whirlaway delivered almost exactly the same race, coming from last in a field of eight to win by five and a half lengths on a track slightly off from recent showers. That set the stage for the 73rd Belmont Stakes in New York on June 7. With only three opponents, Whirlaway was a standout 1-4 favorite. The others tried to slow the early pace to blunt Whirlaway's stretch punch, but after wrestling with his mount through a first half-mile in :49⅘, Arcaro had enough. He turned the big colt loose, and Whirlaway opened a seven-length margin. Then Eddie gathered him together again and cruised through the Belmont Park stretch to win by two and a half lengths, with — in the words of the chart — speed in reserve. A Triple Crown winner for Plain Ben Jones.

About the time that Whirlaway was preparing for his Triple Crown campaign, Bull Lea's first foals were beginning to drop at Calumet Farm. Bull Lea was by Bull Dog out of Rose Leaves and was pur-

Twilight Tear, shown going to the post at Belmont in May of 1944 with Conn McCreary up, had two special distinctions: She was the first filly ever named Horse of the Year, and Ben Jones called her the best filly he ever trained.

chased by Warren Wright as a yearling for $14,000. Trained by Frank Kearns, he won the Blue Grass Stakes of 1938 and was one of the favorites for the Kentucky Derby. Ironically, the winner of the Derby that year was Lawrin, trained by Ben Jones.

Bull Lea won the prestigious Widener Handicap at Hialeah in 1939, added to his credits during the season, and was retired to stud in 1940 at Calumet Farm. From his first crop, those foals of 1941, came the 1944 Horse of the Year, Twilight Tear, regarded as one of the greatest fillies to race in the U.S., and the 1947 Horse of the Year, Armed, who won 41 of 81 starts and $800,000 in purses.

Bull Lea was America's leading sire in 1947, 1948, 1949, 1952 and 1953. In addition to Armed and Twilight Tear, he was the sire

of Triple Crown winner Citation, Kentucky Derby winners Hill Gail and Iron Liege, the Preakness winner Faultless, the brilliant filly Two Lea, and so many other cracks such as Gen. Duke and Mark-Ye-Well.

If there is such a thing as trainers for sires, then Ben Jones' association with Bull Lea was a match made in horse heaven. When Jones brought colts and fillies by Bull Lea to the paddock for important races, they were the center of attention because they looked so good. They were big and dappled and bursting with healthy energy, and they looked like winners before they stepped onto the track. Other trainers with Bull Lea horses couldn't bring them outwith the same resplendence. Nor did they run as well as those trained by B.A.

While he was committed to winning the Kentucky Derby above all other races, Jones never ran a horse for the roses just for the sake of being represented. His measuring stick was: "Can I finish one-two?" and if he couldn't answer "yes," he sat. It wasn't a committee vote, either. In 1944, for example, he felt he could win the classics with a filly, Twilight Tear. But since he had a nice colt named Pensive he chose to play it traditionally.

Pensive, by Hyperion out of Penicuik II, was a moderate 2-year-old who developed early in his 3-year-old season. He was 7-1 when he went to the post at Churchill Downs, and Jones couldn't get Arcaro at those odds. He settled for Conn McCreary, who rode a superb race, waiting patiently at first, far back in a field of 16. Pensive worked his way forward but was still fifth at the head of the stretch. Then he came on like Whirlaway Jr. and won by four and a half lengths.

They went the first half-mile in :47⅕ in the Kentucky Derby. The pace was slowed to :48⅕ in the Preakness, so Pensive's stretch punch was somewhat blunted. He still got up, however, beating George D. Widener's Platter by three-quarters of a length and conjuring thoughts of a second Triple Crown.

And they almost brought it off. McCreary might have moved a trifle soon. Pensive had the lead after the first mile and a quarter but tried to stand off a closing surge by William Ziegler Jr.'s long-winded Bounding Home and missed by half a length.

As for Twilight Tear, she finished third in her 3-year-old debut — against older male horses — and then won her next 11 starts, including the classic Coaching Club American Oaks at Belmont Park. She also beat the colts in the Arlington Classic. Upset in the Alabama Stakes by Mr. Fitz' entry of Vienna and Thread o' Gold, "Suzie," as Twilight Tear was known in the stable, freshened for several weeks and then came back in the fall for several engagements.

Owner Warren Wright and trainer Jimmy Jones greeted Armed in the winner's circle after the gelding beat Stymie in the 1946 Suburban Handicap en route to honors as champion handicap horse. Doug Dodson was the rider.

The most significant of these was the Pimlico Special, in which she beat the handicap champion, Devil Diver, by six lengths. She was later named Horse of the Year.

Twilight Tear bled in her first start at 4 and was retired with 18 wins from 24 starts. There was one other honor for her as she went home to be bred. Her trainer called her the best filly he ever had in his barn, and he never saw fit to change that estimate until the day he died.

One fall morning in 1947, Ben Jones looked down his shedrow at Belmont Park and took stock. An attractive bay head popping out of one stall belonged to the 2-year-old champion, Citation. Another head turning toward the trainer belonged to Bewitch, the 2-year-old filly champion. Faultless, the Preakness winner, looked up from his hayrack to see what was happening, and from an adjoining stall, Fervent, the American Derby winner, indicated he was present and accounted for. Twosy, a top handicap mare, wanted to be sure she was not overlooked, and just beyond her stall stood Armed, the Horse of the Year.

It was Murderers' Row, and what killers they were! Calumet set a record in 1947 by winning 100 races and $1,402,436 in purses, and the earnings mark stood for 22 years. Armed contributed almost $400,000 of that sum as he enjoyed his greatest year, with 11 victories from 17 starts.

Quite a difference from the start of his career. Full of spirit at the farm and relatively small of stature, he convinced the Calumet people to geld him at 2 and he never started. He made his debut as a 3-year-old at Hialeah on February 28, 1944, and won off by eight lengths, a tour de force rarely permitted by Eddie Arcaro. Four days later he won again, and some were saying he was Jones' Derby horse. Jones had Pensive and Twilight Tear, however, and did not need another Derby horse. Armed raced seven times in all that season, winning three times, then was put away.

In 1945, racing was shut down by the government until May 9. Armed didn't make his first start as a 4-year-old until June 2. From that date through the late fall he won 10 of 15 starts, the climax coming in the Pimlico Special, which he won by four lengths.

Armed won 11 races as a 5-year-old of 1946, including the Widener at Hialeah by five lengths and Pimlico's Dixie Handicap under 130 pounds. One of his finest performances came in Belmont Park's Suburban Handicap, which he won by four lengths, carrying 130 pounds and giving Stymie seven pounds.

His Horse of the Year season of 1947 began with four consecutive victories, including a second Widener. Flown to California for the Santa Anita Handicap, Armed misfired, but once he returned to Florida, he regained his form, winning the mile and a quarter Gulfstream Park Handicap under 129 pounds in a track-record 2:01⅖. During the running of the Gulfstream race, Armed was kicked by Concordian, gashing the favorite's right rear pastern. The

The hot-tempered Hill Gail gave Ben Jones his sixth Kentucky Derby victory in 1952 with Eddie Arcaro up.

injury kept him on the sidelines for three months and force him to miss the Suburban, in which he was to have met Assault, the Triple Crown hero of the previous season.

Armed retained his winning ways that summer, capturing the Stars and Stripes Handicap at Arlington Park under 130 pounds and setting a track record of 1:49⅕ for nine furlongs. He carried 130 pounds to win the Whirlaway Stakes in a track-record 1:48⅗ for nine furlongs. He also won the Washington Park Handicap by three lengths from film mogul Louis B. Mayer's great racemare, Honeymoon.

Jones liked to sharpen his horses with a sprint when going to important races. He did it successfully on several occasions for the Kentucky Derby when he ran in the Derby Trial, four days earlier. For the match race with Assault, he was entered in a six-furlong overnight dash and was beaten by America's best sprinter, Polynesian, sire of Native Dancer. However, the race put him on edge, mentally as well as physically.

Unfortunately, Assault was battling a splint on September 27, date of the $100,000 Special. It was no secret, and the Belmont Park people did not permit wagering on the exhibition, which Armed won by eight lengths.

Armed never again was able to reach championship level, but with an overall record of 41 wins from 81 starts, 20 seconds and 10 thirds, he earned a world's record $817,475, a mark that stood for 12 years.

Jimmy Jones trained Armed through much of his career and trained Citation through most of that exceptional horse's racing life.

In the spring of 1948, Jimmy Jones had a unit of Calumet Farm, including Citation, in Maryland for the Chesapeake Stakes at Havre de Grace before coming to the Derby. The senior Jones was at Keeneland with another 3-year-old of sensational promise, Coaltown. Both won their races, and some professed to say they couldn't distinguish between the two. But Ben and Jimmy knew Citation was in a class by himself.

With three Kentucky Derby victories to his credit, Ben Jones needed one more to equal the mark set by Derby Dick Thompson with the Bradley Stable horses in the 1920s and early 1930s. Jimmy Jones graciously stood down but continued to work with his father and the stable during Derby Week. However, Jimmy saddled Citation for the Preakness and the Belmont Stakes, and in all succeeding races until Citation became the first horse to win $1 million at age 6 in 1951.

Ben Jones had his fifth Kentucky Derby winner the following season, and somewhat unexpectedly. Ponder, by Pensive, failed to win in four starts at 2 and wasn't particularly impressive in the spring of his 3-year-old season. However, he began to come to hand as the Derby approached, and after he finished second in the Derby Trial, Ben Jones thought they had a chance at the big one. Few

Iron Liege (Bill Hartack aboard), who gave Jimmy Jones his first Derby victory in 1957, was greeted by Ben Jones and Calumet Farm owner Lucille Markey.

shared his opinion. Ponder was 16-1 under Steve Brooks while Fred Hooper's Olympia was the 4-5 favorite under Eddie Arcaro. But it was Ponder by three at the winning post.

Jones' sixth and last Kentucky Derby winner was Hill Gail in 1952. Hot-blooded and hot-tempered, Hill Gail showed enough at 2 to win the Arlington Futurity and finish second in the Washington Park Futurity. There was no question he had ability, but he was a wild horse as he turned 3. Racing in California that winter, the Joneses devised a strategy to deal with the situation. When Hill Gail came to the track in the mornings, Jimmy, on a pony, would hold one side of his halter, and a pony boy would be on the other side. Hill Gail was strong, but he couldn't shake loose from the two "instructors." Ben Jones, on his pony at the finish line, supervised the training.

Gradually, reluctantly, Hill Gail got the message and behaved himself enough to win the Santa Anita Derby. He won a stakes at Keeneland that spring, and the Derby Trial, and on Derby Day he was the 11-10 choice. Leading most of the way under Eddie Arcaro, Hill Gail got the job done, but not without scaring all concerned. Arcaro saw he was ready to bolt on the turn. Rather than reach for a hold, the Master sent him on his way, initiating instead of reacting. Hill Gail opened a five-length advantage then staggered home, two lengths in front of Sub Fleet.

Ben Jones took the title of general manager of the Calumet Farm racing operation in 1953 so that Jimmy Jones could have full credit for the training. Actually, the younger Jones was responsible for much of the training of the stable over the previous five years, but father and son discussed everything with each other and there was always input from both men, who worked well together.

Toward the end, B.A. would take the grazers to the grass, and while Jimmy was at the track with the gallopers and the workers, his father would hook a leg around the saddle horn on his pony and watch the horses as they munched avidly with their exercise riders up. Most horsemen graze at the end of a shank, without a rider up, but Jones thought a horse's back muscles would be strengthened with weight up.

He particularly loved to be on hand for the Kentucky Derby, and he was a familiar figure at the barn when Calumet's Fabius finished second in 1956 and when Iron Liege accomplished that startling upset in 1957 as a substitute for Gen. Duke. Jones' health was beginning to fail about that time, but that did not mean he was going to be a patsy for anyone. One afternoon, when he was 75, Jones and an old friend, trainer Frank Childs, watched the races from the Calumet Farm box. They left briefly in mid-program to have a cup of coffee, but when they returned, they found two men sitting in their seats. They politely explained their rights but were waved off with a "Get lost, Pops."

That was a mistake. Swinging their heavy binoculars, attached

With two Kentucky Derby winners in hand, H.A. (Jimmy) Jones could afford some quiet moments, as here before the 1970 Run for the Roses.

as usual to their wrists with a leather strap, they hit the men on the top of their heads and knocked them unconscious. Ushers quickly dragged them off to security headquarters, and Jones and Childs resumed their seats for the remainder of the card.

Jones visited the farm in Lexington from time to time and was stricken with a heart attack there on June 10, 1961. A second attack, on June 13, while he was a patient at St. Joseph's Hospital, took his life at 78, but not his fame, which will last as long as men race horses.

∞∞∞∞∞∞

On the showery Saturday afternoon of June 15, 1963, a stooped and wizened old gentleman of 89, supporting himself with an aluminum crutch, waved to thousands surrounding the trackside paddock at Aqueduct. Chairman James Cox Brady of the New York Racing Association, stepping up to a balky microphone, briefly outlined the career of the great trainer, Sunny Jim Fitzsimmons, who was retired that day after 78 years on the racetrack. Mrs. Henry Carnegie Phipps, who had no other trainer but Fitzsimmons during her 37 years of racing, presented him with a silver tray listing 148 of his stakes-winning horses. The presentation touched off an ovation that was without parallel at a New York track in the memory of the oldest observer, and as he raised his hat in salute, Mr. Fitz said simply, "God bless you."

Fitzsimmons trained three Kentucky Derby winners, four winners of the Preakness, six winners of the Belmont Stakes and the Triple Crown winners Gallant Fox and Omaha. He had outstanding horses in his barn through much of his extensive career, but his best horses, Nashua and Bold Ruler, came to him after he turned 80 and following a 10-year dry spell that prompted some to say that the game had passed him by. In victory and in defeat he remained unfailingly cheerful, courteous and friendly, disregarding his physical problems and living up to his nickname which was so appropriate.

Fitzsimmons was born on July 23, 1874, in the Sheepshead Bay district of Brooklyn near the site of what was, in 1880, to become the Sheepshead Bay Race Track. His family's home, in fact, was razed for the project, but the Fitzsimmons clan moved to a nearby house. Mr. Fitz was 6 when he paid his first visit to a track, accompanying his father, George Fitzsimmons, a grocer, who was delivering vegetables and fruit to the Sheepshead Bay track caterer, Thomas Tappan. Tappan had a son named George – his nickname was Fish – who was the same age as Fitz, and the two became lifelong friends. Tappan later served as his chief of staff at the stable.

On March 4, 1885, when he was 11, Fitzsimmons went to work in the stable areas at Sheepshead Bay, walking hots for several stables, mucking out stalls and cleaning stable kitchens at a time when stables fed their own men. He became an exercise rider in 1887 when he joined the Dwyer Brothers stable, and he started to ride in 1889 when he was 15. His first mount, Newburgh, finished fourth. The Dywers were not impressed with his ability and he had only a dozen or so mounts for them – none on their good horses, of which they had many.

Leaving the Dwyers, Fitzsimmons rode on the so-called Iron Hills circuit in New Jersey, Pennsylvania and Maryland, at such tracks as Elkton, Gloucester, Gutenberg, Clifton and Carnegie. He also rode at Alexander Island in Virginia, Patuxent, Maryland, Wheeling, West Virginia, East St. Louis, Illinois, Ivy City in Washington D.C., Batavia, New York and many other "outlaw" tracks not recognized by racing authorities of the time. Only twice was he asked to hold a horse, and his mounts won both races.

He began to "get big" in 1894, tried to reduce with a homemade sweat box which resulted, years later, in the hardening of his spine joints. In his 70s and 80s, he was severely bent forward, but he never permitted his condition to be a problem for anyone else. A popular expression of the time was "I'll pay you when Fitz straightens up," and he laughed a loud as anyone when he overheard it. He bought a couple of cheap horses and trained for a while, but he felt he wasn't making progress and he looked around for other work. His family secured him a job as a motorman on the streetcar line in Philadelphia, but before he could take it he was hired as a trainer by Col. Edward Morrell of Philadelphia, who sent his stable to New York.

Success in his new profession came slowly. He had his first winner, a 2-year-old filly named Agnes D., in a maiden race at Brighton Beach on August 7, 1900. She was one of his two winners the following year, both at Saratoga, but in 1902 he broke out with a dozen winners, three of those victories by Agnes D.

In the winter of 1905 he went to California with a stable of horses for several Eastern owners including Robert Angarola, Albert Stokes and J.J. Morgan. Racing at Ascot Park in south Los Angeles, he saddled seven winners at the meeting, which lasted more than two months. The following winter, Fitz returned to California but this time to the Oakland track near San Francisco as agent for jockey Walter Miller. Miller rode 100 winners during Oakland's 68-day meeting and was to lead the nation that year with 388 winners. The devastating earthquake that leveled San Francisco struck while Fitz and Miller were in the West, and Mr. Fitz recalled for the writer how he and the jockey scurried under tables in their hotel suite for protection. When they returned to New York in the spring, Fitzsimmons resumed training.

When reform legislation closed the New York tracks in 1911, he took his stable to Maryland and Canada. Competition was keen, purses were low and life was a scuffle. But in the fall of 1912 several of the hunt clubs revived the sport, at Belmont Terminal and Piping Rock. Piping Rock had sent a man to Kentucky to buy 50 2-year-olds, and members who subscribed to the race meeting drew a horse by lot. A number of members thus owned a horse but had no trainer, and among those who contacted Fitzsimmons were Herbert L. Pratt, president of Standard Oil of New York; Joseph E. Davis, president of the Island Creek Coal Company, and Vernon Castle, the dancer and an amateur rider of note.

With the re-opening in 1913 of Belmont Park, Aqueduct, Jamaica and Empire City, Mr. Fitz's list of patrons increased and so did his achievements. One of his best wins and one of the most timely for attracting attention to his skills was with Star Gaze in the 1914 Saratoga Cup. In 1915 he saddled 51 winners. He was on his way.

James F. Johnson, active in the sugar trade and a Wall Street star, had one of the largest stables in the U.S. He raced as the Quincy Stable and was well known since his Trojan won the Futurity in 1914. In 1919, Johnson signed Fitzsimmons as his trainer. Fitz sold his own stock, severed connections with his patrons and plunged into his new job. He won stakes for Quincy Stable with Capt. Alcock and had good luck with Copper Demon, Knobbie and Playfellow, a brother to Man o' War. Playfellow, later purchased for $100,000 by oil man Harry

Mrs. Henry Carnegie Phipps had but one trainer during her 37 years as owner of some of America's finest horses and helped honor Sunny Jim Fitzsimmons at a special ceremony on June 15, 1963, at Aqueduct

Sinclair, was the vehicle for a betting coup in 1921 that failed. It was subsequently learned that Playfellow was windy and a cribber. Sinclair sued to return the horse, charging misrepresentation. He won the case, and Quincy Johnson, as he was known, seemed to fade from the racing scene.

Mr. Fitz was at Bowie in the fall of 1923 when he was approached by William Woodward Sr., a New York banker and owner of the Belair Stud in Maryland. Woodward asked if Fitz would like to train his horses. Fitz said he would be honored to do so, and that was the low-key beginning of an association that was to continue until Woodward's death in 1953.

Fitzsimmons' first winner for Belair Stud, and the first horse he saddled for Woodward, was Beatrice, a 2-year-old filly by Jim Gaffney, who led all the way at Jamaica on April 30, 1924, in the last race of the day. The following afternoon, Fitz saddled Priscilla Ruley to capture a maiden race for 3-year-old fillies. Later that summer, Priscilla Ruley won the Alabama at Saratoga. Fitz also developed Aga Khan, a powerful 3-year-old colt by Omar Khayyam, the Kentucky Derby winner, who was to win the Lawrence Realization and finish second in the Travers. In all, Belair had 26 wins that first season under Fitzsimmons — a nice start.

Harry Payne Whitney, America's leading breeder in the 1920s, like to bring new people into racing, particularly those he knew as friends. In the fall of 1926, he selected 10 of his top yearlings and sold them at a bargain price to Ogden Mills and his sister, Mrs. Henry Carnegie Phipps, who had formed the Wheatley Stable. Their trainer was Jim Fitzsimmons.

One of the colts in the package was Dice, by Dominant, a big colt with a sharp way of going. Dice won all five of his starts in 1927, including the Keene Memorial, the Juvenile, the Hudson and the Great American, carrying 130 pounds in the latter stakes. Shipped to Saratoga where he was expected to sweep the 2-year-old series, Dice suffered internal hemorrhage upon arrival at the Spa and died suddenly.

Sunny Jim Fitzsimmons developed Omaha, who became the third Triple Crown winner in 1935. William "Smokey" Saunders rode the son of Triple Crown winner Gallant Fox.

Another colt in the package, Diavolo, developed into a superior stayer and won the Jockey Club Gold Cup at two miles as a 4-year-old in 1929. That was also the year Gallant Fox joined the stable. With his laid-back approach to life, The Fox of Belair tested Fitz's patience. But along with the sunny disposition that earned him his nickname, Fitz had a will of iron and insisted on high standards from his help and his horses.

Fitz developed the 1935 Triple Crown winner, Omaha, a son of Gallant Fox, and a third Kentucky Derby and Belmont winner in 1939, Johnstown, but it was his record in the 1930s as a trainer of stayers that distinguished him as a horseman for the ages. As noted,

he had five winners of the mile and a half Belmont during that decade, including Faireno (1932) and Granville (1936). He won the mile and five-furlong Lawrence Realization with Gallant Fox (1930), Faireno (1932), Carry Over (1934) Granville (1936), and Magic Hour (1938). He won the Jockey Club Gold Cup at two miles with Gallant Fox (1930), Dark Secret (1933, 1934) and Fenelon (1940), and had five of his seven winners of the mile and three-quarters Saratoga Cup during that period.

Such was the breadth of his skill, however, that he also brought off four consecutive runnings of the six-furlong Paumonok Handicap that for a number of years was the opening-day feature.

Mr. Fitz's training style was classic for his time. He started with a sizeable number of horses, identified those he thought had some ability, worked them hard to be sure they were fit and could stand the gaff, and sold or traded those who couldn't measure up. He wasn't always right, of course. After 35 starts during his 2-year-old season, Seabiscuit still hadn't made an impression and was sold to Charles S. Howard as a 3-year-old.

His important colts often worked the full distance of the race but Fitz had a way with fillies and never asked too much of them. He engineered the defeat of the brilliant Princess Doreen in 1924 with Priscilla Ruley and, in 1944, beat another brilliant distaffer, Twilight Tear, with an entry of Thread o' Gold and Vienna. He also won the mile and a quarter Alabama with Vagrancy (1942), Hypnotic (1946), Busanda (1950) and High Bid (1959). His winners in the Coaching Club American Oaks, the filly classic, included Edelweiss (1933), Vagrancy (1942), Hypnotic (1946) and High Voltage (1955).

From 1944 until 1954, Mr. Fitz's stable went into decline. There was a major triumph in 1951 when the fine racemare, Busanda, who was to become the dam of Buckpasser, beat the colts in the prestigious Suburban Handicap. That was one of the few highlights, however, and there were questions in some quarters if Sunny Jim was still able to cope.

He never lost his poise or sense of humor or the warmth that earned him the nickname Sunny Jim, and the cottage on Aqueduct's backstretch, where he made his headquarters, remained a popular destination for racing men.

In 1952, William Woodward Sr. sent his Johnstown mare, Segula, to the court of Nasrullah, and in the spring of 1953 was advised Segula dropped a colt. Woodward, who regularly sent a few horses to England each year, intended the Nasrullah colt to go to Capt. Cecil Boyd-Rochfort, hopefully as an Epsom Derby prospect. But Woodward died that September, and his racing and breeding in-

Nashua (left) was just up in time under Ted Atkinson to neck Summer Tan in the 1955 Wood Memorial at Jamaica.

terests were willed to his son, William Woodward Jr. Tall, handsome and personable, young Woodward was low-key by nature but strong of character. He had been on the fringe of racing but now stepped in as a major player, ready to assume responsibility. He directed that Belair's European operations be concluded. The Nasrullah colt, and the others, would race in the U.S.

The Nasrullah colt, a grand-looking individual named Nashua, made his debut at Belmont Park on May 5, 1954. He was well back early but finished strongly to score by three lengths. Jess Higley, the stable jockey, was in the irons but gave way to Eddie Arcaro for Nashua's second start, the Juvenile Stakes, in which Nashua defeated Mrs. John W. Galbreath's Summer Tan.

Nashua won six of eight starts at 2, with a pair of seconds, and was a solid choice as divisional champion after winning The Futurity by beating Summer Tan and Royal Coinage.

Mr. Fitz brought Nashua out at 3 at Hialeah in a prep for the Flamingo, and the colt's star quality was evident in the tremendous interest of the media and the public in his fortunes. He won it but tried to prop, and the trainer decided to remove the blinkers for the Flamingo. Nashua's principal opponent in the Hialeah stakes was Saratoga, a highstrung individual owned by Marion duPont Scott and trained by Frank (Downey) Bonsal. Nashua, leading most of the way under Eddie Arcaro, won by a length and a half.

Four weeks later, Nashua was to contest the Florida Derby at Gulfstream. Overnight rain had turned the track to a muddy consistency that troubled his trainer. But William Woodward Jr., who spent the morning at the barn, saw the huge crowd streaming into the track at an early hour and made a decision. Rather than disappoint the public, Nashua would run. It was closer than it should have been, but Nashua scored by a neck over the little-known Blue Lem.

Winter-book favorite for the Kentucky Derby, Nashua returned to New York for the Wood Memorial. With Arcaro suspended, Ted Atkinson was aboard as Nashua pursued the front-running Summer Tan. Arcaro, watching from the press box, was impressed when Nashua got up in the final strides to win.

That set the stage for the 81st Kentucky Derby on May 7. Nashua was the 13-10 favorite, and Swaps, the little-known hero of the Santa Anita Derby, was second choice at 14-5.

Summer Tan, third choice at 5-1, lost some of his caste with the public, but after his bravura performance in the Wood Memorial he still enjoyed the healthy respect of both trainer Fitzsimmons and jockey Arcaro. Fitzsimmons said after the Derby that he told Arcaro to concentrate on Summer Tan and to forget about Swaps.

Arcaro says Fitz never gave him any orders and the rider took the blame for his tactics. Whatever the case, Nashua did wait for Summer Tan and beat that colt by six and a half lengths. But in the meantime, Swaps, with Bill Shoemaker up, led all the way and won by a length and a half, the mile and a quarter run in a sprightly 2:01⅕.

Owner Rex Ellsworth and trainer Mesh Tenney, saying they hadn't heard much about the Preakness, took Swaps back to California. Summer Tan also left the Triple Crown circuit, leaving Nashua and Saratoga as principal protagonists at Pimlico. Saratoga set the pace but Nashua closed fastest of all to prevail by a length, with the next closest opponent, a good colt named Traffic Judge, beaten seven lengths for the place. Nashua set a track record of 1:54⅖ for the mile and three-sixteenths.

There was even less opposition for Nashua in the Belmont Stakes on June 11. Without Saratoga, Nashua was heavily favored at 15 cents to the dollar with Portersville the second choice at 9-1. That suggested a waltz, and it was. Nashua won by nine, his mile and a half in 2:29. The Nasrullah colt took on even more stature as a result of the Belmont, and the first calls for a match race against Swaps could be heard on the horizon.

Full of beans despite the rigors of the Triple Crown classics, Nashua was on hand for the traditional Dwyer Stakes in early July. Instead of racing off the early pace as usual, Nashua went to the front this time. Saratoga chased him for a mile but couldn't catch him, and Nashua was an easy winner by five lengths.

In mid-July, Mr. Fitz sent Nashua to Chicago for the Arlington Classic at one mile. The Old Man didn't travel much any more, and his son, John, an accomplished artist, was in charge of the horses on the road. Arcaro flew out to work Nashua five days before his race, and the colt felt better than the rider, who had sipped late the night before. Full of run, Nashua went his five furlongs in :56⅗, slightly better than the world's record at the time.

"The colt was feeling good this morning, Mr. Fitz," Arcaro reported to the trainer moments later by telephone to New York. "How good? Fifty-six and three. Yes, a little bit, but he fooled me. He seems to have come back good, though. I don't think it will hurt him, and he has a few days before the race."

Nashua was the strongest, soundest horse this writer has ever seen. His prep for the Classic would have finished most horses in training for a month – if they could go that fast, which, of course they couldn't. The work did take the edge off Nashua, and Arcaro had to use his whip steadily throughout the stretch but was able to beat Traffic Judge, a good colt, by half a length in 1:35⅕.

William Woodward Jr. came to Chicago to see the Classic and was entertained by Ben Lindheimer, chief executive officer of Arlington and Washington parks. A few days later, Lindheimer escorted Woodward to the press box and announced that an agreement had been reached for a Nashua-Swaps match race at Washington Park on August 31, a mile and a quarter winner-take-all, with both to carry 126 pounds.

It was all smiles in the winner's circle after Nashua won the 1955 Belmont Stakes. The owners, Mr. and Mrs. William Woodward Jr., flanked rider Eddie Arcaro. Harold Talbot (left) presented the trophy, while George D. Widener looked on.

to stroke the face and neck of the well-mannered colt.

Mr. Fitz chose to prepare Nashua for the match race at Saratoga, with the rest of the stable. His jockey, Eddie Arcaro, was riding at the Spa and available for workouts, most of them short, sharp moves as if for a sprint, with an occasional mile for stamina. Nashua was in much more experienced hands. Both Fitz and Arcaro had ridden in match races and had been close to match-race scenes during their careers. Arcaro also practiced coming out of the gate, for he knew the importance of the start in a match.

With less than a week remaining, Nashua traveled to Chicago and took up residence in a special barn that had been arranged by Washington Park officials to maximize security procedures. Swaps was stabled at one end of a long shedrow, and Nashua was stabled at the other. The proximity of the protagonists was also helpful to the huge corps of media in from newspapers and radio and television stations throughout the country.

While Nashua was winning the Dwyer and the Classic, Swaps was enhancing his reputation on the West Coast. He accounted for three stakes at Hollywood Park – the Will Rogers, the Californian and the Westerner – and was impressive in all three. The demand for a match race was on a national level when the two sides were brought together by Lindheimer.

Swaps shipped to Chicago first and prepped for the Match in the American Derby. It was his debut on grass, and he beat Traffic Judge, runner-up to Nashua in the Classic, by one length at a mile and three-sixteenths. Bill Shoemaker entertained the crowd by riding Swaps along the outer rail in the post parade and permitting fans

Mr. Fitz, who wouldn't have missed this one for the world, enjoyed the morning training and daily sessions with the press. Always the epitome of accommodation, he was asked by a battery of photographers to pose for stills with Mesh Tenney. The photographers said they would bring Tenney to Fitz's end of the barn so the Old

The finish of the Aug. 31, 1955, match race between Nashua and Swaps was decisive, with Eddie Arcaro pushing Nashua to a six and a half-length victory.

Man would not have to make the long walk with his crutch.

"Don't bother that man, boys," Mr. Fitz said. "He's got enough on his mind. He's not only got Swaps to care for but a stable full of other horses. I've only got the one horse here. I'll walk down to his end of the barn."

Fitzsimmons may not have known it, but Tenney did have a lot on his mind. Swaps, who had a chronic foot problem, was just about dead lame a few days before the match. Owner Ellsworth discussed the situation with Ben Lindheimer, but a delay or postponement wasn't practical. Time had been cleared for a national telecast, and many thousands were arriving in Chicago to see what was billed as the race of the century. It was the East against the West, the Young against the Old, the Traditionalists against the Newcomers. The lines couldn't have been drawn with more contrast.

On Wednesday, August 31, 1955, a crowd of 35,000 turned out at Washington Park, and every one of them had an opinion or at least a choice. Swaps was the 1-3 favorite, while Nashua was 6-5. Mr. Fitz's final orders to Arcaro were concise: "Get out and go."

Nashua went. With the Master whipping and pushing, Nashua broke on top and held the lead. Swaps tried to take it from him several times, but Nashua would not yield. He got his first five furlongs in 58 seconds, the six furlongs in 1:10⅕ on a drying-out track labeled "good." It was Nashua's day from start to finish, and with Arcaro still keeping his whip busy through the stretch he won by six and a half lengths.

On a Saturday night in late October, William Woodward Jr. walked in the bedroom of his estate on Long Island. Mrs. Woodward, sleeping in an adjoining bedroom, thought she heard a prowler. She reached for a rifle, fired in the dark and accidentally killed her husband.

His executors from the Hanover Bank moved quickly to liquidate his thoroughbred holdings, and Nashua was offered in a sealed-bid arrangement. Leslie Combs 2d of Spendthrift Farm put together a syndicate which bid $1,251,200 and got him for that record price, the first in seven figures.

Nashua was to race as a 4-year-old, and Mr. Fitz sent him to Florida. It was decided he would make his seasonal debut in the Widener Handicap at Hialeah on February 18. To be sure he was fit for the mile and a quarter test after being away almost four months, the Old Man sent him to Tropical Park on the Monday of Widener Week. Ted Atkinson was in the saddle as Nashua drilled a mile and a quarter in 2:01⅗.

Like his brilliant work in Chicago before the Classic, only Nashua could have swallowed this one and come back to win. Giving weight to such fine handicap horses as Social Outcast, Find and Sailor, and favored at 2-5, he had to work to win by a head, provoking a full-throated roar and sustained applause from a huge crowd of 42,000 at beautiful Hialeah.

Perhaps the combination of hard work and hard race took its toll. Favored at 7-10, he was beaten into fifth place in the Gulfstream Park Handicap on March 17. Nashua followed that race with victories in the Grey Lag at Jamaica and the Camden Handicap at Garden State Park, then was upset in the Metropolitan Mile and again in the Carter Handicap.

Mr. Fitz put the blinkers back on a this point, and Nashua ran a corking race to capture the Suburban Handicap at 6-5, carrying 128 pounds and giving 17 pounds to the hard-hitting Dedicate. He won the Monmouth Handicap, was second in the Woodward Stakes, but bid farewell to racing with a second smashing tally in the Jockey Club Gold Cup, setting an American record for two miles of 3:20⅖. That brought his career totals to 22 wins from 30 starts and earnings of $1,288,565.

A week or two after the Gold Cup, a railroad car pulled up to a siding in the stable area of old Aqueduct, and Mr. Fitz looked on

Bold Ruler (left) was forced to race nine furlongs in track-record time to nose out Gallant Man in the 1957 Wood Memorial.

quietly as groom Alfie Robertson led Nashua aboard for the trip to Kentucky and a new career as a stallion. Satisfied the great horse was comfortably bedded down in his temporary stall, Fitz turned and suggested a cup of coffee at the cottage to a young newspaperman alongside. We supposed he was sorry to see Nashua leave.

"Happy as the dickens," Fitz said promptly. "I worried about him every minute this year because of all the money those people put up for him. It is so easy for something to go wrong with a horse. No, I was happy to train him but glad to see him go. Like your coffee black?"

As he worried about the solid-steel Nashua in his final campaign, Mr. Fitz came to realize that he had another star in his stable, a dark bay 2-year-old of racy conformation by Nasrullah out of Miss Disco, by Discovery. Owned and bred by Mrs. Henry Carnegie Phipps, Bold Ruler won his first five starts, including the Youthful and Juvenile Stakes. In beating King Hairan in the Juvenile on June 6, 1956, however, Bold Ruler strained a muscle in his back and was sidelined for three months. In his absence, King Hairan won Monmouth's Sapling and Saratoga's Hopeful.

Returning to competition in late September, Bold Ruler suffered his first defeat in an overnight race at Belmont Park. The winner was another Nasrullah colt named Nashville, trained by Charlie Whittingham, for many years an assistant to Horatio Luro. However, on the same afternoon Nashua won the jockey Club Gold Cup in his

Mr. Fitz had to use all his patience and skill to see Bold Ruler crowned Horse of the Year 1957.

final appearance, Bold Ruler won the Futurity under Eddie Arcaro, speeding down the Widener Chute to beat Fred Hooper's Greek Game and get his six and a half furlongs in 1:15⅕.

Favored to win the Garden State, Bold Ruler had all kinds of bad luck. First he lost his jockey. Arcaro, who had flown to Lexington, Kentucky, for a testimonial dinner honoring John D. Hertz, was asked to stay over a day to ride in the inaugural running of the Spinster Stakes. His mount was disqualified and he was suspended 10 days. Ted Atkinson deputized for him aboard Bold Ruler and got position early, placing his mount directly behind the pacemaker, Jaunty John. Unfortunately, Jaunty John stopped cold at the half-mile pole and Bold Ruler piled up onto his rump. By the time Atkinson got him straightened away, the race was over, won by Calumet's Barbizon, a supplementary nominee who drew an outside post in the field of 18.

It was a different Bold Ruler who made his 3-year-old debut at Hialeah on January 30, 1957. Carrying 126 pounds, he ran seven furlongs in 1:22 to win the Bahamas Stakes while conceding 12 pounds to a handsome Bull Lea colt out of Wistful named Gen. Duke, from Calumet Farm. Federal Hill, runner-up in The Garden State, was third, and an athletic little stayer named Gallant Man was fourth.

Almost every 3-year-old stakes leading to the Kentucky Derby of 1957 was a brilliant show that winter, and Hialeah's Everglades on February 16 was no exception. Gen. Duke was the winner this time under Bill Hartack, his nine furlongs in 1:47⅖, with Bold Ruler only a head farther back while conceding 12 pounds to the winner.

It was evident that Bold Ruler and Gen. Duke were special and might alternate victories. The pattern held for the Flamingo on March 2, which went to Bold Ruler and Eddie Arcaro. Carrying levels of 122 pounds this time, Bold Ruler won by a head in 1:47, track-record time, with Iron Liege again third, behind stablemate Gen. Duke.

Gulfstream's Florida Derby on March 30 went to Gen. Duke, who equaled the world's record of 1:46⅘ for nine furlongs in beating Bold Ruler by a length and a half.

Bold Ruler went to New York for Jamaica's Wood Memorial, two weeks before the Kentucky Derby. He won, but had to race the nine furlongs in a track-record 1:48⅘ to beat Gallant Man by a nose. The game little Gallant Man (by Migoli) was obviously improving steadily for trainer Johnny Nerud.

Round Table was coming to the fore in California. Bred by Claiborne Farm, he raced for that stable until sold for $175,000, on February 9, 1957, to Oklahoma oil man Travis Kerr, whose trainer was Willie Molter. Round Table closed well to finish third in the Santa Anita Derby and improved to win the subsequent Hollywood Derby. After he captured Keeneland's Blue Grass stakes, nine days before the Kentucky Derby, he became a major candidate.

Gen. Duke was scratched from the Derby the morning of the race, and it was later announced that he had broken a bone in one foot. Jimmy Jones said that, in retrospect, he thought the injury might have occurred during the Florida Derby.

The 83rd Kentucky Derby on May 4 was one of the most exciting and eventful of all runs for the roses. Bold Ruler was the 6-5 favorite, with Round Table and Gallant Man almost even as second choice. Federal Hill was next in public affection while Iron Liege, the substitute, was 8-1 on an overcast afternoon with temperatures in the mid-50s.

Federal Hill and Bold Ruler were head-and-head on the lead through a half-mile in :47, with Iron Liege virtually abreast and on the inside. Iron Liege, under Hartack, took command after a mile as Gallant Man, under Bill Shoemaker, charged into contention. Bold Ruler and Gallant Man battled furiously through the final furlong until Shoemaker, misjudging the finish, rose in his irons for a fraction of a second. Iron Liege won by a nose, with Round Table third and Bold Ruler fourth.

Gallant Man and Round Table sat out the Preakness, which was won by Bold Ruler. Mr. Fitz and Arcaro concluded that Bold Ruler may have resented the restraint of their Kentucky Derby tactics. He was turned loose at the start of the Preakness and never headed, finishing two lengths ahead of Iron Liege after stepping a mile and three-sixteenths in a crisp 1:56⅕.

This distinguished gathering before the Belmont Stakes of 1958 included (from left), John W. Hanes of the New York Racing Association; Jimmy Jones, trainer of Tim Tam, who went lame and finished second in the race; Joseph O'Connell, owner of Belmont winner Cavan; George D. Widener, chairman of The Jockey Club, and Sunny Jim Fitzsimmons, who saddled Nasco to run fourth for Wheatley Stable.

Iron Liege and Round Table sat out the Belmont Stakes on June 15, for which Bold Ruler was favored at 85 cents to the dollar. Bold Ruler led out of the gate, easily disposed of Gallant Man's pacemaker, Bold Nero, and was still in front at the end of a mile and a quarter in 2:01⅖. It was a super effort, and he could stay no further. Gallant Man, reserved off the early pace by Bill Shoemaker, came on around the turn, was in front by a length and a half at the furlong pole, and drew out with complete authority to win by eight lengths, setting an American record of 2:26⅗ for the mile and a half. Bold Ruler, who was bothered throughout his career by chronic arthritis, sat out the summer and resumed competition in early September. He won a prep and five days later sped to victory in the Jerome Mile at Belmont Park, carrying 130 pounds in 1:35. When he finished third in the 10-furlong Woodward to Dedicate and Gallant Man, the most common analysis was that Bold Ruler was a one-dimensional sprinter.

Mr. Fitz sent him out next in the Queen's County, which he won smartly, and he followed that with a smashing victory under 136 pounds in the Ben Franklin Handicap for 3-year-olds at Garden State Park, also at a mile and a sixteenth. Mr. Fitz had him ridden from the barn to the paddock that day because of his highweight assignment.

His trainer's faith in Bold Ruler's talent and class was in evidence when Fitzsimmons entered him in the Trenton Handicap at Garden State on November 9. Gallant Man and Round Table were also entered for what was to be the race of the year. Wise Margin and Beam Rider also were entered. Track president Gene Mori asked owners Sam Tufano and Robert Kleberg to scratch them in the interests of history, and they graciously agreed to do so.

Family gatherings were always a major event in the Fitsimmons household in Sheepshead Bay, N.Y., such as Sunny Jim's 75th birthday party on July 23, 1949.

An off track sealed the fate of Round Table, a remarkable racehorse with an Achilles' heel. It was a plus for Bold Ruler, who went to the front at the start and was never headed. He won by two and a half lengths from Gallant Man after a mile and a quarter in 2:01⅗. Gallant Man was a game second and Round Table was a thoroughly beaten third. The Trenton earned Horse of the Year honors for Bold Ruler, who won 11 of 16 starts that season, earning $415,160.

Bold Ruler made seven starts as a 4-year-old, carrying 133 pounds or more in every appearance.

His ankle problems flared up again, and he was retired with 23 wins from 33 starts.

Mr. Fitz had no more Nashuas or Bold Rulers in his final years on the job but continued to come up with hard-hitting stakes-win-

ners such as Broadway, Batter Up, Fashion Verdict, Castle Forbes, Hitting Away, Irish Jay, High Bid, Bold Commander, Progressing, The Irishman and others. He was honored for his many contributions to racing by numerous organizations, but the tribute that seemed to mean the most to him was his annual birthday party, hosted by Monmouth Park. Accompanied by between 50 and 75 children, grandchildren, great-grandchildren, nephews and cousins, he would sail to the New Jersey track on the ferry across the Hudson River and then enjoy lunch with his family in the large Omnibus Box atop the clubhouse. After the seventh race, the entire crowd, cued by the public address announcer, would serenade him with "Happy Birthday," and he always responded with a hearty wave and a tip of his fedora.

He was a great trainer but a greater human being, and he had the quality of making one feel better just by talking with him for a while. He was a very charitable man in his typically quiet fashion, and his good deeds took many forms. Once he received a letter from an American clergyman posted in a remote district of India, who was responsible for a large geographical area of mountainous country. He said he needed transportation, so Mr. Fitz purchased a mule and sent it to him. Some time later, the Old Man received another letter which brought a broad smile to his face. In it, the priest recounted that on a recent trip, he'd fallen off Mr. Fitz's ass and onto his own.

His legs began to go on him in 1963, at the age of 88, and in an orderly way he stepped down in June of that year, with Bill Winfrey as his successor. In the next three years his routine didn't vary all that much from the norm when he was working. He spent the Winters in Miami, with guests invited to the comfortable house in Miami Springs to hear those wonderful stories over dinner: how he bet $100 once in his life, on Man o' War in the Sanford Stakes, the only race Big Red ever lost; how he advised Mrs. Phipps not to buy Grey Flight, who produced nine stakes-winners for her; how he mistook dollar bills for Kleenex at the movies one night and literally blew his wad.

He began to wind down in Miami in March 1966 and died on a Friday morning, March 11. All of racing mourned in sadness until someone recalled a funny story Fitz told, and then another, and another, and everyone was smiling again. He was always Sunny Jim.

∞∞∞∞∞∞∞∞

Max Hirsch saddled his first winner, F.J. Buckdevitz's Gautama at the Fair Grounds in New Orleans on March 21, 1902. He sent out his last winner, King Ranch's Heartland, on April 2, 1969. In the intervening 67 years, he built a reputation as one of the smartest and

Robert Kleberg (right), master of King Ranch, picked a winner when he retained fellow Texan Max Hirsch as his trainer.

most successful horsemen racing has known, and one of the most colorful.

He trained three Kentucky Derby winners – Bold Venture, Middleground, and Triple Crown winner Assault – two winners of the Preakness; four winners of the Belmont Stakes, and four winners of the Coaching Club American Oaks. He developed a long series of champions, including Sarazen, But Why Not, Gallant Bloom and High Gun.

He was a rugged individualist, outspoken, sure of himself and self-sufficient. He affected a gruff manner, but he was the most generous host on the racetrack and in the kitchen at his barn, whether in New York, Saratoga or South Carolina, where he often wintered his horses.

He trained for more wealthy owners than anyone else. His patrons included Bernard Baruch, Adm. Cary T. Grayson, William duPont Jr., Mrs. F. Ambrose Clark, Morton L. Schwartz, A.H. Cosden, Arnold Hanger, Mrs. Adele Rand, Walter Salmon, Robert J. Kleberg, Ed Lasker, John McEntee Bowman, Sam Harris, and Breckinridge Long. They thought the world of him, though he was the absolute boss when your horse was in his barn. He brooked no interference, and if an owner questioned him the wrong way, he could and did tell them to have their horses out of his barn in an hour or he'd turn them loose.

"He showed us how to race," Kleberg of King Ranch said when notified of Hirsch's death in April 1969. "He had character, guts and heart. The last horse he ran won. That's where he came from. He always ran his best."

He was born in Fredricksburg, Texas, on July 12, 1880. His father, Jacob Hirsch, was born in Germany, fought for the Union during the Civil War and served as postmaster in Fredricksburg. The Morris brothers, Alfred, David and John, owned a ranch near his home, and young Hirsch was riding quarterhorses there at age 10. When he was 12, he accompanied a draft of Morris horses shipping to Maryland tracks. He had his first ride, at age 14, at Morris Park in Westchester, New York, in 1894. In 1896 he rode 60 winners and had 50 winners the following year.

"I was a whoop-de-do rider," he recalled years later. "I went to the front as fast as I could and stayed there as long as I could."

Weight drove him from the saddle, and he obtained a trainer's license when he was 20, in 1900. His first winner came two years later, and his first stakes winner was Beauclere, a 2-year-old of 1906. Hirsch ran him against older horses at a mile and a quarter at the Bennings course near Washington, D.C., and Beauclare won. After that victory, Hirsch would try any horse in any situation.

He came to New York in 1913, after racing resumed in that area following a blackout of several years because of reform legislation. His first stakes winner on the circuit was Norse King, who won the Brooklyn Derby (later known as the Dwyer Stakes) of 1915. Hirsch, who had a keen eye for value in a horse, had purchased Norse King for $750 from August Belmont and won eight races with him.

Norse King's exploits, widely reported in the newspapers, brought Hirsch his first wealthy patron, candy maker George Loft, whose business motto was "Penny a Pound Profit." He had a horse named Papp, whom Hirsch trained to win the Futurity of 1917. Loft's Donnacona, trained by Hirsch, finished second in the 1920 Belmont Stakes, but only two horses ran, and the other horse, Man o' War, won by 20 lengths.

Hirsch frequently bought yearlings from John E. Madden, a leading Kentucky breeder and one of the most knowledgeable horsemen of his era. In 1919, he bought a colt from Madden by the leading stallion Starshoot, sire of Triple Crown winner Sir Barton. Hirsch gave $10,000 for this fellow and named him Grey Lag.

Grey Lag was not an instant success. He raced five times before breaking his maiden, but then he finished third in The Futurity and aroused the interest of Sam Hildreth, who was putting together a powerful stable for oilman Harry Sinclair. Hildreth asked for a price and Hirsch said $40,000. Hildreth inspected Grey Lag and turned him down. So Hirsch entered the colt in the Champagne Stakes.

Sinclair, a wild bettor, came by Hirsch's box on Champagne Day and said he needed a winner badly. Hirsch replied that he liked his horse and that was all the encouragement Sinclair needed. He sent runners to the bookmakers and loaded up on Grey Lag. When Grey Lag won, Sinclair returned to the box and asked Hirsch to price the colt. Hirsch explained that Hildreth had already turned him down, but Sinclair shook his head. "How much?" he persisted. Hirsch thought a moment and said $60,000. Sinclair nodded his assent.

With money in his pocket and a desire to make more, Hirsch returned to John Madden's farm and bought another Star Shoot colt named Sidereal. At 2, Sidereal raced three times and showed nothing. But then, one morning, Sidereal outworked another of Hirsch's young horses, Morvich, and the trainer thought he saw an opportunity. He entered Sidereal in the last race at Aqueduct on the Fourth of July program in 1921. Sidereal was stabled at Belmont, but horses could then be scratched at post time.

Hirsch saw that big bettors were in town for the heavyweight championship bout between Jack Dempsey and Georges Carpentier. He knew that there would be a lot of action. When he saw Arnold

Rothstein, the gambler, at the races that day, he discussed a proposal. Rothstein agreed, and Hirsch phoned his wife at Belmont, instructing her to send Sidereal to Aqueduct. He arrived with only seconds to spare.

Rothstein's eight runners hit the books hard. Sidereal opened at 20-1, and when the runners bet the hour was late and there was no time to check the situation. Sidereal closed at 5-1, won by a length and a half, and Rothstein's runners returned to the bookmakers to collect. They stuffed their pockets with wads of bills and went to the barn at Aqueduct, dumping the money into a big tack trunk which was locked and transported back to Belmont in the horse van that brought Sidereal home.

Hirsch, Rothstein and Hirsch's young son, Buddy, counted the money in Hirsch's cottage at Belmont. As Buddy Hirsch, a Hall of Fame trainer in his own right, recalled recently, the total was $770,000, regarded as the record for a betting coup. Of that sum, Rothstein took $570,000, since he had put up the betting money. Hirsch, who supplied the horse and the know-how, took $200,000.

Racing is a game of ups and downs. After the Sidereal episode, Hirsch sold Morvich for $6,500, representing a $500 profit. For his new owner, Ben Block, Morvich won 12 consecutive races, including the Kentucky Derby of 1922. Nobody wins 'em all.

Grey Lag, who went on to glory as an older horse with Earl Sande riding, won the 1920 Champagne and helped finance Max Hirsch's activities in the early 1920s.

One of many prominent businessmen who placed their stables with Max Hirsch in the 1930s was Morton L. Schwartz. Schwartz bred many of his own horses, and one of the homebreds was a St. Germans colt out of Possible by Ultimus who was a 2-year-old in 1935. Named Bold Venture, he showed some promise at 2, winning three of eight starts but finishing unplaced in Saratoga's Hopeful Stakes and the Arlington Futurity that preceded it. Still, the colt finished well, and Hirsch thought he might have a 3-year-old of 1936.

The trainer was right, again. Bold Venture won his seasonal debut nicely but was dismissed at 20-1 when shipped to Louisville for the Kentucky Derby. The 4-5 choice was Joe Widener's Brevity, who had won the Florida Derby (renamed the Flamingo) at Hialeah, equalling the world's record for nine furlongs of 1:48⅕.

To ride Bold Venture, Hirsch called on apprentice Ira Hanford, who was under contract to another trainer named Hirsch, Max's daughter, Mary, the first woman to receive a trainer's license, in 1932. Bold Venture had never won a stakes and no apprentice had ever won the Kentucky Derby, but Max Hirsch always made his own way. Starting far back in a field of 13, Bold Venture improved his position steadily, took the lead entering the far turn, and withstood a late charge by Brevity to register by a head.

Two weeks later in the Preakness at Pimlico, Bold Venture had George Woolf, the Iceman, in the saddle. There was another jam at the start, and Bold Venture was 10th in a field of 11 down the backstretch. Granville had the lead through most of the first mile but Bold Venture took it away from him near the furlong pole. The two colts dueled bitterly to the wire and the newly installed photo-finish camera gave the decision to Bold Venture by a nose.

Back in New York and preparing for a sweep of the Triple Crown, Bold Venture bowed a tendon and was retired.

King Ranch came into racing in August 1935 when New York stock broker Morton Schwartz dispersed his breeding stock at Saratoga. Sy White, a prominent Kentucky horseman, boarded the Schwartz bloodstock at his farm in Lexington, and it was White who directed the dispersal. Two of those who went to Saratoga for the dispersal were Robert J. Kleberg, head of King Ranch, and his one-time roommate at the University of Wisconsin, Howard Rouse, who later was to manage King Ranch.

Kleberg acquired a weanling filly, Dawn Play, who won the Acorn Stakes and the classic Coaching Club American Oaks for King Ranch. White brought Kleberg together with Schwartz' trainer, Max Hirsch, and Kleberg decided to retain the fellow Texan as his trainer.

It was a happy decision from the outset. The two men became fast friends, and the winners came in a steady stream. Dawn Play, the champion 3-year-old filly of 1937, was the first to gain national

Mary Hirsch and her brother Buddy carried home the silver at Hialeah in February of 1937. Mary was the first woman ever licensed as a trainer, while Buddy, like their father Max Hirsch, was a Hall of Famer.

prominence, followed over the next 30 years by But Why Not, Resaca, Here and There, Curandero, Dotted Line, Rejected, High Gun, Buffle, Middleground and Gallant Bloom.

None enjoyed more stature than Assault, the Triple Crown winner of 1946. When Bold Venture's racing career was concluded so abruptly with his injury after winning the Kentucky Derby and Preakness, he was purchased by Kleberg as his first important stallion prospect and stood in Kentucky. Kleberg later moved Bold Venture to Texas, where he kept some of his mares. One of these was Igual, whose granddam, Masda, was a full sister to Man o' War. Igual was almost put down as a foal because of poor health, but an abscess was discovered in a stifle and treatment was successful, though she never raced.

A cloud hung over Igual's foals. Clean Slate, her first foal by Bold Venture, had wind problems. Air Lift, her second foal, fractured an ankle in his first start. Assault didn't wait that long. As a weanling he stepped on a nail, which went right through his right front foot. He acquired a habit of protecting the foot with an awkward gait. The injury never seemed to give him any pain. He was awkward when he walked or trotted, but when he ran his action was excellent.

Assault started slowly, He didn't break his maiden until his fifth race, but then showed improvement and won the Flash Stakes down the Widener Chute at Belmont Park at odds of 70-1.

Max Hirsch trained his horses to be fit, and Assault made his 3-year-old debut at Jamaica on a winning note. On April 9, 1946, he won the six-furlong Experimental Free Handicap Number 1 by four and a half lengths and on April 20 defeated the favored Hampden in the Wood Memorial, winning by more than two lengths. Had he won the Derby Trial at Churchill Downs, he might have been a short price when he ran for the roses. Instead he finished fourth on an off track, and he was lightly regarded at 8-1 on Derby Day.

Spy Song, as anticipated, set the pace on a slow track, the half-mile in :48, the six furlongs in 1:14⅕, the mile in 1:40 Warren Mehrtens, riding Assault, lurked just off the pace, and when Spy Song was through at the head of the lane, Assault swept past. He was more than two lengths in front at the furlong pole and drew out to win by eight, timed in 2:06⅗ for the mile and a quarter.

One week later, in the Preakness, Mehrtens moved a bit prematurely, sending Assault to the lead on the turn. Assault was four lengths in front at the eighth pole and running out of gas very quickly while Lord Boswell was closing like the wind. Eddie Arcaro on Hampden bothered Doug Dodson on Lord Boswell just enough to give Assault the victory by a neck.

Lord Boswell left the impression he had a great chance to catch Assault at a mile and a half and he was favored to win the Belmont Stakes on June 1. But Assault, racing off the pace, came on at the proper moment and won by three lengths, with Natchez and Cable second and third, and Lord Boswell fifth. King Ranch had a Triple Crown winner.

Max Hirsch had Assault ready for the Belmont Stakes in 1946 and the colt swept the Triple Crown by three lengths.

Assault was in such good condition, that just two weeks after the Belmont he came out for the mile and a quarter Dwyer and won by four and a half lengths. However, after shipping to Chicago for the Arlington Classic he ran poorly against colts who shouldn't have been able to warm him up. Tests were taken, and it was discovered Assault had a kidney infection. He was freshened for the remainder of the summer.

When he returned in early fall, Assault placed in the Discovery and Jersey handicaps for 3-year-olds and then had his first meeting with older horses in the Manhattan Handicap at a mile and a half. Stymie beat Pavot, and Assault finished third. He followed with a second in the Roamer and a third in the Gallant Fox.

Hirsch put in a call for the Master.

Assault had been making his move prematurely. With the prestigious Pimlico Special coming up, Hirsch wanted the best rider on his horse, and he wanted to beat Stymie. Arcaro waited like a statue

Assault may have reached his peak as a racehorse in the 1947 Butler Handicap at Empire City, when he carried 135 pounds to a head victory over Stymie, with the top racemare Gallorette third.

as Bridle Flower and Turbine opened a long lead. It was only when Basil James brought Stymie abreast of Assault that Arcaro went about his business. Business was good. Assault won by six lengths in a sparkling 1:57, with Stymie second.

One week later, at Empire City, Assault beat the hard-hitting Lucky Draw in the Westchester Handicap at a mile and three-sixteenths, nailing down Horse of the Year honors and setting a single-season earnings record of $424,195.

Assault won five of seven starts as a 4-year-old and reached his peak as a racehorse in the Butler Handicap at Empire City on July 12, 1947. Topweight under a steadying 135 pounds, he was asked to give nine pounds to Stymie, 14 pounds to Rico Monte and 18 pounds to the great racemare, Gallorette. Once again, Arcaro waited for Stymie and the two raced up outside of Gallorette, with the 15.2-hands Assault in the middle, inches behind the other two.

Bobby Permane, on Stymie, kept Assault in check to the sixteenth pole and there was nothing Arcaro could do. But coming to the wire, Gallorette gave way, Assault had room and zoomed ahead to score by a head, with Gallorette third. The ovation was as stunning as the race.

Early in his 5-year-old season, Assault wrenched an ankle and developed a splint, and it was decided to send him to stud. When he proved sterile, he was returned to training and resumed his career in June 1949, at age 6. He won the Brooklyn Handicap at Aqueduct in his only victory of the year, raced briefly as a 7-year-old, then was turned out at King Ranch to enjoy the remainder of his life in a spacious paddock.

Assault was probably the best horse trained by Hirsch, but he developed many other good ones after the Triple Crown winner left the scene, including Middleground. Like Assault, Middleground was the son of Kentucky Derby winner Bold Venture, and he was a top 2-year-old, winning four of five starts, including Saratoga's Hopeful Stakes.

Christopher T. Chenery's Hill Prince, a keen rival of Middleground at 2, beat the King Ranch colt by two lengths in the Wood Memorial, and both colts were shipped to Louisville for the Kentucky Derby. Max Hirsch prepped his colt in the Derby Trial, with Middleground finishing a good second to Black George. On that same afternoon, Hill Prince had an impressive public workout.

Yet, as good as they looked, neither went off favorite in the run for the roses. That honor went to Santa Anita Derby hero Your Host, who was 8-5 under Johnny Longden. Owned by film executive William Goetz, Your Host arrived in Louisville on a railroad car bearing a sign that proclaimed him the prospective winner of the Kentucky Derby. Hill Prince was second choice at 25-10 and Middleground, ridden by apprentice Bill Boland, was third choice at 8-1.

Your Host flattered his backers early, leading by two lengths after the first half-mile. He gave way to Mr. Trouble, winner of Keeneland's Blue Grass Stakes, after five furlongs, but regained the lead at the head of the stretch. Meanwhile, Middleground was racing just off the pace and was never far back. He saved ground, moved boldly on the stretch turn, was a length and a half back at the eighth pole, and came on to prevail by a length and a quarter over Hill Prince. It became known later that trainer Hirsch had warned young Boland that if he asked his horse to run before reaching the three-sixteenths pole it would be better for all concerned if he just kept on going. It was, of course, a Pattonesque gesture: First you have to get their attention.

Middleground, Bill Boland up, won two of the classics in 1950 for King Ranch.

Middleground and Hill Prince, with nothing to do on the weekend between the Kentucky Derby and Preakness, competed in the Withers Mile at Belmont Park, with Hill Prince victorious. Hill Prince won again the following weekend, capturing the Preakness from Middleground by a resounding five lengths on a slow track. How slow? The mile and three-sixteenths in 1:59⅕ was more than three seconds – 15 lengths – off the track record.

Hill Prince sandwiched an appearance against older horses in the Suburban Handicap on May 30 between the Preakness and Belmont. Conceding 12 and eight pounds to Loser Weeper and My Request, respectively, he finished third to those good 5-year-old handicap horses in an upbeat performance.

It may have taken some of the edge off his form, however, for he finished seventh in a field of nine in the Belmont Stakes on June 10. The odds-on favorite, Hill Prince went to the front under Eddie Arcaro, led through six furlongs in 1:12⅗, and then began to back up steadily. Middleground came off the pace under Boland to win by a length from Lights Up.

Thus, honors in the classics went to Middleground by a 2-1 count. But Hill Prince won the war. Middleground injured an ankle in training shortly after the Belmont Stakes and was retired. Hill Prince, after a holiday, won the American Derby and Jerome Mile, and capped his season with a victory in the Jockey Club Gold Cup, earning Horse of the Year honors.

King Ranch bred most of the horses it raced, but there was the occasional purchase, such as High Gun. A Heliopolis colt, he was out of Rocket Gun, whom King Ranch bred, raced and sold. Rocket Gun, in turn, was out of Sunset Gun, one of the mares purchased from the Morton Schwartz dispersal in 1935. Max Hirsch saw the colt at the Keeneland sales ring and bought him for King Ranch for $10,200.

High Gun showed promise at 2, winning two of three starts.

Turning 3, he finished third in the Wood Memorial and Withers Mile before winning the Peter Pan at Belmont Park, beating C.V. Whitney's Fisherman. The two colts met again on June 12, 1954, a week following the Peter Pan, in the Belmont Stakes. Correlation was the 17-10 favorite under Eddie Arcaro, but only two of the 13 starters were genuine stayers: High Gun and Fisherman. Both came from well off the early pace, Fisherman first. He had the lead after a mile and led by two and a half lengths at the furlong pole under Hedley Woodhouse. However, he couldn't stave off the fast-closing High Gun, who prevailed by a neck under Eric Guerin to give Max Hirsch his fourth Belmont Stakes victory.

Bob Kleberg, whose King Ranch came into thoroughbred racing in 1935, was a powerful force in the sport for several decades.

High Gun concluded his campaign with three good tallies. First, he beat older horses in the weight-for-age Sysonby Mile. Then he beat older horses again in the Manhattan Handicap at 12 furlongs. And just to show he had it down pat, he scored a third victory over older horses in the Jockey Club Gold Cup at two miles. He was voted champion 3-year-old and would have been Horse of the Year except for the great popularity of Native Dancer, who only raced three times that season, winning one stakes.

Another good 3-year-old to carry the King Ranch colors was Buffle, who was third in the Wood Memorial of 1966. He developed slowly, and Max Hirsch knew it wouldn't do to put too much pres-

sure on him early. That's why he planned to pass the Kentucky Derby. However, a member of the Kleberg family was eager for the stable colors to be represented in the Run for the Roses and her point of view was made known. Ever accommodating to ladies of all ages, Max shipped Buffle to Churchill Downs. A few days later, Buffle was announced as ailing – a case of frammis on the cram – and he was returned to New York in time to make a quick recovery. He was second in the Belmont Stakes to Amberoid and won the rich New Hampshire Sweepstakes.

Well into his 80s now, Hirsch's lifestyle hadn't changed that much. He still wintered in Columbia, South Carolina, and was quartered in the old Wade Hampton Hotel where he had a suite of rooms and unparalleled status with the hotel staff. He still put a shotgun over his shoulder and went into the fields and woods for partridge or pheasant, which he kept in the freezer of the hotel for the arrival of guests.

His last good horse was a filly, Gallant Bloom (by Gallant Man) who was champion of her division at 2 after coming to hand in the fall and winning the Matron and the Gardenia. She won six of 10 starts that season and displayed considerable ability, which pleased the old man very much. He thought she was going to make a terrific 3-year-old filly and, of course, he was right, as he usually was. But it was Buddy Hirsch, who had been ordered east from his California headquarters, who trained her to an undefeated season, in which she won all eight of her starts. She was so dominant that she not only was voted 3-year-old filly queen but champion handicap racemare as well.

Max went hunting in the winter of 1969, tripped and fell, and was hospitalized. Full of spirit to the end, he commanded a reporter who phoned to "tell those so-and-sos I'm not dead yet." But a week later, on April 3, he was gone at 88. Gone but not forgotten. Never.

∞∞∞∞∞∞∞

Of all the great horse trainers of the 20th century, the one

By 1968, at age 87, Max Hirsch barely had room at home for all the pictures, trophies and mementoes he had collected in a lifetime of training great horses.

He was different in other ways, as well, notably in his approach to racing. He believed in racing over training. His horses started more often than those of other men because he preferred to give them a chance to earn some money when he put them at risk. Through much of his career, he backed his thinking with his own money, working with homebreds. The bottom line was that he was a great success, one of a very few men to make a personal fortune through owning, breeding and training his own horses. From 1933 through 1939, he was

who looked least like a professional stereotype was Hirsch Jacobs. He was born and raised in New York, while so many of his contemporaries came from small towns in the Midwest and the South. When his fellow trainers took their horses to the track for morning gallops or workouts, most rode ponies or had ridden at one point in their careers. Jacobs was never on the back of a horse in his life.

Horsemen of his era dressed in jeans, some with chaps and heavy parkas or windbreakers, to be shucked with the arrival of good weather. Jacobs was invariably dressed in a business suit and tie, with overcoat in harsh weather, and could have been mistaken for an accountant or attorney on his way to work. His face was smooth and serene; his features were not weatherbeaten or sunscorched.

America's leading trainer in races won, and he regained that title from 1941 through 1944. He was leading trainer in money won three times, and, with his lifelong partner, Isidor Bieber, was leading money-winning breeder four times.

No partners ever offered greater contrast. Bieber was a gambler all his life and a man of strong and frequent opinion on every conceivable topic. The names of his horses were thundering editorials on his outlook at the moment: Nothirdchance, Hail to Reason, Humane Leader, Paper Tiger, Shedontsmoke, Pufawaysister, Burnt Throat. In his younger days, he was handy with his fists, and his friend, Damon Runyon, nicknamed him Kid Beebee. Even when he wasn't so young he was ready to swap punches with anyone who publicly disagreed with his global thinking. He believed in universal love but didn't speak to his brother, Phil, for 35 years.

Jacobs, at work, said little. While considering a million details in his mind, he'd hum a tune to himself and go about his business at a steady pace. He was not without opinion, either, but expressed it in the context of his work. He was particularly interested in racing surfaces and the safety of his horses. He always carried a small pocket knife, and when the opportunity arose he would walk to a point several feet from the inner rail and attempt to stick the knife in the ground. Very often the blade met resistance, and Jacobs would shake his head at the evidence that had just been unveiled.

Jacobs usually held his own council, but he was a man of quiet strength who would not be bullied. On one occasion a chief executive of racing in New York became annoyed at Jacobs' comments about track safety. "If you don't like our tracks, go somewhere else to race," he was told. "I was here before you came," Jacobs replied coolly. "I'll be here after you're gone, and I'll say what I want when I want." He was, and he did.

Jacobs, whose brothers Sid and Gene were also to become successful trainers, was born April 8, 1904. There was no horseracing in his background, but pigeon-racing consumed him in his teens and he did well with his birds. When he was 22 he spent time at the

Hirsch Jacobs was sartorially correct as ever when he conferred with jockey Walter Blum in the Aqueduct paddock.

barn of a friend, trainer Charlie Ferraro, at Jamaica Race Track, and liked what he saw. Ferraro claimed a horse named Reveillon for him for $1,500 late that fall, and Jacobs ran the horse 14 times in the next month. One of those races took place at the small track in Pompano, Florida, on December 29, 1926. Reveillon, a Fair Play gelding, won, and Jacobs collected the winner's share of $700 for his first victory.

A couple of winters later, while racing in Havana, Jacobs was strolling in front of the National Hotel when he was hailed by a fellow American who mistook the young redhead for one of the Harvey Brothers, who were riders.

"I'm Hirsch Jacobs," the trainer said, offering his hand. "I'm Izzy Bieber," came the reply "but my friends call me Beebee."

Though Jacobs was only 24 to Bieber's 41, the young redhead was serious in manner and the two men spoke at length. This led to several more informal meetings, and it was finally agreed they would be partners in a stable. Bieber liked Jacobs' thinking on expanding the stable and financed the acquisition of more horses. By the conclusion of the 1928 campaign, Jacobs racked up 38 winners, and the new Bieber-Jacobs Stable earned $38,770.

New Yorkers soon realized that Jacobs had a way with horses, and the rest of the country was served notice at the end of the 1933 season when Jacobs was the nation's leading trainer with 116 winners. He was to repeat the championship in 10 of the next 11 years, a record of remarkable achievement. In 1936 he set a record with 177 winners, cracking the old mark by three winners.

Jacobs won so many races that people were beginning to talk. He would claim a horse for $1,500, keep him in a stall for four or five days and then run him back for $2,500 or even $3,500 and win. He had to be doing something illegal. The stewards hired private investigators to watch the barn around the clock. Jacobs was under surveillance for months, but no one could find anything amiss. He kept his horses well-fed and happy, and they did the best they could.

On June 2, 1943, Jacobs claimed yet another horse for $1,500, an Equestrian colt named Stymie, from King Ranch. Stymie hadn't won in three starts when claimed from Max Hirsch and didn't win for Jacobs, either, in his next 10 starts. He managed a victory at Belmont on August 18, 1943, while racing with a $3,500 claiming price but they still weren't comparing him with Man o' War.

He won four times from 28 starts as a 2-year-old and three times from 29 starts at 3. After 57 starts, Stymie still looked like a cheap claimer, but was paying his way and Jacobs persevered with him. Then, at 4, Stymie started to win stakes. The wartime ban on racing was lifted in May 1945, and in his third appearance of the season

Stymie, champion handicap horse of 1945, brought years of joy to Ethel and Hirsch Jacobs. Bobby Permane was the regular rider of Stymie that season.

Stymie came from well off the pace to capture the Grey Lag Handicap, his first stakes victory.

Second to Devil Diver in the Suburban Handicap, Stymie, with a 16-pound pull, won the Brooklyn Handicap and began to pick up weight. He was one of the topweights for the Butler Handicap at Empire City and won, was beaten in the Yonkers and Whitney handicaps, and then scored by three lengths in the historic Saratoga Cup over a mile and six furlongs at the Spa. He carried 126 pounds that afternoon.

In all, Stymie won nine of 19 starts at 4, with earnings of $225,375. He concluded his campaign with his best performance in the Pimlico Cup at two and a half miles. Carrying 128 pounds, he won in spectacular fashion by eight lengths, and was voted champion handicap horse of the U.S..

Stymie was equally effective at 5, winning eight of 20 starts, out of the money only once while earning $238,650. He won seven of 19 starts and earned almost $300,000 as a 6-year-old, including a memorable victory in the International Gold Cup at Empire City when, under Conn McCreary, he came flying late to beat Natchez, Endeavour II, Talon, Phalanx, Assault and Ensueno at a mile and a half. This was one of the greatest field of stayers assembled in the U.S.

Stymie won the Metropolitan Handicap for the second time as a 7-year-old of 1948, and had two other stakes victories carrying 130 pounds before fracturing a sesamoid in the Monmouth Handicap. He served about a dozen mares in the spring of 1949, then was put back in training and raced five times that fall, placing in stakes. Retired permanently at season's end, he left the scene with an overall record of 35 wins from 131 starts and record earnings of $918,485. Not bad for a $1,500 claim.

Much of Stymie's earnings went into the purchase by Jacobs and Bieber of a 300-acre farm near Monkton, Maryland, which they named Stymie Manor. It was stocked with mares and, within a few years, its homebreds became an increasing higher proportion of the racing stable. Jacobs was able to recognize every horse he owned and bred, could absent himself as long as a year and match every colt and filly with their dam and, without written notes, could inquire about specific illnesses and injuries.

In 1955, Jacobs was saddling a horse at Belmont Park while in the next stall, Ogden Phipps, a well-known owner and breeder, stood watching as Jim Fitzsimmons and his assistants were saddling a maiden filly. A granddaughter of La Troienne, Searching had run 20 times and hadn't won a race. She wasn't an object of envy but she did have the marvelous bloodlines, and Jacobs asked Phipps if she was for sale. Phipps always bred on a major scale and had to sell horses every year or be swamped by sheer numbers. "You can have her for $15,000," he told Jacobs.

It was a momentous acquisition. Racing through her 6-year-old season, Searching won $327,381 and was eventually voted into rac-

Isidore Bieber formed a profitable alliance with Hirsch Jacobs.

ing's Hall of Fame at Saratoga. She was the dam of Admiring, winner of the rich Arlington-Washington Lassie of 1964, and of Affectionately, who had 28 victories and earnings of $546,659 and was voted into the Hall of Fame. A third significant daughter of Searching was Priceless Gem, who won the Futurity Stakes of 1965 at the expense of Phipps' favored Buckpasser. Later sold to the Wildenstein family of Paris for a substantial sum, Priceless Gem became the dam of Allez France, who beat the colts in the Arc de Triomphe of 1974. It is fair to say that the Bieber-Jacobs partnership benefitted from the $15,000 purchase of Searching to the extent of several million dollars.

Perhaps the most talented horse Hirsch Jacobs ever trained was the homebred Hail to Reason, champion 2-year-old of 1960 and America's leading stallion of 1970. In 1947, Jacobs and Bieber paid $12,000 for an unraced mare by Sir Gallahad III. They bred her to Blue Swords and the resulting filly was named Nothirdchance, winner of a division of the Acorn Mile in 1951. Bred to Turn-to, first winner of the Garden State Stakes – at one time the world's richest race – Nothirdchance produced a robust but plain-looking colt, Hail to Reason.

He won nine of 18 starts in his juvenile campaign, beat Carry Back and other cracks in Monmouth Park's rich Sapling that summer and also made light work of the Hopeful at Saratoga. He dominated his generation but went wrong in early fall and never raced again. Yet, his name will light up the pages of racing history for centuries, thanks to the deeds of such sons as Roberto, who not only won the Epsom Derby of 1972 for America's John W. Galbreath but later that summer handed the brilliant Brigadier Gerard his only defeat in the Benson and Hedges Gold Cup at York.

Another Hail to Reason colt of substance resulted from Jacobs' mating of that stallion with his fine filly, Affectionately, in 1966. A year or two earlier, Jacobs had been in Louisville with Flag Raiser for the Kentucky Derby and was staying with Mrs. Jacobs at the Brown Hotel. In those days, Derby weekend was a time for serious partying, and it was a good-natured but raucous group which celebrated in a room adjacent to the Jacobs. The hit tune of the day was "With Personality," and the partiers loved it. They sang it all night long, and just before Jacobs dropped off to sleep, he commented to his wife that they would never forget that song, and that it wasn't a bad name for a horse. Thus, the Hail to Reason colt out of Affectionately was named Personality.

Troubled by a vascular condition, Jacobs suffered a stroke in the summer of 1966, and attending physicians recommended a revision of his work load. A total of 153 yearlings, weanlings, broodmares, horses in training and stallion shares were sold at various reduction sales for slightly more than $3 million. Admiring, then a 4-year-old filly, brought a record price of $310,000 from the partnership of Paul Mellon and Charles Engelhard. Jacobs' eldest son, John

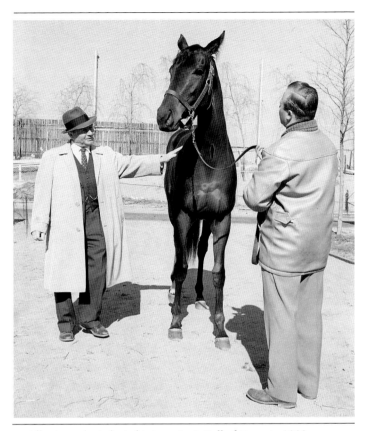

Affectionately, inducted into racing's Hall of Fame in 1989, was a special filly for Hirsch Jacobs and his son, John, who assisted in her training in 1963.

William Jacobs, his assistant for a number of years, took active charge of the racing stable with the senior Jacobs as chairman of the board. A younger son, Tom, worked with the stable briefly but left to pursue varied other interests. A daughter, Patrice, who at one time wrote a column on racing for *Daily Racing Form*, married financier Louis Wolfson and has been active in the operation of Harbor View Farm.

Personality only ran once as a 2-year-old and did not distinguish himself, while a contemporary, High Echelon, won the Futurity at Belmont Park and the Laurel Futurity. That winter of 1970, Personality broke his maiden at Hialeah and six days later won again. Hirsch Jacobs, hospitalized in Miami in mid-January with a blocked artery, was delighted. When son John brought photos of the colt to the hospital, Jacobs, barely able to speak, said: "He'll do better with blinkers." Then the great horseman lapsed into a coma and died shortly after, on February 13.

At the time of his death, Jacobs held a world's record, having saddled 3,596 winners. That figure subsequently has been surpassed, but Jacobs' achievements as a total horseman have yet to be equalled. He has been hailed as the Federico Tesio of America: a

As Hirsch Jacobs had predicted before his death in February of 1970, Personality went on to become a major stakes winner. The entire Jacobs clan – (from left), John, Ethel, Tom and Patrice – was on hand to greet the colt after his victory in the Jersey Derby at Garden State Park.

great success in every aspect of the racing business. Nor did his success end with his death. That spring, after track conditions compromised his chances in the Kentucky Derby, Personality won the Preakness. Then, when an injury prevented his appearance in the Belmont Stakes, John Jacobs saddled High Echelon to capture that classic.

"You'll never be the trainer your father was," some lout once told John Jacobs. "You're right," Jacobs replied. "And no one else will, either."

∞∞∞∞∞∞∞∞

In the Golden Era of Sports– the roaring 1920s that produced

baseball's Babe Ruth, football's Red Grange, boxing's Jack Dempsey, golf's Bobby Jones and tennis' Bill Tilden – racing's most celebrated and successful personality was jockey Earl Sande.

He rode three winners of the Kentucky Derby (Zev, Flying Ebony and Gallant Fox), five winners of the Belmont Stakes (Grey Lag, Zev, Mad Play, Chance Shot and Gallant Fox), was America's leading money-winning rider in 1921, 1923 and 1927, and rode 968 winners from 3,673 mounts for an unusually high lifetime percentage (26).

His achievements were exceptional, and yet without the marvelous poem by Damon Runyon his star would not have shined quite as bright. Nor would the memory of his exploits been handed down the corridors of time be recalled with quite the same fervor.

"Maybe there'll be another
Heady an' game an' true –
Maybe we'll find his brother
At drivin' them horses through.
Maybe – but, say, I doubt it,
Never his like ag'in –
Never a handy
Guy like Sande
Bootin' them babies in.
Maybe we'll find another,
Maybe in ninety years!
Maybe we'll find his brother
With brains above his ears.
Maybe – I'll lay against it,
A hundred bucks to a fin –
Never a handy
Guy like Sande
Bootin' them babies in!"

Paul Revere was a great patriot, but he wasn't the only American riding on that magic night to spread the alarm that the British were coming. Yet, his name is the one we remember, thanks to Longfellow's immortal lines: "Listen my children and you shall hear/ of the midnight ride of Paul Revere ..."

But Revere had the right stuff, and so did Sande, who was born November 13, 1898, in Groton, South Dakota. His family moved to American Falls, Idaho, when Sande was eight, and he was a 12-year-old growing up on a working ranch when a horseman named Burr Scott dropped by one day, en route to the races. Not the races at recognized tracks in Chicago and New Orleans but the bush races, matching horses for private bets, in Arizona, Colorado and Utah.

Scott saw young Sande on a horse, liked his relaxed appearance, and offered to take him along as a riding prospect. Sande was a natural, and it wasn't long before his services were in demand. On one occasion, in Flagstaff, Arizona, he rode 23 races before nightfall. He prospered while learning his profession in a rough-and-tumble school. The headmaster was a sagacious veteran, Charley Thompson, who knew all the tricks and used them to good advantage.

Sande was 19 in the fall of 1917 when he made the big jump from the outlaw circuit to the traditional racing at the Fair Grounds in New Orleans. No one knew him on the big circuit, but Joe Goodman took a chance and gave him some rides.

Earl Sande's prowess as a rider moved Damon Runyon to flights of poetry.

That was the only break he needed. He rode his first official race on January 5, 1918, and finished second. On January 25, he had his first official winner when Prince S. cruised to victory. He had 158 winners in all that first year at a recognized track, and signed for the 1919 season with the powerful stable of Commander J.K.L. Ross. Aboard Ross' Billy Kelly, Sande had his first stakes victory at Laurel In the Columbus Handicap. He also rode Milkmaid and Sir Barton to stakes triumphs, but he split with the stable in the fall of 1920 when taken off Sir Barton in favor of Frankie Keough for the match race against Man o' War at Kenilworth.

Sande's feelings may have been hurt, but he could not have expected to win. He had an opportunity to ride Man o' War that August in the mile and three-sixteenths Miller Stakes at Saratoga. Carrying 131 pounds, Man o' War won off by six lengths, and later Sande hailed him as the "best I ever rode."

Shortly after leaving the Ross stable, Sande signed to ride for Rancocas Stable, whose horses were trained by Sam Hildreth. This collaboration of racing greats proved profitable for both parties. Sande was the leading money-winning jockey of 1921 when he rode Grey Lag to capture the Belmont Stakes. He had a fantastic season in 1923 when he rode Zev to win the Kentucky Derby and Belmont. He rode the winners of 39 stakes, a mark not duplicated for more than 20 years, and his mounts earned almost $570,000, more than double the sum with which he topped the list two years earlier.

A bad spill at Saratoga in 1924 and a subsequent gallstone operation had Sande on the sidelines for eight months. Upon his return he experienced trouble obtaining mounts, but then friends persuaded Gifford Cochran, owner of Flying Ebony, to give Sande the mount in the 1925 Derby. Flying Ebony, part of an eight-horse mutuel field, was prominent throughout the mile and a quarter and won by a conclusive length and a half on a track so sloppy the winner was timed in a pedestrian 2:07⅗. Several weeks later, Sande rode Mad Play to win the Belmont, and his services once again were at a premium.

He led the nation in money won for a third time in 1927, just missing in the Kentucky Derby with Joe Widener's Osmand and winning the Belmont for the same owner with Chance Shot. Osmand was a very fast horse but had stamina limitations. Sande had him prominent throughout the Derby, took the lead at the furlong pole, and was just nipped at the wire by Whiskery, the favorite, who scored by a head on a slow track in 2:06. Sande thought it was the best race he ever rode.

That fall he was suspended indefinitely for a foul he – and others – contended that he did not commit. In the Pimlico Futurity, the track was very deep along the rail and most riders received instructions to stay away from the inside. Walter Jefford's Bateau, with Sande up, was away first and had a two-length lead down the backstretch while racing in the middle of the track. At the five-furlong pole, Chick Lang moved up on the inside with John D. Hertz's Reigh Count. Sande moved Bateau, a Man o' War filly, over towards Reigh Count, intending to keep Reigh Count in the deeper and tiring going on the rail.

Lang reached out and grabbed Sande's silks, perhaps wary that Sande, no angel, might try to put him over the infield fence. As Lang grabbed his jacket, Sande shifted in the saddle. Bateau bobbled then bumped Reigh Count, nearly knocking him down. Mrs. Payne Whitney's Glade won the race, with Petee-Wrack second, Bateau third and Reigh Count fifth. Lang claimed foul, Bateau was disqualified, and Reigh Count was moved up to fourth.

Largely through the influence of Joe Widener, who was president of Belmont Park and a member of The Jockey Club, Sande was restored to good standing in March 1928. While he missed only a couple of months of riding, the suspension was costly in other ways. His weight became a problem, and he apparently agonized over the unfairness of the ruling to the extent he developed stomach trouble. He retired from the saddle in September of 1928 and bought some horses to train.

His venture as an owner-trainer – he occasionally rode his own horses under the special license issued to him – was disastrous. Although he saddled Nassak to win Bowie's Prince Georges Handicap, the stable's earnings for the season from eight victories was only $12,000. At the close of the 1929 campaign, most of the horses were sold to satisfy creditors.

At the start of the 1930 season, William Woodward Sr. invited Sande to ride Gallant Fox in his 3-year-old campaign. In his earlier years, Sande asked for and received $1,500 a month, a sizeable sum at the time, as his flat riding fee. Woodward inquired and Sande, realizing the potential of Gallant Fox, said he wanted a flat 10 percent of all purses won by the Fox of Belair. Sande rode Gallant Fox to a sweep of the Triple Crown and record earnings of $308,275.

Sande retired for a second time in 1931, landed some movie roles and did some singing at New York's Stork Club as well as some broadcasting. He resumed riding in 1932, had 13 more winners, and then retired a third time to train for Maxwell Howard. For a change, luck was with him, and in the next several seasons he developed such stakes winners as Polycletus, Fencing, The Chief, Heather Broom, Stagehand and Sceneshifter. In 1938, Stagehand won both the Santa Anita Handicap and the Santa Anita Derby, victories which propelled his trainer to top national honors in money earned. Howard died in 1944 and left Stagehand and his brother, Sceneshifter, to Sande, who went into breeding. It was a bust, and Sande was in financial difficulties once again.

Clifford Mooers came up with some horses for Sande, who trained for him with little success through 1949. Over the years he talked continually of making another riding comeback. He turned down several attractive offers in racing and television. In 1953, he managed to reduce sufficiently to ride and had 10 mounts. The highlight of this last romantic gasp was his photo-finish victory over Eddie Arcaro at Jamaica on October 14, with thousands of fans voicing their approval via sustained cheers.

Sande was 55 at the time, and the effort to reduce from 140 pounds to 113 had taken a toll. He had to back off, and he became a recluse, declining numerous job offers. Instead he lived in a small apartment over Nino's Restaurant in Westbury, New York, where the proprietor, a friend and racing fan, gave him room and board gratis. Occasionally he would sing for the restaurant's dinner guests but refused opportunities to appear on local television.

In 1964, he left Long Island to live with his 90-year-old father in Salem, Oregon, and died in a nursing home on August 19, 1968, at the age of 69. The Handy Guy was history.

Perhaps even more brilliant than Earl Sande, Laverne Fator, by every standard and testimonial one of the greatest riders in American racing history, killed himself on May 16, 1936, by jump-

Jockey Laverne Fator's star shone brilliantly for 14 years, but he came to a tragic end.

ing out of a window at New York's Jamaica Hospital. He was 36, married and the father of three children.

Don Meade, himself one of the outstanding jockeys of the era before being ruled off in Mexico City during World War II, has frequently alluded to Fator as the best he ever saw. Leading American rider in money won for 1925 and 1926, his career extended from 1919 to his retirement in 1933, during which he rode 1,183 winners from 5,403 mounts. His most outstanding season was 1926, when he rode 143 winners from 511 mounts for a sparkling winning percentage of 28.

Fator was born in Picabo, Idaho, in 1900, and went to work on a cattle ranch in the area when he was 15. He spent three years on the job, and on weekends rode in informal races, at the many half-mile tracks that dotted the countryside. Fator's natural ability caught the eye of Ace Smith, a veteran racerider, who brought the youngster to the attention of horseman Stuart Polk, who had developed some good riders of the day. Polk went to see Fator ride and was impressed.

Fator was happy on his job and had no thought of becoming a professional jockey. But after talking with Polk several times, he became interested. Polk said he would teach Fator how to ride races and Fator agreed to accompany Polk to Havana, where Polk had a stable of horses. Fator's first mount was a mare, Pauline Crowley, who touched heels and fell. Fortunately, Fator bruised only his feelings. He studied hard, listened to Polk, who stressed waiting off the pace with horses, and also benefitted from official supervision. The Havana stewards were strict about rough riding, and newcomers had reasonable protection.

Fator, five feet in height and under 100 pounds in weight, demonstrated remarkable hands and an empathy with his mounts, as Bill Shoemaker was to do years later. He made a name for himself and attracted the attention of the great trainer, Sam Hildreth, who always wanted the best possible rider on his horses. Hildreth had Earl Sande riding for him but offered Stuart Polk $15,000 for Fator's contract, and the deal was consummated.

Fator rode for Rancocas through the 1930 season and had many notable winners from that well-stocked barn. The best of these was Grey Lag, with whom he collaborated to bring off several handicaps. His one disappointment was that he never had a Kentucky Derby victory.

In 1931, Fator signed to ride for the Idle Hour Stock Farm of Col. E.R. Bradley at the largest salary he ever received, an estimated $30,000. On June 24 of that year, riding Col. Bradley's Blind Cowboy at Aqueduct, Fator registered the 1,000th victory of his career.

He retired in 1933, held several racing jobs, and was admitted to Jamaica Hospital on May 11, 1936, with an infected appendix. Because of his condition, doctors ruled out immediate surgery. He became delirious and startled his nurses by riding imaginary races from his past. Quieted, Fator requested some medicine. When the duty nurse returned with it, she found his bed empty and the window wide open. Looking down to the ground below, she saw Fator lying in the courtyard, his skull fractured and his leg broken by the fall. The flame had expired.

Put two racing men together and they will argue endlessly: the

George Edward Arcaro was better known as "The Master."

greatest horse, the greatest race, the best racing surface; almost every aspect of the sport. But there isn't much argument when it comes to the greatest rider. Professionals, amateur experts, jockeys, trainers, the media – almost all are in agreement that the finest rider America ever produced is George Edward Arcaro.

There are others with more imposing statistics, though Arcaro's 4,779 winners from 24,092 mounts over 31 seasons of riding, for a winning percentage of almost 20, stands up nicely under scrutiny. His $30,039,543 in career earnings is a sign of his times against Laffit Pincay's $170 million in 27 seasons and Angel Cordero's $164 million in 31 seasons. But when it comes to accomplishment, the picture moves into perspective: Five Kentucky Derbys (a record). Six Preaknesses (a record). Six Belmonts (a record). Two Triple Crowns (a record). Ten Jockey Club Gold Cups (a record). Nine Wood Memorials (a record). Eight Suburban handicaps (a record).

Even relentless success isn't what distinguished him from a dozen more of the saddle greats. He was the rare combination of physical strength and agility, coupled with a superior intelligence. He rarely moved for an opening without a contingency plan, he was rarely beaten in a photo finish, he handled all type of horses and could adapt strategy to fit any situation.

His personality was another major asset. Gregarious, articulate and well-read, he could walk into a room full of strangers and leave with a room full of friends. Many of the great riders, some because of continual dieting, had personality problems and were introspective. Arcaro was the born extrovert and a natural leader. His riding

Lawrin carried Eddie Arcaro to the first of his five Kentucky Derby victories in the 1938 running.

"Mr. Arcaro," the agent said. "Can you please change the name of this place? It doesn't look good to have the name of a top jockey linked with bookmaking."

"Absolutely not," stormed the senior Arcaro. "I had the name first. Let him change *his* name."

The old Latonia racetrack, located near his home, attracted Eddie and many of his contemporaries who were seeking to make a few dollars as a hotwalker or stable assistant. Arcaro found a niche, liked the romance of the scene and signed on as an apprentice exercise rider with trainer Odie Clelland. A superb horseman, Clelland was able to teach Arcaro a few things but wasn't in a position to start Eddie as a rider. In the spring of 1931, Arcaro landed a job with trainer Alvin Booker. Booker raced in two divisions during the summer. He sent one unit to Ohio with his assistant, Bill Brennan, and Arcaro was assigned to that group.

Eddie got up for the first time on May 18, 1931, at Bainbridge Park near Cleveland. Julius Reeder was racing secretary and Buddy Wingfield was the starter. A faded chart book of the era shows that Golden Bu finished sixth in a field of 11 in the second race under jockey E. Acaro (a typo).

Arcaro had three rides at Bainbridge and then shifted activities to old Thistledown. He rode in Ohio throughout the summer, accepted some 30 mounts, and was still looking for his first winner. In the late fall of 1931, when Booker shipped his combined stable to

style became the model for all apprentices, and his living style became the model for all veterans. When the first warnings about the danger of smoking were published, he switched to a filtered holder. In a week's time almost every rider at Belmont Park looked like FDR at a fireside chat, holder waving jauntily from between clenched teeth. They called him The Master, and he was.

He came out of Cincinnati, born February 19, 1916, at 414 Reading Street. When he was 11, the family – Eddie had two sisters – moved across the river to Southgate, Ky., a suburb of Covington. Eddie's father was a feisty little guy who wouldn't back up an inch. He opened a handbook in Covington some years later, with a big sign overhead that read "Arcaro, Bookmaker." By that time his son was one of the leading jockeys in the country. A representative of the Thoroughbred Racing Protective Bureau, racing's security service, went to see him.

Agua Caliente for the winter, Arcaro went along. On January 14, 1932, he rode a horse named Eagle Bird in a cheap claiming race at seven furlongs. Eagle Bird came off the pace to win by a length, and Arcaro was no longer a maiden. In that same race, by the way, Johnny Longden finished fourth on Webster, while others who rode included George Woolf, Willie Molter, Frank Coltilletti and Johnny Beech.

When the Caliente meeting closed, Arcaro was broke. The job with Booker was washed up and prospects were dim. Enter veteran horseman Clarence Davison. He'd watched Eddie ride and thought he had possibilities. Davison shipped the stable to Tanforan near San Francisco and Arcaro, making $50 a month, went along.

Davison grew fond of Arcaro, took him into his home, kept close tabs on all his activities, and rode him on a lot of horses. He gave Eddie a sound professional education, and it was one of the best breaks of Arcaro's career.

He had 557 mounts in 1932, his first full year of riding, and won with 62 of them for a modest winning percentage of 11. But he was learning something every day. In 1933 he accepted more than 1,000 mounts and more than doubled his number of wins. In 1934, he had a successful winter in New Orleans, and when the stable arrived in Chicago for the summer, Warren Wright of Calumet Farm purchased Arcaro's contract from Davison for $6,000, a big price in that era.

From his $50-a-month salary with Davison, Eddie was jumped to $350-a-month by Wright, plus the usual 10 percent of 1-2-3 finishes. More importantly, he had a chance to ride good horses.

"Seventy percent of horses don't want to win," Arcaro said several years later. "Horses are like people. Everyone doesn't have the ambition to knock himself out to succeed. Many horses will dog it if you let them get away with it. Even horses with reputations."

In 1935, Arcaro rode in his first Kentucky Derby and finished fourth aboard the Calumet Farm filly Nellie Flag. Bert Williams was training for Calumet at the time and was preparing Nellie Flag for the Derby at the farm in Lexington. Wright asked him to ship her to Louisville for a prep race, and Williams reluctantly agreed. Nellie Flag started to "horse" and sulked during the running of the Derby.

His original contractual obligation having run its course, Arcaro was now a seasonal employee of Calumet Farm in 1936 and was receiving a salary of $750 a month. That fall, Greentree offered him $1,000 a month and Eddie agreed. He was of little immediate help to his new employer, however, for he was under a six-month suspension. In the Pimlico Futurity, he'd pushed one horse and collided with another. He was no angel. He had a hair-trigger temper and loved to gamble.

In 1938, Plain Ben Jones was coming to the fore as a trainer with a national reputation in his capacity with the Woolford Farm Stable of Kansas City's Herbert Woolf. His best 3-year-old was Lawrin, ridden by Wayne Wright, but Wright rode Lawrin in the Derby Trial and wasn't impressed with his Derby chances. He thought he could do better in New York on Derby Day. Jones contacted Arcaro, who checked with Greentree, found no conflict, and accepted the offer. Eddie flew to Louisville.

"When I got there," he recalled some years ago, "Jones told me that Lawrin, who was very unsound, had been racing in a bar shoe. He planned to take the bar shoe off for the Derby, however, and thought it would move his horse up five or six lengths. We had a long strategy session, and Jones had all the early speed pegged exactly right. He calmed me down a lot, too, and when the field went to the post for the Derby, I was very settled and confident. The race came up exactly as he predicted, and I'll never forget the thrill of winning that first Kentucky Derby."

Jones also trained Eddie's second Derby winner, Whirlaway, in 1941, but the two had to bury the hatchet first. That winter at

Hialeah, Arcaro, riding for Greentree, was accused by Jones of rough-housing the Calumet Farm entry in a major stakes. Whirlaway, a rogue with ability at 2, also gave Jones a lot of trouble and he thought Arcaro was the ideal rider for his troublesome horse.

Jones and Arcaro worked hard with Whirlaway in the weeks before the Derby. Then, a few days before the race, B.A. took a knife out of his pocket at the barn and whittled most of the leather away from the left cup of the blinkers Whirlaway wore.

"It was the first time I recall seeing a one-eyed blinder," Arcaro says. "He told me he thought that by giving Whirlaway full vision in his left eye, the colt would naturally be inclined to follow the turn of the track and pursue a straight course. I thought to myself this was a hell of a time to be experimenting, but it worked like a charm."

B.A. was right as usual. Whirlaway won by eight lengths, set a track record, and went on to sweep the Triple Crown.

The worst year of Arcaro's great career was 1942, when two incidents caused him plenty of grief. The first involved the selection of a Kentucky Derby mount. As Greentree's contract rider, he had his choice of mounts and selected Devil Diver over Shut Out. Devil Diver proved the best horse in the long run but ran a dull race in the Derby and finished sixth. Wayne Wright, the same rider Arcaro replaced on Lawrin, rode Shut Out to a Derby victory. The two riders had an agreement to split all monies won, but a win in the Derby is a pearl beyond price.

Helen Whitney, who owned Greentree Stable, wrote the letter in 1943 that got Eddie Arcaro reinstated from what could have been a never-ending suspension.

The second incident was even more costly and marked a turning point in his life.

That fall, riding favored Occupation in the Cowdin Stakes at Aqueduct, Arcaro was placed in jeopardy leaving the gate when another horse came in on him and almost put him over the fence. The horse was Breezing Home and the rider was Vincent Nodarse.

Arcaro's temper boiled over and he flailed savagely at Occupation in an effort to catch up with Breezing Home, and Nodarse. Eventually he drew abreast and rammed Occupation into Breezing Home, sending Nodarse over the inner rail.

Arcaro was still burning when he climbed to the stewards' stand after the race. He was asked to explain his actions.

"I was trying to kill the son-of-a-bitch!" Eddie said.

The stewards hit him with the book; in fact, the entire library. He was suspended indefinitely on the spot, and 10 days later, The Jockey Club revoked his license. The revocation was announced September 29, 1942, and Arcaro didn't ride again until September 19, 1943. If William Woodward Sr., chairman of The Jockey Club, had adhered to his original opinion of the incident, Eddie would never have ridden again.

"That year was tough to take," Arcaro said later. "I worked at Greentree Farm but I was left with more free time than I really wanted, and I had ample opportunity to reflect and take stock. I began to realize that I hadn't changed with the times; that the rough-house school of riding in which I was raised was a thing of the past. I made a vow to myself that if I ever got another chance I'd behave myself."

It was Helen Whitney, owner of Greentree, who was instrumental in getting Arcaro the chance he wanted. She wrote a letter to Woodward, explained she didn't have long to live, and that before she died she wanted to see Eddie ride again in her colors. Woodward relented and a chastened Arcaro reappeared on the scene in the fall of 1943.

Arcaro rode his third Kentucky Derby winner in 1945 with Hoop Jr. and had his fourth – and a second Triple Crown – with Citation in 1948. As was so often the case, fate intervened in the latter instance. Albert Snyder, a bright young rider, was Citation's regular jockey. But he went on a fishing trip to the Florida Keys after riding Citation to victory in the Flamingo Stakes. When he was lost in local waters following a fierce tropical storm, the Joneses put in a call to Eddie.

His fifth and last Derby winner, Hill Gail in 1952, showed Eddie at his tactical best. The highstrung Hill Gail was always eligible to explode in a race. He got off well at Churchill Downs and was stalking the 76-1 pacesetter Hannibal, when Arcaro sensed his horse was ready to blow. He reached down, smacked Hill Gail and surprised him. Hill Gail took off like a scalded rabbit, opening a lead of five lengths at the quarter pole. The Joneses were aghast as Hill Gail began to get "late" through the stretch, but he had just enough left to win.

One of his most important triumphs was the victory on Nashua over Swaps in the match race at Washington Park on August 31, 1955. Nashua had been favored to win the Kentucky Derby that spring but Swaps led all the way. The match race, in which Nashua led all the way, was sweet redemption.

Arcaro, who had ridden the great gelding Kelso to Horse of the Year honors in 1960 and 1961, retired at 46 in the spring of 1962 while still committed to more good horses than any other jockey. Feeling he could no longer give his physical best, he stood down, to a national ovation from the racing industry. In departure, as in battle, he was still The Master.

CHAPTER THREE

New Concepts

1941 to 1960

The growth and expansion of *Daily Racing Form* during the 1940s and 1950s continued along traditional lines, with the West Coast the focus of greatest change. Racing in California had early development in the San Francisco area. There was no formal racing in Southern California for many years between closing of the original Santa Anita track operated by Lucky Baldwin and the opening of the new Santa Anita by Dr. Charles Strub and associates on Christmas Day 1934. Thus, *Daily Racing Form*'s activities were largely centered in the Bay area, with bundles of papers shipped south each evening by train and bus.

The success of Santa Anita and the prospects of additional tracks in Los Angeles and environs prompted a decision in 1936 to move *Daily Racing Form* offices to southern California.

A plant was built on North Vermont Avenue, and now bundles of papers were shipped north every evening to San Francisco.

Daily Racing Form was one of the earliest and biggest shippers by air freight in the West. At one

Oscar Otis, "Double O" to his friends, was the mainstay of DRF's California columnists.

time, United Air Lines would delay departure of its planes from Los Angeles to San Francisco in the evening if *DRF* bundles were late off the press. Chief of operations in the Los Angeles office for many years was Jerry O'Brien, a genial, white-haired man who made friends easily. Well-respected throughout the racing industry, he was on a number of occasions called in by the managements of West Coast tracks to help settle labor disputes. His pleasant manner and innate fairness were well-received by all parties involved and he played a key role in several important agreements.

O'Brien was a traditionalist in many aspects of life, none more so than his evening meal. Every night of his adult life he ate a shrimp cocktail, sirloin steak (medium-rare), baked potato, apple pie with vanilla ice cream and coffee.

In the 1940s and 1950s, the Four Horsemen of *Daily Racing Form* were its columnists Nelson Dunstan, Evan Shipman, Charles Hatton and Oscar Otis, whose daily commentary dominated the paper. Each had a different style and area of expertise.

Dunstan, blockily built, emphasized breeding and breeders. His favorite track was Saratoga, where, installed in a suite at the Rip Van Dam or United States Hotel, he would receive visitors each morning after training hours. Prominent racing men from all parts of the country would drop by for a chat and a cup of coffee or something stronger, and by post time Dunstan had enough material for his next column. His writing style was measured and picturesque. He died in 1959.

Shipman, a member of the prominent Biddle family of Philadelphia, was a physical contrast: thin and fragile. He was, however, a man of great courage. He drove an ambulance for Republican troops during the Spanish Civil War, was wounded several times and cited for bravery. While in Spain, he struck up a friendship with Ernest Hemingway, and the author devoted a chapter to Shipman in his book "A Moveable Feast."

Shipman had a lifelong love of horses and a superb command of the language. His descriptions of great races in the pages of *DRF* were masterpieces. He was also an insatiable player. If he had $998 in his pockets, he would borrow $2 and bet the entire bankroll on the horse of his choice, but he never permitted his wagering to affect his writing. He died in 1957.

Charles Hatton (left), one of DRF's preeminent writers for several decades, visited Man o' War and groom Will Harbut at Faraway Farms in Lexington, Ky., in 1940.

Hatton was a Midwesterner who worked for several newspapers in Kentucky before joining *DRF*. A keen student of the thoroughbred and its ways, Hatton's commentary on the racing scene and his word portraits of great horses entertained generations of readers until his death in 1975.

Soft-spoken, dapper and handsome, Hatton exhibited a courtly manner with acquaintances from every level of racing, from Chicken Sadie, the lady who sold fried chicken near the administration building at Belmont Park, to the chairman of The Jockey Club. He drank gallons of hot, black coffee while composing every morning, and he had an aversion to air-conditioning that was the bane of his press box colleagues during sweltering summer days at Saratoga.

Otis, who worked on several California newspapers as a young man, also held various jobs on the racetrack, including announcer. He joined *Daily Racing Form* in the early 1940s and quickly proved an indefatigable reporter. He roamed the stable areas every morning, speaking to everyone and coming away with at least a bit of news that went into his widely read column. He had so much news and material at hand that he was always two weeks ahead with his column, while his colleagues rushed to make their daily deadlines.

A convivial drinker at one time, Otis – known to his friends as Double O – gave it up completely in later life in favor of iced tea.

On a tour of European racing centers, he horrified English restaurateurs by requesting a bowl of ice cubes for his steaming cup of Earl Gray. When he gave up whiskey, he doubled his smoking and went through several packs of Camels a day. He and his wife, Ticky, operated a walnut and almond farm in Manteca, California, which they sold to the Diamond Corporation for a sizeable sum. Otis died at 85 in 1992.

When racing was legalized in Texas in the early 1930s, the sport was conducted at Epsom Downs in Houston, Arlington Downs, located between Dallas and Fort Worth, and Alamo Downs in San Antonio. To serve the new and growing market, *DRF* opened a plant in Houston which printed editions for a number of tracks in the Southwest. Reform legislation closed racing down after only a few years, however, and the Houston office of *DRF* was closed. A Spanish-language edition was printed in Mexico City during World War II when a number of American stables raced at the Hipodromo de las Americas.

Other editions were published in Miami, Seattle and Vancouver, cities located hundreds of miles from one of the three main plants in New York, Chicago and Los Angeles. When bad weather interfered with the arrival of the main edition, these special editions, on sale in early evening, proved invaluable to local fans. They also

J. Samuel Perlman (center), publisher of DRF for 20 years, was a familiar figure at racetracks and racing functions. A Canadian, Perlman was always on hand for Horse of the Year festivities in Toronto. In 1963, he presented a painting of Windfields Farm's champion Canebora to the horse's connections, from left, trainer Gordon (Pete) McCann; Mrs. E.P. Taylor; E.P. Taylor, and jockey Hugo Dittfach.

helped *DRF* maintain one of its proudest boasts, that no American has ever attended a track in the U.S. in this century where *Daily Racing Form* was not for sale.

In the early 1940s, one of the most popular racing newspapers published in Winnipeg, Canada, was a tabloid owned by J. Samuel Perlman. A tall, red-headed handicapper with a neat mustache, Perlman grew up in that prairie city, learned to love horses and racing, and decided to make racing his life's work. His newspaper was purchased by the Annenberg family and one of the sale provisions was a job for Perlman.

He was sent to New York, became general manager shortly after World War II, and soon after was named editor and publisher by Walter Annenberg, succeeding Ken Friede, a member of the Annenberg family. Perlman gradually added personnel and upgraded both the collection and dissemination of statistics and the coverage of industry news. Under his direction, and with the support of owner Annenberg, the modern era of *DRF* became a reality.

Perlman made two key appointments. Sol Rosen, a top handicapper and newspaperman, was named managing editor of all editions of *The Morning Telegraph* and *Daily Racing Form*, succeeding Dan Lyons, who moved upstairs as editor until his death in 1961. Rosen knew racing and he knew the newspaper business, and added many innovations to both the coverage of the sport and the past performances. Rosen also had the theatre in his blood. He wrote a musical comedy about racing that was produced off Broadway, and was the author and director of the Jockeys' Guild Follies, a *divertissement* each fall at the Waldorf-Astoria Hotel to raise money for injured riders.

To improve the coverage of racing, Rosen hired a number of young reporters and columnists, some recent college graduates. One of these was Fred Grossman, originally assigned to the editorial desk. Grossman became Rosen's assistant and succeeded him when Rosen retired in 1972.

The other appointee was Lou Iverson, the office manager for *The Morning Telegraph* when it was located at 26th Street and Ninth Avenue in New York. Iverson was named head of the extensive track and field division, including chart callers, call takers, correspondents and clockers located at tracks throughout the U.S. and Canada. He was required to shift personnel at the end of every meeting, and the maps and colored pins on the walls of his office resembled those of a commanding general.

Iverson succeeded former racing official Lincoln Plaut and brought a more businesslike approach to the post, which he held for more than 30 of his 54 years of service with *DRF*. He was succeeded in 1985 by his longtime assistant, Joe Laskowski.

Walter Annenberg succeeded his father in ownership of Daily Racing Form.

Saul Rosen, better known to all as "Sol," brought an infectious enthusiasm to his job as editor of DRF *and* The Morning Telegraph.

Shortly after Perlman's arrival in New York from Winnipeg, another Canadian, Michael Sandler, arrived from Toronto to begin his career with *DRF*. Sandler, with a business education, was sent to Los Angeles as assistant circulation manager. He advanced to circulation manager of the West Coast edition, then general manager, and, finally, in 1974, became publisher of *Daily Racing Form*.

Daily Racing Form was America's racing newspaper in the Midwest and West, but in the East it had to share the market with *The Morning Telegraph*. Both were Annenberg publications; they shared common business, statistical and editorial staffs, but as a concession to the New York print unions they had separate press rooms in the same building. Perhaps because of tradition, *The Morning Telegraph*, with its broadsheet format, was more popular with the public. However *Daily Racing Form*, a tabloid, continued to be offered in the East until a decision to discontinue in 1951.

In a similar vein, *The Morning Telegraph* was briefly offered to the racing public in the Midwest and West during the 1950s. Its broadsheet mode, so popular in the East, was rejected by those to whom the tabloid size was the norm. Broadsheet remained the choice in the East until 1993.

∞ ∞ ∞ ∞ ∞

The three most significant racing developments during the period 1941 to 1965 were, chronologically: the return of the sport to New Jersey, the case of Jule Fink versus The Jockey Club and the creation of the New York Racing Association.

Racing in New Jersey had its origin in the southern portion of the state during the early days of the 19th century. Philadelphia spawned active racing enthusiasts during the latter part of the 18th century, and elements of this enthusiasm found their way across the Delaware River. During the period before, during and immediately after the Civil War, New Jersey racing flourished just across the Hudson River from New York in cities like Paterson and Hoboken. America's oldest derby, the Jersey Derby, was inaugurated in Paterson in 1865, 11 years prior to the first Kentucky Derby.

In 1870, the first Monmouth Park opened on the Jersey Shore, a resort area some 50 miles south of New York. It was a great success, the quality of the racing was high, and the crowds followed. A second and third Monmouth Parks were built during a 20-year period, each a little more elaborate than its predecessor. Ironically, as New Jersey was challenging Saratoga for patronage and prestige, reform forces were active throughout the state and they would soon force racing from the scene.

In 1939 and 1940, the political climate in New Jersey was right for a return of racing, and several groups began to maneuver for the

New Jersey racing giants Gene Mori (left), who built Garden State Park, and Phil Iselin, who operated Monmouth Park, often relaxed at Hialeah in the winter.

franchise. The successful group, many of them wealthy farmers from the area around Vineland, was headed by Gene Mori. The son of a farmer, he exhibited a keen business sense from the outset. When he was 19, at the end of World War I, he made $100,000 from the sale of tires, at a time when there was a shortage of rubber products due to the war effort.

After the war Mori toured Europe, then returned and plunged into the automobile business. He organized tours of rural New Jersey by a fleet of 20 cars of varying design so that buyers could have a choice and buy them on the spot. Mori was able to sell cars even during the Depression, and he became interested in real estate. When the racing movement began to make headway, Mori and his friends started assembling parcels of land not far from Camden.

Mori's group, one of the few able to come up with cash to meet the requirements of earnest money, was selected to build the track for racing's return. Construction began in 1941 and was proceeding well when the Japanese attacked Pearl Harbor. Suddenly there was a federal freeze on building materials, and the outlook was glum. Mori called on Mayor Frank Hague of Jersey City, a power in Democratic circles. Hague made a few calls, and Mori soon had all the building materials he needed. Garden State opened July 18, 1942.

Wartime restrictions on the use of gasoline forced many patrons to arrive by horse-drawn carriages. Yet, Garden State was a hit and other groups in the state began making plans. Approximately a year from the cessation of hostilities in Europe, two new tracks opened, and with Garden State formed a Golden Triangle of New Jersey racing.

Near the site of the original Monmouth Park, in Oceanport, a borough of Long Branch, the 20th century version of Monmouth opened July 19, 1946. Many patrons from New York arrived by boat to enjoy the racing from air-conditioned dining rooms and lounges.

The Monmouth Park management was headed by Amory Haskell Sr. and Phil Iselin. Haskell, scion of an old-line family, had many Victorian attributes. Courtly of manner, he always addressed his business associates as "mister" and always had a freshly cut flower in his lapel. He always dressed for dinner, even when dining alone on his estate near Red Bank following the loss of his first wife. For years, post time at Monmouth was 2:30 p.m. because Haskell always rode his horses for an hour each morning, followed by 18 holes of golf. His frequent companion on the links was Monmouth's colorful starter, Eddie Blind, who startled

In September 1954 (above), John B. Kelly, president of Atlantic City Race Course, was joined at the track by his daughter Grace, who had a successful career outside of racing. Dr. Leon Levy (below, with his wife Blanche) was one of the men responsible for building the Shore track.

pedestrians with his Maryland license plate which read: BLIND.

Iselin, a New Yorker, manufactured women's sports clothes and had a summer home in Oceanport, near the site of the track under construction. He met Haskell, who invited him to participate. He soon headed the track's business operations while Haskell supervised the racing and the track's rigorous social schedule. A fine host, he enjoyed serenading his guests with his signature song: "Makin' Macon My Home."

Atlantic City Race Course, located about a dozen miles inland from the famous resort, opened four days after Monmouth, on July 22, 1946. Noted for its spectacular landscaping and superb turf course, it was headed by an interesting trio. John B. Kelly was a noted oarsman, a prominent brick manufacturer and the father of Princess Grace of Monaco. Leon Levy helped his brother-in-law, William Paley, organize the Columbia Broadcasting System (CBS) and served as vice chairman of the board. He conceived the United Nations Turf Handicap, the track's signature race. Frank Fiore, a restaurateur and hotel owner in New Jersey with many excellent political connections, was also part of the trio.

Monmouth and Atlantic City followed

Garden State's success with triumphs of their own. All three tracks offered modern facilities and fine racing, and they attracted considerable patronage from New York. The Jersey tracks also attracted stables and riders from the Maryland and New England circuits. Havre de Grace closed its doors in 1952, unable to compete for the critical Philadelphia market. In New England, the loss of horses to New Jersey helped speed the decline of that once-vital circuit. The return of racing to New Jersey cast a long shadow across the sport.

One of the most significant legal cases involving thoroughbred racing – Fink versus The Jockey Club – began in 1949.

Jule Fink grew up in Cincinnati where his father had a barber shop. The senior Fink, like many of his customers, was a keen racing fan, and often visited the nearby Latonia track. His son soon came to enjoy horses and racing as much, and showed surprising skill at his age as a handicapper. He cashed some big tickets and, as a young man, bought a horse or two.

Toward the end of World War II, Fink moved to New York and started the Marlet Stable, his trainer a young Kentuckian named Woody Stephens. Several of Fink's friends and fellow handicappers from Cincinnati also came to New York, and with one or two locals formed a group to pool their wagers. They liked horses with speed and became known as the "Speed Boys."

With Fink directing activities, the Speed Boys struck hard and often. Authorities at the New York tracks, reacting to stories in the papers, expressed interest in the activities of the Speed Boys, and Fink in particular. In 1949, The Jockey Club, which issued all li-

Jule Fink turned the racing world upside down with his victory in the New York court system.

censes in New York, tabled Fink's application for an owner's license. Fink appealed to the New York Racing Commission and brought Bernard Baruch as a character witness. The commission denied the appeal.

Fink went to court. The appellate division upheld the denial but handed down no decision, and the case moved to the Court of Appeals, New York's highest tribunal. On March 8, 1951, by a vote of 7 to 2, the Court of Appeals reversed the appellate division and upheld Fink's contention that the action of The Jockey Club, in licensing individuals, was unconstitutional.

With the opening of the New York racing season less than a month away on April 2, immediate action was required. A bill transferring the power to issue occupational licenses from The Jockey Club to the State Racing Commission was passed by both houses of the legislature and was signed into law by Gov. Thomas E. Dewey on March 30.

Racing commissions throughout the U.S. gained new respect as an aftermath of the Fink case. Realizing that they alone held the power to license, many passive commissioners became activists, and the national organization, the National Association of State Racing Commissioners – later the Racing Commissioners International – tackled major problems such as uniform rules and medication with enthusiasm.

As for Fink, he was denied a license by the New York Racing Commission, and it wasn't until 1967 that he was finally licensed. He raced several good horses, some in partnership with Dr. William

O. Reed, a prominent veterinarian, until his death at 77 in August 1990.

The formation of the New York Racing Association had its origins in Saratoga. Each summer The Jockey Club hosts a dinner for its members at the Spa toward the end of Sales Week, at which time a guest speaker addresses important racing matters. The guest at the 1953 dinner was Ashley

Ashley T. Cole was a major influence on racing in New York.

Mr. and Mrs. John Galbreath (left) were guests of Monmouth Park president Amory L. Haskell in 1963.

Trimble Cole, chairman of the New York Racing Commission and general counsel for the Union Carbide Corporation.

A formidable man on his feet, Cole took note of the alarming decline of New York racing with its aging facilities, and the contrasting success of the neighboring New Jersey tracks with their modern plants. Cole challenged the leaders of racing to deal with the situation and warned that if racing did not act, government would step in and do it.

John Hanes, a former under secretary of the Treasury and CEO of the Olin-Mathieson Corporation; Capt. Harry Guggenheim of the copper family and founder of the Guggenheim Museum, and Christopher T. Chenery of the huge Commonwealth and Southern utilities, were appointed a committee of three to draft plans. After a series of meetings, they proposed formation of the Greater New York Association, the purchase of Aqueduct, Belmont Park and Saratoga and their consolidation into a nonprofit corporation, and the rebuilding of Aqueduct and Belmont. Trustees of the GNYA – later renamed the New York Racing Association – would receive no

emoluments of any kind and all profits would go to the state.

John Hanes was named first chairman of the GNYA. He and his board of trustees had no trouble persuading banks to loan them $60 million as a start-up fund. The franchises of the existing tracks were purchased, popular Jamaica Racetrack was closed and the property sold to developers, and Aqueduct was rebuilt, the new state-of-the-art facilities opened in September 1959. John W. Galbreath of Darby Dan Farm, president of the Pittsburgh Pirates, was chairman of The Jockey Club building committee. He completed construction of Aqueduct on budget (about $30 million) and on time, and then did the same thing with Belmont Park, which reopened in 1968. Improvements were also made at Saratoga, including installation of a sprinkler system, both in the ancient stands and the stable area.

The formation of the NYRA saved racing in New York, which once again became the bellwether of the American turf and the supply depot from which many tracks throughout the nation consistently drew horses with box-office appeal to head their major stakes. The two most influential American racing men during the period

1941 to 1965 were John Wesley Hanes of the New York Racing Association and Arthur B. "Bull" Hancock Jr. of Claiborne Farm.

Hanes, a quiet man of steely determination, was born in Winston-Salem, North Carolina, on April 24, 1892. His father was an associate of R.J. Reynolds, the tobacco magnate, and a substantial shareholder in Reynolds' firm. In 1903, the senior Hanes borrowed on the stock to launch Hanes Hosiery Company. John Hanes graduated from Yale, began his business career as a salesman for the American Tobacco Company, and rose to district manager by the time he enlisted in the Navy during World War I.

In 1922, he joined Charles Barney & Co., a Wall Street investment firm, and rose to become a senior partner. His sense of finance was so widely regarded that he served on the boards of 30 corporations. In 1938, he became a member of the Securities and Exchange Commission and sold his seat on the Exchange. A year later he switched to the Treasury Department and in 1940 was named undersecretary of the Treasury in the Roosevelt Administration.

Breaking with FDR over the third-term issue, Hanes left Treasury in 1941 to back Wendell Wilkie's memorable bid for the White House. Later he was asked to reorganize the financial empire of William Randolph Hearst, with its 90 corporations, a challenging assignment he handled brilliantly. He followed that triumph by merging Olin Industries with Mathieson Chemical Company. The Olin-Mathieson Corporation became an international powerhouse.

In 1949, Hanes was invited to sit on the board of Belmont Park by George D. Widener, chairman of The Jockey Club. Hanes' wife,

John Hanes was instrumental in the creation of the New York Racing Association.

Hope Hanes, had raced a stable of horses since the 1930s, and the Haneses made frequent trips to Belmont. His appointment to the Belmont board stimulated Hanes' interest in racing and by 1952 he had joined his wife in assembling a broodmare band of 20 head. That was also the year he became a partner with Leslie Combs of Spendthrift Farm in a venture that included the purchase of My Babu for $600,000, the importation of Epsom Derby winner Arctic Prince and the breeding for the commercial market of yearlings with outstanding pedigrees.

The timing was spectacular. When Ashley Cole of the New York Racing Commission challenged the membership of The Jockey Club at Saratoga in 1953 to do something to halt the slide of racing in New York, John Hanes was ready, willing and able. Named to head the club's planning committee, he met frequently with the other members, Harry Guggenheim and Chris Chenery, and devised the intricate corporation mechanism that became the New York Racing Association. He was its first chairman, solicitous of what he termed "a rare example of government and private enterprise joining hands in a venture from which only New York State can receive all profits and benefit."

It was Hanes' participation that enabled the just-formed NYRA to borrow millions of dollars from the banks. Bank officers, many of whom knew him from his stint at Treasury, held him in great regard and respect. When former President Eisenhower came to the Belmont Stakes in 1961, it was as the guest of his good friend, John Hanes. Racing's debt to Hanes for his services, time and enthusiasm as chairman is considerable, and was only partly repaid with such honors as the F. Ambrose Clark Award from the National Steeplechase Association, an Exemplar of Racing citation from the National Museum of Racing, a Man of the Year award from the Jockeys' Guild and a selection as Guest of Honor at the annual testimonial dinner of the Thoroughbred Club of America.

When he stepped down as chairman of NYRA, Hanes served as president of the National Museum of Racing and also as president of the National Steeplechase and Hunt Association. He was also a key figure in the group assembled by John Galbreath in 1972 to buy Hialeah from Gene Mori. He gave generously to racing without regard for his personal health, and when he could give no more, at 95, he died at his home in Millbrook, New York, just before Christmas in 1988.

Few racing transactions involving track managements and finance were consummated in America during John Hanes' watch at NYRA without his advice and/or participation and fewer important bloodstock transactions were conducted in this country between 1945 and 1972 without some input from Bull Hancock. He was, perhaps, the most respected horseman in America, the first to be elected to The Jockey Club, a member of the Kentucky State Racing Commission, a director and shareholder of Churchill Downs, a director of Keeneland.

As president of the American Thoroughbred Breeders Association and vice president of the American Thoroughbred Owners Association he brought about the merger of the two groups in 1961 to form the Thoroughbred Owners and Breeders Association (TOBA). He was a director of the Grayson Foundation, a founder and director of the Thoroughbred Breeders of Kentucky, an organizer of the American Horse Council and president of the Thoroughbred Club of America.

He was close to many of the nation's leading owners and breeders, men who owned and/or controlled the best racehorses and the most popular stallions. All called on him frequently for his valued opinion. Some never made a move in racing or breeding without him.

Everyone enjoyed his company. Outgoing and gregarious, he moved easily between the corporate worlds of the bankers and oilmen who bought expensive yearlings from him to the locker rooms and the world of sports he enjoyed through his friendship with Bear Bryant and other prominent coaches and personalities.

The son of nationally known Virginia breeder Arthur Boyd Hancock Sr., Bull Hancock was born on January 24, 1910, in Paris, Kentucky, on property inherited by his mother. For some years the Hancock family operated two farms, one in Virginia and the other in Kentucky. The Virginia operation was eventually closed out in 1946. Hancock was educated at Princeton, where he lettered in football and baseball. He stood 6-feet-2, weighted more than 200 pounds, and no one had to ask how he got his nickname.

Graduating in 1933, Hancock returned to Claiborne Farm in Kentucky as assistant to his father. In 1937 he was put in charge of Ellerslie Farm in Virginia.

In 1939 he met Waddell Walker of Nashville and they were married in 1941, shortly before his enlistment in the Army Air Corps. He was discharged as a captain in 1945 when his father suffered the first of a series of heart attacks that led to his death in 1957. Bull Hancock was now in charge at Claiborne Farm.

He found the stallions old (Blenheim was 18, Sir Gallahad III was 25) and the 250 broodmares an undistinguished bunch. The first stallion he brought in as a replacement was Princequillo. When Hill Prince became a star in the U.S. and Prince Simon was a champion in England, Princequillo was on his way. Hancock then bought Ambiorix in France for $250,000 and Nasrullah in Ireland for $350,000. The turnaround was complete. Stallions brought to Claiborne Farm by Bull Hancock led the U.S. general sire list for 15 consecutive years.

Hancock had successful foal-sharing agreements with Howard Keck and then William Haggin Perry, raced such nice horses as Moccasin, Dike and Drone, and was America's leading breeder four times. He flew to Scotland in September 1972 for some shooting, went racing in Ireland, and became ill. He died on September 14, with all of American racing in morning.

While Edward P. Taylor's principal sphere of influence was his native Canada, his impact on the American racing scene was considerable. As chief executive officer of the Ontario Jockey Club, his many successful innovations were often years ahead of the industry, and were widely copied in the U.S. At one time the only Canadian member of The Jockey Club, Taylor was widely admired for his accomplishments and was sought out for his ideas and point of view by fellow members.

He was also an owner and breeder of thoroughbreds on a world-class level. He raised purses and stakes at Ontario tracks to new heights, attracting American stables. He sold much of his well-bred produce at public auction in Toronto, with American buyers in the audience, and sent his top horses across the border to win major U.S. stakes. His Northern Dancer was the first Canadian-bred to capture the Kentucky Derby.

For several decades, Bull Hancock (left) and E.P. Taylor were two of the most important figures in North American thoroughbred racing.

Taylor was born on January 29, 1901, in Ottawa. A mechanical engineering student at McGill University in Montreal, he helped pay his way through college by inventing a pop-up toaster. Upon graduation, he organized a fleet of buses and cabs to provide the first real transportation services to Ottawa. Within a year he was able to sell out for a profit. After his father joined an investment firm, Taylor took a job as a securities salesman and, with his gregarious personality, did well. After the market crashed in 1929, Taylor did even better. He began buying, at cut-rate prices, small, struggling breweries and consolidated them into major firms such as Carling's.

Taylor served as a supplies and munitions expediter during World War II, speeding Canadian goods to Britain. On one perilous trip he was torpedoed in the North Atlantic and drifted for several days before being rescued. He was subsequently cited for his contributions toward the Allied victory.

Taylor had been interested in racing early in life and started a small stable under George Alexander in the 1930s. He came back to the sport on a more substantial basis after the end of hostilities in Europe and gradually involved himself in the affairs of the many small racetracks near Toronto. They each raced two meetings a year for a total of 14 days. When Taylor became chairman of the Ontario

Opening day of the new Woodbine Racetrack in 1956 gave Canadian sport a boost.

Queen's Plate, Canada's premier horserace, with Eddie Arcaro in the saddle. Canadiana (by Chop Chop) went to the U.S. later in the year to win the Test Stakes at Saratoga and the Vagrancy at Aqueduct.

As his homebreds grew in number, Taylor developed a unique method of selling some while convincing buyers he wasn't keeping the best for himself. All his yearlings were priced, and when half were sold, the sale was over. It was from this apparatus that he came to race his greatest horse, Northern Dancer.

George Blackwell, the outstanding bloodstock agent, bought Taylor a Hyperion mare, Lady Angela, in England. She was bred to the undefeated Nearco and imported to Canada where she produced a colt named Nearctic. He was Canada's Horse of the Year in 1958. Bred to the Native Dancer mare Natalma, Nearctic got a white-stockinged, muscular little colt whose size and coloring were against him. Priced by Taylor at $25,000, he failed to arouse interest and eventually went into training with a colorful Argentinian, Horatio Luro, who saddled the 1962 Kentucky Derby winner, Decidedly, for George Pope of San Francisco.

A stakes winner at 2 in Canada and the U.S., Northern Dancer developed a quarter-crack late in the year. Taylor's farm people wanted to take the colt out of training, cut out the quarter-crack in traditional fashion, and permit the hoof to grow back. The colt

Jockey Club, he followed the same pattern that proved so successful with the breweries. He bought up the racing dates of the small tracks such as Thorncliffe and Dufferin to concentrate racing at three sites in the province: Woodbine, Fort Erie and the new track. He rebuilt Woodbine and renamed it Greenwood, refurbished the Fort Erie track near Buffalo, and in June 1956 opened New Woodbine, a magnificent state-of-the-art track on several hundred acres of land near the Toronto airport he purchased quietly at bargain prices.

Simultaneously, he was upgrading his breeding operation, which was to become a supply source for Canadian racing. He purchased the National Stud Farm in Oshawa from Col. R.S. McLaughlin and established Windfields Farm in Willowdale. Taylor began accumulating stallions and broodmares, and one of his first international successes was the filly Canadiana, winner of the 1953

Northern Dancer managed to beat The Scoundrel a length in the 1964 Florida Derby at Gulfstream despite a too-fast work just days before the race. Bill Shoemaker rode, but gave up the mount for the Kentucky Derby.

would be forced to miss the first six months of the campaign, including the classics. Luro demurred and sent for Bill Bane, a West Coast blacksmith who developed a vulcanized rubber patch for quarter-cracks. After winning Taylor's approval for the new technique by offering to pay Bane's fee himself, Luro had the blacksmith flown to Belmont Park. Bane worked on the patching all day, collected his check and returned to California. Northern Dancer missed about a week of training instead of many months, shipped to Florida, and began to get ready for his 3-year-old debut.

With Bill Shoemaker in the saddle, Northern Dancer won Hialeah's Flamingo Stakes and the Florida Derby at Gulfstream Park. However, a misjudged workout a day or two prior to the Florida Derby took the edge off the blocky, little colt. Actually, it was

to the credit of Northern Dancer that he won at all, but Shoemaker didn't see it that way. He was offered the Kentucky Derby mount on Hill Rise, the Santa Anita Derby winner, and promptly took himself off the little Dancer from Canada in favor of the hulking Hill Rise, owned by George Pope of Decidedly fame.

Just as promptly, Luro was on the phone to Bill Hartack, who rode Decidedly to victory in the Kentucky Derby of 1962. Hartack and Northern Dancer collaborated to win the Blue Grass easily and then brought off a masterful partnership in the Kentucky Derby to score by a neck in the record time of 2:00 for the mile and a quarter. Northern Dancer also won the Preakness (Hill Rise finished third) but found the mile and a half of the Belmont simply too far for him. He finished third, half a length in front of Hill Rise.

Returning, to Canada, Northern Dancer was paraded up Yonge Street and received a hero's welcome from the city of Toronto. Then he earned a second ovation with a smashing victory in the Queen's Plate. Training in New York later that summer for a major stakes in Chicago, he bowed a tendon and was retired. He enjoyed unparalleled success at stud, siring 146 stakes winners. A sire of sires, his successful sons include Lyphard, Danzig, Nijinsky II, Nureyev, Sadler's Wells, Sovereign Dancer, Storm Bird and Vice Regent.

In 1977, Taylor passed Harry Payne Whitney as the all-time

leading breeder of stakes winners, and at the time of his death, in May 1989, was credited with 325. He was North America's leading breeder by earnings nine times, including a run of seven consecutive years, from 1974 through 1980.

Where many American racing executives were initially opposed to off-track betting, Taylor, following a world-wide tour of leading racing centers, predicted it would become essential to the sport. When he stepped down as chairman of the OJC in favor of his hand-selected successor, Lt. Col. Charles Baker, Taylor organized The Jockey Club of Canada, became it first chairman, and undertook a long battle with the bureaucracy in Ottawa to obtain OTB. He influenced many racing men in this country to change their thinking.

John D. Hertz proved an American success story in his business endeavors and in racing.

Chicago, and quickly learned to box and to defend his territory. He later worked as an office boy at the Chicago *Record*, briefly covered the boxing beat for the newspaper, and then worked as a valet and bookmaker's clerk at the Roby track on the Illinois-Indiana border. He became an auto salesman, founded the Yellow Cab Company of Chicago, and later the Hertz rental car company.

One of the nation's leading industrialists, he became a partner in the internationally prominent investment banking firm of Lehman Brothers. He was also a member of the executive committee of Paramount Pictures, and served as special adviser on transportation to the Secretary of War during World War II.

Hertz came into racing in 1921 at the urging of a friend, Roy Carruthers, whom he had known since they both worked at the Roby track. Active in Chicago sporting circles, Hertz helped finance Matt Winn in the construction of the Lincoln Fields track which opened in 1926, and a year or two later organized a group of Chicago civic leaders who purchased Arlington Park to prevent it from falling into the hands of a local entrepreneur, Alphonse Capone. Hertz asked Roy Carruthers to manage Arlington.

⧜⧜⧜⧜⧜⧜⧜⧜

Four remarkable horses made headlines frequently during the period 1941 to 1965. How remarkable? On anyone's list of the greatest American horses of all time, all four would be included among the top dozen. Their names reverberate through the corridors of time: Count Fleet, Citation, Native Dancer, Kelso.

In the summer of 1927, John D. Hertz of Chicago was at Saratoga to see some racing. His attention was attracted by a maiden race in which a Sunreigh colt, Reigh Count, came from behind to win, pausing only at the sixteenth pole to bite the runner-up on the neck. Hertz, born in Czechoslovakia, came to the U.S. when he was 10. He ran away from home, sold newspapers on the streets of

But back to Saratoga and that maiden race. Hertz admired the spirit of the horse who bit his rival and bought Reigh Count for $12,000, a serious sum at the time, from Willis Sharpe Kilmer of Exterminator fame. That fall, Reigh Count, trained by Ben Mitchell, won the Kentucky Jockey Club Stakes at Churchill Downs. It was a prophetic victory, for Reigh Count returned in the spring to win the 1928 Kentucky Derby with jockey Chick Lang in the saddle.

Hertz sent Reigh Count to England as a 4-year-old and the American colt distinguished himself by winning the Coronation Cup and finishing second in the Ascot Gold Cup. Retired to stud in 1930, he stood in Illinois for six years, then at Claiborne Farm in Kentucky for three seasons. Hertz purchased Stoner Creek Stud near Claiborne in 1939 and Reigh Count was transferred to the new property in 1940.

One of his first covers at Stoner Creek was Quickly, a Haste mare who won 32 races in six campaigns. The mating of Reigh Count and Quickly produced a brown colt Fanny Hertz named, with some prescience, Count Fleet. He looked rapid and he was rapid, winning 10 of 15 starts at 2. One of the highlights of his season was a pre-Futurity work at Belmont down the Widener Chute in which he was timed in 1:08⅕ for six furlongs. For some reason, it took the edge off his performance in the stake four days later. Another highlight was his six-length victory in the Champagne Stakes, also at Belmont, when he ran the fastest mile of the year: 1:34⅘. No 2-year-old ran a faster Champagne until 1976 when Seattle Slew was timed in 1:34⅖.

Fannie Hertz named Count Fleet, who lived up to her hopes for him by winning the Triple Crown in 1943 with Johnny Longden aboard.

Count Fleet had an easy time of it in winning the Pimlico Futurity, then added a dramatic punctuation to the season by winning Pimlico's mile and a sixteenth Walden Stakes as a 1-10 favorite by 30 lengths. Little wonder he was honored by handicapper John Blanks Campbell with topweight of 132 pounds on the Experimental, six pounds above scale and still the highest assignment since the Free Handicap was inaugurated in 1933.

If he was awfully good at 2, Count Fleet was perfect at 3 with a record of six for six and the admiration of every horseman in the country as among the best ever seen.

Trainer Don Cameron brought him out on April 13, 1943, at Jamaica in a mile and 70-yard overnight race on a sloppy track. With the familiar Johnny Longden in the irons, Count Fleet won easily by three and a half lengths. Four days later, sent off as a 1-4 choice, he made light work of the Wood Memorial at Jamaica, beating runner-up Blue Swords by three and a half lengths.

With the Kentucky Derby two weeks away, Count Fleet was in trouble. A foot problem peaked at Churchill Downs, and for a day or two there was real doubt Count Fleet would be ready to run for the roses. But Longden recalls that a major effort by Cameron and

Before Secretariat's tour de force in 1973, the Belmont Stakes most talked about was Count Fleet's total domination of the 1943 running when he romped by 25 lengths.

his stable staff turned the tide. Those were the days of stable secrets, so Count Fleet was 2-5 on Derby Day. He made it look easy. Taking the track at the start, he led past every pole, winning by three lengths.

Only three faced Count Fleet in the Preakness a week later, and Count Fleet was awesome. After a half-mile in :47⅖ he was in front by four lengths, and galloped home to register by eight lengths. With the Belmont Stakes a month away, Cameron, who believed in fitness, saddled Count Fleet for the Withers Mile at Belmont and wasn't disappointed. Racing on a muddy track, The Count was a five-length winner.

He completed his sweep of the Triple Crown on June 5. Sent off at 1-20 and facing only two others, Count Fleet was brilliant. He drew off through the stretch, won by 25 lengths, and accomplished the mile and a half in a near-record 2:28⅕. But it was an expensive triumph. He rapped himself in the ankle of his right foreleg, and later in the summer it was announced that he had been retired. His record showed 16 wins from 21 starts, with four seconds and a third. He was one for the ages.

He was a great success at stud, too. He was champion sire in 1951 when his son, Counterpoint, was Horse of the Year, and was leading broodmare sire in 1963. At one time during his career at stud he was insured for a then-record sum of $500,000.

The Hertzes had many other good horses, but none could replace Count Fleet in their esteem. A devoted couple, they celebrated their 50th wedding anniversary with a big dinner for hundreds of friends plus the publication of a private book, written for them by *Daily Racing Form*'s Evan Shipman. It concluded with a poem written by John D. Hertz himself:

"She's my Fanny and I'm her John;
She's my Fanny, though life goes on.
Golden weddings to me don't so often occur,
But boy, oh boy, what I would give
To live it all over again with her."

When he died a few years later, Hertz left $50 million to the United States of America for the privilege of being a citizen. His bequest stated the money should be used for the training of engineers. A provision of the scholarship was that the graduate donate a year of service to the country.

The 20th century produced five truly exceptional 3-year-olds – Sysonby, Man o' War, Count Fleet, Citation and Secretariat. While each has his opinionated advocates, there is some unanimity that Citation's 3-year-old campaign of 1948, when he won 19 of 20 starts from one side of the country to the other, was the paradigm: the best of the best.

Citation was owned and bred by Warren Wright of Calumet Farm, heir to the Calumet baking powder fortune, who sold the company in the 1930s for a reported $60 million and began an odyssey into thoroughbred racing. Wright set high standards in all his activities, hired Ben and Jimmy Jones as his trainers in 1939, and was rewarded with his first classic victories in 1941 when Whirlaway swept the Triple Crown. His stable was the leader in earnings that year, and repeated as champion in 1943, 1944, 1946 and 1947.

With Bull Lea an instant success at stud, Wright continued to buy broodmares through the 1940s. One acquired in England was Hydroplane II. She wasn't a distinguished runner, but it was her pedigree that made her attractive. She was by Epsom Derby winner Hyperion, a proven source of quality. Bred to Bull Lea, she produced a handsome bay colt, graced with a significant name, Citation.

Trained from the outset by Jimmy Jones, Citation was a marvelous 2-year-old who only lost once in nine starts, and that to his stablemate, the filly Bewitch.

"We ran three horses in the Washington Park Futurity that year," Jones recalls, "and we figured we'd take the first three places with Citation, Bewitch and Free America. So we told the riders before the race that we would split the fees three ways. That way nobody would do anything foolish in the drive. Bewitch, with Doug Dodson up, got the lead and finished a length in front of Citation, with Free America third. Later, Steve Brooks, on Citation, said he could have gone by the filly at any time. But Jack Westrope, who rode Free America, said he could have beaten them both without going to the whip."

Citation underscored his class in the Futurity at Belmont Park, a race that attracted almost every top juvenile in the country. Six of

SEVENTH RACE
4 7 7 3 0
May 1-48—C.D

1 1-4 MILES. (Whirlaway, May 3, 1941—2:01⅖—3—126.) Seventy-fourth running KENTUCKY DERBY. $100,000 added. 3-year-olds. Scale weights. (Owner of winner to receive gold trophy.)

Gross value, $111,450. Net value to winner $83,400; second, $10,000; third, $5,000; fourth, $2,500. Mutuel Pool, $670,833.

Index	Horses	Eq't	A	Wt	PP	St	½	¾	1	Str	Fin	Jockeys	Owners	Odds to $1
(47451)	CITATION	w		126	1	2	2ʰ	2³	2⁵	1²	13½	E Arcaro	Calumet Farm	a-.40
(47189)	COALTOWN	wb		126	2	1	1⁶	13½	1½	2⁴	2³	N L Pierson	Calumet Farm	a-.40
(47326)	MY REQUEST	w		126	6	3	4ʰ	4³	31½	3¹	31½	D Dodson	B F Whitaker	3.80
47189²	BILLINGS	w		126	5	6	5½	3½	4⁸	4¹⁵	4²⁰	M Peterson	Walmac Stable	14.70
47282³	GRANDPERE	w		126	4	4	3²	6	6	5½	5ⁿᵏ	J Gilbert	Mrs J P Adams	17.80
47451²	ESCADRU	wb		126	3	5	6	5⁶	51½	6	6	A Kirkland	W L Brann	7.10

a-Coupled, Citation and Coaltown.

Time, :12⅕, :23⅗, :34⅗, :46⅗, :59⅕, 1:11⅖, 1:24⅖, 1:38, 1:51⅖, 2:05⅖. Track sloppy.

Mutuel Prices
	—$2 Mutuels Paid—		—Odds to $1—		
CITATION (a-Entry)	2.80	….	….	.40	…. ….
COALTOWN (a-Entry)	2.80	….	….	.40	…. ….
NO PLACE OR SHOW MUTUELS SOLD.					

Winner—B. c, by Bull Lea—Hydroplane II., by Hyperion, trained by B. A. Jones; bred by Calumet Farm
WENT TO POST—4:32. OFF AT 4:32½ CENTRAL STANDARD TIME.
Start good from stall gate. Won handily; second and third driving. CITATION, away forwardly and losing ground while racing back of COALTOWN to the stretch, responded readily to a steady hand ride after disposing of the latter and drew clear. COALTOWN began fast, established a clear lead before going a quarter and, making the pace on the inside in the stretch, continued willingly, but was not good enough for CITATION, although easily best of the others.

As Daily Racing Form's chart of the 1948 Kentucky Derby shows, the Calumet Farm entry of Citation and Coaltown dominated the Run for the Roses.

Jimmy Jones led Citation, Eddie Arcaro up, to the winner's circle after the race.

the 14 were still in the thick of the fight at the furlong pole when Citation suddenly quickened and drew off, winning by three lengths. Whirling Fox was second and Bewitch was third.

Citation, incredibly, received only 126 pounds as the topweight on the Experimental Free Handicap, possibly attributable to strained relations between Ben Jones of Calumet Farm and handicapper John B. Campbell. Jones groused publicly about high weights in handicaps assigned to Armed. Campbell, in reply, nailed a "crying towel" to the bulletin board in the racing secretary's office.

Citation developed an osselet, did not race at 4, and never again regained the scintillating form he displayed throughout his 3-year-old season. But he was still a major drawing card and led the Calumet team under topweight of 132 pounds in the Santa Anita Handicap. It was a nightmare. Johnny Gilbert, on Two Lea, had the rail in the drive and wouldn't let Arcaro through on Citation. Big Cy had to take up and go around, and was beaten a length and a quarter by Noor, who was in receipt of 22 pounds..

There was another memorable meeting between Noor and Citation in the San Juan Capistrano Handicap eight days later. For the mile and three-quarter test, Big Cy was asked to concede "only" 13 pounds (130 to 117). In a field of eight, Citation took the lead after the first mile. Noor drove up abreast with half a mile remaining and the two continued head and head to the wire, with Noor the winner by a nose. So sensational were the two leaders they clipped more than five seconds from the track record.

A third extraordinary confrontation took place at Golden Gate

A familiar scene: Alfred Vanderbilt leading Native Dancer to the winner's circle.

Fields on June 17 in the Forty Niners Handicap at nine furlongs. This time Citation gave Noor five pounds. They staged another thrilling duel through the stretch, Noor prevailing by a neck in the world-record time of 1:46⅘.

Seeking to make Citation the first equine millionaire, Jones kept the horse in training as a 6-year-old. He was beaten in his first four starts by horses who couldn't warm him up when he was right. Then he won the Century Mile at Hollywood Park on June 14, came back on July 4 to win the American Handicap, and ran a corking race in the Hollywood Gold Brooks he won by four lengths, his 10 furlongs in 2:01. With total earnings of $1,085,760, he was retired to stud.

As a sire, his best horses were probably Silver Spoon, a champion filly who beat colts in the Santa Anita Derby, and Fabius, who won the Preakness and might have been best in Needles' Derby. Citation never got a horse of his own quality, but that would have been impossible.

Geisha, a Discovery filly owned, bred and occasionally trained by Alfred Gwynne Vanderbilt, was not herself a champion. She started 11 times and won one race. But she had credentials in bloodstock. Her granddam, La Chica, produced Planetoid, dam of Grey Flight, a mare who dropped nine stakes winners for the Phipps family.

Polynesian was a Preakness winner and an agent of speed and versatility. Vanderbilt thought he had potential as a sire and made the decision to send Geisha to Polynesian's court in 1949. The result of that tryst was a gray colt with a striking presence, ability and style. Undefeated at 2 in nine starts, Native Dancer won nine of 10 races at 3, finishing second by a head to Dark Star in the controversial Kentucky Derby of 1953. After winning his three starts at 4, evidence sufficiently impressive to earn him Horse of the Year honors for 1954, he was retired to stud as one of the finest racehorses of the century, with a record of 21 wins and a second from 22 starts.

Despite the esteem in which he has always been held, no horse has ever paid as dearly for one circumstantial

Bill Winfrey (center) checks out some Hialeah information in 1954 with two other railbirds – trainers Tommy Root Sr. (left) and Sunny Jim Fitzsimmons.

York racing season. Native Dancer was favored, but they didn't come from Outer Mongolia to bet him down as with some "good things." They love the chalk in old New York and they should have come. They did thereafter. In every other race, except for one betless exhibition, The Dancer was odds-on. Under Eric Guerin, Native Dancer won by four and a half lengths after stepping five furlongs in :59⅗, the price a generous 7-5.

Only four days later, Winfrey, an ex-Marine, had Native Dancer back in the pits

defeat as the Gray Ghost of Sagamore Farm. The loss, which never should have happened, came in America's most celebrated horserace. Though *Daily Racing Form's* chart told the story succinctly – "Native Dancer, roughed at the first turn by Money Broker . . . was eased back to secure racing room . . . finished strongly but could not overtake the winner, though probably best" – and though as the country's first equine television star he was extremely popular, the public perception of his talent changed by degrees in the wake of the loss. Had he retired undefeated, it is fair to say that history would have slotted him as the second of what would be three superstars of the century, together with Man o' War and Secretariat.

Bill Winfrey, a Hall of Fame horseman and the son of a Hall of Fame horseman, brought Native Dancer to the races at Jamaica just a few weeks after the traditional April 1 opening of the 1952 New

for his first stakes appearance, the five-furlong Youthful. This time Dancer was 4-5 and he won by four lengths at Jamaica. The Youthful helped buck the grey colt's shins and he was sidelined for more than three months, returning at Saratoga August 4 in the Flash Stakes at five and a half furlongs. He was the winner by more than two lengths.

Native Dancer raced four times at the Spa that month and added the Saratoga Special, the Grand Union Hotel Stakes and the Hopeful to his growing collection.

After capturing a prep race at Belmont Park, Dancer was 1-3 in the Futurity down the Widener Chute. He was impeded during the early stages but recovered with agility and displayed a fearsome acceleration to win by two and a half lengths. Remarkably, Guerin never hit Native Dancer, who equaled the world's record for a straight course of 1:14⅖. He concluded his undefeated campaign in Jamaica's mile and a sixteenth East View Stakes on October 22. Favored at 1-5, he registered another easy tally for his ninth victory and became the leading money-winning 2-year-old with record earnings of $230,495.

Handicapper John B. Campbell, who gave Count Fleet 132 pounds on the Experimental and assigned Citation 126 pounds, topped his Free Handicap with Native Dancer at 130 pounds. Trainer Winfrey raced in California that winter, and The Dancer went west with the stable. His ankles were fired as a precaution, delaying his 3-year-old debut until April 18, 1953, when he won a division of the mile and a sixteenth Gotham Stakes at Jamaica. Favored at 1-6, he won by two lengths, but not impressively.

A week later, in the Wood Memorial, Native Dancer was favored at 1-10. His time for the nine furlongs was a pedestrian 1:50⅗, but he scored by a convincing four and a half lengths and shipped to Louisville as the hottest Kentucky Derby choice in years.

Native Dancer, who came from off the pace, was away casually, as one might anticipate in a mile and a quarter race. Guerin, with a chance to sit back and choose his route, found a comfortable opening between horses on the inside and was preparing to go through

Trainer Bill Winfrey supervises Native Dancer's exercise at Churchill Downs just days before the fateful 1953 running of the Kentucky Derby.

when he caught a look from the young rider on the outside horse, Money Broker. His name was Al Popara and the look was trouble.

As the gray horse moved through, Popara brought Money Broker into Native Dancer, "roughed him" in the words of Don Fair's graphic footnotes. Native Dancer dropped back, then raced wide into the far turn, and "cut" the final corner. He settled in on the rail behind Dark Star, the 25-1 leader. At the furlong pole, the difference between the two horses was a length and a half. Native Dancer continued to stalk Dark Star until Guerin suddenly moved him to the outside. As though galvanized, the grey horse accelerated and hurled himself forward. He missed by a head.

There is newsreel footage but no film patrol record of the first-turn incident. The film patrol was installed at Churchill Downs the following year. The description of the incident cited here represents a consensus of the recollections of a few surviving witnesses who were in various ways involved. To a man they concluded: What a shame.

The Kentucky Derby was run on May 2 and the Preakness wasn't until May 23. Bill Winfrey decided to sharpen Native Dancer's speed with an appearance in Belmont Park's Withers Mile, a week preceding the Preakness. Bet down to 1-20 off his only defeat, The

Dancer galloped to a four-length victory.

In the 78th Preakness, however, Jamie K., who passed the Derby, gave Native Dancer and his people a real scare. Coming from far back in a field of seven, Jamie K. pursued Native Dancer across the wire, separated by only a neck. Dark Star, the Kentucky Derby winner, set a lively pace for a mile, then gave way and finished fifth. He'd broken down, never to race again.

The Belmont on June 13 was of a pattern with the Preakness. Jamie K., with the opportunistic Eddie Arcaro aboard, moved first and had the lead after a mile in 1:39⅖. Native Dancer, put on alert, was just a head back at the eighth pole and a neck in front at the winning post.

Three weeks after completion of the demanding Triple Crown campaign, Native Dancer was back to the racing wars in Aqueduct's Dwyer Stakes on July 4. Favored at 1-20 by an enthusiastic holiday crowd, the gray horse won smartly by almost two lengths. He caught a heavy track two weeks later when he went west to contest the Arlington Classic Mile. Chicagoans had some suspicions, sending The Dancer off at 2-3, but these anxieties were quickly relieved when he won by nine lengths.

Native Dancer trained nicely at Saratoga for the Travers on August 15. Among those who knew him best, he was 1-20 going into the race, and they were right. He won easily by more than five lengths and promptly shipped back to Chicago for the American Derby the following weekend at Washington Park. During the week it was announced by the New York stewards that jockey Guerin was suspended 10 days for a riding infraction. Eddie Arcaro got the call.

Perhaps the gray horse wanted to test The Master, or perhaps Eddie relaxed him so much. In any event, he was six lengths off the pace at the head of the stretch as a 1-5 favorite. Arcaro, realizing he was the only rider other than Guerin to sit on Native Dancer, had no intention of losing and communicated that thought to his part-

The footnotes of Daily Racing Form's chart of the 1953 Kentucky Derby spell out the cause of Native Dancer's only career defeat.

ner through the whip. The gray sprung forward, and making light work of his 128 pounds, was up to score by two lengths, the nine panels in 1:48⅖. Interviewed after the American Derby, Arcaro described his new friend as "sheer power."

Native Dancer was nine for 10 at that point in the 1953 season while Greentree's 4-year-old Tom Fool was eight-for-eight, en route to a brilliant campaign in which he went undefeated in 10 starts. Every racing executive in the United States made an effort to bring them together but Native Dancer had bruised his left foreleg during the American Derby and was sidelined for the remainder of the year. Tom Fool, with his spotless record, was voted Horse of the Year, and Native Dancer was forced to settle for the 3-year-old championship.

He made his 4-year-old debut at Belmont Park on May 7, 1954, in a six-furlong overnight event, the Commando Purse, and won smartly at 1-6. The gray received a hearty ovation from the public, which had learned to pick him out on television with the help of his color and his fantastic record.

Native Dancer made his second start of the season in the Metropolitan Mile on May 15. This traditional feature, which has been run for more than a century, has had some storied renewals but the 1954 edition must rank with the finest races of the century. Anyone who witnessed it, either in person or on television, will never forget The Dancer's performance.

Straight Face, a very solid handicap horse from the Greentree Stable, had a margin of seven lengths as he turned for home under 117 pounds. Native Dancer, carrying 130 pounds, appeared to have no chance to catch him but he persevered, whittling away at Straight Face's margin with that huge, sweeping stride. And when he got up in the last jump to score by a neck, the racing world exploded with admiration.

Assigned 133 pounds for the Suburban, Native Dancer developed some soreness in his right foreleg which forced him to pass

that engagement. During the period of recuperation, trainer Bill Winfrey, at owner Vanderbilt's suggestion, flew to Paris to inspect the Longchamp course in the event Native Dancer went to Paris that fall for the Arc de Triomphe.

Winfrey returned in time to ship Native Dancer to Saratoga, where his main objective was the Whitney Stakes. Prepping for that traditional test, the gray carried 137 pounds to win an exhibition race, the seven-furlong Oneonta Handicap. On a sloppy track he won by nine lengths, but soreness returned to his right front foot.

That Sunday morning, attending the annual Jockey Club Conference on Racing Matters, Vanderbilt tore a sheet of paper from the pad that had been placed in front of every seat at the conference hall. He scribbled a note to Robert Fulton Kelley, the Belmont Park publicity director, sitting nearby. The note read: "ND NG." A few days later, Native Dancer's retirement to stud was announced.

His son, Kauai King, led all the way to win the 1966 Kentucky Derby. His grandson, Northern Dancer, won the Derby in record time in 1964. Another son, Dancer's Image, finished first in the 1968 Derby but was subsequently disqualified for use of the then-forbidden Butazolidin to relieve a sore ankle. Another grandson, Majestic Prince, won the Derby in 1969.

In November 1967, after undergoing surgery to relieve intestinal blockage, Native Dancer died at 17. He was almost perfect.

One of the most remarkable racehorses of any era was a foal of 1957. Almost totally obscure at 2 during a brief fall campaign, Kelso began to come to hand in the summer of his 3-year-old season. By fall he was the best horse in the country and went on to Horse of the Year laurels, an award he was to win a record five consecutive seasons.

During his five-year reign, some 67,000 foals were registered in this country. Kelso proved himself superior to all of them, in sprints, in middle-distance events, at cup distances, on dirt and grass. He won under high weights consistently, carried as much as 136 pounds successfully, and met every challenge by which superior horses are recognized. Was he the greatest horse ever to race in America? Horse for horse, possibly not, but in totality of accomplishment over an extraordinary period of time, he was one of a kind.

The Kelso story begins in 1956 when Allaire duPont, widow of a highly-decorated glider pilot in World War II, sent her mare Maid of Flight, by Count Fleet, to the court of Your Host, standing at the New Jersey farm of Mrs. F. Wallis Armstrong.

Your Host, by Alibhai, had won the Santa Anita Derby of 1950 under Johnny Longden and was shipped to Kentucky by rail to prepare for the Kentucky Derby

Sharpening at Keeneland over seven furlongs, Your Host beat Flamingo winner Oil Capitol and Blue Grass winner Mr. Trouble in the record time of 1:22⅖, and his margin of victory, more than six lengths, sent him into the Derby as the 8-5 choice. He led for six furlongs, gave way to Mr. Trouble, then came again gamely to regain the lead, but tired in the drive and finished ninth of 14.

Your Host enjoyed considerable success during the remainder of the season, with stakes victories in the East, Midwest and West. He came out smoking as a 4-year-old, winning the Santa Catalina at Santa Anita under 130 pounds and setting a track record of 1:48⅕ for the nine furlongs. But a week later, in the San Pasqual Handicap,

Ismael "Milo" Valenzuela became Kelso's regular rider when the gelding was a 5-year-old.

Your Host clipped heels with Renown and fell, fracturing his right foreleg in four places.

Veterinarians despaired of his life and a $250,000 insurance policy was paid, but he was not put down. Thanks to his own determination and the devoted care of attending personnel, Your Host lived and was eventually sent to New Jersey to stand at stud. He was syndicated by Mrs. Armstrong ,and one of the shareholders attracted to Your Host by his courage was Allaire duPont. Maid of Flight had good bloodlines, had placed in several stakes on the Jersey circuit, and was added to the Bohemia Stable broodmare band on the farm in Chesapeake City, Maryland. With Your Host close by in New Jersey, and with access through her participation in the syndicate, Mrs. duPont made the fateful decision.

Dr. John Lee was Kelso's first trainer. A licensed veterinarian, he was essentially a horseman and well-known for his professional skills in the Maryland-Delaware area. Mrs. duPont kept some of her mares at Claiborne Farm in Paris, Kentucky. That's where Kelso was foaled, and when he turned 2 he was sent to the duPont Farm in Chesapeake City. Mrs. duPont named him for a close friend, Mrs. Kelso Everett.

He wasn't a physical beauty. He had a decent frame but he was on the rangy side, with his ribs prominent. Lee saw immediately he in the Hawthorne Gold Cup, running the mile and a quarter in 2:02 carrying 117 pounds. Kelso was giving weight on the scale to all his opponents.

The Hawthorne Gold Cup marked Arcaro's fourth consecutive win in four rides on Kelso, and The Master cemented the relationship in Kelso's final start at 3, the Jockey Club Gold Cup, held that year at Aqueduct on October 29. Favored at 4-5 in a field of eight, Kelso won by more than three lengths and set a record of 3:19⅖ for the two miles on a sloppy track. Don Poggio and Bald Eagle, two fine handicap horses, were second and third, respectively.

Kelso romped by five and a half lengths in taking his fifth straight Jockey Club Gold Cup in 1964, which led to a fifth consecutive Horse of the Year title.

With eight victories from nine starts and dominance over older horses firmly established, Kelso was voted Horse of the Year in 1960 for the first time.

His 4-year-old season brought confirmation of the widely held suspicion that Kelso was special. In his second start of the year, he won the Metropolitan Mile under 130 pounds and gave 13 pounds to runner-up All Hands. He won the Suburban under 133 pounds, with a margin of five lengths on Nickle Boy, who was in receipt of 21 pounds. Then Kelso swept the NYRA handicap series by capturing the Brooklyn under 136 pounds.

There was another unhappy experience in Chicago that summer when Kelso finished fourth on a muddy, holding track in the

Washington Park Mile. But Kelso re-established his dominion with an eight-length victory in the Woodward Stakes, during which he equaled Aqueduct's track record for a mile and a quarter of 2:00. He also polished off the Jockey Club Gold Cup by five lengths, setting the stage for his turf debut in the Washington D.C. International at Laurel. In an outstanding performance, he finished second to T.V. Lark, beaten less than a length in the course-record time of 2:26⅕ for the mile and a half.

Arcaro retired after the 1961 season and recommended Bill Shoemaker as his successor. But Kelso was a horse who needed a physically strong rider while Shoemaker's success emanated principally from his light touch. Their partnership never flourished, and after Kelso was upset in the Metropolitan, the Suburban and Monmouth handicaps, Ismael (Milo) Valenzuela succeeded Shoemaker. The occasion was an allowance race on the grass at Saratoga on August 22. Kelso, highweight at 124 pounds and a solid 1-4 favorite, won smartly from grass specialist Call the Witness while conceding seven pounds, the mile and a sixteenth run in a near-record 1:41⅘.

That fall, Kelso and Milo competed in six stakes, won all four on the dirt, and were second twice in two grass stakes. They worked together particularly well in the Jockey Club Gold Cup, which Kelso needed time and Kelso didn't make his debut until September 4, 1959, at Atlantic City. Mildly regarded at 6-1 in a six-furlong maiden race, he stood a hard drive under John Block to beat 11 opponents, getting up to score by a length and a quarter. Ten days later, he finished second in a nonwinners of two, rallying to be beaten a length and a half.

Lee thought he saw something. He ran Kelso a third time, nine days after that, and Kelso was second again, this time under Walter Blum. Kelso got the lead, probably should have won, but gave way to be beaten three-quarters of a length as the 19-10 favorite. Lee was now convinced that Kelso was not moving freely and ordered him gelded. In later years, as Kelso built an incredible record, Lee took a kidding from friends as the man who gelded Kelso, but as he pointed out, Kelso probably wouldn't have been the caliber of horse he was if he hadn't been cut.

Lee wanted to devote more time to his veterinary practice and gave up his small stable that winter. Mrs. duPont set about finding another trainer, and when the word circulated she received a call from Carl Hanford, member of a well-known family of riders. One of the brothers, Babe Hanford, rode Bold Venture to victory in the 1936 Kentucky Derby. Another brother, Buddy Hanford, was killed in a race when his horse fell. Low-key, knowledgeable and thorough, Carl Hanford got the job with Bohemia Stable.

Hanford trained Kelso carefully in the spring of 1960 and liked what he saw of the raw-boned brown gelding. Kelso was working crisply, and when he made his 3-year-old debut at Monmouth Park on June 22, he was sent off at even-money. Bill Hartack, a three-time riding champion in the late 1950s and a regular on the Jersey circuit, had the mount. Kelso came from of the pace to win by 10 lengths, and people began to notice. Three weeks later, Hanford shipped Kelso to New York for an allowance race at Aqueduct. Hartack declined to make the trip so Hanford got Walter Blum.

Favored at 13-10, Kelso won by 12 lengths and raced a mile in 1:34⅕. New York turf writers gave the gangly gelding high marks.

Now it was time to test Kelso in stakes competition. Hanford chose the Arlington Classic Mile as a suitable engagement, sent Kelso to Chicago and engaged Steve Brooks to ride. Venetian Way, the Kentucky Derby winner, was in the field, and so was a promising runner named T.V. Lark. All eyes were on Kelso in the Classic, but he showed absolutely nothing in a dull effort. Nor was it the only occasion on which he would disappoint Chicagoans.

Kelso regained winning ways in his next start, the Choice Stakes at Monmouth Park on August 3. With Hartack once again in the saddle, Kelso flew, winning off by seven lengths from Careless John. Hartack and Kelso seemed made for each other. In their two collaborations, the margin of victory totaled 17 lengths. Hanford penciled Kelso in for the Jerome Mile at Aqueduct on September 3, and two weeks before the race began phoning Hartack for a commitment. He could never reach him, and messages produced no response, so the trainer called on a familiar and reliable figure in New York, Eddie Arcaro.

Picking up seven pounds from the Choice Stakes, Kelso won the Jerome, but it was close. After a mile in 1:34⅖, Kelso had a head on Careless John, the same horse he'd beaten easily in the Choice. Arcaro knew his mount a little more in the subsequent Discovery Handicap and Kelso, though forced to swerve in the drive, won by a length and a quarter from Careless John, conceding eight pounds this time.

Belmont Park's Lawrence Realization at a mile and a five furlongs on September 28 was a rout. Favored at 1-2, Kelso equaled the track record with a 2:40⅕, winning by more than four lengths over the Santa Anita Derby winner, Tompion. Two weeks later, Kelso and Arcaro triumphed again, this time in Chicago. Making light work of a muddy track and moderate field, Kelso sped to a six-length tally

SEVENTH RACE **1 1-4 MILES. (Gun Bow, July 25, 1964, 1:59$\frac{3}{5}$, 4, 122.)**
Aqu 21725
October 3, 1964

Eleventh running WOODWARD. Weight for age. $100,000 added. 3-year-olds and upward. By subscription of $200 each, which shall accompany the nomination; $1,000 additional to start with $100,000 added. The added money and all fees to be divided 65 per cent to the winner, 20 per cent to second, 10 per cent to third and 5 per cent to fourth. 3-year-olds, 121 lbs.; older, 126 lbs. Mrs. William Woodward, Sr. has donated a trophy to be presented to the owner of the winner; trophies will also be presented to the winning trainer and jockey. Closed Tuesday, Sept. 15, 1964 with 16 nominations.
Value of race $108,200. Value to winner $70,330; second, $21,640; third, $10,820; fourth, $5,410.
Mutuel Pool, $583,934.

Index	Horses	Eq't	A	Wt	PP	¼	½	¾	1	Str	Fin	Jockeys	Owners	Odds to $1
21452Aqu[2]	Gun Bow	b	4	126	2	1^{1}	$1^{1\frac{1}{2}}$	$1^{1\frac{1}{2}}$	1^{h}	$2^{1\frac{1}{2}}$	1no	W Blum	Gedney Farm	1.45
21452Aqu[1]	Kelso		7	126	3	2^{4}	$2^{3\frac{1}{2}}$	2^{h}	2^{1}	1^{h}	2^{4}	I Valenz'ela	Bohemia Stable	.95
21551Aqu[3]	Quadrangle		3	121	4	3^{3}	3^{5}	3^{12}	3^{20}	3^{25}	3^{25}	M Ycaza	Rokeby Stable	5.45
21578Aqu[6]	Guadalcanal		6	126	5	5	5	5	4^{8}	4^{10}	4^{18}	J Ruane	R L Dotter	51.45
21542Atl[10]	Colorado King		5	126	1	4^{7}	4^{8}	4^{5}	5	5	5	W Hartack	R W Hawn	11.00

Time, :23$\frac{4}{5}$, :48$\frac{1}{5}$, 1:12$\frac{1}{5}$, 1:37$\frac{1}{5}$, 2:02$\frac{2}{5}$ (no wind in backstretch). Track good.

$2 Mutuel Prices:			
2-GUN BOW	4.90	2.40	2.10
3-KELSO		2.30	2.10
4-QUADRANGLE			2.10

B. c, by Gun Shot—Ribbons and Bows, by War Admiral. Trainer, E. A. Neloy. Bred by Maine Chance Farm.
IN GATE—4:50. OFF AT 4:50 EASTERN DAYLIGHT TIME. Start good. Won driving.
GUN BOW, taken in hand leaving the gate, saved ground drawing clear on the first turn and raced with neck bowed when taken under double wraps entering the backstretch. Jockey Blum gradually loosened restraint approaching the half-mile pole and had him under pressure rounding the stretch turn. He was headed briefly by KELSO at the three-sixteenths marker and was gradually forced in by that rival passing the furlong marker, where he regained a slight advantage which he maintained narrowly under extreme hand urging. KELSO, lightly hustled to show first away from the gate, was taken under restraint when joined by GUN BOW after the opening furlong and dropped back until clear on the first turn.

Daily Racing Form's *chart of the 1964 Woodward Stakes describes one of the most dramatic races of the decade.*

won by 10 lengths in 3:19$\frac{4}{5}$ for the two miles, and in the Washington D.C. International, which he lost by half a length to France's Match II after gamely putting away several leading contenders. With six wins and four seconds from 12 starts, Kelso was Horse of the Year for the third consecutive season.

At age 6 in 1963, Kelso ran off a string of eight consecutive stakes victories in top-class features such as the Gulfstream Park Handicap, Bowie's John B. Campbell, the Nassau County and Suburban handicaps at Aqueduct, the Whitney at Saratoga, the Aqueduct and Woodward stakes at Aqueduct, and a fourth victory in the Jockey Club Gold Cup. But he finished second in the Washington D.C. International for the third straight year. Mongo won by half a length after Kelso broke sluggishly and lost position. Despite the defeat, he was Horse of the Year a fourth time with nine wins and two seconds in 12 starts.

Kelso, now 7, began the 1964 campaign in California with two appearances designed to have him at tops for the Hollywood Gold Cup. It didn't work out well at all. In his seasonal debut, the seven-furlong Los Angeles Handicap at Hollywood on May 23, Kelso was the 17-10 favorite, despite being topweight at 130 pounds. In a dull effort he beat one horse in the field of nine. Cyrano was the winner under 124. Kelso came back in the mile and a sixteenth Californian on June 6, this time a 7-5 choice. Impeded at a crucial point, he finished sixth under 127 pounds, the race going to Mustard Plaster, who carried 111 pounds.

A decision was made to pass the Hollywood Gold Cup and return to New York. Kelso prepped for the Suburban Handicap in a nine-furlong overnighter on June 25 and won nicely, beating Tropical Breeze and Sunrise Flight. The Suburban on July 4 drew an outstanding field including Cain Hoy Stable's Iron Peg, who was sent home from England with the notation "Not very genuine," and Olden Times, versatile winner of the San Juan Capistrano at 14 furlongs and the Metropolitan Mile. Kelso was the favorite despite 131 pounds and gave it a big try, but was a head shy at the finish. Iron Peg – he was "Iron Pig" in England – won under 116 pounds.

Two weeks later, in the Monmouth Handicap, the situation was the same. Kelso was topweight at 130 pounds and favored at 3-5. He raced strongly, was in good position and attacked the leaders but began to fade and finished second, beaten a neck by the top-class Mongo, who carried 127 pounds. Gun Bow, under 124 pounds, finished third in the brilliant field. Kelso failed to improve his record in the Brooklyn Handicap, as well. One week after the Monmouth race, he was favored in the ancient Brooklyn while carrying 130 pounds. There was some bumping leaving the gate, and Kelso lost his position. He was never really a factor after that and finished fifth in a race won easily by Gun Bow, with Olden Times second.

With six races of the season gone by the boards, Kelso had only one victory, and that in an allowance race. Some asked the question: Is Kelso through? Carl Hanford kept his own council, shipped the horse to Saratoga, and gave him a brief working holiday. Late in the meeting, on August 27, Kelso came out in an allowance race on the grass and won by two and a half lengths at nine furlongs.

Kelso's retirement years were tranquil as he served as the world's most esteemed riding horse for his owner, Allaire duPont, at her Maryland farm.

It was a different story, however, on October 31 when Kelso won his fifth consecutive Jockey Club Gold Cup. Favored at 1-2 in a field of six, he galloped to a five and a half-length tally over those classy 3-year-olds, Roman Brother and Quadrangle.

It was a memorable score, for Kelso broke his own record with a time of 3:19⅕ for the two miles. He also became the leading money-winning thoroughbred, breaking Round Table's record of $1,749,869 set in 1958. Round Table ran in 66 races while Kelso broke the mark in his 56th start.

Kelso was all business on September 7 in the Aqueduct Handicap. He was away smartly, stalked the pace, and then came on to win by three-quarters of a length from Gun Bow, who was equally weighted at 128 pounds. The Labor Day crowd of 65,000 treated Kelso to an ovation which lasted a full five minutes. The stage was now set for the 10-furlong Woodward at Aqueduct on October 3. Kelso was favored in the weight-for-age test, which was one of the great races of the era. Gun Bow, under Walter Blum, set the pace, with Kelso right alongside. They were a head apart as they turned into the stretch, Kelso put his head in front at the eighth pole, and the two came down the lane together as the crowd went into frenzy. It took a camera to separate them, with the decision to Gun Bow by half an inch.

After three consecutive seconds in the Washington D.C. International, and every one of them a superb effort, sentiment was high in Kelso's favor when he returned to Laurel for the November 11 race. Favored at 6-5 in a field of eight, Kelso took the lead midway in the race and then, after battling Gun Bow fiercely, won by four and a half lengths in the record time of 2:23⅘. Gun Bow was second and Russia's Analine was third, but the crowd could see only one horse, and as he cantered back to the winner's circle they hollered "Kelso, Kelso, Kelso!"

A fifth straight Horse of the Year title was the prize.

Kelso raced at 8, started six times, and won three. Carrying 130 pounds at Saratoga, he won the Whitney Stakes for the third time, getting up in the final stride to beat Malicious by a nose while conceding 16 pounds. He ended his season on September 22, winning the Stymie Handicap at Aqueduct by eight lengths under 138 pounds. Some thought he was ready for another top fall campaign and a sixth Horse of the Year title but old age was beginning to catch up, and Kelso was forced to the sidelines.

After one start at Hialeah in the winter of 1966, Kelso was retired to Mrs. duPont's Farm in Chesapeake City where he hacked through the fields and made occasional appearances to raise money for equine research. One such occasion took place at Belmont Park on October 15, 1985, when Kelso and another great gelding, Forego, greeted the public in a parade past the stands. Returned to the farm that evening, Kelso took ill the next day and was dead at 26 in 48 hours. Tributes poured in from around the world but the greatest tribute to Kelso was his unparalleled record. Once upon a time there was a horse named Kelso. But only once.

∞ ∞ ∞ ∞ ∞

The two dominant horsemen of the era, Woody Stephens in the East and Charlie Whittingham in the West, created distinctive records in major races not likely to be duplicated. Stephens, a Kentuckian who rose to fame in New York, saddled five consecutive winners of the classic Belmont Stakes, an incredible achievement. California's Whittingham has a series of signature accomplishments, including 14 victories in the San Juan Capistrano Handicap, 10 victories in the Santa Anita Handicap and eight victories in the Hollywood Gold Cup.

Woodford Cefis Stephens, born September 1, 1913, in Stanton, Kentucky, grew up on a horse. His father, Lewis Stephens, was a farmer and share-cropper, and one of Woody's chores was taking care of the farm horses. He received a pony when he was six, rode him the three miles to school every morning and fed him during the lunch break. By the time he was 10, Woody could handle a wagon and team of horses.

In 1926, the Stephens family moved to Midway, Kentucky, not far from the heart of the horse country centered in Lexington. Woody landed a job at 13 breaking yearlings for town banker, J.M. Parrish, and it was at the Parrish farm that he got his first chance to ride thoroughbreds in various stages of training.

At 15, Stephens signed on as an exercise rider for the veteran horseman John S. Ward. He had his first ride as a jockey in September 1930 at Lincoln Fields near Chicago and broke his maiden at Hialeah in January 1931 on the opening-day program. John Ward's son, Sherrill, had taken over the training of the stable and put Woody up on a filly named Directly. At 18-1 she got up to score by a nose, and he had $20 on her, more than half his monthly pay of $35. Unfortunately, there weren't too many paydays like that one.

Stephens was still with the Ward family in 1936 when Sherrill Ward suggested Woody be listed in the program as the trainer of a horse he'd been galloping: Deliberator. Racing at the old Latonia track in Covington, Kentucky, just across the Ohio River from Cincinnati, Deliberator got up to win by a neck. "If you have a future in this game, it's as a trainer and not as a rider," John Ward told Woody.

Stephens married Lucille Easley of Lexington in 1937, left the Wards and tried to make a living for his new bride and himself. He scuffled, galloped horses for 50 cents each, broke a few yearlings, and hoped to get a horse to train. The Depression was in full swing and times were hard. Earl Horn gave him a few horses to take to Latonia but they couldn't run very fast.

In 1940, Stephens went to work as an assistant to Steve Judge, a veteran horseman who trained the stable of his old friend, Royce Martin, chairman of the Auto Lite Corporation. Judge asked Stephens to take Martin's promising 3-year-old prospect, Our Boots, to Oaklawn Park for the winter and train him for the Kentucky Derby. Woody spent three months with Our Boots in Hot Springs, brought him back to Judge in Lexington, and Judge ran him to win the Blue Grass Stakes at Keeneland, beating Whirlaway, who raced erratically. Between the Blue Grass and the Derby, however, Whirlaway's trainer, Ben Jones, outfitted his horse with blinkers. That proved to be the key to success.

After two years with Judge, Woody was ready to move on. Judge helped him get a job as assistant to Ross Higdon, who was training the large stable of Herbert Woolf of Kansas City. Higdon, however, trained every horse as a sprinter and the stable went downhill fast. Woody left in 1944 and signed on as assistant to trainer Earl Snyder in Chicago. But Snyder's horses couldn't run much, either, and Woody was pondering his future when he

By the late 1940s, Woody Stephens was on his way to a national reputation as a trainer to reckon with.

met a bright young horseplayer from Cincinnati named Jule Fink. Fink wanted to buy horses and bring a stable to New York. He offered a salary of $1,000 a month, plus 15 percent of all first money won. Trainers usually received 10 percent, but Fink bet on his horses and he wanted his trainer involved, too. Stephens accepted.

Fink and his associates, who became known as the "Speed Boys," claimed horses with speed and hoped Stephens could improve them. In a bit more than two years with Fink's Marlet Stable, Woody saddled 157 winners, and in April 1945 had his first stakes winner when Saguaro won the Excelsior Handicap at Jamaica.

A lot of success attracts attention, and racing authorities were soon looking into the affairs of the Marlet Stable. Stephens was questioned about some of the horses he claimed, and he could see

problems ahead. He left Fink's employ shortly before Fink was ruled off for associating with gambling interests.

Stephens landed a job with New York business man Frank Frankel, but it wasn't until he was hired by Royce Martin to train the Woodvale Farm stable that he began to win races in clusters again with such horses as Sports Page, Lady Dorimar and Tall Weeds.

Woody's first horse to gain some national recognition was Blue Man, owned by Arthur Abbott, who had the ice cream concessions at several busy amusement parks. Blue Man was trained by Woody's old boss, Steve Judge, but at 80, Judge was ready to retire, and he turned the horse over to Stephens. Woody found the colt washy and nervous, so he gave him plenty of time to settle down, put on some weight and regain confidence.

Blue Man ran in a division of Hialeah's Flamingo Stakes – the only time that stake was split – and won his race under Conn McCreary. That earned him a trip to the Kentucky Derby, in which he finished third to the winning favorite, Hill Gail, and Sub Fleet. Blue Man had better luck in the Preakness. Coming from last in a field of 10, he took command at the furlong pole and went on to win by three and a half lengths, Woody's first score in the classics.

Favored at 1-2 in the Belmont, Blue Man was upset by the 12-1 One Count and had to settle for second. But with a first, second and third in the Triple Crown, Blue Man acquitted himself well.

Royce Martin had a horse named Goyamo who was one of the favorites for the 1954 Kentucky Derby. Thanks to a fine ride by Eddie Arcaro, Goyamo finished well but could do no better than fourth in a race won by Determine. Martin, confined to a hospital bed in Lexington because of a heart condition, died that afternoon.

Following Martin's death, Stephens put together a public stable and did well with horses owned by Alton Jones, chairman of Cities Service; John A. Morris, an investment banker and breeder; international sportsman Raymond Guest, later U.S. Ambassador to Ireland; breeder Mildred Woolwine; and the colorful Clifford Mooers, whose Traffic Judge, winner of the Ohio Derby, the Withers and the Jerome Handicap, was the best horse in the barn.

Toward the end of 1956, Woody took a private job as trainer of the Cain Hoy Stable owned by Capt. Harry Guggenheim, whose family wealth came from copper. The Captain, a naval officer in two World Wars and a former U.S. Ambassador to Cuba, had been seeking Woody's services for some time. The Captain corraled him with an offer of $50,000 a year, 20 percent of all profits, but no share of the purses. The Cain Hoy Stable expenses ran to $450,000 a year.

It was Capt. Guggenheim's custom to send a couple of yearlings to Europe every year, trained in England by Capt. Cecil Boyd-Rochfort, who had horses for Queen Elizabeth and a number of American clients. Bald Eagle was a Nasrullah and did not enjoy certain aspects of racing abroad. But he did show considerable ability, which made his lack of success all the more frustrating. In despair, Boyd-Rochfort sent him home in the fall of his 3-year-old season with the comment, "Not very genuine."

Capt. Harry Guggenheim had his hands on a champion in 1962 with Never Bend, ridden by the fiery Manuel Ycaza.

Woody gave Bald Eagle almost a year before putting pressure on him, and patience on the part of owner and trainer paid dividends. Led by Bald Eagle, winner of the Suburban Handicap, the Gallant Fox and the Washington D.C. International at Laurel, Cain Hoy became the nation's leading stable with earnings of $742,081. At Christmas, Capt. Guggenheim sent Woody a turkey and a check for $75,000.

A portion of Cain Hoy's success was attributable to its stable jockey, Manuel Ycaza. Ycaza came from Panama to the United States in the mid-1950s and began riding for the Maine Chance Farm of Elizabeth Graham, the cosmetics executive. A natural talent with a pleasant manner, he mastered English quickly but not the rules of racing. Highly competitive by nature, he was constantly being suspended for infractions such a rough riding or careless riding, but between suspensions, rode a number of stakes winners.

Ycaza signed a contract in 1959 to ride for Cain Hoy and did well with Bald Eagle and One Eyed King. Bald Eagle won the International again in 1960 and Make Sail won the Kentucky Oaks. Other horses in the stable won stakes as well and Cain Hoy had another strong season. Woody's strong suit was always the fitness of his horses. He never sent a half-fit horse to the post in his life. He didn't believe in those long, demanding works so popular at the turn of the century. He took note of Ben Jones' success with six-furlong works and adapted that principle to his style. But he always insisted on fitness, and won races.

Never Bend, the 2-year-old champion of 1962, was the 3-year-old prospect Capt. Guggenheim had been looking for since he won the 1953 Kentucky Derby with Dark Star. The handsome Nasrullah colt out of Lalun enhanced his status with a five-length victory in the Flamingo at Hialeah, then tuned up for the Derby with tallies in a pair of seven-furlong allowance races at Keeneland and Churchill Downs. The Derby favorite, however, was an undefeated colt, Candy Spots, winner of the Santa Anita Derby and the Florida Derby. The oddly marked Nigromante colt was owned by Rex Ellsworth, trained by Mesh Tenney and ridden by Bill Shoemaker.

Never Bend set the pace in the 89th Kentucky Derby. There was plenty of speed in the small field of nine and they went the first six furlongs in 1:10, with No Robbery second and Candy Spots a close third. After a mile in 1:35⅕ the three horses were still prominent, but now the huge crowd was aware of movement on the outside. Darby Dan's Chateaugay, 9-1 despite the fact he won all three of his starts that season including Keeneland's Blue Grass Stakes, was starting to pick up the field. Under Braulio Baeza, he got up to score by a length and a quarter from Never Bend, with Candy Spots third.

As Never Bend was resting from his Triple Crown campaign, Capt. Guggenheim's Iron Peg was sent home from England after a series of disappointing performances, including the Epsom Derby. Iron Peg was a sound, good-looking individual with an even disposition, and Stephens, recalling his success with Bald Eagle, gave his new charge more than six months to acclimate before returning him to training. In May 1964 he won at first asking on the dirt in New York and two months later won the Suburban Handicap. A frac-

Angel Cordero Jr. doffed his cap after guiding Cannonade to victory in the centennial Kentucky Derby in 1974.

tured leg ended Iron Peg's career shortly after the Suburban, but his development from reject to Grade 1 stakes winner was another triumph for Woody.

It was also his last major winner for Cain Hoy Stable. Lucille Stephens had raced a small stable of homebreds for a number of years. Initially they were trained by Woody, but when he began his association with Cain Hoy, Capt. Guggenheim stipulated that only his horses could be in the barn. That was all right with the Stephenses, who gave the small stable to an old friend, Sherrill Ward. When the horses began winning races, however, the New York stewards intervened. They said they saw the situation as giving the appearance of a conflict of interest, and said Woody must either train the horses himself or sell them.

Neither Woody nor Lucille saw any reason to sell, and since Capt. Guggenheim refused to yield on having non-Cain Hoy horses in the barn, the only alternative was for Woody to leave. Capt. Guggenheim asked him to stay on until he could find a successor, and that fall he chose Roger Laurin, son of trainer Lucien Laurin.

Woody put together a public stable for racing in 1966 that included such prominent owners as John A. Morris, Louis Lee Haggin, John Olin and John Gaines. Bold Bidder, a 4-year-old, was the stable leader, winning the Monmouth Handicap and several other stakes, each with a value of $100,000. Bold Bidder was retired to stud, and many prominent racing men bred to him. Among those sending mares to his court was John Olin, who with John Hanes and John Gaines had purchased Bold Bidder in mid-career for $600,000.

One of the mares sent by Olin was Queen Sucree, who won one of four starts. She foaled Bold Bidder's colt in the spring of 1971 and Olin named him Cannonade.

Woody had two major classic prospects in the spring of 1974. One was Cannonade for John Olin and the other was Judger for Claiborne Farm's Seth Hancock. Judger, a Damascus colt, was bred by Claiborne and was bought back for $90,000 by Hancock in an effort to win the Kentucky Derby.

A record field of 23 turned out for the 100th Kentucky Derby. Everyone wanted to participate in the centennial Run for the Roses and that included the public, which arrived in record numbers. The day's attendance of 163,628, including England's Princess Margaret, is still the all-time high at an American racetrack. The stands were so jammed with people that it was difficult to move, and the same held true for the racetrack in the Derby.

Darby Dan Farm's Little Current was stopped half a dozen times en route. Yet, he went from last to finish fifth and then followed the Kentucky Derby with victories in the Preakness and Belmont stakes. Judger was squeezed back at the start, lost his position in the run to the first turn, and was hemmed in on both sides for much of the mile and a quarter. Cannonade also experienced trouble at the start, but he was an agile colt in the hands of the chilly Angel Cordero Jr. Picking his way between horses like a football running back, Cordero got Cannonade home first by more than two lengths over the hard-hitting Hudson County. Owner-breeder Olin, ill at home in St. Louis, could not be present, but trainer Stephens, a Kentucky

Conquistador Cielo pulled off a remarkable double for Woody in 1982.

boy, proudly accepted the trophy on his behalf for winning the 100th Kentucky Derby.

Woody was elected to racing's Hall of Fame in Saratoga in 1976 for his accomplishments as a trainer over three decades. Ironically, the greatest accomplishment of his career had its climax 10 years later, and the start of this remarkable story was still three years off. John Olin's death in 1979 and the dispersal of his thoroughbred holdings marked the entrance into racing of Henryk de Kwiatkowski. A colorful Pole who escaped from the Russians and flew with the Royal Air Force in England during World War II, he came to America via Canada, and worked for Pratt and Whitney. He then set himself in the business of converting used civilian air liners into bombers for third-world nations, and converting used military aircraft into luxury planes for rich shiekhs and princes.

Having sold a package of planes to the Shah of Iran in a deal reportedly worth $150 million, de Kwiatkowski decided to get into racing and attended the Olin dispersal. He bought several horses, including the filly Kennelot, and was recommended to Woody Stephens for training by E. P. Taylor.

One of the yearlings subsequently purchased for him by Stephens for $300,000 was named Danzig. He won his first three starts, failed to stand further training, and was retired. He became one of the most successful stallions of the era.

Another purchase, the filly Sabin, cost $750,000. Under Stephens' direction, she won 18 of 25 starts and earned almost $1.1 million.

And then there was the Mr. Prospector colt. Purchased at

Saratoga for $150,000, he was named Conquistador Cielo, after an aviation society in which de Kwiatkowski was a member. He broke his maiden in Maryland, winning by nine lengths. Then he was shipped to Saratoga and won the Special, but Stephens discovered a small knot building on one of the colt's shins. After he was beaten a head in the Sanford, Conquistador Cielo was X-rayed and found to have a saucer fracture. Dr. William Reed drilled a small hole in the cannon bone to enhance circulation. Stephens also purchased a machine known as the Blue Boot to send weak currents of electricity through the area of the fracture.

In time, Conquistador Cielo began to gallop and work. Woody sent him to Baltimore to win the Preakness Prep, going a mile and a sixteenth at Pimlico. He was impressive, and Stephens decided on the Metropolitan Mile as his next start. He'd face older horses but would receive a break in the weights. It was an electrifying performance. Leading all the way, Conquistador Cielo ran a mile in 1:33 to score by more than seven lengths. He was hailed as the epitome of speed, but the next morning Stephens said he would bring the speed king right back in the mile and a half Belmont Stakes, five days later. The racing world was stunned.

A prominent racing figure went to see de Kwiatkoski and strong-

Caveat, a son of Cannonade, gave his trainer a second straight Belmont Stakes victory in 1983 with Laffit Pincay Jr. aboard.

ly advised him not to permit the attempt to win two major races five days apart. He predicted disaster. But when de Kwiatkowski relayed the story to Stephens, Woody told him to get his shoes shined, put on his blue suit, and meet his horse and trainer in the winner's circle.

It was an eventful few days. The afternoon preceding the Belmont, Conquistador Cielo's regular rider, Eddie Maple, went down in a spill at Belmont Park, fracturing several ribs. Laffit Pincay Jr. had called a few days earlier, asking consideration as a backup. Woody phoned him promptly and learned Pincay was named on six mounts at Hollywood Park the next day. Stephens placed a call to Hollywood's chief executive officer, Marje Everett, an old friend. When she called back a few minutes later, Pincay was released from his engagements and was on his way to New York.

Conquistador Cielo, off at 4-1, led much of the way on a track turned sloppy by daylong rains and won by 14 lengths, the mile and a half in 2:28⅕. Woody had won his first Belmont Stakes, and later that summer the stable hit another big one when Conquistador Cielo was syndicated by Seth Hancock for $36.4 million and retired to stud.

Cannonade was the sire of Woody's second Belmont Stakes winner, Caveat. The colt was owned by August Belmont IV, whose grandfather was the founder of Belmont Park. Belmont had two partners in the ownership of Caveat, Jim Ryan and Bob Kirkham, both of whom raced with Woody.

Slew O' Gold, the Peter Pan winner, was the favorite for the 115th Belmont Stakes on June 11, 1983, at 25-10, with Caveat second choice and High Honors third after an encouraging performance in the Preakness. Au Point set the pace and was joined in the upper stretch by Slew O' Gold and Caveat. Angel Cordero Jr., riding Slew O' Gold, squeezed Au Point into Caveat leaving the three-sixteenths pole, and Caveat hit the fence. Recovering quickly under Laffit Pincay Jr., Caveat took command and drew out to win by three lengths, the mile and a half in a stylish 2:27⅕. It was back-to-back Belmonts for Woody Stephens, but Caveat came out of the race the worse for wear. Indeed he never ran again, and Woody was very unhappy with Cordero's role in the incident.

There were a number of promising 2-year-old prospects in Woody's barn that summer of 1983, but the two who stood out were Devil's Bag (by Halo), owned by the Hickory Tree Stable of Jimmy and Alice Mills, and Claiborne Farm's Swale (by Seattle Slew). Swale broke his maiden first, at Belmont Park on July 21, and came back to win the Saratoga Special. But from the moment Devil's Bag made his debut during Saratoga's final week, he was the center of attention – not only in the barn but in the nation. The word went out that this fellow was special, and everything he did drew headlines. He won that first race by seven and a half lengths, with Eddie Maple sitting chilly.

Woody will test a horse he likes, and eight days later, despite an off track, Devil's Bag raced again, this time at Belmont Park. He won by more than five lengths. But he really established himself as an extraordinary 2-year-old in capturing the subsequent Cowdin Stakes by three conclusive lengths.

Devil's Bag did even better in the Champagne Mile, winning by seven lengths from hard-hitting Dr. Carter. Devil's Bag was the most publicized horse in America, and he lost little caste by going to Maryland and winning the Laurel Futurity by more than five lengths. Unfortunately, he stepped on a stone while training for the Remsen at Aqueduct and was through for the season.

In the meantime, Swale finished third in the Hopeful at Saratoga, but rebounded to win the Futurity Stakes at Belmont, the Breeders Futurity at Keeneland, and the Young America at The Meadowlands, giving him a record of five wins from seven starts and earnings of almost $500,000. But the public knew only Devil's Bag, who was syndicated for $36 million by Seth Hancock of Clairborne Farm.

Devil's Bag returned to competition in mid-February, winning a Flamingo prep by seven lengths and coming off the pace nicely. It made him an even shorter price for the Flamingo, but after going to the front at the start in that race, he began to fade in the stretch and finished fourth.

A deeply disappointed Stephens turned his attention to Swale, who opened his 3-year-old campaign with an impressive, eight-length victory in Gulfstream Park's Hutcheson at seven furlongs. However, Swale failed as the 2-5 favorite in the subsequent Fountain of Youth Stakes. Eddie Maple noticed he got his tongue over the bit, reducing his intake of air. Maple mentioned it to Woody, who had Swale's tongue tied down for the Florida Derby. Ironically, Maple was not a beneficiary of his suggestion. He was committed to Devil's Bag, and Laffit Pincay Jr. was engaged for Swale. Swale ran well and won by three-quarters of a length from Dr. Carter.

Despite that victory, which he watched on television from a hotel room in Cincinnati, Stephens was uncharacteristically gloomy that spring. He was bothered physically by fractured ribs, the result of a fall at his home in Miami earlier in the winter. The ribs, coupled with his emphysema condition, aggravated by cigarettes, made sleeping difficult.

Stephens was also concerned about the steady rain in the New York area. Following his defeat in the Flamingo, Devil's Bag was shipped to New York for the Gotham Mile and Wood Memorial, but the rains were so steady that Stephens felt he couldn't get the colt ready. The $36 million syndication price was an albatross around his trainer's neck.

A few days prior to the Gotham, Woody shipped Devil's Bag to Keeneland, where Swale was headquartered. Then he took himself to Miami to try and get some rest

The ill-fated Swale provided Stephens and Pincay with a third straight Belmont Stakes success in 1984.

and relief from his physical problems. Mike Griffin, the yearling manager at Claiborne Farm, was put on detached duty at the barn in Kentucky as supervisor in Stephens' absence.

Swale started first, going off as the 1-10 favorite in the Lexington Stakes. On a sloppy track, and carrying 123 pounds, Swale struggled and finished second to the lightly regarded He Is A Great Deal, rigged at 111 pounds. The crowd expressed displeasure over the favorite's performance.

Two days later, it was Devil's Bag's turn, and he came out in the seven-furlong Forerunner Purse under Eddie Maple. On a sloppy track, Devil's Bag was reserved off the early pace, went to the front on the turn, and drew out through the stretch to win by 15 lengths. Howver, Woody, who had flown back to Lexington, was too sick to

come to Keeneland for the race. His cousin, Dr. David Richardson, a prominent physician, drove from Louisville to examine Woody, found he had pneumonia, and transferred him by ambulance to a Louisville hospital.

With Woody still hospitalized and restricted to one phone call a day to Mike Griffin at the barn, Devil's Bag got ready for the Derby Trial. He won by two lengths from Biloxi Indian, but Maple was forced to go to the whip in the drive and Devil's Bag appeared to be trying to get out.

The first set of X-rays showed calcium deposits on the right knee, the result of an injury several months earlier. Seth Hancock and Stephens decided to pass the Kentucky Derby with Devil's Bag and await the Preakness Prep. Dr. Richardson permitted Woody to leave the hospital for a press conference in the Churchill Downs stable area where the trainer, with remarkable grace under pressure, explained the situation.

Stephens was released from the hospital the day before the Derby, and arrangements were made for him to watch the race on television from the director's room. Incredibly, two fillies went off as the favored entry trained by Wayne Lukas. Life's Magic and Althea were both unplaced while Swale, attacking the pace-setting Althea aggressively, took command on the turn, led by five lengths at the eighth pole, and cruised home to beat the surprising Coax Me Chad a bit more than three lengths. Weak as he was, Stephens raced to the winner's circle to grab Swale's shank and pose for the official photo.

Less than 24 hours after his trip to the winner's circle with Swale, Stephens was in a stall at Churchill Downs with Devil's Bag. The trainer felt heat in the left shin and asked Dr. Alex Harthill to take X-rays early Monday morning. Dr. Harthill took pictures and returned in an hour with a print that confirmed a loose chip in the right foreleg. Devil's Bag had been trying to get off that leg and, in doing so, stressed the left leg.

Specifics of the syndication called for Devil's Bag to enter stud in 1985. If the chip was removed, the 1984 season would be over before Devil's Bag was ready for significant racing. The colt couldn't race with the chip loose, so Seth Hancock announced his immediate retirement.

Woody remained in Louisville that week to visit the barn briefly as Swale rebounded from the Derby. Both he and Seth Hancock had reservations about the Preakness because of track conditions but felt an obligation to the Triple Crown. Actually, the issue was moot a week before the Preakness. Preparing to travel to Baltimore, Swale worked a mile at Churchill Downs on Saturday morning. Stephens asked for a mile in 1:41. He got a mile in 1:37, almost enough to send the trainer back to the hospital.

Understandably dulled by the extraordinary work, Swale didn't measure up in the Preakness. After displaying some of his customary verve, he began to tire and finished seventh in a field of 10.

Both Woody and Swale were delighted to return to New York. They seemed invigorated by a taste of the Big Apple as they prepared for the Belmont Stakes, and the public concurred with their enthusiasm. Despite his defeat at Pimlico, Swale was sent off the 3-2 favorite, while the Preakness winner, Gate Dancer, was third choice at almost 5-1.

The 116th Belmont on June 8, 1984, was played against a background of intolerable heat and humidity. Under a penetrating sun, the thermometer kept nudging 100 degrees all afternoon, and with the humidity factored in the discomfort index was near an all-time high.

It didn't seem to bother Swale, who led the entire mile and a half and drew out to score by four lengths under Laffit Pincay Jr. The crowd cheered as Stephens appeared in the winner's circle after the Belmont for the third consecutive year, a major accomplishment. Woody and Swale both relaxed the week following the Belmont and were together the following Sunday morning at Belmont Park for a gallop. It was Swale's first exercise since the Belmont, and he went well after the brief freshening. Walking back to the barn he was kicking and playing, and Stephens nodded in approval at the display of verve, for many horses are knocked out by the Triple Crown campaign and need months to rebound.

As Swale was being bathed on a grassy plot alongside the bar, Woody sat in his car and relaxed for a moment with the Sunday papers. Suddenly, he was summoned to the washing area by his assistant, Sandy Bruno. For no visible reason, Swale had gone into the air on his hind legs and fallen over backwards. When he landed, he did not move. Stephens took one look at the colt and asked Sandy to phone for a vet. As Woody kneeled to try and comfort Swale, with no response, three veterinarians arrived. They examined the colt and confirmed Stephens' fears. Swale was dead, probably since the moment he went in the air. Preliminary diagnosis: heart attack.

Swale's body was shipped to Paris, Kentucky, for burial at Claiborne while certain organs were removed and sent to the University of Pennsylvania for laboratory analysis at New Bolton Center. No definitive conclusions were reached, but foul play was ruled out and scientists were in general agreement that Swale was carried off by natural causes: an attack, stroke or seizure.

Some four months after Swale's death, Stephens saddled a husky little 2-year-old named Creme Fraiche for his racing debut on a muddy track at Aqueduct. Owned by the Brushwood Stable of Betty Moran, a Pennsylvanian and a member of the family that operates the Smith, Kline and French pharmaceutical company. Creme Fraiche (by Rich Cream), a $160,000 yearling purchase, was unruly when he first joined the stable and was gelded at that time.

Mrs. Moran raced steeplechasers for half a dozen years with modest results before she decided to switch to the flat sport. Woody Stephens was recommended to her as a trainer and Creme Fraiche was one of the first horses she sent him. Dismissed at 20-1 in a field of 13, Creme Fraiche, breaking from the rail going seven furlongs, had the lead after half a mile and went on to score by three and a half lengths under Jean Cruguet. The winner seemed to revel in the mud.

There was no thought on Stephens' part to run Creme Fraiche in the Kentucky Derby, unless the track was a sea of mud. Stephens thought he had a solid Derby prospect in Stephan's Odyssey, and he was right. Spend A Buck ran away from the field at the start and won by almost six lengths but Stephan's Odyssey was best of the others and finished second. Later that month, Woody ran Creme Fraiche in the Jersey Derby at Garden State Park. Once again Spend A Buck's speed was the difference. He didn't run off at the start of

Eddie Maple was ecstatic after Creme Fraiche made it four straight for Stephens in the 1985 Belmont Stakes.

the Jersey Derby but did lead all the way at 1-20 to score by a neck over the 16-1 Creme Fraiche.

With the forecasts threatening rain for the 117th Belmont on June 8, 1985, Stephens entered two horses. Laffit Pincay Jr. was named on Stephan's Odyssey and Eddie Maple on Creme Fraiche. It rained on the morning of the Belmont and the track was muddy most of the day. In a field of 11, Stephens' twosome were last and next-to-last for the first six furlongs. They moved up on the turn, were a head apart at the furlong pole and then staged a pretty duel through the last eighth of a mile with Creme Fraiche, on the outside, prevailing by half a length. For the fourth consecutive year, Stephens walked to the winner's circle after the Belmont, and the ovation from the crowd was stirring.

Six weeks after Creme Fraiche's victory, Woody ran a first-time starter at Belmont for Henryk de Kwiatkowski in a maiden race at five and a half furlongs. Under Jerry Bailey, the Danzig colt out of Gdynia, appropriately named Danzig Connection, won by four lengths after going to the front on the turn. He was the 8-5 favorite on his works and connections.

After successful surgery to remove a chip in his right knee at the end of his 2-year-old season, Danzig Connection was back in training by the end of January. Employing all his skill and experience,

Woody had the colt ready to run on Derby Day, May 3, 1986, but not at Churchill Downs. This was a seven-furlong event at Aqueduct. Making his first start in six months, he was a respectable third and Jerry Bailey was careful not to be stressful. It was a good return to the races, but time was running out if Stephens was going to bid on winning a fifth consecutive Belmont.

Two weeks later, Danzig Connection ran in a mile at Belmont Park and showed considerable improvement. He finished second, beaten a neck,

Nothing could dampen Henryk de Kwiatkowski's spirits in the winner's circle after his Danzig Connection provided trainer Stephens a fifth straight Belmont in 1986.

after coming off the pace with Jerry Baily in the saddle. The critical race was the Peter Pan at Belmont on May 25. Clear Choice, trained by Wayne Lukas, was the 2-1 favorite but had to settle for second money in a field of eight. The winner, after leading all the way under Pat Day, was Danzig Connection, timed in 1:48⅖.

Despite that victory, and despite his trainer's incredible record in the Belmont, Danzig Connection was 8-1 when the final leg of the Triple Crown was run on June 7. Rampage, an unlucky fourth in the Kentucky Derby, was the mild choice at almost 3-1. Ferdinand, the Derby winner, was second choice at 18-5. Mogambo, second in the Jersey Derby, was third choice at 4-1.

Rain had begun to fall during the night. It was pouring by first light, and though it slackened to a drizzle by post time, the track

was sloppy for racing. Mogambo set the early pace, the half-mile in :47⅘. Danzig Connection raced second under his new jockey, Chris McCarron, who sent him to the lead near the half-mile pole. Danzig Connection remained in front around the turn and past the eighth pole, and now the shouts of "Wood-ee!" began emanating from the stands.

Danzig Connection continued strongly to the wire, holding off stretch challenges by John's Treasure and Ferdinand to win by more than a length, the mile and a half of slop in 2:29⅖. Fans on the apron began crowding around the winner's circle and the shouts of "Wood-ee!" "Wood-ee!" grew in intensity. The man they were shouting for was having a difficult time making his way from the box section, where everyone wanted to shake his hand, to the winner's circle. And even before he finally arrived to pose with Danzig Connection and a jubilant de Kwiatkowski, the crescendo kept increasing in volume. "Wood-ee!" "Wood-ee!" "Wood-ee!"

∞ ∞ ∞ ∞ ∞

Charlie Whittingham was born in San Diego on April 13, 1913, and grew up on a small farm in suburban Otay while living with an aunt and uncle. His older brother, Joe, became a jockey at Tijuana, just across the border, when he was 16. Charlie, 11, tagged along and soon was walking hots and mucking out stalls. A few years later, after Joe grew too big to ride, he began to train a small stable, and Charlie was his staff and assistant.

In 1930, after assembling eight or nine useful horses, Joe Whittingham shipped to Ohio and Canada for an extended stay. Two of Joe's horses weren't worth shipping so he gave them to Charlie, along with a $5 bill and a pat on the back. At 17, Charlie was a horse trainer and on his own.

Racing his small stable at the county fair in Monterey, California, he did well. The two horses showed to sufficient advantage that Charlie was able to sell them for $325. He also earned a well-done from his brother when Joe Whittingham returned in the fall.

California legalized pari-mutuel wagering in 1933, and when Santa Anita opened in late December 1934, Charlie Whittingham was there as a jockey agent. He had a few horses, however, when Del Mar opened in July of 1937 and Hollywood Park opened in June, 1938. It was a scuffling existence but everyone was in the same boat and you did what you had to do to eat and live.

It was in the spring of 1940 that Whittingham encountered Horatio Luro in a night club in Tijuana. The two men had met several times previously at California tracks, but this was the first time they had a chance to sit down together and talk. They discovered a communality of interests, including girls, and decided on a racing partnership. Luro would supply the horses, which he brought from

Charlie Whittingham, the "Bald Eagle," became one of the century's top trainers.

South America, and would round up and entertain prospective buyers. Charlie would train the horses.

It was a match made in heaven, and for the next two years these free-wheeling bachelors had a hell of a time, ranging up and down the West Coast, racing their horses and ducking out of back doors – and windows – when unable to pay their hotel bills. Every horse in the stable was for sale, and when they were all gone,"The Senor" and "Chawk," as Luro used to address his partner, would go to Argentina for replacements.

They were at the Fair Grounds in New Orleans on Dec. 7, 1941, when the Japanese attacked Pearl Harbor, and early in 1942 Whittingham enlisted in the Marines. He served on Guadalcanal, was promoted to sergeant, was struck down by malaria, and was evacuated to Honolulu for treatment. After a tour of duty on Johnston Atoll, he was posted back to Honolulu and was assigned to a military police unit. Sent back to the mainland in the spring of 1944, he was ordered to Camp Lejeune in North Carolina. With Lejeune as his headquarters, Sgt. Whittingham of the Marine Military Police patroled the streets of half a dozen neighboring cities, including Rocky Mount.

It was in Rocky Mount that he met an attractive local girl named Peggy Boone. They were married in October 1944. Discharged the following year, he phoned Luro, who asked him to rejoin the stable as soon as possible. Luro's health was not good, and after Whittingham and his bride came to New York in the spring of 1946,

Luro turned the stable over to him and left for a lengthy visit and recuperation in his native Argentina.

During Charlie's tour of duty with the Marines, Luro attracted several wealthy patrons whose purchases upgraded the quality of the stable substantially. Charlie enjoyed handling top-notch bloodstock and dealing with prominent owners. He did an outstanding job and helped Luro prepare Dick Tyan's imported Talon to win the Santa Anita Handicap of 1948.

Convinced that Whittingham was ready to train his own stable, Luro urged him to leave their partnership that spring. Charlie did, and later in the season took on his first major patron, the Llangollen Farm of Liz Whitney. The beautiful Liz, one of America's foremost equestriennes, was divorced from Jock Whitney and raced a small stable with her good friend, Horatio Luro. She had encountererd Charlie Whittingham in this fashion, was impressed with his knowledge of the game and with his dedication. She also felt her horses would receive more attention from Whittingham, eager to get off to a good start, than from Luro, who had horses for many individuals.

With Luro's assistance, Liz Whitney in 1947 imported the South American crack Endeavour II. He had several starts in this country, was subsequently retired to stud and in 1951 produced his first champion. Porterhouse, owned by Liz and trained by Charlie, set the seal on his 2-year-old title by winning the 1953 Futurity Stakes

Horatio Luro, "El Gran Senor," provided early guidance – and good times – for Whittingham.

at Belmont Park.

Another Llangollen Farm horse to do well under Whittingham's supervision was Mister Gus, who, on a never-to-be-forgotten fall afternoon in 1956, upset the mighty Nashua at Belmont Park in the prestigious Woodward Stakes. On that same program, Whittingham saddled Nashville, a 2-year-old by Mister Gus' sire, Nasrullah, to upset the brilliant 2-year-old Bold Ruler in a small stakes race.

Charlie was building a national reputation as a good man with a horse, and construction was completed the next spring after he won the Santa Anita Handicap, one of America's most prestigious races, with a steeplechaser. Corn Husker, a gelded son of Endeavour II, ran in $10,000 claiming company at 2 (no takers), broke his maiden at 3 in New York on the flat and later that season won over jumps.

Because the Louis E. Stoddard Steeplechase was named for a family friend, Liz Whitney wanted a runner in the stakes. Corn Husker, on hand and available, was chosen for the assignment – and won.

Charlie took over the training of Corn Husker in the fall of 1956, found he had a runner with genuine stamina, and began a long-range plan designed to have the versatile horse ready for the Big 'Cap. In those days the Santa Anita Handicap was weighted about the time the meeting started in late December. Corn Husker was thrown in the race at 104 pounds and Whittingham pounded the

Winter Book at Caliente when quoted a price of 100-1.

On New Year's Day 1957, Corn Husker won the San Gabriel Handicap, letting everyone in on the secret. Two months later, with Ralph Neves in the saddle, Corn Husker won the Santa Anita Handicap and Charlie was widely hailed for his major achievement.

In subsequent years Whittingham's public stable expanded dramatically. He acquired horses owned by John Gaines and Bob Hibbert. When Liz Whitney moved on with her Llangollen Farm string, Charlie replaced them with the stable of Major C.C. Moseley. When Moseley attempted to dictate stable policy, his horses were transferred out and were replaced by those of Howard Keck, chief executive of Superior Oil Company. Keck, who bred at Claiborne Farm in Kentucky, supplied Charlie with at least half a hundred stakes winners, including his first Kentucky Derby winner, Ferdinand, in 1986.

Whittingham had his first major season in 1967 when Pretense, Forli, Tumble Wind, Drin, Saber Mountain and Spinning Around were in the barn. Forli, undefeated winner of the Carlos Pellegrini in his native Argentina, was the star of the stable. Imported by a syndicate headed by Bull Hancock which purchased him for just under $1 million, he was the first of what was to be a parade of interna-

Greer Garson and Buddy Fogelson had reason to admire Ack Ack, who brought them an Eclipse Award as Horse of the Year 1971.

tional heroes trained by Whittingham, including Dahlia, Exceller, Cougar II and Tobin Bronze.

But Forli needed time to become acclimated, and Pretense, a 4-year-old Endeavour II colt, filled the bill. Unraced at 2, he learned at 3. Charlie added blinkers to his equipment and he opened the winter campaign by capturing the six-furlong Palos Verdes Handicap on opening day at Santa Anita. He also accounted for the San Pasqual Handicap, the San Antonio Handicap, and he gave Charlie his second Santa Anita Handicap victory by beating the legendary Native Diver. Bill Shoemaker rode Pretense, who was pulling seven pounds from the Diver.

Forli, after a six-month freshening, made his American debut on the turf at Hollywood Park, winning the Coronado Stakes under Bill Shoemaker. Then he won an exhibition race and flew to Arlington Park in Chicago for the Citation Handicap. Unfortunately, he fractured the cannon bone in his left foreleg during the race, finished second to a horse who couldn't warm him up, and was retired to Claiborne Farm.

Drin, who won the Charles Strub Stakes at Santa Anita, Tumble Wind, who won the Hollywood Derby, and Pretense all went wrong before the year was out, but the stable passed the $1 million mark in earnings for the first time. Whittingham was the country's leading money-winning trainer for the first time in 1970 with earnings of $1.3 million, thanks to the exploits of New Zealand's Daryl's Joy, Chile's Cougar II, Howard Keck's fine filly Turkish Trousers, and Ack Ack, a colt who had been purchased from the Harry Guggenheim dispersal by actress Greer Garson and her husband, oilman Buddy Fogelson. Whittingham also owned a substantial interest.

Early in 1971, Ack Ack, now 5, and Cougar II, also 5, met in the Santa Anita Handicap. Ack Ack, full of speed, carried 130 pounds. Cougar II, a strong finisher, carried 125 pounds. Ack Ack began to tire on the lead, and

Exceller caught Seattle Slew on the turn in the 1978 Jockey Club Gold Cup, but was all out to hold off that rival through the stretch and prevail by a nose in the sloppy going.

Cougar II, under Laffit Pincay Jr. gave it a big try but his bid fell short by a length and a half. Both were entered for the Hollywood Gold Cup that summer, Ack Ack at 134 pounds and Cougar II at 130, but Cougar was a late scratch, leaving the spotlight to Ack Ack. What a show he put on! Leading all the way, he cruised home a four-length winner under a Hollywood record impost.

The first Eclipse Awards voting was conducted at season's end by *Daily Racing Form*, the Thoroughbred Racing Associations and the National Turf Writers Association. Standing tall at the Waldorf Astoria Hotel in New York in January, Whittingham accepted awards on behalf of Ack Ack, who was voted champion sprinter, best older horse, and Horse of the Year. Turkish Trousers, whom he

also trained, was voted champion 3-year-old filly, and Charlie got a trophy for himself as racing's outstanding trainer.

He gave another illustration of his skills in the winter of 1973. Cougar II bruised a foot the previous summer and came back that fall to win the Carleton Burke Handicap during the Oak Tree meeting. Charlie, seeing how well his horse performed after a long absence, decided to point him for the Santa Anita Handicap. Cougar lost his regular rider when Bill Shoemaker fractured his right thumb in a spill. Whittingham called on Laffit Pincay Jr. to deputize, while Don Pierce had the mount on an entrymate, Kennedy Road. Kennedy Road emerged from a tightly bunched field at the head of the stretch and drove to the wire. But Cougar was coming on now, too, and after dueling side-by-side for a sixteenth of a mile, Cougar stuck his neck out to win it by a nose.

You don't make racing history by losing the big ones, and there weren't many bigger than the Jockey Club Gold Cup of 1978, which attracted two Triple Crown winners, Seattle Slew and Affirmed. Those two appeared to be standouts, but Whittingham, who had been inducted into the Hall of Fame at Saratoga in 1974, felt he had a good chance with Nelson Bunker Hunt's Exceller, who had raced in Europe.

Cougar II (outside) beat Kennedy Road a nose in the 1973 Santa Anita Handicap, giving Charlie Whittingham the fourth of his nine Big 'Cap victories.

On a rainy weekend, with the track a sea of slop, Seattle Slew set the pace, stalked by Affirmed, with Exceller racing off the pace. At the quarter-pole, Seattle Slew was moving smartly, more than two lengths ahead on the turn. Exceller edged past Affirmed and was almost on even terms with Seattle Slew. Then Exceller moved ahead. Seattle Slew fought back gamely and drew even for an instant but couldn't quite sustain his drive after an exhausting run in front. Exceller registered by a nose under Bill Shoemaker.

Whittingham has saddled three winners of the Arlington Million. The first of these was Perrault in 1982. Another import from Europe, Perrault was owned by Serge Fradkoff and Baron Thierry von Zuylen. Though he had no experience on dirt, Whittingham trained him to be versatile and Perrault won the Hollywood Gold Cup that summer, carrying 127 pounds. After a prep at Del Mar, Perrault flew to Chicago, was favored in the Million under Laffit Pincay Jr., and won it convincingly by more than two lengths.

Charlie was a legend in racing when he showed up at Churchill Downs in the spring of 1986 with a colt for the Kentucky Derby. He hadn't brought a horse to run for the roses in 26 years, and the colt he brought in 1960, Divine Comedy, finished ninth. Several promising prospects in the interim, such as Saber Mountain and Balzac, were injured before they could ship east. But Howard Keck's Ferdinand was different. A big, rugged colt by English Triple Crown winner Nijinsky, he broke his maiden in November and attracted some attention by finishing third in the rich Hollywood Futurity.

After an in-and-out winter at Santa Anita – he won a small stakes but finished third in the Santa Anita Derby – Ferdinand left for Louisville three weeks before the Derby, Whittingham at his side. He prospered at Churchill Downs and trained smartly, capped by a mile in 1:38⅖. Then, early in Derby Week, Ferdinand drilled five furlongs in :58⅗. Ferdinand obviously proved he could handle the Churchill Downs strip, an ability many good horses do not share.

Whittingham was growing increasingly confident, but the public perception of Ferdinand was less flattering. Generally, he was painted in the press as a plodder, to be ridden by an aging jockey who hadn't been on a Derby winner in 21 years. Ferdinand was dismissed at 17-1.

Breaking from post 1, Ferdinand was bothered as he came out of the gate and was last of 16 runners as the field swept to the first turn. Shoemaker moved him to the outside for the run down the backstretch, during which he passed some horses. He accelerated notably around the turn, split horses in the upper stretch, and then was party to

Experience was the key as Ferdinand, trained by the 73-year-old Charlie Whittingham, won the 1986 Derby, with Bill Shoemaker, 54, aboard.

an inspired turn of events. Racing behind a wall of horses, Shoemaker saw a small opening, which closed behind him, frustrating Pat Day and Rampage, who had also endeavored to shoot through. Ferdinand won by two and a quarter lengths, giving Whittingham his first Kentucky Derby at age 73. Shoemaker, at 54, became the oldest rider to pilot a Derby winner.

Whittingham won the Kentucky Oaks of 1988 with Goodbye Halo, a daughter of Halo owned by breeder Arthur Hancock and sportsman Alex Campbell. Later that spring, a 2-year-old colt by Halo, in whom Whittingham had purchased a half-interest for $25,000, was shipped to the trainer by co-owner Arthur Hancock. The black colt lived an eventful life. He almost died as a weanling after developing a severe case of diarrhea. He failed to sell at a yearling auction, and it was at that point that Hancock bought him for

$17,000 from the breeders, the Oak Cliff Stable. He failed to meet his reserve price at a 2-year-old sale in California, and on the way back home to Kentucky, the van driver suffered a heart attack and the van went off the road in Texas. The Halo colt emerged with a few cuts and bruises, was given first aid by a local veterinary clinic, and continued on his way. Whittingham, delighted with Goodbye Halo, agreed to take a half-interest but later hedged his bet. He sold half of his half-interest to an old friend, Dr. Ernest Gaillard.

Sunday Silence, a black beauty, made his debut at Santa Anita on October 30, 1988, the same day Ferdinand had a retirement gallop at Churchill Downs. Sunday Silence did well, leading most of the way before being caught at the end. He broke his maiden in his second start, then finished second to Houston, a $2.9 million son of Seattle Slew, in his third race. Charlie began to suspect the colt had ability, but Sunday Silence was so full of himself that he tested the health, sanity and poise of the Whittingham staff.

He made his 3-year-old debut on March 2, 1989, and won smartly on a muddy track. Seventeen days later, in an impressive step forward that reflected his trainer's confidence in him, Sunday Silence ran in Santa Anita's Grade 1 San Felipe Stakes. He broke poorly, surrendered position early, but regrouped and came on to win under Pat Valenzuela.

Meanwhile, Easy Goer, the 2-year-old champion of the previous season, was making progress in Florida. He won his 3-year-old debut impressively and was shipped to New York for the Gotham Mile at Aqueduct on April 8. He had his running shoes on, too. He won the Gotham by 13 lengths and raced the mile in 1:32⅖, a fifth of a second off Dr. Fager's world record.

April 8 was also Santa Anita Derby Day, and Sunday Silence won by 11 lengths. It was obvious the Kentucky Derby was going to have major intersectional overtones.

As he did with Ferdinand, Whittingham relied on a mile work at Churchill Downs as Sunday Silence's principal preparation for the Kentucky Derby. On April 29, the black colt drilled in 1:39⅗ on a sloppy track. Whittingham was pleased with his colt's work and was even more pleased on the Thursday morning prior to the Derby when Sunday Silence zipped a half-mile in :46⅗. It was the best Derby blowout of the day and indicated to Charlie that his horse was sharp at the right time.

The signs were right. Although forced to steady coming out of the gate, when Northern Wolf angled in from post 15, Sunday Silence, at 3-1, quickly recovered and got good position on the first turn, directly in front of Easy Goer, the favorite at 4-5. The track was muddy and tiring on a chilly, overcast afternoon, with the temperature hovering just above the 40-degree mark. Sunday Silence moved toward the pace-setting Houston on the turn, stood a long drive gamely and was a length and a half in front at the eighth pole. Valenzuela asked him for more, and Sunday Silence swerved under pressure but won by a convincing two and a half lengths, the mile and a quarter in 2:05. Easy Goer was best of the others, edging his entrymate, Awe Inspiring, by a head.

The trip to Baltimore was uneventful, but on the weekend between the Derby and Preakness, and following a gallop over the Pimlico strip, Sunday Silence was partially lame in his right front

In one of the greatest Preakness battles of all time, Sunday Silence (left) proved just a nose better than Easy Goer in the 1989 running at Pimlico.

foot. Whittingham phoned Louisville and Dr. Alex Harthill, veterinary adviser to many well-known horsemen, quickly traveled to the scene. After inspecting and X-raying the patient, Harthill found no evidence of a fracture and suspected a bruise. He phoned the noted veterinarian and blacksmith, Dr. Ric Redden, who arrived from Lexington with a pair of bar shoes for support. In addition, hot and cold compresses were alternately applied to the hoof, almost around the clock.

After walking the shedrow for three days, Sunday Silence went to the track for a gallop Wednesday morning and was full of himself. He galloped boldly, showed no sign of lameness, and his people drew a deep breath.

The 114th Preakness on May 20 drew a field of eight, and despite the results of the Kentucky Derby, Easy Goer was an even shorter price at 3-5. Sunday Silence was 2-1. Once again there was an incident at the start as the aggressive Northern Wolf bumped Sunday Silence, but the Derby winner, after encountering heavy traffic on the first turn, settled in stride down the backstretch, again in front of Easy Goer. Nearing the far turn, Pat Day, on Easy Goer, accelerated suddenly and moved past Sunday Silence to take the lead. Day had been criticized in Louisville for delaying his challenge too long. He wanted to seize the initiative this time.

It was a daring move, designed to stun. But quick-thinking Pat

In their final head-to-head struggle, Sunday Silence (right) proved a neck better than Easy Goer to take the 1989 Breeders' Cup Classic at Gulfstream Park.

Valenzuela responded with the reaction of a cat on a hot tin roof. He instantly sent Sunday Silence after Easy Goer, caught him in a sixteenth of a mile, with Day moving his colt to the inside for the drive instead of drifting and carrying Valenzula wide. And what a drive it was! As 90,000 screamed their approval and millions of others sat transfixed in front of their television sets, those two marvelous colts thundered down the stretch at ancient Pimlico, neither giving an inch. As they approached the wire in the greatest Preakness ever run, Sunday Silence seemed to lunge at precisely the right instant to snatch victory by a nose.

The 121st Belmont on June 10 was to be a coronation, with Sunday Silence the Prince of Wales at 9-10. But the script was rewritten by Easy Goer, who sat off the pace for the first mile as a French invader, Le Voyageur, led in fractions of :23⅕, :47, 1:11⅕ and the mile in 1:35 ⅕. Sunday Silence stalked Le Voyageur, but Easy Goer, accelerating on the turn, swept past both of them entering the stretch and was some four lengths in front at the eighth pole. As the New York crowd cheered for its favorite, Easy Goer drew out to register by eight lengths, the mile and a half in a crisp 2:26.

Sunday Silence, upset in the Swaps Stakes at Hollywood Park by the improving Prized, regained winning ways in the Super Derby at Louisiana Downs and then pointed for the Breeders' Cup Classic at

Gulfstream Park on November 4. It was a classic confrontation, with everyone well aware that this was for all the marbles: Horse of the Year, Trainer of the Year, the whole nine yards.

The Breeders' Cup program ran long that afternoon, and the sun was beginning to set when the horses assembled at the gate for the 5:36 p.m. post. It was an all-American field of eight that went postward in the Classic, but even the overseas trainers, caught up in the confrontational nature of the publicity surrounding the Classic, leaned forward in their seats to see who would win this shootout.

Slew City Slew set the pace, the first six furlongs in 1:10⅖. Blushing John, who was stalking the pace, moved up boldly to take command at the far turn and led to the eighth pole. Now it was the black colt, Sunday Silence, who charged to the lead, and as the huge crowd roared, Easy Goer began to come on. Would Sunday Silence get there or would Easy Goer catch him? The roar was deafening as Sunday Silence, with Chris McCarron up, passed the winning post a neck to the good of Easy Goer.

That evening, as Whittingham, his wife and friends walked into Tiberio's restaurant in Bal Harbour, Florida, some five miles south of Gulfstream Park, the room full of diners rose as one to accord Charlie the ovation he richly deserved.

The dominant riders of the era, each brilliant in his way, were as different as night and day. Bill Shoemaker was easy-going, even-tempered, unflappable in crisis, gregarious and light-hearted, with a feathery touch in the saddle. Bill Hartack was serious, intense, cool under fire, a private person and introspective. His rides were a test

Bill Shoemaker in 1953.

of wills between him and his horses, and he insisted on prevailing, with a busy style in the saddle that defied convention. Yet, both riders achieved remarkable results in lives that were tinged with sadness.

The jewel of the crown for Shoemaker was the 8,833 winners he accumulated from April 20, 1949, when he broke his maiden on Shafter V. at Golden Gate Fields, to his last score on Beau Genius at Gulfstream Park, Jan. 20, 1990. He accepted 40,349 mounts and thus rode at a 21.9 percent average, higher than almost any other major jockey of his time. His mounts earned a total of $123,368,624.

He rode four winners of the Kentucky Derby, five winners of the Belmont Stakes, 11 winners of the Santa Anita Handicap, eight winners of the Santa Anita Derby, and seven winners of the Hollywood Gold Cup.

His remarkable success exerted a profound change on his profession. He was the smallest and lightest of all the great riders in American racing history. Prior to his celebrity, trainers articulated a strong dislike for dead weight: lead pads in the saddle. They preferred live weight in the person of a rider, feeling he could shift the weight as the occasion demanded. On October 2, 1976, Shoemaker piloted Forego to victory by a head over Honest Pleasure in the Marlboro Cup at Belmont Park. Forego carried 137 pounds to Honest Pleasure's 118, and it took two valets to lift the winner's lead pad so that Forego could be saddled.

Shoemaker weighed two and a half pounds at birth on August 19, 1931, in Fabens, Texas, 25 miles southeast of El Paso on the Rio Grande. His father was tenant farmer, and family means were modest. His brother, Lonnie, and his parents were of average size but Shoe was always tiny. His parents were divorced when he was 3 and a few years later he went to live with a grandfather, Ed Harris, foreman of a ranch in Winters, Texas.

His father, who remarried, moved to El Monte, California, not far from Santa Anita, and obtained a job in a tire factory. Shoe went to live with his father when he was 10, liked California, and attended school. He wasn't big enough for football or baseball but made the boxing and wrestling teams at El Monte Union High. He won a Golden Gloves tournament at Legion Stadium in El Monte, beating a taller opponent in the 90-pound category. As a wrestler he was undefeated in two years of competition.

One of his schoolmates dated a jockey riding at Santa Anita. The rider was Shoe's size, and the girlfriend suggested Shoe might want to ride, too. She introduced him to her friend, Bud Bailey, who took him to the Suzy Q Ranch in nearby La Puente, where thoroughbreds were boarded and trained. Shoe was hired. He was 16 and had found a career.

At first he attended school in the mornings and went to the ranch in the afternoon, but later he gave up school and spent all his time with the horses, covering his action with a spurious letter of transfer to a school in La Puente. When his father learned of the deception, Shoe went to live at the ranch full time. He was making $475 a month, with room and board.

Shoe spent two years at Suzy Q Ranch, learning about horses and riding. In 1948, when he was 17, he decided to leave the ranch and try his luck at the racetrack. He went to Bay Meadows near San Francisco where he landed a job as exercise rider with trainer Hurst Philpot. Johnny Adams, the stable jockey and a future Hall of Famer, was able to teach Shoe about the importance of pace.

When Philpot shipped south to Hollywood Park, Shoe went to Del Mar and got a job with George Reeves, a veteran horseman.

Reeves had only a dozen horses and was able to pay more attention to Shoe. He also introduced the young riding prospect to the only agent Shoe ever had, Harry Silbert. In the winter of 1949, Silbert dropped by the barn at Santa Anita to chat, and Reeves suggested he take Shoemaker's book. Silbert shook hands on an association that ended with his death in March 1987.

Reeves and his stable were at Golden Gate Fields in the spring of 1949 when he put Shoemaker up for the first time on March 19. Waxahachie, a filly, finished fifth. For his third ride, on April 20, Shoe rode a 3-year-old filly named Shafter V. in a six-furlong claiming race for horses worth $3,000. Though she had won the week before with an older rider, Shafter V. was 9-1 with Shoe. Prominent throughout, she won by more than two lengths and paid $21. The whole barn bet on her, and it was Christmas in April.

In that first abbreviated season of 1949, Shoe rode 219 winners form 1,089 mounts, attracting attention with a winning percentage of 20. The next year, his first full campaign, he tied with Joe Culmone for the national championship, each with 388 winners.

Shoemaker rode the winners of more than 250 stakes with a value of $100,000 or more during his career. The first of these was Great Circle in the Santa Anita Maturity of 1951. Several days later, he was awarded the George Woolf Memorial Award for exemplary character and at season's end was the country's leading money-winning jockey with a total of $1,329,890. He was to gain that distinction 10 times in all.

Of all the laurels early in his career, though, the one that meant the most to him was the praise of The Master, Eddie Arcaro, who repeatedly told the world that Shoe was going to be the greatest rider anybody had ever seen. The two became close friends — as well as keen competitors — and remain close to this day.

Shoemaker rode some of the greatest horses of the century, including Spectacular Bid, Round Table, Forego, Damascus and John

Henry. The first of the great ones, however, was Swaps. John Burton was Swaps' regular rider when the copper-colored 2-year-old colt won two of his first five starts. Trainer Mesh Tenney stopped on him in July after his fifth race, and when he brought him back, late in December 1954, Shoemaker was on him. Swaps, who to that point had shown little of the speed that was to carry him to five world records, was close to the pace throughout, won by a nose, and raced six furlongs in 1:10.

Shoe wasn't impressed, but three weeks later, when Swaps showed acceleration and won the San Vincente Stakes by three and a half lengths, it was a different story. Committed to Blue Ruler for the Santa Anita Derby, Shoe saw Johnny Longden win on Swaps while Shoe's mount finished third. But owner Rex Ellsworth had promised Shoe he could have the mount in the Kentucky Derby and kept his word. Swaps prepped for the Derby in a six-furlong allowance race the weekend before and won easily.

It wasn't easy for Shoe. He had a spill at Golden Gate Fields a week earlier and a horse kicked him in the knee. Shoe was hospitalized, and doctors told him he wouldn't ride for three weeks. His agent, however, had other ideas. Harry Silbert brought Shoe's clothes to the hospital, spirited him out of the building, and the two flew to Louisville.

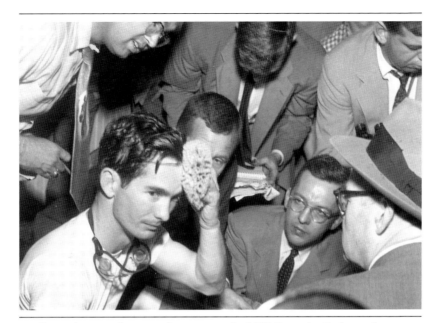

Shoemaker met the press after winning the 1955 Kentucky Derby on Swaps.

The knee blew up in flight, and Silbert almost had to carry Shoe to a Turkish bath near their hotel. The steam didn't help much, but Silbert chatted with a man at the bath who invited him to bring Shoe to the University of Louisville's athletic department to use a whirlpool. The whirlpool was a big help, and Shoe was able to ride Swaps in the prep race. Had he missed the prep, he might have lost the Derby mount, too, for most horsemen want the same rider for the prep and the main event.

Nashua, having won the Flamingo, Florida Derby and Wood Memorial, was the solid 13-10 favorite for the 81st Kentucky Derby. Swaps was second choice at 14-5. Swaps took command soon after the start, and Shoe found to his delight that no one was putting much pressure on his horse. He just kept Swaps going and going and going while Eddie Arcaro on Nashua waited for Summer Tan to move while Eric Guerin on Summer Tan waited for Nashua to move.

Arcaro swung into gear around the turn and Nashua ranged up outside of Swaps at the furlong pole. But Shoemaker always had some horse left, and Swaps went on to triumph by a length and a half in a lively 2:01⅘. Hailed for a superb ride in America's premier horserace, Shoe was now a national sports figure.

That first Kentucky Derby victory was relatively easy, but Shoe didn't have many easy moments at the Downs after that. Consider his experience in 1957, when his mount was Gallant Man, owned by oilman Ralph Lowe of Midland, Texas, with Johnny Nerud as trainer. Gallant Man was second to Bold Ruler in the Wood Memorial, and was about equal with Round Table, winner of Keeneland's Blue Grass Stakes, as second choice in the Derby.

Lowe had a dinner party in his Louisville hotel the night before the Run for the Roses and told his guests of a dream he'd had a few nights earlier, in which the rider of his horse stood up in the saddle prematurely and lost the race. Shoemaker commented that, having been alerted, he would pay particular attention to the finish and told Lowe not to concern himself about the dream any longer.

Bold Ruler was never a key factor that day, but Iron Liege ran the race of his career. After sitting off Federal Hill's pace for the first mile, Iron Liege went to the front and led at the eighth pole. Gallant Man ranged up alongside and the two were head and head as the crowd cheered when suddenly Shoe rose in the irons. Realizing his mistake, he was down in an instant and riding his horse again but Iron Liege finished a nose in front.

There was more Derby drama for Shoemaker two years later. As usual, he had his choice of several prospects, but Harry Silbert had given his word to an old friend, veteran horseman Frank Childs, that if Tomy Lee won the Blue Grass, Shoe would ride him back in the Derby. The horse Shoe wanted to ride was Sword Dancer, who appeared to be coming to hand for Elliott Burch after an in-and-out winter in Miami.

First Landing, the 1958 2-year-old champion, was a slight favorite over Tomy Lee in the 85th Kentucky Derby on May 2. Triolus, who stopped badly after half a mile and died shortly thereafter of stress, set the early pace. Tomy Lee, racing just off the pace, inherited the lead and went the first mile in 1:36.

Sword Dancer, never far away, moved up at this point under Bill Boland and, racing outside, took the lead from Tomy Lee. Suddenly, Sword Dancer lugged in on Tomy Lee, who had a reputation for bearing out. The two colts bumped, and then bumped again several more times through the stretch, with Sword Dancer the aggressor. As the battling twosome neared the wire, Tomy Lee spurted and won by a nose. Shoemaker revealed later that Tomy Lee had been tiring on the same lead until bumped onto the other lead by Sword Dancer in the shadow of the winning post.

Tompion, the Santa Anita Derby winner, was the favorite for the 1960 Kentucky Derby with Shoemaker up but lost a shoe on the backstretch, then flattened out in the drive and finished fourth. Candy Spots, winner of the Santa Anita Derby, was the favorite for the 1963 Kentucky Derby under Shoemaker, was forced to check three times in the race, and was beaten a neck for second.

It was even more frustrating in 1964 for Shoe, who had the mount on Northern Dancer, with whom he won the Flamingo and Florida Derby. A botched workout just before the Florida Derby, however, took the edge off the Canadian colt. Shoe was disappointed with his performance and told trainer Horatio Luro that he was going to accept the mount on Hill Rise for the Kentucky Derby. In a courageous stretch drive, Northern Dancer, the "Good Little Horse," won by a neck under Bill Hartack from Hill Rise, the "Good Big Horse," with Shoe in the saddle.

Just when he was beginning to wonder about his Derby luck, Shoe rode Lucky Debonaire to win the 1964 Santa Anita Derby for Dan and Ada Rice of Wheaton, Illinois. Trained by Frank Catrone, one of the few trainers who could look Shoe in the eye – they both stood about five feet tall – Lucky Debonaire won the Blue Grass at Keeneland and then came to Churchill Downs to win the Kentucky Derby. He had to give it everything he had to stave off a late challenge by Dapper Dan, who missed by a neck.

One of Shoe's strangest Derby rides came aboard Damascus in 1967. A standout favorite at 17-10 in a field of 14, Damascus came to the Derby off a solid victory in the Wood Memorial and appeared to be a cinch. He trained nicely for Frank Whiteley, was stabled in seclusion at Churchill Downs with no press or visitors permitted, and made a splendid appearance on Derby Day. Shoe rode him perfectly, reserving him off the early pace and then producing him at the head of the stretch with a clear shot at the finish and only two moderate horses to catch and pass. But when Shoe asked the question, Damascus came up empty. He was beaten by the 30-1 Proud Clarion and the 15-1 Barbs Delight.

Damascus, owned by Mrs. Tom Bancroft, came back to win the Preakness and Belmont stakes. He should have been a Triple Crown winner, but then racing is full of couldas, wouldas and shouldas.

Full of them. Shoe's ride in the 1969 Kentucky Derby was to be Paul Mellon's Arts and Letters, 15-length winner of the Blue Grass Stakes. Three days prior to the Derby, Shoe was to ride in a maiden filly race at Hollywood Park when his mount, Poona's Day, flipped over backward in the paddock. Shoe attempted to jump off but was trapped under the filly. His pelvis was fractured in five places, his bladder was ruptured and his left leg was paralyzed.

Even worse, he had resumed riding that February 11 after another accident that cost him a full year. His first major injury occurred January 26, 1968, at Santa Anita when his mount, Bel Bush, went down. Struggling to get up, Bel Bush kicked Shoe in the right thigh, fracturing the femur. Dr. Robert Kerlan, the famed orthope-

The camera caught Shoemaker rising in the saddle for just an instant as he misjudged the finish line aboard Gallant Man in the '57 Kentucky Derby.

dic surgeon, inserted a steel pin into the marrow of the bone for stabilization but the fracture took a long time to heal.

Shoe returned in spectacular fashion, winning with all three of his mounts, and quickly resumed prominence in his profession. But the second major injury, occurring so soon, was a downer. Nor did it help to watch the Derby telecast and see Arts and Letters miss by a neck to Majestic Prince under a rider who didn't know the horse. The doctors said six months. Shoe was back in four.

Shoe wondered for a long time if there was another Derby with his name on it and had just about concluded there wasn't when Ferdinand came along. Whittingham had great confidence in the big Nijinsky colt though he was a late bloomer and went off at almost 18-1 in the Run for the Roses. Bothered at the start of the Derby, Ferdinand dropped back, then came on briskly around the turn. Momentarily, after straightening for home, Ferdinand raced behind a wall of horses. Shoe noticed an opening on the rail, slipped through quickly, and then drove Ferdinand to a two and a quarter-length tally over the British invader, Bold Arrangement. At 54, Shoe became the oldest rider of a Derby winner. A few weeks earlier, Jack Nicklaus, at 46, won the Masters. Was this, the newspapers asked, to become the Year of the Codger?

As dramatic as they were, Shoemaker's Kentucky Derby experiences represented just a small part of his professional career, which was marked by brilliance and achievement from start to finish. Consider the first Arlington Million of 1981. Shoe was riding a 6-

year-old gelding named John Henry, who had won the Sword Dancer Handicap at Belmont Park. However, John Henry didn't care for soft ground and the Chicago area was hit by rain storms for several days prior to the race. The course was a bog and John Henry was 11-10, while The Bart, at 40-1, was one of a few horses in the race who loved soft turf.

"It was terrible," Shoe recalls. "He wasn't handling it at all down the backstretch and I didn't think we'd be close. I was trying to urge him a little, without making him sour, but

One of Shoe's finest hours came in 1981, when he guided John Henry (left) to a dramatic nose victory over The Bart in the inaugural Arlington Million.

he was struggling. He began to pick it up on the turn and moved through the upper stretch pretty good, although he was still a beaten horse at the eighth pole. I was trying to hold him together at that point, for he was working very hard and beginning to tire."

The Bart had the lead and appeared home free, but John Henry never gave up. He kept coming for Shoe, lunged forward at precisely the right moment, and got the decision by a nose to the screams and cheers of the crowd, although the NBC commentators called it a victory for The Bart until the photos proved otherwise.

That was a big one, and so was the Marlboro Cup of 1976, in which Shoe rode Forego, topweight under 137 pounds. Honest Pleasure, impressive winner of the Travers at Saratoga that summer, carried 119 pounds in the mile and a quarter test. With his devastating speed, Honest Pleasure took command and appeared to have

the Marlboro Cup at his mercy. But Forego kept cutting into the margin between them. Looping the field, he drove through the stretch and, despite the great difference in weight, got up in the final stride to win by a head, touching off an ovation from the crowd that lasted 10 minutes.

Shoe is emphatic that Spectacular Bid, whom he rode as a 4-year-old to nine victories in nine starts, is the best horse he ever sat on. The grey horse was so dominant that there weren't many close finishes for him that memorable season and in one important test, the Woodward, he had no opponents at all: a walkover.

Shoe had his final ride at Santa Anita on February 3, 1990, after a farewell tour of the nation's racetracks that lasted almost a year. Hailed as one of the greatest riders in American racing history, he retired at 58 and almost immediately launched a training career. In the spring of 1992, his car went off the road. The accident almost cost him his life and left him confined to a wheelchair. But champion that he is, he has refused to permit disability to interfere and conducts business as usual with his successful public stable.

∞ ∞ ∞ ∞ ∞

Bill Hartack: He wanted to win them all. Every one. It was no act; no pose. There was no false modesty. He knew he had ability, and he was so successful from the beginning that he knew his agent had him on a horse with a chance. He did his homework. He studied the past performances in *Daily Racing Form* and knew what his horse could do and what the others in the race could do.

He studied the other riders. He knew their strengths, their weaknesses, their habits. He ran each race in his mind with great objectivity, and if he thought he should win and didn't, he was upset. If he felt the horse didn't perform, he was upset with the horse. If he felt the horse wasn't fit enough to win, he was upset with the trainer. If he felt the horse was overmatched and should have been racing in different company, he was upset with his agent. And if he felt he had not ridden as well as he should, or could, he was angry with himself.

Racing is one of the few sports where even the champions lose much more often than they win. The best riders average one winner from every five mounts. Eddie Arcaro rode for 31 years and averaged 19.8 percent winners. Bill Shoemaker rode 42 years and averaged 21.9. Johnny Longden rode for 40 years and averaged 18.6. Angel Cordero Jr. rode for 31 years and averaged 18.3. Hartack rode for 22 years and averaged 19.8, which means he was unhappy four-fifths of the time.

Win. He had an obsession with winning, but, surprisingly, not at all costs. He was one of the cleanest riders ever to get on a horse.

A fierce determination to win marked Bill Hartack's riding style.

Rough riding or careless riding appalled him. He considered it the mark of an inferior professional and wanted no part of it. He knew the rules and rode by them and rarely lost an important race in the stewards' stand.

Win. When he stepped into the racetrack for a day's work it was the only thing he thought about. Jimmy Jones recalls an incident from the period in the 1950s when Hartack was riding regularly for Calumet Farm. A stakes-winning horse who had been sidelined by injury for many months was making his return appearance.

"Win if you can," Jones said to Hartack in the paddock, "but try not to beat this horse up today. He's been away a long time."

Hartack was furious. "If you don't want me to win with this horse, put somebody else on him," he said. "I only know one way to ride, and that's all out."

Hartack was born December 9, 1931 in suburban Johnstown, Pennsylvania. His father was a coal miner at a pit near Colver, Pennsylvania, and Hartack and two sisters lived in a nearby house. Their mother died on Christmas morning, 1940, when a car parked on a hill near their home suddenly rolled down the hill, crushing Mrs. Hartack. A year later, the Hartacks' house burned down, and William Hartack Sr. moved his family to his father's farm near Belsano, Pennsylvania.

Hartack performed chores on the farm every morning, took the bus to Black Lick Township High School and played drums in the school band. Although homework was not his strong point, he graduated at 17 in the upper third of his class. At 18 he would have been eligible for a job at Bethlehem Steel, but shortly before his birthday he received a letter from a friend of his father, who suggested that because of his size, he might be able to work at a racetrack. Hartack caught the next bus to Charles Town, West Virginia.

He was hired by Morman (Junie) Corbin, a good horseman and a patient teacher. Hartack served as a combination groom and exercise boy, was a quick study and enjoyed the work. Corbin could see he had the makings of a racerider, but Hartack was happy exercising horses and was reluctant to change jobs. Eventually, Corbin sent him home to Pennsylvania for a day to get his father's signature on a contract and, without mentioning it, named him to ride a horse at Waterford Park in Chester, West Virginia.

This was on October 11, 1952. The first ride, on a 65-1 shot named Hal's Play, went as expected. Hartack's mount was last out of the gate, he forgot to pull his goggles down and had trouble crossing his reins. But Corbin wasn't disappointed. Two days later, on a 50-1 shot, there was some improvement, and the next day, Oct. 14, aboard the 8-1 Nickelby, Hartack broke his maiden. In the remaining two weeks of the Waterford meeting, he had six more winners and was on his way.

In 1953, his first full year as a rider, Hartack was second in the national standings with 350 winners. The leader, with a record 485 winners, was Bill Shoemaker. For the first time in his life, Hartack had money and purchased a farm in Charles Town. Then he phoned his father to give up his job in the mines and come to Charles Town to manage the farm.

At about the same time, one of Junie Corbin's horses came back positive for a prohibited medication. Corbin needed money and was forced to sell Hartack's contract. He received $15,000 for it from the stable of Ada L. Rice, Tom J. Kelly trainer.

The sale moved Hartack from the smaller tracks in West Virginia frequented by Corbin to the larger tracks of the East and Midwest were Kelly raced. But though the competition was keener, Hartack was a better rider and improving steadily. In 1954, he was second again in the national standings to Shoemaker, 380 to 323, but where Hartack's mounts earned $587,330 in 1953, he was fourth on the money list in 1954 with $1,330,121. Shoemaker topped the money list with $1,876,760.

The first major victory of Hartack's career came in September 1954 at Belmont Park. Kelly had a classy but crippled old warrior named Pet Bully for Dan and Ada Rice and nominated him for the first running of the $75,000 Woodward Stakes, honoring the memory of the late chairman of The Jockey Club, William Woodward Sr. The 6-year-old Pet Bully, by Petrose out of Camelina, by Bull Dog, responded to hard work by Kelly and his staff and recaptured some of the past glory by winning, under Hartack, the Washington Park Handicap in Chicago – the Rices made their home in Wheaton, Illinois – and the Fall Highweight at Belmont Park.

Carrying topweight of 126 pounds, the courageous Pet Bully won the Woodward by half a length from the hard-hitting Joe Jones while conceding 15 pounds. Hartack handled him with the poise of a veteran and was well received by New York fans who were never slow to voice displeasure or to salute a championship performance. He also gained himself a top agent about this time in Charles (Chick) Lang, whose father rode Reigh Count to win the 1928 Kentucky Derby. Lang was diplomatic and good with trainers before going to work for Hartack, but his skills were polished after he came on board and was forced to "cool out" horsemen who had been guilty, in the rider's opinion, of putting him on a "short" horse – one not fit enough for the job.

Hartack, whose contract with the Rices had expired, gained the first of a then-record three consecutive national riding titles in 1955 when he had 417 winners and his winning percentage was a gaudy 25. His cause was helped by a winning streak in Chicago that summer when he and Shoemaker rode against each other on a daily basis for about six weeks. He repeated as champion rider in 1956 with 347 winners and, for the first time, also led in purses won with $3,060,501. It was the first time the $3 million level had been reached.

That 1956 campaign was memorable for him in many ways, not the least of these being his first appearance in the Kentucky Derby. He began the weekend by attending the turf writers dinner at the Kentucky Hotel and gleefully cleaning out the scribes in a post-prandial poker game. That was on Thursday night. On Friday he gave one of his greatest riding performances aboard Princess Turia in the Kentucky Oaks. With Steve Brooks on Claiborne Farm's Doubledogdare, the two exceptional fillies duelled the length of the stretch before Princess Turia scored by a nostril.

Earlier that season Hartack had agreed on a first-call relationship with Calumet Farm, and Jimmy Jones put him on the better half of his entry, the Citation colt Fabius. The veteran Robert Lee Baird rode the stablemate, Pintor Lea. Needles, the Flamingo and

Owner E.P. Taylor (left) and trainer Horatio Luro were on hand to greet Northern Dancer and Bill Hartack after the 1964 Preakness

Florida Derby winner, was the Kentucky Derby favorite under Dave Erb, though he refused to train very much for an exasperated Hugh Fontaine.

Ben A. Jones, a horse named for the great Calumet trainer, and Terrang, the Santa Anita Derby winner, set the early pace, with Fabius immediately behind them in a field of 17. Needles was far back, in front of only one horse. Fabius put Terrang away, took the lead at the head of the stretch, and looked like the one to beat. But now Needles was in gear, accelerated around the turn, and passed horses to be second at the eighth pole. The Florida-bred colt went on to win by three-quarters of a length, with Fabius second and Come On Red, a field horse, third.

Two weeks later at Pimlico, Fabius and Hartack turned the tables. Once again, Fabius stalked the early pace and Needles was at the rear of the field of nine. Fabius took command at the head of the stretch and led by three lengths at the furlong pole. Needles came on late as usual, was third at the furlong pole but couldn't get to Fabius, who scored by a length and three-quarters. Admiral and Mrs. Gene Markey got the good news from Jimmy Jones via radio-telephone on the Queen Elizabeth, as they were sailing for Europe and their customary summer holiday in France.

After another successful summer at Arlington and Washington

parks, Hartack came east to clinch the riding title with a brilliant fall meeting at Garden State Park. Calumet's Bardstown established himself as a top handicap horse when Hartack rode him to win the Trenton Handicap at the expense of such hard hitters as Summer Tan and Find.

Hartack reached the heights, however, aboard a colt named Barbizon in the Garden State Stakes for 2-year-olds as the meeting drew to a close. By Polynesian, sire of Native Dancer, out of the stakes-winning Good Blood, Barbizon came to hand late in the season for trainer Jimmy Jones, who decided to supplement him to the Garden State, then the world's richest race, at a cost of $10,000.

When Barbizon drew an outside post, Jones despaired, fearing he had squandered the $10,000. But things worked out surprisingly well. First, the heavily favored Bold Ruler, ridden by Ted Atkinson in place of the suspended Eddie Arcaro, ran up on the heels of the stopping leader, Jaunty John, down the backstretch. Meanwhile, Hartack kept improving his position with Barbizon, who outfinished Federal Hill to win by a nose.

Though 1955 and 1956 seasons were outstanding for Hartack, 1957 was even better, bringing a third consecutive riding title with 341 winners and a remarkably high winning percentage of 28.

He opened the campaign with an impressive triumph in Hialeah's Widener Handicap aboard Bardstown, who was topweight under 126 pounds and conceding considerable weight to all. Then, to show it wasn't a fluke, Bardstown came back to win the Gulfstream Park Handicap under 130 pounds.

The highlight of the winter for Hartack wasn't Bardstown's Widener or Gulfstream Park Handicap, however. As good as he was – and Hartack always rated the speedy, classy Bardstown among the greatest he rode – Bardstown had to take a back seat to a handsome bay son of Bull Lea and Wistful named Gen. Duke. If there was ever

a four-legged matinee idol it was Gen. Duke, whose sire was one of the top stallions of the century and whose dam was a brilliant stakes winner. Even casual fans with little or no knowledge of conformation remarked at his perfect balance. He wasn't robust on the order of Secretariat; his was more of a classic beauty.

The experienced Bold Ruler, under Eddie Arcaro, won the Flamingo that winter of 1957, but the improving Gen. Duke was finishing fastest of all, beaten a neck in a track-record 1:47 for the nine furlongs. By the time of the Florida Derby at Gulfstream, four weeks later, Gen. Duke was the better horse. He won the Florida Derby by a length and a half, his nine furlongs equaling the world's record of 1:46⅖.

Even Hartack was impressed with Gen. Duke, who was to have one race at Keeneland and a final prep for the Kentucky Derby at Churchill Downs – in all likelihood the Derby Trial that had served Calumet so well over the years. The Keeneland race, the seven-furlong Forerunner on April 19, had a shocking result. With only three horses it was classified as a betless exhibition and was won by Iron Liege, with Gen. Duke third.

No one knew why Gen. Duke, a stickout on class, didn't win, but there were plenty of theories. After the race, Hartack said he thought that Gen. Duke bobbled or took a back step at one point during the race. The Joneses said little but had plenty of X-rays taken. The pictures were inconclusive, and a week after his Keeneland race Gen. Duke worked six furlongs at Churchill Downs in 1:12⅖.

Four days after that work, Gen. Duke ran in the Derby Trial as part of an entry with Iron Liege favored at 2-5, Dave Erb on Iron Liege. Federal Hill, who had won the Kentucky Jockey Club Stakes at Churchill Downs the previous fall, set the pace from the outset. Gen. Duke raced off the pace and Iron Liege, who led all the way to

Hartack (left) had a very brief career as a jump jockey, starting and ending aboard Meilaison in this hurdle race at Monmouth Park in 1958.

win at Keeneland, was almost as far back as his stablemate. Federal Hill, under Willie Carstens, went on to triumph by two and a half lengths. Gen. Duke closed fairly well to be second but was never a serious threat to the winner. Iron Liege was a disappointing fifth. More X-rays were taken of Gen. Duke's feet and a young veterinarian, Dr. Alex Harthill, was called into the case. He found what ap-

peared to be a fracture in one hoof. The Joneses went into a huddle. Gen. Duke was so good he was probably better on three legs than most of the others on four. Was it worth the risk to try him with bar shoes in front? That was ruled out. Barbizon had contracted a respiratory ailment over the winter and was to be sold. He wasn't available. So it was do or die in the Derby with Iron Liege. Hartack would ride, replacing Erb. And one point of information. Erb, experimenting in the Trial, had taken hold of Iron Liege to try him off the pace. The colt didn't care for those tactics. He wanted to run his own race.

On a raw, cold May 4, 1957, the finest Kentucky Derby field of the century went to the post. Bold Ruler was the 6-5 favorite under Eddie Arcaro. Round Table, the Blue Grass winner, was second choice under Ralph Neves. Gallant Man was third choice under Bill Shoemaker and Federal Hill was fourth choice under Willie Carstens.

Federal Hill set the pace as expected, the half in :47, the first mile in 1:36⅘. Bold Ruler and Iron Liege were both close to the pace, followed by Round Table, with Gallant Man well back. Iron Liege took command at the head of the stretch and led past the eighth pole as Federal Hill began to retire. Bold Ruler failed to stay in the drive and Round Table couldn't reach the leader but Gallant Man was coming fast. The crowd roared as he drew abreast of Iron Liege, and the two colts matched strides briefly until Iron Liege inched ahead and won by a nose.

Few in the crowd noticed that Shoemaker had risen in the irons briefly a sixteenth from the finish, realized his mistake instantly, and got into his mount, who never really broke stride. Of course, Gallant Man was beaten only half an inch, and that incident might have been the difference.

Bold Ruler came back to win the Preakness and Gallant Man won the Belmont, so there was glory for all that spring. But Hartack's ride in the Derby earned him high praise and was the start of a remarkable series during which he was to win the Derby five times in 12 years and earn the well-deserved reputation as the greatest Derby rider of them all.

Hartack rode Calumet Farm's Tim Tam to victory in the Flamingo and Florida Derby of 1958 and the handsome son of Tom Fool and Two Lea looked to be a solid choice for the spring classics. However, during Derby Week, Hartack rode a 2-year-old filly named Quail Egg for trainer Henry Forrest. She flipped in the starting gate and Hartack's right leg was fractured. Jimmy Jones phoned friends throughout the country and Ismael (Milo) Valenzuela was the name most recommended as a replacement for Hartack.

With Valenzuela up, Tim Tam won the Kentucky Derby on a muddy, tiring track, the winner's time 2:05. Tim Tam also won the Preakness, and the following week Hartack appeared at Garden State Park with a light cast on his injured leg and a keen desire to ride Tim Tam in the Belmont Stakes. As a good will gesture, Mrs. Markey had sent him a check for $5,000 on Derby Day so money was not the issue. He wanted to get his mount back and Jimmy Jones, aware of his ability and his singlemindedness, didn't know what to do.

To demonstrate his fitness, Hartack rode at Garden State that weekend and did well. But Jones said he didn't see how he could take Valenzuela off Tim Tam after he won the Derby and Preakness. Mrs. Markey settled the matter with a letter to Jones saying she wanted Valenzuela to ride her horse in the Belmont. Hartack took exception to the decision and ended his agreement with Calumet Farm.

As for Tim Tam, he was 1-20 in the Belmont, was reserved off the pace, and then moved up smartly. The Irish-bred Cavan was moving to the lead at the head of the stretch when Tim Tam ranged up. As Valenzuela asked him to accelerate, Tim Tam swerved under pressure and swerved again. Cavan was an easy winner and Pete Anderson, who rode him, appeared to have something left in his horse. Valenzuela didn't. Tim Tam had shattered the sesamoids in his left leg. He underwent surgery a few days later at the University of Pennsylvania's veterinary clinic, then located in Philadelphia. Dr. Charles Raker and the brilliant Swiss surgeon, Dr. Jacques Jenney, extracted 13 pieces of bone from the leg and saved Tim Tam for stud duty.

Hartack gained his fourth riding title (with 307 winners) and his second Kentucky Derby in 1960 aboard Sunny Blue Farm's Venetian Way, who was by Royal Coinage out of Firefly. Mike Gonzalez had ridden him throughout his 2-year-old season but the colt disappointed in his first two races at Hialeah the next winter and trainer Vic Sovinski opted for a change of pilots. Hartack rode Venetian Way in the Florida Derby and the colt missed by a nose to Bally Ache.

Bally Ache won a seven-furlong prep race at Churchill Downs on opening day, a week before the Derby, and once again Venetian Way was second. The colt's stifles were bothering him, but Sovinski was able to stablize them by Derby Day. Sovinski, a big, burly Chicagoan with a heart of gold, had finished second to Tim Tam in 1958 with Lincoln Road and really was into the classic scene. "If I

Hartack tied Eddie Arcaro's mark of five Kentucky Derby winners aboard Majestic Prince in the 1969 Run for the Roses, and gave Johnny Longden the distinction of being the only man to win the race as a trainer and a jockey.

could win the Kentucky Derby," he said, "I wouldn't care if I never won another race."

That's almost the way it turned out. C.V. Whitney's Tompion, the Santa Anita Derby winner, was the 11-10 favorite for the 86th Run for the Roses but lost a shoe down the backstretch and did well to finish fourth. Hartack rode a superior race on Venetian Way, was in perfect position and saved his colt for the drive. Venetian Way won by three and a half lengths, and Sovinski was beside himself.

Hartack's third Kentucky Derby came in 1962 aboard Decidedly. The slender grey son of Determine didn't show much at 2 until he was transferred in mid-summer to veteran trainer Horatio Luro. When he turned 3, Bob Ussery rode him at Hialeah but used his whip in contradiction to orders in the Flamingo and Decidedly finished second to Sir Gaylord. Hartack rode him in a prep at Keeneland, in which he finished second to Roman Line, but Luro was pleased with the ride.

The 1962 Kentucky Derby was full of speed. Hartack, following orders to the letter, was well back in the early stages, went wide into the stretch, and Decidedly stood a long drive gamely to win by two and a quarter lengths.

The grey colt didn't have the constitution to stand up to the rigorous demands of the Triple Crown, but Hartack's serious approach to his job impressed Luro. Thus, two years later, when Bill Shoemaker took himself off Northern Dancer after winning the Flamingo and Florida Derby in order to ride Hill Rise, Luro promptly picked up the phone and called Hartack. By this time, 1964, Hartack wasn't as active or successful as in the past. He rode only 115 winners that year, but two of them were in the Kentucky Derby and Preakness aboard Northern Dancer.

Hartack's fifth Derby winner, tying him with Eddie Arcaro, came in 1969 when he wasn't getting many choice mounts and had only 55 winners the entire season. He'd moved from the East to California, which is why Johnny Longden asked him to stop by the barn one morning to work a 2-year-old named Majestic Prince. Longden sent the $250,000 Raise a Native colt to Bay Meadows in late November and Hartack rode him to break his maiden at first asking.

He never lost all winter, accounted for the Santa Anita Derby, and was the 7-5 favorite for the Kentucky Derby. Once again, Hartack was superb, moved just ahead of his principal rival, Arts and Letters, and won by a neck.

Hartack's weight, a problem he overcame through much of his career, was getting the best of him, and when his mounts all but dried up he took his tack to Happy Valley Race Course in Hong Kong in 1975. Highly regarded by Chinese horsemen, he spent five productive winters in China, returning to the States every spring for a long summer holiday.

A knee knjury ended his riding career, and he became a racing official at California tracks beginning in 1980. He rose through the ranks, was particularly effective as a reader of films, and was called upon by the Hollywood Park stewards to conduct an extraordinary post-mortem for the owners, trainers and the press on the morning after the first Breeders' Cup and the controversial finish of the Classic.

He served as a steward at California fairs, landed a better job in Florida, and was a steward at Chicago area tracks for several years before moving to the Fair Grounds. Everywhere he's served, his knowledge of the rules and his firm adherence, have impressed his colleagues and licensees alike.

Complex Times

1961 to 1994

Picture, if you can, a long wall with a great many shelves running the length of the wall from floor to ceiling. On those shelves were thousands of metal trays and cans, each holding 10 lines of type describing the last 10 races of every horse in training in America. One of these walls was the dominating feature of the composing room at every office of *Daily Racing Form.*

When a horse was entered, his tray would be taken from the shelf by a printer and locked into a steel chase, along with the 10 lines of type for all the other horses in the race. When the horse ran, linotype operators punched out a new line of type with information derived from the chart, and the line of type, in lead, was added to the horse's tray.

These lines of type were the past performances that are the principal ingredient of *Daily Racing Form.* Before November 1971, that is how the statistical portion of the paper was printed. It would have been impossible to set 10 lines of type for each horse every time he ran, so the lines were saved and placed on the shelves against the long wall in the three main offices of *Daily Racing Form,* in New York, Chicago and Los Angeles, and in the Toronto office of the Canadian edition.

In that era, and even today, although transportation of horses has improved considerably, stables had regional bases. For most of the year, at any rate, stables headquartered at tracks in the East, the Midwest, and the West. So the shelves at *The Morning Telegraph* office, located for many years at 26th Street and Ninth Avenue in Manhattan, and later at 52nd Street and 10th Avenue, contained the past performances for the thousands of horses at Eastern tracks, from New England to Florida.

Similar arrangements prevailed at the Chicago offices of *DRF,* located at 731 Plymouth Court, and later at 1301 North Elston Avenue, and in Los Angeles, where *DRF* was published at 1540 North Vermont Avenue, and later at 170 South Bimini Place. If there were close to 100,000 horses in training in those years, perhaps 50,000 were based at Eastern tracks, 30,000 at Midwestern tracks, and 20,000 at Western tracks. That's a lot of shelves and a lot of type, and a lot of opportunity for trouble: fire, theft, mischief, etc.

Fortunately, there was little trouble. Occasionally a printer would drop some lines of type, but they were quickly recovered and accurately put back in place. Virtually everybody working for *Daily Racing Form* was a horseplayer. They knew the horses and their form as well, if not better, than the editorial staff.

In the 1960s, a technological revolution swept through the nation's newspapers, doing away with the hot metal of the linotype era and substituting the cold paper of the photo-copy process. Essentially, text was composed by computer, the printed matter emerging in column form from a photo typesetter, and then the columns were pasted into page form. The pages were photographed, plates were made and then transferred to presses for printing.

Reporters on the majority of papers in the 1960s and early 1970s had begun using computers to file their stories to their papers but *Daily Racing Form* staff was still using typewriters into the 1980s. Stories filed at the racetrack were transmitted by teletype machines punched by an operator. The first crude facsimile machines, some requiring six minutes to send a single page of copy, were in use in the 1970s.

Despite the outdated nature of the equipment, *Daily Racing Form's* appearance, editorial content, distribution and sales improved steadily in the 1950s and 1960s under the direction of editor and publisher J. Samuel Perlman and managing editor Saul Rosen. Both were based in New York and conferred continually throughout the day on matters of editorial content and staff.

The size of the staff grew steadily and gave *DRF* the capability of covering major racing events in depth. No event in American racing, at least until the advent of the Breeders' Cup, commanded greater coverage than the Kentucky Derby. Several times during the 1950s, *DRF* had a crew of almost 20 at Churchill Downs, including the editor and publisher, three columnists, two reporters, two chart callers, two calltakers, two operators, three clockers, the chief of

"Frenchy" Schwartz was DRF's chief of clockers for decades.

clockers, and the field supervisor of the track and field division.

The chief of clockers for many years was Eugene "Frenchy" Schwartz of New Orleans. The son of a successful baker, he grew up near the Fair Grounds on Gentilly Boulevard and was an early victim of its seductive ways, as were a number of his brothers and cousins. Some became trainers, some became racing officials and Frenchy became a clocker; the best clocker of them all. He had a great eye for recognition, confidence in his ability, serenity in the midst of daily chaos, and the character to withstand temptation, all essential to the job.

Schwartz and *Daily Racing Form's* senior Maryland clocker, Frank Robinson, who also enjoyed an outstanding reputation for accuracy and probity, were standing on the press-box porch during the 1973 Preakness, a dozen feet apart. Since Secretariat set a track record in the Kentucky Derby two weeks earlier, they were alert to all possibilities. At the finish of the race that they timed independently, they compared watches and found that they were in agreement on a time of 1:53⅖ for the mile and three-sixteenths. The official time on the board, however, was 1:55, a second slower than the Pimlico record of 1:54.

Schwartz immediately came to the *DRF* office in the Pimlico press box and without a word showed his stopwatch to the writer, who was punching out the lead on a typewriter. When Schwartz added that Frank Robinson had the same time, the writer asked Ed Schuyler of the Associated Press and Ray Ayres of the United Press to confer with him. The situation was explained and the two wire-service stories, carried by papers throughout the country, detailed the findings of the *DRF* clockers.

Not only the Kentucky Derby and Preakness, but the Belmont Stakes as well, was part of *DRF*'s Triple Crown coverage. Prior to the start of the classic season of 1958, I proposed a daily detailed story on the Kentucky Derby, updating the status of the leading candidates. Such stories had been written in the past but mostly concerned the Derby horses stabled at Churchill Downs and did not cover Derby prospects in all areas of the country. Under the heading of "Derby Doings," the daily report began, and was sufficiently acceptable to be continued through the Preakness and Belmont Stakes. It is still an annual feature, written since the spring of 1994 by Steve Haskin, who supplements these daily accounts with weekly previews of the Kentucky Derby scene beginning in early January.

The advertising manager of *Daily Racing Form* and *The Morning Telegraph* for almost half a century was Leo Waldman. A remarkable man of energy, reliability and detail, his style was to start his day at noon and work well into the evening. Time and occasion meant little to Leo. One advertiser recalls receiving a phone call from Waldman on New Year's Eve, asking about an ad that was to go in the weekend edition and taking details of the ad over the phone as an orchestra in the background played "Auld Lang Syne."

Waldman was honored at an elaborate retirement dinner in New Jersey in 1990 – and was back in the office the next day. Eventually, he went into semi-retirement, restricting his advertising duties to the breeding farms in New York State and writing a lively weekly column on breeding activities in the area.

Sam Perlman retired as editor and publisher in 1965. He was succeeded as publisher by Stewart Hooker, who served as chief labor negotiator for *Daily Racing Form* after an earlier tenure in Cleveland as head of the Newspaper Publisher's Association. Walter Annenberg also appointed Saul Rosen as editor.

Both men moved to strengthen *Daily Racing Form*. Dave Schultz,

general manager of the Canadian edition, was brought to Chicago to take charge of the Midwest Edition of *DRF*. Mel Schrier, an outstanding professional in his field, continued as editor in Chicago and was now assisted by John McEvoy. Michael (Mickey) Sandler was named general manager of the Western edition of *Daily Racing Form*, succeeding the retiring Jerry O'Brien, while Matt Taylor retired as editor in the West and was succeeded by Don Fleming. Bill Dow moved from Toronto to Los Angeles in an executive capacity as assistant to Sandler, and Fred Grossman was named managing editor of *The Morning Telegraph*.

In the 1950s, New York City was served by eight daily newspapers: the *Times*, *Herald-Tribune*, *Daily News* and *Daily Mirror* in the morning and the *World-Telegram*, the *Sun*, the *Post* and the *Journal-American* in the afternoon. One by one these papers closed, in part due to pressure from the International Typographical Union under the direction of Bert Powers.

Daily Racing Form management, seeking to avoid the kind of long, debilitating strikes that preceded the closing of the majority of New York's newspapers, purchased a piece of property in Hightstown, New Jersey, just off the New Jersey Turnpike. Midway between New York and Philadelphia, the property was just outside the jurisdiction of the New York ITU.

A modern newspaper plant was constructed, and it opened in November of 1971, just as talks were under way between *The Morning Telegraph* and the New York Typographical Union. The paper that was printed at the Hightstown plant was *Daily Racing Form*'s first venture into "cold type" and was sold in Mid-Atlantic locations while the New York office of *The Morning Telegraph* continued to print that paper.

Negotiations between the paper and the union were stalemated and going downhill in the spring of 1972. As the New York union called for a strike, it was announced on April 1 that *The Morning*

Telegraph would no longer be published and that the Hightstown office would henceforth print the Eastern edition of *Daily Racing Form*, but in a broadsheet mode with which readers of *The Morning Telegraph* were familiar.

The union reacted by throwing a picket line around the 52nd Street office, barring passage in and out of the building. Some union members also journeyed to Hightstown and attempted to picket there, but an injunction was obtained and the pickets were removed to a location from which they were no longer effective. Because ground transport of records and certain equipment was barred by the picket line in New York, essential items were taken to the roof of the building and removed by helicopter. Those tin cans and trays full of type on the wall in the composing room were no longer needed. The past performances of all the horses in training had been entered into a deck of computers at Hightstown, with a backup set of computers in another location to safeguard the information against fire or theft. These banks of computers were located in air-conditioned rooms under 24-hour security.

Most staff members at *The Morning Telegraph* in New York were offered comparable jobs at Hightstown. Some accepted, and most of this group switched residences from New York to New Jersey. Some, reluctant to leave New York, chose a buyout.

In June of 1972, two months after the death of *The Morning Telegraph*, Saul Rosen retired as editor. He was succeeded by an editorial board consisting of Fred Grossman, Harold Tannenbaum, William C. Phillips and the writer. This group met periodically and conferred more frequently by telephone, but the plan was unwieldy and in 1973, Grossman was named editor of *Daily Racing Form*, headquartered in Hightstown but with national responsibilities. The writer was named executive columnist, a title Frenchy Schwartz habitually mangled into "exclusive communist."

Hooker died suddenly in 1975 and was succeeded by Mickey

Sandler, first as national general manager and then as publisher. William H. Williams, who had come on board in 1970 to handle labor negotiations, took on added executive responsibility in the East. Many innovations followed, both editorially and in upgrading the past performances. There were advances, as well, on the technological front. In 1980, the Hightstown editorial operation switched over to computers, followed by the offices in Chicago and Los Angeles. David Schultz retired as general manager in Chicago and was succeeded by Stan Shulman.

In 1982, *DRF* utilized satellite technology for the first time, from Los Angeles to Seattle. The editions for the Longacres track near Seattle and several other tracks in the area were now being made up in the Los Angeles office and bounced off the satellite to a printing plant in Seattle. Other satellite printing programs followed in the East and Midwest.

As Walter Annenberg passed his 80th birthday in 1988, and with no successor in the family as head of the Triangle Publications Corporation which included *Daily Racing Form*, the incredibly successful *TV Guide* and *Seventeen* magazine, he pondered his options. In the spring of that year he received a phone call from Rupert Murdoch, the international publisher, who came to Philadelphia to see him. That was the start of negotiations which led, in August, to the announcement that Murdoch had purchased Triangle Publications for $3 billion.

The actual transfer of *Daily Racing Form* took place that fall, at which time Sandler retired as publisher. Martin Singerman, for many years president of Murdoch's News Corporation, became president of *Daily Racing Form*, while Bill Williams was named national general manager in charge of business and administrative functions and Fred Grossman was named editor in charge of editorial operations. Shortly thereafter, George Bernet, who served for a number of years on the editorial staff, was named associate editor.

In June 1991, K-III Communications purchased eight magazines and *Daily Racing Form* from Rupert Murdoch for a reported $650 million. When he purchased Triangle Publications from Walter Annenberg, Murdoch was primarily interested in *TV Guide* as a complement to his Fox Television Network. Annenberg, however, was not interested in a piecemeal sale, so it was all or nothing for Murdoch, and he took it all. But nothing in the conditions said he had to keep the properties that didn't hold his interest. He was involved, briefly, when an old business rival, Robert Maxwell, started a racing newspaper, *The Racing Times*, in competition with *Daily Racing Form*, in April of 1991. But that fall, Maxwell was lost at sea and both direction and funds were subsequently in short supply.

The Racing Times published its last edition in February 1992, and it was subsequently announced that *Daily Racing Form* had purchased its assets, real estate and equipment. Many staff members of *The Racing Times* were hired by *Daily Racing Form* including Neil Cook and Katherine Wilkins.

K-III Communications, which purchased *Daily Racing Form*, is headed by chairman William F. Reilly and vice chairmen Charles McCurdy and Beverly Chell. Harvey Miller was appointed president of *DRF* after the sale but policy differences caused Miller to leave that fall. He was succeeded by Jack Farnsworth. Concurrent with the transfer from Murdoch to K-III, Bill Williams was named pub-

Bill Reilly (left) and Jack Farnsworth led K-III Communications' drive to upgrade DRF's operations.

lisher and Grossman continued as editor.

When Farnsworth came on board, he found the three regional editions of *Daily Racing Form* notably different in many aspects and sorely behind times in technology and equipment. K-III pledged $35 million to upgrade the operation and many changes followed in 1992 and 1993. Grossman stepped down as editor in March 1992, succeeded by George Bernet. Williams left as publisher later that summer and Bill Dow was appointed chief operating officer.

Modernization of the paper was undertaken, beginning in 1992, with the introduction of desktop-publishing procedures. Instead of pasting columns of paper into a page, articles were called up on a computer screen and maneuvered into place. Half a dozen production people were now doing the work of 25. Between retirements and buyouts, the size of the *DRF* staff was cut in half.

In major break with tradition, the broadsheet format of the Eastern edition of *DRF* was changed to tabloid size in August of 1993. Neil Cook, who signed on as editorial director, was named editor-in-chief. The Chicago office was closed and modern facilities in Lexington, Kentucky, took over responsibility for publishing the Midwest Edition. There are no printing presses in the building. Instead, *DRF*'s Midwest edition is now printed at a commercial press near Cincinnati. A number of staffers came from the Chicago office to live and work in Lexington.

The Los Angeles riots during the summer of 1992 took place near the offices of *Daily Racing Form*. The threat of further civil unrest and possible disruption of operations prompted the closing of the Los Angeles office early in 1993, and the opening of state-of-the-art facilities in Phoenix, Arizona. Here, too, there are no presses at the offices and the printing is done in suburban Los Angeles by commercial press.

Another major change involved a reduction in work force and responsibility at the huge plant in Hightstown, New Jersey. Early in 1994, the Eastern edition was made up at the Phoenix office, with the Lexington office assuming responsibility for certain pages.

For the first time in its history, *Daily Racing Form* has a promotions staff and department. Operating under the direction of Katherine Wilkins and Mandy Minger, the paper conducts handicapping seminars at tracks throughout the country, sells merchandise with the *DRF* logo and owns a hot-air balloon, fashioned in the shape of a rolled front page, which makes appearances at major racing events. *DRF* also conducts spring and fall Fantasy Stables contests in which readers assemble imaginary stables based on actual horses. The "manager" with the highest earnings on a certain date can win thousands of dollars or receive an all-expenses trip to the Kentucky Derby or Breeders' Cup. Some 15,000 persons participated in the first such

This is how Daily Racing Form's *distinctive artist Pierre "Peb" Bellocq sees himself.*

promotion in 1993.

With the updating of equipment well under way, emphasis was placed on the improvement of *DRF*'s editorial content. Many new features were introduced including personalization of racing stables and their staffs, and many new columns of news, features and commentary on breeders and breeding under the direction of bloodstock editor Sid Fernando.

One of the most popular features of *Daily Racing Form* today, as it has been for more than 40 years, is the work of the racing world's best-known artist, Pierre Bellocq, most readily identified by his pen name, Peb. An amateur rider and poster artist in his native Paris, Peb's charming depictions of the thoroughbred came to the attention of John Schapiro, then-president of Laurel Race Course, who made frequent trips to Europe on behalf of his Washington D.C. International, the first successful international race. In the mid-1950s, Schapiro brought Peb to Laurel to do some work for the track in connection with the International and recommended the young artist to Sam Perlman, editor and publisher of *DRF*.

Perlman immediately offered Peb a full-time job as staff artist, and his success was assured by the popularity of an early series of sketches known as "The Equine Comedy." Saul Rosen, the managing editor, had Peb create special cartoons commemorating major races, and they are still among the highlights of *DRF*. Peb's son, Remi Bellocq, is also a skilled cartoonist and his sketches often illustrate another new and popular *DRF* feature, the weekly "Racing Forum" pages with columns of opinion and additional pages of letters from the public.

In commemoration of *Daily Racing Form's* centennial, a program of events was held throughout the year, highlighted by a deluxe reception for many of racing's leading personalities at the Metropolitan Club in New York during Belmont Week, and the special 100th anniversary edition published on November 17. With all the changes that have taken place in the interim, the paper's proudest boast remains the same: that no one in this country has ever in his lifetime attended a track in the U.S. where *Daily Racing Form* is not on sale, carrying complete statistics and stories of the sport.

The most significant racing developments of this era were the introduction in 1984 of the Breeder's Cup and the dramatic changes in the business of racing from a virtually non-competitive industry to one with keen competition in every direction.

By every standard, the Breeders' Cup was a rousing success from the outset. The first running, at Hollywood Park on November 10, 1984, attracted a huge turnout of 64,254 during a time of the season when the interest of most sports fans centered on football and racing never had crowds of that size. On-track wagering totalled $11,466,941, while on-track wagering at the Kentucky Derby that year (with an attendance of 126,453) was $11,488,130. Millions of others watched the four-hour telecast, and one can guess an occasional dollar changed hands on man-to-man wagers. Perhaps the greatest indication of success was the four-hour telecast itself. For a

The Breeders' Cup was one of many contributions John Gaines made to racing.

major network (NBC) to commit so much time to another sport during the football season boggled industry thinking for a long time, both before and after the fact.

The Breeders' Cup story essentially is the story of one man: John R. Gaines, who was raised in upstate New York where his father, Clarence Gaines, was in the animal feed business.

One of the elder Gaines' employees was a genius in animal husbandry, Lao Brosemer, who interested Clarence Gaines in expanding the company by including dog food. As Brosemer traveled on behalf of Gaines Feed Company, John Gaines went along, fascinated with Brosemer's knowledge of animals, his theories and insights into inheritability.

Gaines recalls a typical week at the New York State Fair in Syracuse. They would check out every breed of animal on the grounds, and while young Gaines absorbed information like a sponge, Brosemer would judge them all: What was good about them, the weak points, etc. Each afternoon the savant and his pupil would attend the trotting races at the fair to study yet another breed, and in the evening they went to the horse show. It was total immersion and a great influence on John Gaines' life and career.

He attended Culver Military Academy, majored in English at Notre Dame and then studied genetics at the University of Kentucky. He was called to service, attended the language school of the ultra-secret National Security Agency, and briefed high-ranking officers of the Department of Defense on information gathered by U-2 surveillance flights over the Soviet Union during the height of the Cold War.

His father decided to sell a farm in Kentucky he'd owned for more than 20 years, and John Gaines, back in civilian life, went to Lexington to participate in the residential development of the property. Brought up in a trotting horse environment, he bought a farm of his own in the Lexington area and stocked it with broodmares. It was an attractive and successful operation, and a few years later he sold it at a nice profit.

Subsequently, at a public sale of some of the bloodstock he raised at the farm, he purchased a filly he'd always liked. She cost $16,000, and doing business as Kerry Way won the Hambletonian, trotting's premier prize, for her entrepreneurial young owner. But his father was closely identified with standardbreds and young Gaines wanted to make his own way. He decided on a venture into thoroughbred racing.

In 1962, he made his first significant thoroughbred purchase when he bought the 4-year-old stakes-winning filly, Oil Royalty, from Max Gluck's Elmendorf Farm. He had the good sense to send her to Charlie Whittingham in California, where she promptly won the Las Flores Handicap at Santa Anita.

In May 1963 he bought the old Keene Farm adjacent to Keeneland Race Course on the Versailles Pike and changed the name to Gainesway Farm. Then he purchased the broodmare, Cosmah, dam of Tosmah, from Gene Mori, and bred her to Turn-to. The resulting foal brought the highest price in history for a yearling filly sold at Keeneland when John Olin was the successful bidder in 1965 at $140,000. That was also the year Gaines leased Bold Bidder from owner Paul Falkenstein, raced the good handicap horse in partnership with John Hanes and John Olin under the supervision of Woody Stephens, and then sent Bold Bidder to stand at stud at Gainesway Farm.

Gaines was now in high gear. He gave Rex Ellsworth $3.75 million – making it the largest racing transaction ever – for three stallions: Candy Spots, Prove It and Olden Times. He then syndicated

them. Gaining recognition, he was elected a director of the Thoroughbred Breeders of Kentucky, and he concluded the 1965 season by buying half of C.V. Whitney's 1,000-acre farm on the Paris Pike, plus 30 of Whitney's broodmares, though he didn't move his Gainesway Farm operation to its new location until 1974.

He was elected a director of the Thoroughbred Club of America, was named a director of the Keeneland Association, and in 1970 was named by Gov. Louis Nunn to the committee planning the Kentucky Horse Park in Lexington. He was honored for his contributions to this project when the park was dedicated, late in 1978.

Gaines hired New York architect Theodore Giraldi to design the stallion barns at his new Gainesway Farm, incorporating artistic touches as well as equine comfort and safety. The four-stall barns, with high-pitched tile roofs, excellent ventilation and attractive metal doors, won critical acclaim and several architectural awards.

He sought stallions from all over the world that met his discerning standards and imported Lyphard, Blushing Groom, Riverman, Green Dancer, Lypheor and Faraway Son to stand with such American acquisitions as Cannonade, Dr. Carter, Exceller, Temperance Hill, Icecapade, Cozzene, Mt. Livermore and Broad Brush. Literally thousands of mares were bred at Gainesway each spring on an around-the-clock basis.

During the 1970s and into the early 1980s, foal registrations, yearling prices and stallion fees all rose precipitously in the U.S. In 1970, registrations totalled 24,367. By 1980, that figure reached 35,613. Yearlings that were selling for $500,000 in 1970 were bringing $1 million in 1981. Stallions that were standing for $10,000 in 1970 were commanding $25,000 and $35,000 a decade later.

Life was good for breeders of thoroughbred racehorses in the late 1970s, but John Gaines was restless and cogitative. Despite rising prices for horses and increased purses, racing's presence on the

American sporting scene was all but invisible. There was a little television coverage of the Triple Crown classics in the spring, but virtually no racing on television in late summer and fall, and none in the newspapers. Gaines turned the picture over in his mind and gradually, during a period covering a couple of years, the idea of a breeder-sponsored championship day of racing in the fall began to take shape. The bulk of the funding would come from fees to make stallions and their progeny eligible to participate.

From time to time, Gaines discussed his idea with staffers at Gainesway Farm and with a few fellow breeders such as Nelson Bunker Hunt. It was Hunt who pushed Gaines off his reflective dime.

"I've heard enough about this idea of yours," Hunt said one day in the spring of 1982. "When you going to do something about it?"

When Gaines swings into action he is impressive. First he spoke to a number of prominent breeders and received informal approval and pledges of support. Then he made arrangements to address the annual "They're Off Awards Luncheon," hosted in Louisville by the Kentucky Derby Festival Committee. The luncheon attracted a large and influential audience and received wide coverage by the media.

On a Tuesday afternoon, April 20, he placed a call to me in the press box at Keeneland. "I'd like to have breakfast with you this week," he said. "I've got something on my mind."

When he heard a reply about busy schedules and Triple Crown coverage, he replied that this would be the most important story of the writer's career.

The next morning, at 7 a.m., Gaines led the way into his study,

Marje Everett played a prominent role in the first Breeders' Cup.

produced coffee and rolls, and told a fascinating tale of his idea for a championship day of racing in the fall, at a time appropriate to the winding down of major racing. He answered all the questions with contagious confidence and enthusiasm and chalked up another convert. By agreement, *Daily Racing Form* had the story first in editions that appeared on Friday morning, April 23, hours before the general announcement at the luncheon in Louisville.

Gaines continued his mission. He rounded up stallion managers at all the leading farms in Kentucky to brief them on the program. In August, at Saratoga, he received a visit from Art Watson, President of NBC Sports, who said his network was interested in televising the Breeders' Cup races. Gaines, seeking exposure for racing, was delighted.

That fall, Gaines pitched his proposal to a group of racetracks, including the New York Racing Association, Santa Anita, Hollywood Park, Gulfstream Park, Woodbine, the Fair Grounds and Atlantic City. Many of the executives present expressed different ideas, and some wanted the big races spread out over the year, instead of being packaged on one afternoon. But Gaines held a few aces: overwhelming approval from the press and NBC's interest in televising the Breeders' Cup.

Hollywood Park expressed the most interest in hosting the new concept, to the point that Mrs. Marje Everett, the track's chief executive officer, pledged $200,000 of her own money to the Breeders' Cup organization if her track gained approval. Money was an important item at that point because there was little of it – perhaps $25,000 – in the Breeders' Cup funds for operations.

The matter came to a head that fall at a meeting of directors in Lexington. C. Gibson Downing, a Lexington attorney, was named first president of the Breeders' Cup because of differences several directors had with John Gaines. Gaines gracefully stepped aside in the interests of harmony, and a formal organization was put together.

At a subsequent meeting of the newly organized Executive Committee, the matter of funding operations was pre-eminent. Finally seven – not all – of the committee members pledged $50,000 each, with no guarantee of any kind. The $350,000 in the bank enabled the work of the Breeders' Cup to go forward.

The marketing committee was headed by Johnny Nerud, a top horseman who developed Dr. Fager and many other fine horses for the Tartan Farm of W.L. McKnight, chief executive officer of Minnesota Mining and Manufacturing Co. Nerud also had a keen business sense, built Tartan Farm in Ocala, Florida, for McKnight and organized every detail of its operation. He was aware of the importance of marketing to the success of the Breeders' Cup and was determined to hire a top company. Through contacts, he was introduced to Robert Landau Associates, a pioneer firm in the sports marketing field. He liked their presentation but wanted a professional opinion.

Nerud went to see Sonny Werblin, racing enthusiast, horse owner and breeder, former executive of Monmouth Park, former president of the New York Jets, president of Madison Square Garden, former president of MCA-TV, former chairman of the New Jersey Sports and Exposition Authority and former agent for film and television star, Ronald Reagan, who now held an important post

Leah Ray and Sonny Werblin were enthusiastic in their racing endeavors.

in Washington D.C.

Werblin knew Mike Letis and Mike Trager, two of the key executives of the Landau firm, liked their work and approved Nerud's intention to hire them. A year later, the Landau firm went into bankruptcy, but Nerud offered Letis and Trager an opportunity to continue their fine work on behalf of the Breeders' Cup under their own banner. Sports Marketing and Television International was organized and immediately went into action.

Commercial sponsorship of the Breeders' Cup events was deemed an essential element of a successful plan. Letis and Trager went to work, and by the summer of 1984 were able to announce some important participants, including Mobil Oil, DeBeers diamonds, Chrysler Corporation, Anheuser-Busch and First Jersey Securities.

Preceding the confirmation of sponsorship, and indeed a vital element of the sales pitch to the sponsors, was completion of an agreement under which NBC Sports signed a multiyear contract to telecast all seven Breeders' Cup races live over a period of four hours.

Meanwhile, officials at Hollywood Park were rushing to complete the project they undertook after being named to host the first Breeders' Cup. Their eight-furlong track was increased to nine furlongs, and the seven-furlong grass course was enlarged to a full mile in circumference. This was a major undertaking by itself, but Hollywood was also building a five-story turf club, adjacent to the new finish line and located some 50 yards from the clubhouse end of the present stands.

A key piece of equipment was a giant tamping machine, designed to tamp down loose earth around the end embankments and the chute for the enlarged track. Only one such machine was available on the West Coast and was located in Seattle. At considerable expense it was driven down Highway 101 and placed in operation at the track, saving countless man hours of labor at a time when time was of the essence.

Finally, on November 10, 1984, racing entered a new era with the presentation of the first Breeders' Cup and its melodramatic climax, the Classic. Representing a combined effort by many segments of the industry, it was hailed as an example of racing's full capabilities. And, of course, it was just the beginning. As the competition built in intensity, business rose steadily. The total wagering on the first Breeders' Cup, $16,452,179, increased to $79,744,742 by Breeders' Cup X.

Howard Samuels was the first president of New York City OTB

∞∞∞∞∞∞∞∞

For those too young to have gone racing in the U.S. in the 1950s and 1960s, it would be taxing credulity to tell them of the large and enthusiastic crowds that jammed the nation's racetracks on a regular basis. With casinos limited to Las Vegas, with no state lotteries, with no off-track betting and with bookmakers feeling public heat as an aftermath of the Kefauver Hearings, the racetrack was a magnet for those who loved to gamble as well as those who loved racing.

The rebuilt Aqueduct, which opened in September 1959, hosted a record crowd of 73,435 on Memorial Day, May 31, 1965. Belmont Park regularly hosted Saturday crowds of 40,000 and 50,000. The Labor Day crowd at Atlantic City in 1953 was 33,404. Garden State Park attracted 51,077 on Memorial Day, 1967, for its

Jersey Derby program and a re-enactment of a Civil War skirmish. When Monmouth Park closed its meeting on August 4, 1962, it drew a record crowd of 43,591.

Arlington Park regularly had weekend crowds of 30,000 to 40,000 and weekday crowds of more than 20,000, while Washington Park was almost as popular. Hialeah Park in Miami attracted 42,366 on February 18, 1956, the Washington Birthday holiday in the height of the tourist season. Santa Anita and Hollywood Park in Los Angeles, during the era before the advent of Sunday racing, had Saturday crowds of 40,000 and 50,000, and midweek crowds of 25,000.

This idyllic situation turned slowly, with several landmark dates worth noting. New Hampshire was the first state in modern times to institute a lottery, in 1964. Other states followed, slowly at first and then in considerable numbers, offering games popular with the public, easy to understand, and rich in prize money. Hundreds of millions of dollars, some of which routinely passed through mutuel windows at the nations tracks, is now diverted.

And then, in 1971, off-track betting first came to the U.S. The French had been wagering for years at the PMU counters in their tobacco shops. For a much longer period, Englishmen had their neighborhood bookmakers or turf accountants, with whom they placed wagers when not at the racetrack. But off-track wagering was not traditional in this country. The betting windows ended at the track gates, and many executives, aware of the value of a live customer – parking, attendance, program, concessions etc. – wanted to keep it that way.

A superior force thought otherwise. State Legislatures, desperate for additional sources of revenue, wanted racetracks to expand their market areas via OTB. New York acted first, hoping the New York Racing Association would go along. NYRA's board of trustees kept a firm grasp on the past and the die was cast. OTB legislation was passed anyway, with the operation assigned to corporations organized by cities, counties and regional jurisdictions.

New York city's OTB Corporation grew quickly, from a single outlet to more than 100 betting shops, and then almost 200. Attendance at the New York tracks began to evaporate as more and more regulars found it easier and cheaper to bet at OTB than to go to the track, even with a 5 percent surcharge on OTB wagers. The loss of patronage was costly to the tracks, which were not properly compensated for the diverted wagers and sustained a total loss on the missing customer.

OTB came to other jurisdictions in a variety of modes, almost all of them an improvement over the original New York scene. In many instances, the tracks themselves operated their own off-course facilities. Some states incorporated minimum-distance provisions into their laws to protect the patronage base of the host track. States with widespread population centers, such as Florida, seemed to fare well.

The Phipps family, from left, Ogden, Dinny and Cynthia, concentrated on racing from their box at Saratoga.

Gulfstream Park, racing the choice mid-winter dates, saw its daily purse distribution rise substantially as a result of its simulcast activities.

Racing's share of the gaming dollar suffered another blow in 1978 with the introduction of casinos in Atlantic City. The ancient resort on the Jersey shore was quickly transformed into Las Vegas East, and a dozen glittering casinos followed the first, Resorts International. In two years, the impact of casino gaming on the handle and at the gate was felt by tracks throughout the mid-Atlantic area and particularly in New York, New Jersey, Pennsylvania, Delaware and Maryland.

Developments in Atlantic City led to the introduction of casinos in states throughout the country, gambling halls operated by Native American tribes, and adaptations such as river boats, card clubs and video poker clubs provided additional competition for racetracks, who were forced to expand their marketing operations in order to survive and compete.

∞∞∞∞∞∞∞∞

Ogden Phipps, who celebrated his 86th birthday on November 26, 1994, was one of the great American breeders of the 20th century. He bred more than 100 stakes winners, including the brilliant Buckpasser, Horse of the Year 1966, and winner of 25 races from 31 starts. He also bred Easy Goer, winner of $4,873,770; Personal

Ensign, undefeated in 13 starts over three seasons and the first major horse with a perfect record since Colin, who was retired in 1908 and such well-known stakes-winners as Seeking the Gold, Dancing Spree, Personal Flag, and Polish Navy, all of whom earned more than $1 million.

His son, Ogden Mills (Dinny) Phipps, raced his first horses with trainer Sunny Jim Fitzsimmons in 1962, when he was 20 and still an undergraduate at Yale. Five years later, at 25 and an executive with Bessemer Trust, he was elected to membership in The Jockey Club. In 1975, he was named vice chairman of the New York Racing Association under chairman Jack Dreyfus. In July of 1976, when he was 35, he was elected chairman. Dealing with politicians in Albany, labor leaders in New York and horsemen in the stable area, Phipps held the post until early in 1983. When he stepped down as NYRA chairman, he was elected chairman of The Jockey Club almost immediately, succeeding August Belmont, who served an interim term after chairman Nicholas Brady was appointed a United States Senator from New Jersey.

Under Phipps' leadership, The Jockey Club was re-established as the parent body of the American turf. At the Club's centennial dinner in August 1994, at the National Museum of Racing's Hall of Fame Auditorium in Saratoga, representatives of every major racing country in the world were on hand to pay tribute to the Club's ac-

An Aqueduct paddock strategy session had owner Ogden Phipps (left) and trainer Eddie Neloy conferring with jockey Braulio Baeza.

complishments and the respect in which it is held.

Many outstanding horses raced in America during the period from 1966 to 1994. The era, in fact, started with just such a crack in Buckpasser. The Tom Fool colt out of Suburban winner Busanda had been 2-year-old champion of 1965 when trained for owner-breeder Ogden Phipps by Bill Winfrey of Native Dancer fame. Winfrey, who had succeeded Sunny Jim Fitzsimmons during the 1963 season, retired from training in the fall of 1965 to spend more time with his large family, though he knew Buckpasser had tremendous potential. His successor was veteran horseman Eddie Neloy.

Neloy was a groom for many years before moving up the ladder. After taking out his trainer's license, he joined the Army, served as an infantryman during the bitter Italian campaign in World War II, and caught a bullet in an eye at Anzio beachhead. When he recovered and was discharged, he returned to the racetrack and developed some nice horses, including Gun Bow, who defeated Kelso in the memorable Woodward Stakes of 1964.

Buckpasser had three races at Hialeah in the winter of 1966, winning the nine-furlong Everglades as a prelude to the Flamingo, in that era the most prestigious of all 3-year-old events on the Kentucky Derby trail. And it was not just your ordinary Flamingo. This was the famous "Chicken Flamingo," so named by the press

SEVENTH RACE **1 1-4 MILES. (Gun Bow, July 25, 1964, 1:59⅗, 4, 122.)**
Aqu 32432
Sept'ber 30, 1967

Fourteenth running WOODWARD. Weight for age. $100,000 added. 3-year-olds and upward. By subscription of $100 each, which shall accompany the nomination; $1,000 additional to start, with $100,000 added. The added money and all fees to be divided 65 per cent to the winner, 20 per cent to second, 10 per cent to third and 5 per cent to fourth. 3-year-olds, 120 lbs.; older, 126 lbs. Mrs. William Woodward Sr. has donated a trophy which will be presented to the owner of the winner and trophies will also be presented to the winning trainer and jockey. Closed Friday, Sept. 1 with 18 nominations.
Value of race $107,800. Value to winner $70,070; second, $21,560; third, $10,780; fourth, $5,390.
Mutuel Pool, $648,902.

Index	Horses	Eq't	A	Wt	PP	¼	½	¾	1	Str	Fin	Jockeys	Owners	Odds to $1
32225Aqu^{1}	—Damascus		3	120	5	5^{1}	$5^{1\frac{1}{4}}$	4^{1}	$1^{\frac{1}{2}}$	1^{5}	1^{10}	W Sho'aker	Edith W Bancroft	a-1.80
31769Aqu^{2}	—Buckpasser	b	4	126	6	6	6	5^{3}	3^{4}	3^{6}	$2^{\frac{1}{2}}$	B Baeza	O Phipps	b-1.60
32217Rkm^{1}	—Dr. Fager		3	120	2	$1^{\frac{1}{2}}$	1^{h}	$1^{1\frac{1}{2}}$	2^{3}	2^{3}	3^{13}	W Boland	Tartan Stable	1.80
32229Det^{4}	—Handsome Boy	b	4	126	4	4^{5}	4^{5}	3^{1}	4^{3}	4^{12}	4^{20}	E Belmonte	Hobeau Farm	10.50
32341Atl^{1}	—Hedevar		5	126	1	2^{1}	2^{5}	2^{6}	5^{8}	5^{3}	5^{6}	R Turcotte	Edith W Bancroft	a-1.80
32377Aqu^{8}	—Great Power	b	3	120	3	3^{3}	3^{2}	6	6	6	6	R Ussery	Wheatley Stable	b-1.60

a-Coupled, Damascus and Hedevar; b-Buckpasser and Great Power.

Time, :22⅖, :45⅕, 1:09⅕, 1:35⅗, 2:00⅗ (with wind in backstretch). Track fast.

$2 Mutuel Prices:			
1-DAMASCUS (a-Entry)	5.60	2.60	..
2-BUCKPASSER (b-Entry)		2.80	...
NO SHOW MUTUELS SOLD.			

B. c, by Sword Dancer—Kerala, by My Babu. Trainer, F. Y. Whiteley, Jr. Bred by Mrs. T. Bancroft (Ky.).

IN GATE—4:50. OFF AT 4:50 EASTERN DAYLIGHT TIME. Start good. Won easily.

DAMASCUS, steadied after beginning alertly, saved ground while in hand for three-quarters, moved up determinedly thereafter and, taking command from DR. FAGER near the stretch turn, drew clear without the need of urging. BUCKPASSER, outrun until near the stretch turn but saving ground, responded readily during the drive but was no match for DAMASCUS and was under brisk handling to best DR. FAGER for the place. The latter went to the front before a quarter, was much used racing HEDEVAR into defeat and faltered when challenged by DAMASCUS. HANDSOME BOY tired before entering the stretch. HEDEVAR, away alertly, engaged DR. FAGER for three-quarters and had nothing left. GREAT POWER was finished early.

Daily Racing Form's *chart of the 1967 Woodward Stakes shows why it is considered it one of the great races of the century.*

after Hialeah's management, fearful of a huge minus pool on Buckpasser, ran the race as a betless exhibition despite a field of 10.

As it turned out, Buckpasser cut it close. He looked beaten for sure at the sixteenth pole when he suddenly lunged forward near the wire to nail the tough little Abe's Hope by three-quarters of a length. Pointing for Gulfstream's Florida Derby, however, he developed a quarter-crack and not only missed the Derby but the entire Triple Crown. He returned to action at Aqueduct on Belmont Stakes Day, winning an allowance race. Then he ran the table.

On the final day of the year, Buckpasser was at Santa Anita to capture the seven-furlong Malibu, his 10th consecutive stakes victory since mid-June. Little wonder he was a standout choice as Horse of the Year, despite his absence from the classics.

Buckpasser competed against two exceptional horses: Dr. Fager and Damascus. Damascus, who won 21 of 32 starts, was by Sword Dancer out of Kerala, by My Babu. He was owned by Edith Bancroft and was trained by Frank Whiteley. A promising 2-year-old, he disappointed in the Kentucky Derby but won the Preakness and Belmont comfortably. He cinched Horse of the Year laurels in 1967 with victories in the Dwyer, American Derby, Travers, Woodward and Jockey Club Gold Cup, among others. Carrying weights of as much as134 pounds, Damascus was a first-class 4-year-old, winning six of 12 starts and almost always a major factor.

Dr. Fager was one of the most brilliant horses of the century and still holds the world's record for a mile (1:32⅕) set at Arlington Park on August 24, 1968, when he won the Washington Park Handicap under 134 pounds by a margin of 10 lengths. After winning four of five starts at 2, he won seven of nine as a 3-year-old. The one that hurt the most was the Jersey Derby at Garden State Park. Pounds the best, he finished first by more than six lengths but was disqualified and placed last in a four-horse field when jockey Manny Ycaza herded him into his three opponents in the early stages of the race.

Bred and owned by William L. McKnight of Tartan Farm and trained by Johnny Nerud, Dr. Fager reached a peak at 4, winning seven of eight starts, including the Californian at Hollywood Park, the Washington Park Handicap in Chicago, the Whitney at Saratoga, and the United Nations Handicap at Atlantic City. The last-named event was his first and only appearance on grass, and he won carrying 134 pounds. He followed it up by winning the Vosburgh at Aqueduct under 139 pounds with seven furlongs in 1:20⅕. At season's end he was named Horse of the Year 1968 and also champion handicap horse, champion grass horse and champion sprinter. This was a coup de force without parallel.

During the 12-year period 1973 through 1984, the racing careers of two of the greatest geldings in American racing history overlapped and left a rich vein of records and memories. Between them, Forego and John Henry earned Horse of the Year honors five times and accumulated total purses of $8.5 million. They were decidedly dissimilar in appearance. Forego was an equine giant of 17 hands and fairly robust, a striking individual. John Henry barely reached 16 hands and was somewhat on the dumpy side, very plain. Buty fiery determination burned bright in both, and they reached a level few attain.

Sherrill Ward, whose byword was patience, trained the young Forego.

On the Tuesday prior to the 99th Kentucky Derby, Forego electrified the scene at Churchill Downs by drilling five furlongs in :57. But on Derby Day 1973, it was Secretariat who did the electrifying, winning off by two and a half lengths from Sham, with Forego fourth, beaten 11 lengths after racing wide through the stretch.

Forego had some time off that summer, resumed racing at Saratoga, and won three consecutive allowance races that fall at Belmont Park. Later that fall, in top form, he won the Roamer Handicap under 123 pounds and the Discovery under 127. In all he recorded nine victories that season from 18 starts.

Forego, by the imported Argentine crack Forli, was bred and owned by the Lazy F Ranch of Martha Farish Gerry, who purchased the dam, Lady Golconda by Hasty Road, from Hall of Fame horseman Harry Trotsek. Forego's size was against him at 2, and he was also bothered by chronic sesamoiditis. Veteran trainer Sherrill Ward, who saw raw ability, bided his time.

Three weeks after his third birthday, Forego made his debut at Hialeah in a seven-furlong maiden race and finished fourth at 10-1. He ran back in less than two weeks to win by eight at 6-5. He won two more races in allowance company before moving up smartly in class, trying the Florida Derby at Gulfstream. Trainer Jimmy Croll saddled the victorious Royal and Regal, who led all the way with Walter Blum aboard to win by three lengths from Forego.

Forego gained national recognition in Florida as a 4-year-old by winning the nine-furlong Donn Handicap and the Gulfstream Park and Widener handicaps, both at 10 furlongs. Arbees Boy upset him in the Metropolitan Handicap at Belmont, but it should be noted Forego was carrying 134 pounds and was conceding 22 pounds to the winner. He won the Brooklyn, was third in the Suburban, and freshened during August at Saratoga. Trainer Sherrill Ward was always cognizant of his sesamoiditis.

It was Forego's three consecutive victories that fall that earned him the first of his three Horse of the Year awards. He began with a narrow victory over Arbees Boy in the Woodward Stakes at a mile and a half. Three weeks later, he dropped back to seven furlongs for the Vosburgh and, carrying topweight of 131 pounds, won easily. Three weeks after the Vosburgh he ran two miles to win the Jockey Club Gold Cup, run that season at Aqueduct. He was rewarded for his versatility.

As a 5-year-old in 1975, and now trained by Frank Whiteley following Sherrill Ward's retirement, Forego won a second Widener Handicap, this one under 131 pounds. He also accounted for the Brooklyn under 132 and the Suburban under 134 but missed a sweep of the Handicap Triple when he finished third in the Metropolitan under a steadying 136. He sustained a narrow defeat under 129 pounds in the Marlboro Cup but clinched Horse of the Year laurels a second time with a decisive triumph in the Woodward.

Forego may have reached a peak as a 6-year-old of 1976, when he won six of eight starts with a second and a third. Eschewing a Florida campaign, Frank Whiteley kept Forego in South Carolina for the winter, playing an endless stream of water on the leg with the troubled sesamoid. After a mid-May prep at Belmont, Forego won his first Metropolitan Mile under 130 pounds. Carrying 125 pounds and pulling nine from Forego, Foolish Pleasure edged him a nose in the Suburban, costing Forego a handicap sweep. He won the Brooklyn very smartly, carrying 134 pounds. Concluding the campaign, he won the nine-furlong Woodward with a flair and then earned himself immortality with his signature victory in the 10-furlong Marlboro Cup, for which he carried an incredible 137 pounds.

Forego had a good season as a 7-year-old of 1977, winning four of seven starts, including the Metropolitan under 133 pounds, and

Trainer Frank Whiteley and jockey Bill Shoemaker whooped it up many times with the magnificent exploits of Forego.

his fourth consecutive Woodward Stakes. Horse of the Year honors, however, went to Seattle Slew for his sweep of the Triple Crown. Once again, Forego got a lengthy holiday, from mid-September to mid-June, and Frank Whiteley had him ready to run in his seasonal debut as an 8-year-old. Going seven furlongs in allowance company at Belmont Park, Forego won in 1:21⅗. He was assigned topweight of 132 pounds for the Suburban Handicap on July 4, but showed little and finished fifth. That was enough of a message for Martha Gerry and trainer Whiteley, who promptly announced his retirement. He went home with 34 victories from 57 starts, remarkable longevity for a horse with chronic sesamoiditis, and earnings of $1,938,957.

There has never been a horse quite like John Henry, who ran his greatest race at age 6, who was Horse of the Year again at age 9, and who worked better at 10 than most outstanding horses but was retired out of concern for his safety.

The bizarre tale begins in 1976 at the Keeneland Fall yearling sale when Mrs. Robert Lehmann of Golden Chance Farm sold a homebred colt by Ole Bob Bowers for $1,100 to J.E. Colloway. Colloway either had second thoughts or was pin-hooking when he sold the Ole Bob Bowers colt at Keeneland in January for $2,200 on a bid by Hal Snowden. Even at that modest price, the colt was no prize. Snowden recalls he was back at the knee, ungainly in appearance and had a fiery temper. Snowden had him gelded after he destroyed several hundred dollars worth of feed tubs and water buckets.

The surgery helped a little, but three months after his purchase, John Henry was sold to Mrs. Akike McVarish for $7,500. Mrs. McVarish sent her veterinarian to the farm to inspect the new purchase. We don't know what he reported, but we do know Mrs. McVarish was on the phone to Snowden, inquiring if he would take the horse back at the same price. Snowden, with a sigh, agreed.

A few weeks later, Mrs. Colleen Madere was on the phone to Snowden, wondering if he had a horse for sale. It turns out he did, for $10,000.

John Henry and the Shoe were a perfect match.

Mrs. Madere sent her exercise boy to Keeneland where John Henry was ready to breeze. The boy liked the work, and the deal was made. That was in early May of 1977. Later that month, on May 20, John Henry made his first start and won in Mrs. Madere's colors at Jefferson Downs in Kenner, Louisiana. He was involved in a spill in his second start but rebounded that summer to win the Lafayette Futurity at Evangeline Downs, which netted Mrs. Madere $43,225.

That fall, at the Fair Grounds in New Orleans, John Henry was entered in a $25,000 claimer and showed little. When he was dropped to $20,000 and showed even less, Mrs. Madere was on the phone to Snowden again, asking if he would be willing to trade her a couple of untried 2-year-olds for John Henry. Patiently, Snowden agreed and owned John Henry for a third time.

In the spring of 1978, John Henry, now 3, was working nicely

at Keeneland. Snowden began looking around for a small 3-year-old stakes and found one in the Sportsman's Park condition book. He was making plans to ship the gelding to Chicago when his phone rang. Jimmy Ferraro, a bloodstock agent from New York, had a customer for a 3-year-old in the neighborhood of $25,000.

Sam Rubin, an importer of bicycles from the Far East, had been a horseplayer all his life. Every so often he talked about owning a horse, and when Ferraro approached him at Aqueduct and said he had a prospect for $25,000, Rubin told him to go ahead and buy. As Rubin figured it, he would have his little fling, and the most it could cost him was $25,000 and a year's training fees. If the horse was able to run a little, he might break even.

John Henry was shipped to trainer Bob Donato in New York. Rubin had met Donato at the track, they talked, and Rubin invited the Philadelphian to train his small stable. Donato selected a $25,000 claiming race on May 21 for John Henry's debut in the Dotsam (Dorothy and Sam) Stable's brown and blue colors, and it was winning effort. Then, experimenting one morning, the trainer tried John Henry on the grass for a gallop and liked what he saw. He ran him back on the turf for $35,000, and John Henry won by 14 lengths.

The story was unfolding rapidly. Three weeks after that claiming victory on turf, John Henry returned to the grass for an allowance win, his third tally in three starts since his acquisition by Rubin. On July 1 he was at Monmouth Park for the Lamplighter Handicap and almost won it, finishing a close third. That was followed by a pair of seconds in two grass stakes at Belmont Park and, finally, on September 16 at Arlington Park in Chicago, a 12-length victory for John Henry in the Round Table Handicap. He also won a grass stakes at Penn National that fall and concluded the season with earnings of $120,319, most of it for Dorothy and Sam Rubin.

Rubin and Donato disagreed over stable policy as John Henry prepared for his 4-year-old campaign, and John Henry was transferred to the care of Victor (Lefty) Nickerson, a veteran horseman who developed the Marlboro Cup winner Big Spruce and other good ones. John Henry had another useful campaign, finishing first or second in nine of 11 starts and earning almost $130,000.

A high-stakes poker player all his life, Rubin saw his $25,000 investment return $250,000. He thought, however, that John Henry could do better. He took note of the many rich grass races at Santa Anita and told Nickerson he wanted his horse on the West Coast for several months. Nickerson had commitments in the East and proposed that his good friend, Ron McAnally, train John Henry for his engagements in the West. The recommendation was approved by Rubin and was endorsed by John Henry, who responded to McAnally's low-key approach and his apple and carrot treats by running off a string of six consecutive stakes victories, five of them on the grass. This was a key element of his first championship as America's best grass horse.

He was transferred back to Nickerson's care in mid-season of 1980, made five starts and won only once. Shipped west again that fall to McAnally, he won the rich Oak Tree Invitational and from that point on spent most of his time with McAnally. For his part, McAnally continued to split his 10 percent trainer's commission with Nickerson throughout the remainder of the gelding's career.

John Henry at 5 won more than $900,000. He doubled that sum as a 6-year-old of 1981, underlining his versatility and class by capturing the prestigious Santa Anita Handicap on the main track under 128 pounds and the Hollywood Invitational Turf Handicap under 130 pounds. But everything else he did that year paled in comparison with his incredible performance to win the first Arlington Million, a victory immortalized by a stunning bronze depiction of the finish entitled "Against All Odds." Commissioned by Arlington chairman Dick Duchossois, it captures the desperate nature of John Henry's amazing triumph.

It rained every day of Million Week, and the course was unbelievably boggy for the world's first million-dollar race. At that time the track was owed by Gulf + Western Corporation. David (Sonny) Werblin, chairman of G + W's Madison Square Garden division and the man who, as president of the New York Jets, signed Joe Namath to football's first $400,000 contract, felt the huge purse would attract attention, and he was right. Major newspapers from all parts of the U.S. and Europe covered the inaugural Million.

Having won five of his first six starts of the campaign – he finished fourth in the Hollywood Gold Cup under 130 pounds – John Henry was the solid choice for the Million at 11-10. Early on, however, it was obvious the favorite didn't care for the soft turf and was in trouble. He was many lengths back in last place while The Bart, reveling in the going, was cruising in front.

A sense of urgency was indicated by Bill Shoemaker as The Bart led the field into the final half-mile. Shoe sat quietly most of the time, but was moving in the saddle now, trying to rouse John Henry. There seemed to be some communication between the two because John Henry began to pick up horses at last. Still, he was a badly beaten horse turning into the stretch, many lengths behind The Bart.

The Bart gave no indication of slowing down, but John Henry seemed to have solved the riddle at last and was eating into the margin with every stride. On and on he came, and now the crowd was beginning to hope aloud. The shrill cries and shouts washed down from the packed stands like a tidal wave, engulfing the two horses as they flashed past the wire together. NBC televised the Million nationally and an announcer called The Bart a narrow winner, but the photo-finish pictures clearly showed it was John Henry's victory by a nose, and when the announcement was made, the cheering could be heard in the Loop, 15 miles away.

Physical problems kept him on the sidelines through much of his 7-year-old season of 1982, when he won twice in six starts.

Raced sparingly as an 8-year-old, his form in four appearances on grass continued to be top class, with victories in the American Handicap and Hollywood Turf Cup. Turning 9 in 1984, he trained smartly for McAnally, went off the favorite in the Santa Anita Handicap, and stumbled at the start. It cost him position and he finished fifth. After a third-place finish in the San Luis Rey on the turf, he won the Golden Gate Handicap in San Francisco and the Hollywood Invitational, both on grass.
Second in the Hollywood Gold Cup as the topweight, John Henry rebounded with a victory in the Sunset Handicap. He returned to Chicago for a second tally in the Arlington Million and went on to New York to add Belmont Park's Turf Classic to his souvenirs. He made his final start of the season under the lights at The Meadowlands in the Ballantine's Scotch Classic as the 3-5 favorite in a field of 12, and for a while the large and enthusiastic crowd feared

Ron McAnally's training style fit John Henry the best.

an upset. He was far back in the early stages and going nowhere. Then, rising to the occasion, he got in gear, passed one horse after another, and won off by almost three lengths as the topweight under 126 pounds. He was conceding 11 pounds to the runner-up, the hard-hitting Who's For Dinner.

That was the year of the first Breeders' Cup, and everyone wanted to see John Henry in the Turf. He had not been nominated, however, and Sam Rubin expressed reluctance to post the large supplementary fee. He finally made the first payment, only to have his horse go wrong a week before the race. Despite being forced to miss the Breeders' Cup, his six victories in nine starts and earnings for the season of $2,336,650 made John Henry a prominent candidate for Horse of the Year honors, an incredible prospect at age 9. The Eclipse Awards were announced at the annual Eclipse Dinner that year, and when Ted Bassett of Keeneland tore open the envelope and said "Like fine old wine . . ." the ballroom packed with almost 1,000 dinner guests roared its approval.

Both Sam Rubin and Ron McAnally had often said that if John Henry were ever perceived to be at physical risk, he would be retired. The old war-horse returned to training in the spring of 1985 as a 10-year-old, and McAnally proceeded carefully, putting no pressure on him and announcing no goals or schedule. By summer John Henry was getting fit and he electrified clockers at Hollywood Park on the morning of July 4 by drilling a mile in 1:35⅖. He was equally sharp a week later when he worked a mile on the Hollywood turf course and was timed in 1:36⅕.

But he injured himself leaving the course, and a few days later his retirement was announced. He would be the star boarder in a special paddock and barn at the Kentucky Horse Park in Lexington, Kentucky, where people could visit him daily and marvel at his record of 39 victories, 15 seconds, nine thirds and earnings of $6,597,947, at the time a world's record. Gov. Martha Layne Collins of Kentucky gave a special party in his honor upon his arrival in the Blue Grass and hundreds of prominent luncheon guests turned out to greet him, a reception he took in stride like everything else.

Seattle Slew, Affirmed and Spectacular Bid, who were 3-year-olds respectively in 1977, 1978 and 1979, were other outstanding individuals of this period.

Seattle Slew, possibly the most brilliant of the three and undefeated through his sweep of the Triple Crown, came out of the yearling sales for $17,500. The brown colt by Bold Reasoning out of My Charmer, by Poker, was originally listed as the property of Mickey and Karen Taylor of White Swan, Washington, where Taylor directed a lumber operation. Shortly after the colt's Kentucky Derby victory, it was revealed that Dr. Jim Hill, Seattle Slew's veterinarian, and the man who selected him at Keeneland, was a full partner in the ownership, together with his wife, Sally.

Seattle Slew's first trainer was Billy Turner Jr., a tall, young former steeplechase rider who developed several nice horses at Maryland tracks before moving his public stable to New York. Turner saw considerable ability in Seattle Slew early on, though the tallish, leggy youngster was also a bit ungainly. It was hoped to unveil him at Saratoga, and he worked smartly enough to have the clockers talking. But Turner decided to wait a bit longer, and Seattle Slew didn't make his debut until September 20 at Belmont Park.

By that time he was an International Good Thing and was bet down to 2-1 in the six-furlong maiden race. With Jean Cruguet, who had been working him, in the saddle, he romped home a five-length winner in 1:10⅕, an impressive first race. His second start, on October 5, was even more impressive as he sped seven furlongs in 1:22 to register by three and a half lengths as a 2-5 choice.

Encouraged, Turner brought Seattle Slew back in 11 days in the prestigious Champagne Stakes. Sent off at 6-5 despite his relative inexperience, he won off by almost 10 lengths, his mile in an eye-catching 1:34⅖. By way of comparison, this was the fastest mile in New York by a 2-year-old since Count Fleet won the 1942 Champagne in 1:34⅘, and though his campaign consisted of three races, Seattle Slew was voted America's champion 2-year-old.

A red-hot Winter Book favorite for the classics, Seattle Slew made only one start prior to the Flamingo, winning at Hialeah on March 9. He was 1-10 and made the odds look like a bargain as he won off by nine lengths, his seven furlongs in 1:20⅗. He was 1-5 in the glamorous Flamingo on March 26 and was punctual as ever, winning by four lengths with his nine furlongs in a crisp 1:47⅖. Then he was shipped back to New York and completed his classic preparation in the Wood Memorial at Aqueduct on April 23, winning by more than three lengths as a 1-10 favorite.

The large crowd on hand at Churchill Downs on May 7 came to see the coronation of a four-legged king in the 1977 Kentucky Derby and gasped when the 1-2 Seattle Slew, breaking from Post 1, appeared hemmed in on the rail going past the stands for the first time. Then they saw him push aside a horse blocking him in front, take the lead with his prodigious speed, and win by almost two lengths for his seventh consecutive victory without a defeat.

His Preakness at Pimlico on May 21 was another triumph. Bet down to 2-5, he won by a length and a half and arrived in New York as a star of the first magnitude for the Belmont Stakes June 11. The muddy track on Belmont Day didn't make a bit of difference. Favored at 2-5, he won by four lengths, Cruguet jubilantly shaking his whip in the air as he passed the winning post. It was his ninth consecutive victory and the principal impetus behind his selection as Horse of the Year 1977.

Turner announced plans for a lengthy rest and pulled Seattle Slew's shoes, but the colt's owners had a different agenda and ordered him sent to California for the Swaps Stakes on July 3. It was a dreadful mistake. Favored at 1-5, he sustained his first loss, finishing fourth in a race won by the English crack, J.O. Tobin. Horse and trainer, both completely drained, were through for the year. Turner was replaced by another young horseman, Doug Peterson.

Sent to Florida as he turned 4, Seattle Slew almost died at Hialeah. He contracted a form of colitis, taxed the skills of several prominent veterinarians, but pulled through and made his seasonal debut at Aqueduct on May 14. Favored at 1-10, he looked like the Slew of old, winning by more than eight lengths on a sloppy track. Then another set-back kept him in the barn for three months until August 12, when he won at Saratoga going seven furlongs. His 1:21⅗ on a sloppy track signaled his sharpness.

Thus there was disappointment when he finished second by a neck to Dr. Patches in the Paterson Handicap at the Meadowlands on the evening of September 5. Dr. Patches carried 114 pounds to Slew's 128, but most observers felt it was Angel Cordero Jr,. aboard Dr. Patches, that made the major difference. Seattle Slew's owners felt the same way. Cruguet was replaced by Cordero for the Marlboro Cup at Belmont, 11 days later, and Seattle Slew, favored at 2-1, won by three lengths, the nine furlongs in a sprightly 1:45⅘ under topweight of 128 pounds.

Slew certified his form in the subsequent Woodward Stakes on

Jean Cruguet waved his stick crossing the finish line with Seattle Slew in the 1977 Belmont Stakes, then returned to the winner's circle where trainer Billy Turner Jr. and a blanket of carnations awaited the Triple Crown winner.

September 30, winning by four lengths as the 3-10 choice and accomplishing the mile and a quarter in a sprightly 2:00. That set the stage for the memorable Jockey Club Gold Cup of 1978, one of the great races of our time. It featured two Triple Crown winners in the 4-year-old Seattle Slew and the 3-year-old Affirmed, plus the imported Exceller. Slew raced Affirmed into defeat in the mile and a half test but couldn't hold off the late-charging Exceller who prevailed by a nose in 2:27⅕ on a sloppy track.

Seattle Slew made a triumphant farewell to racing at Aqueduct on November 11, winning the nine-furlong Stuyvesant Handicap. Favored at 1-10, he won by more than three lengths in 1:47⅖ while carrying topweight of 134 pounds. Jumping Hill, the runner-up, was pulling 19 pounds at 115. A nice stakes-winner, he wasn't in the same league with Seattle Slew, who went home to Kentucky with a record of 14 wins from 17 starts and earnings of $1,208,726.

Affirmed, one of the most determined horses ever to race in this country, never lost a photo, and the only time he finished out of the money in 29 starts was when his saddle slipped in the Jockey Club Gold Cup of 1978. That was the season he swept the Triple Crown and was voted Horse of the Year, the first of two consecutive championships for the the home-bred Exclusive Native colt out of Won't Tell You, by Crafty Admiral, owned by the Harbor View Farm of the Louis Wolfsons and trained by Laz Barrera.

Barrera was born in Cuba, became a teen-aged handicapper for a Havana newspaper, and then a horse trainer. When Castro came to power, Barrera moved to Mexico City where he quickly became leading trainer at Hipodromo de las Americas. He moved to California in the early 1960s, then went to New York where he began to fashion a top reputation in a third country. He rose to prominence in the late 1960s, and when he saddled the smallish Bold Forbes to win the Kentucky Derby and Belmont Stakes of 1976, he became a national figure. He was elected to the Hall of Fame in 1979.

Three days after Seattle Slew won the Preakness of 1977, en route to a sweep of the Triple Crown, Affirmed made his debut at Belmont Park. Sent off at 14-1 in a field of 10, he led all the way

Trainer Laz Barrera (right) and jockey Laffit Pincay Jr. were ecstatic with the prowess of Affirmed in 1979.

under Bernie Gonzalez to win by more than four lengths at five and a half furlongs. They may have overlooked him the first time, but Affirmed was 3-1 for his second start on June 15, the Youthful Stakes, with Angel Cordero Jr. in the irons. This time he was reserved just off a lively pace, took command at the furlong pole and stood a hard drive to register by a neck.

With two wins from two starts, including a stakes victory, Affirmed would normally have been favored when he came out for his third appearance in Belmont's Great American Stakes on July 6. Instead the wiseguys and the figure men went for a big, rugged Calumet FarmRaise A Native colt named Alydar who was impressive in his debut. They were right. Alydar won by more than three lengths with a five-pound pull in the weights.

That was the start of thoroughbred racing's greatest rivalry: an extraordinary sequence of major races over a two-season period in which Affirmed and Alydar were always the principal protagonists. Their most glamorous stage, of course, was the Triple Crown competition of 1978, and the climax of this melodramatic cut-and-thrust was the Belmont Stakes, in which the two colts were at each other's throats for the last mile of the mile and a half distance, with Affirmed the better of the two by precisely half an inch.

Affirmed made his first transcontinental trip as a 2-year-old in late July to capture the Hollywood Juvenile Championship by seven lengths and three weeks later was at Saratoga to win the Sanford. Steve Cauthen, America's leading apprentice of 1976, had the mount on Affirmed for the first time in the Sanford.

Affirmed and Alydar got together for the second time in Saratoga's Hopeful Stakes on August 17. His victory in the Great American made Alydar the favorite in the Hopefu, but this time they were head-and-head much of the way and Affirmed never was beaten under such circumstances. You could charge past him with a sudden move and beat him that way, but you could not look him in the eye and win. He was one of the most determined horses we ever had the pleasure of watching.

At the end of the Hopeful, with Affirmed clocked in a speedy 1:15⅖ for the six and a half furlongs, the Harbor View colt had half a length on Alydar. Two weeks later, at Belmont Park, they were at it again. Once more it was hand-to-hand combat in the streets, and this time Affirmed's margin was a nose.

By now the nation was aware of the rivalry, and great attention was focused on the two colts whenever they raced. Alydar's people were also aware of the relentless nature of Affirmed, and they moved to deal with it in the next meeting of the two in the Champagne Stakes at Belmont on October 15. Affirmed was the 6-5 favorite but Alydar was reserved off the pace, finished strongest of all, and

Steve Cauthen – "The Kid" – guided Affirmed to a Triple Crown in 1978.

rushed past Affirmed to tally by a length and a quarter on a muddy track.

The Laurel Futurity on October 29 was the final start of the season for both colts. With the results of the Champagne in mind, both camps planned an easy first half-mil,e and they were one-two after four furlongs in :48⅕. That left them both with plenty of energy for the drive and they staged a beauty, Affirmed winning by a neck. Star de Naskra, a nice colt who would win the Whitney at Saratoga in 1979, finished 10 lengths behind Alydar in third place. Affirmed and Alydar were simply at another level.

Affirmed went to California for the winter while John Veitch, Alydar's trainer, followed his usual custom and went to Florida. Florida had the better weather, and Alydar was ready for his 3-year-old debut on February 11 at Hialeah in a seven-furlong allowance race. He won easily under Jorge Velasquez, timed in a crisp 1:22⅕. California, by contrast, had one of its wettest winters and the constant rains kept Affirmed in the barn at Santa Anita. To give the colt a little exercise, Laz Barrera took to daily jogs around the shedrow. Barrera waited as long as he dared and finally put Affirmed in a race March 8, almost a month after Alydar's first appearance of the year and four days following Alydar's four and a half-length victory in Hialeah's important Flamingo Stakes. Alydar rocketed the nine furlongs in 1:47.

The rivals each had one more appearance prior to the Triple

Crown, and they made the most of their opportunity. Affirmed won the Hollywood Derby on April 16 by two convincing lengths under Cauthen, timed in 1:48⅕ for the mile and an eighth after leading all the way. Alydar went to Keeneland for the Blue Grass Stakes on April 27, a traditional date nine days before the Kentucky Derby. Favored at 1-10 in a field of nine, he came from off the pace to win by a spectacular 13 lengths, timed in 1:49⅗ on a "good" track.

Admiral and Mrs. Gene Markey of Calumet Farm, owners of Alydar, were in their 80s and in relatively poor health. The Keeneland management made arrangements for them to drive from their farm, just down the Versailles Pike, to the track, and to park their station wagon alongside the outer rail across from the eighth pole to see the race as quietly as possible. During the post parade, Jorge Velasquez brought Alydar over to the Markeys so they could see him up close, and he even got the colt to bow to Mrs. Markey as a salute.

On the basis of Alydar's impressive tally in the Blue Grass, and with the unparalleled success of Calumet Farm in the Kentucky Derby, it was not surprising to find Alydar the 6-5 favorite as the annual Triple Crown drama opened at Churchill Downs. Affirmed was 9-5 second choice in a field of 11, and there was solid support as well for Sensitive Prince and Believe It.

Sensitive Prince, with his speed, was the leader by three lengths at the half-mile pole, timed in :45⅗. Believe It surged on the turn, took command at the quarter-pole, but raced wide through the stretch. Affirmed, lurking off the pace, moved with Believe It and relieved the latter of the lead near the three-sixteenths pole. The Harbor View colt was in front by two lengths at the eighth pole and stood a hard drive gamely to hold Alydar safe by a length and a half. Alydar was not as effective as usual during the initial stages but got back into gear toward the end to finish purposefully. The winning time of 2:01⅕ was a full second faster than the previous year's Derby

won by Seattle Slew.

The exciting rivalry between Affirmed and Alydar reached new heights in the Preakness on May 20 before a record Pimlico crowd of 81,261. Only five challenged the Big Two, and four of the five had no business in the classic. Affirmed went to the front down the backstretch, rated easily on the lead, getting the first six furlongs in 1:11⅘. Alydar, far back during the early stages, moved up around the far turn and was almost abreast of Affirmed as they straightened for home. Affirmed led by a head at the eighth pole and the crowd, in a frenzy, cheered both colts to the echo as they passed the winning post a neck apart. Good horse though he was, Alydar couldn't gain a fraction of an inch on Affirmed from the furlong pole home.

The Belmont on June 10 drew 65,417, most of whom anticipated a fitting climax to an absorbing drama. They were not disappointed. Affirmed went to the front at the break from post 3 while Alydar, from post 2, settled in stride early and then went after Affirmed with seven furlongs remaining. They were virtually even after the first mile, and a head apart after a mile and a quarter in 2:01⅗. Affirmed held that margin to the centimeter for the final quarter-mile under incredible pressure. Leaving the furlong pole, when Alydar appeared ready to assert himself, Cauthen reached down and, for the first time, hit his colt left-handed, a surprise he'd been saving for a long time. He received a heartening response and Affirmed won by a head, the mile and a half in 2:26⅘.

There was a brief respite after the classics, but Alydar, showing amazing recuperative powers and a deep reservoir of energy, gave one of his most impressive performances in late June when he galloped to victory in the Arlington Classic. Then, in early August, he beat older horses handily in the Whitney at Saratoga, carrying 123 pounds or four pounds above scale. These exceptional efforts indicated just how good a horse he was, and how good a horse was the one who beat him.

Affirmed had only one race between the Belmont and the Travers but it was sensational. Saratoga's Jim Dandy on August 8 drew a field of five including the swift and talented Sensitive Prince. Affirmed was the 1-20 favorite despite topweight of 128 pounds, but when Sensitive Prince, pulling nine pounds, opened an eight-length advantage down the backstretch, the natives became restless. At the eighth pole, Sensitive Prince was still four lengths ahead of Affirmed but at the wire, with applause ringing in his ears, it was Affirmed in front by half a length.

Thus the stage was set for the ancient Travers on August 19, and the Big Two looked so formidable that only two other opponents entered. Cauthen injured a knee in a spill a few days prior to the Travers and Laz Barrera put in a phone call to Laffit Pincay Jr., who had ridden Affirmed twice before and won the Hollywood Juvenile and the Santa Anita Derby in collaboration. Fans began to descend on Saratoga Springs early that Saturday morning and by post time some 50,000 — a record number — were on the grounds, with cars parked everywhere, up and down Union Avenue.

Affirmed, with his speed, was forwardly placed from the outset, and led down the backstretch, with Alydar settling into stride and well back initially. Then Alydar started to move, and as he approached Affirmed near the five-eighths pole, Pincay appeared agitated. Suddenly, in what appeared to be a spasmodic gesture, Pincay reined Affirmed toward the rail and Alydar, striking Affirmed on the rump, was thrown off stride.

The incident brought to mind a situation in the Preakness of 1962 when Manual Ycaza, on the co-favorite Ridan, stuck his elbow out in an apparent attempt to impede the on-coming Greek Money, with John L. Rotz in the saddle. Greek Money got up to win by a nose, sparing the gentlemanly Rotz from lodging a complaint. But many of the news photographers lining the inner rail area had the shot, and the whole world knew the next morning.

Affirmed (right) had a tenacious rival in Alydar, but proved good enough by inches to win his Belmont Stakes and sweep the 1978 Triple Crown races.

Affirmed, recovering quickly from the bumping incident, regained command of the Travers, was two lengths in front at the furlong pole and won by a length and three-quarters from Alydar. The stewards immediately posted the "inquiry" sign, however, and after reviewing the video tape disqualified Affirmed for interference and awarded the race to Alydar. Since Alydar lost all chance because of Pincay's action, the officials had little choice.

It was an unsatisfactory ending to what could have been a great race, and it was even a greater shame when, a couple of weeks later, Alydar fractured the wing of a coffin bone in his right front foot and was retired. That was the conclusion of thoroughbred racing's greatest rivalry, which deserved a more dramatic denouement. As for Affirmed, he went from the Travers into the rich Marlboro Cup at Belmont on September 16. Billed as a rare battle of Triple Crown winners, the Marlboro Cup field of six was headed by Affirmed and Seattle Slew, and it was a mark of respect that the 3-year-old went off the favorite at 1-2. The more mature Seattle Slew was the better horse that day, however, and won their personal battle by three lengths.

Affirmed made one more start as a 3-year-old, in the Jockey Club Gold Cup on October 14, but lost all chance on the first turn when his saddle slipped. In a memorable finish, Exceller won by a nose over Seattle Slew.

Steve Cauthen, rebounding from the spill at Saratoga, rode Affirmed in the Marlboro Cup and Jockey Club Gold Cup. When Affirmed came out at 4 in the seven-furlong Malibu at Santa Anita on January 7, Cauthen was in the saddle again. But Affirmed, hemmed into the stretch, found racing room too late and had to settle for third money as the 3-10 favorite.

Two weeks later, the nine-furlong San Fernando, Affirmed drifted through the stretch run and was beaten by Radar Ahead, who couldn't warm him up under normal circumstances. Cauthen, unable to ride a winner of any kind, was under heavy pressure from the media and the public. When he was taken of Affirmed by Laz Barrera, he accepted an offer from Robert Sangster to ride in England, where he created a brilliant new career for himself.

The switch from Cauthen to Pincay also proved effective for Affirmed, who, as 9-10 favorite, won the Charles Strub Stakes on February 4 by 10 lengths. Then, to prove that tally no fluke, Affirmed came back in the Santa Anita Handicap on March 4 and carried topweight of 128 pounds to a four and a half-length victory, setting a track record of 1:58⅗ for the mile and a quarter.

Affirmed was better than ever at 4 and never lost another race. From the Big Cap he went to the Californian at Hollywood Park on May 20 and gave a dazzling performance under 130 pounds. He led from start to finish in the mile and a sixteenth test, won by five lengths as a 3-10 choice, and conceded 16 pounds to the runner-up, Syncopate. Five weeks later, in the Hollywood Gold Cup, he again made use of his speed and just missed a track record with a mile and a quarter in 1:58⅖ under 132 pounds.

Barrera give him a holiday during the summer's hottest two months, shipped East for fall racing, and sharpened him in a betless exhibition at Belmont on August 29. Affirmed waltzed home by six lengths and was favored at 2-5 in the Woodward on September 22. He made it look easy, winning by two and a half lengths with something left. Facing Kentucky Derby and Preakness winner Spectacular Bid in the Jockey Club Gold Cup on October 6, Affirmed's maturity was decisive. He led most of the way as Pincay slowed the pace to a first half-mile in :49, then had plenty left and tallied by three-quarters of a length, the mile and a half in 2:27⅖. Coastal, the Belmont winner, finished third.

The Gold Cup was Affirmed's seventh consecutive victory, and he went to stud with a formidable collection of honors, including consecutive selections as Horse of the Year. His overall record was

22 wins from 29 starts and earnings of $2,393,818. He was 2-year-old champion, 3-year-old champion and handicap champion, and won important races on the East Coast and the West Coast. If Seattle Slew enjoyed a slight edge in brilliance, and that is clearly subjective judgment, Affirmed had the edge in achievement.

The third horse in this trilogy of the '70s was Spectacular Bid, a rugged grey colt by Bold Bidder from Spectacular, by Promised Land, owned by Baltimore's Harry Meyerhoff in partnership with his son, Tommy, and wife, Theresa. Meyerhoff's family were developers, and he worked building homes for a time before retiring to the Eastern Shore. Harry and his brother, Robert, raced a stable together in the '60's and had some success, but then went their separate ways.

Trainer Grover (Bud) Delp, a Maryland native, grew up in racing and saddled his first winner at age 30 in 1962. He was leading trainer at Delaware Park from 1963 to 1972, and was also leading trainer at such tracks as Arlington Park, Hawthorne, Pimlico, and Monmouth Park. By 1990 he registered his 3,000th winner. Of these, Spectacular Bid, purchased as a yearling for $37,000, was a standout.

Spectacular Bid came to the races on June 30, 1978, at Pimlico, winning at first asking. Sent off at 6-1, he was prominent early, led the rest of the way under stable rider Ron Franklin, and won by more than three lengths in a lively 1:04⅗, just two-fifths of a second off the track record. He must have left an impression because he dropped from 6-1 to 3-10 for his second start on July 22, again at Pimlico. This time he equaled the track record, going five and a half

Bud Delp called Spectacular Bid the "best horse to ever look through a bridle."

furlongs in 1:04 ⅕, and drawing away toward the end to score by eight lengths.

People were beginning to talk about the grey colt when he went to Monmouth for the August 2 running of the Tyro. In a field of eight, Spectacular Bid was favored at 17-10. However, he was permitted to race wide early and couldn't overcome the handicap he gave himself, finishing fourth. He made his next appearance in the Dover Stakes at Delaware Park on August 20, closed well from off the pace to finish second to Strike Your Colors, a colt he beat easily the day he broke his maiden.

Spectacular Bid turned the corner in time for the World's Playground Stakes at Atlantic City on September 23, leading much of the way and winning off by 15 lengths after seven furlongs in a near-record 1:20⅘. He was to win his next 11 starts as well, making for a string of 12 that ended in the Belmont Stakes the following June.

His World's Playground tour de force earned him a berth in the Champagne Stakes at Belmont Park. His people wanted a New York rider and Jorge Velasquez, then in his prime, took over from the relatively inexperienced Franklin. Spectacular Bid was as good as his name in the Champagne, winning off by almost three lengths from the well-regarded General Assembly, the mile in 1:34⅘. Nothing could stand in his way. He followed his Champagne appearance with triumphs in the Young America at the Meadowlands, the Laurel Futurity, and the Heritage at Keystone Park, trainer Delp proclaiming Spectacular Bid to be the greatest horse ever to look through a bridle. Completing his 2-year-old campaign, he cominated the picture for the spring classics.

Spectacular Bid made his 3-year-old debut on Feb. 7, 1979, in the Hutcheson Stakes at seven furlongs. Favored at 1-20 in a lackluster field of four, he rated off a sizzling pace – the first half-mile in :44⅘ – then surged entering the stretch. He was in front by three lengths at the furlong pole and won by almost four lengths with Ronnie Franklin aboard, timed in 1:21⅖.

The Hutcheson set him up perfectly for the Fountain of Youth Stakes on February 19, and Spectacular Bid won easily by eight and a half lengths as a 1-10 choice. The big grey colt stood out over the local 3-year-olds and was 1-20 again when he faced six opponents in the Florida Derby on March 6. It should have been a cut-and-dried deal, but Franklin managed to inject some melodrama with possibly the worst ride in the history of horseracing. The Bid visited every part of the track except the Directors' Room, was tugged and shuffled this way and that, and still won by more than four lengths, his nine furlongs in 1:48⅖.

"I think I'll have a chat with the rider," Delp said later. Whatever he said was effective, for Franklin rode a sensible, businesslike race in Hialeah's Flamingo on March 24, and The Bid won easily by 12 lengths. Nor did he harm his prospects in Keeneland's Blue Grass Stakes. Favored at 1-20 in a field of four, Bid led most of the way to tally by seven lengths.

The 105th Kentucky Derby on May 5 attracted a relatively small field of 10, and the Churchill Downs crowd liked Spectacular Bid at 3-5. There was a murmur when Bid, ducking in slightly from post 3, left the gate well toward the rear of the pack. Racing in the middle of the track, he rallied strongly down the backstretch, accelerated around the turn, and was head-and-head with General Assembly at the head of the stretch. Bid was best, leading by a length and a half at the furlong pole and almost three lengths at the wire.

The trip to the Preakness was a homecoming for Spectacular Bid and his connections, and it was a joyous two weeks in Baltimore, capped by the middle jewel of the Triple Crown on May 19. Bid, his reputation bigger than life, personally reduced the field to four opponents, and he was favored at 1-10. By way of comparison, Secretariat was a 3-10 favorite in his Preakness and Count Fleet was favored at 15 cents to the dollar when he ran for the Black-Eyed Susans.

Only five ran in that Preakness, but there was still trouble leaving the gate when Flying Paster, breaking from post 1, angled out and bumped The Bid, breaking from post 2. The favorite was well back in the early stages but moved up around the turn and had the lead at the quarter pole. Exploding at that point, Bid led by six at the furlong pole, was roused by Franklin with six left-handed strokes of the whip and finished first by five and a half lengths.

Having enjoyed Triple Crown winners in each of the two preceding seasons, it was taken for granted by most racing men that Spectacular Bid would follow the example of Seattle Slew and Affirmed for the 111th Belmont on June 9.

An 85-1 shot, Gallant Best, opened a lead of five lengths at the start of the Belmont, and Ronnie Franklin, on Spectacular Bid, quickly took after him. It was an irrational pursuit, and The Bid paid for his exertions through the stretch run. Coastal and Golden Act, racing in the middle of the field, moved together. They were third and fourth to Spectacular Bid and General Assembly at the head of the stretch. When those two gave way under pressure, Coastal and Golden Act took over, and Coastal had the most in reserve, winning by three and a quarter lengths.

In retrospect, Spectacular Bid had several excuses for this defeat. On Monday of Belmont Week, he had a severe work on a sloppy, tiring track and came back breathing deeply, though he was a dead fit horse after the Derby and Preakness. Then, on the morning of Belmont Day, there was the incident of the safety pin. The groom reportedly found that Bid stepped on a pin during the evening. A veterinarian was called in and treated the foot, but nothing was said about the matter until after the race. Finally, there was Franklin's witless ride, chasing a horse who had no chance.

The Bid had a lengthy holiday after the stress of the Triple Crown campaign, and during that period, Delp conferred with the Meyerhoffs. The owners wanted a change of riders, specifically to Bill Shoemaker, and Delp found it difficult to raise an objection. So it was that Shoe was in the irons when Spectacular Bid returned to competition at Delaware Park on August 26 in a mile and a sixteenth overnight race that drew a field of five. Favored at 1-20, he won by 17 lengths and bettered the track record by a fifth of a second. That was his preparation for the Marlboro Cup at Belmont Park on Sept. 8. Once again, Bid was spectacular. He ran a mile and an eighth in 1:46⅗, won off by five lengths from General Assembly and by more than six lengths from Coastal, to whom he was conceding two pounds.

Bid suffered the last defeat of his career a month later in the Jockey Club Gold Cup. The 4-year-old Affirmed, favored at 3-5 over the 3-year-old Spectacular Bid, led all the way at a mile and a half to score by three-quarters of a length, weight for age.

Two weeks after the Jockey Club Gold Cup, Bid won the Meadowlands Cup in New Jersey by three lengths, setting a track record with his 2:01⅕. Favored at 1-10 in a field of five, he con-

Spectacular Bid was in a class by himself and nothing proved it more than his walkover in the 1980 Woodward at Belmont Park.

cluded his season with a record of 10 wins from 12 starts, a second and a third.

As a 4-year-old, Bid did even better: He was undefeated in nine starts.

Spectacular Bid's final victory that year was one of the most memorable. When it was announced that he would run in Belmont Park's Woodward Stakes at weight for age on September 20, the news was greeted by deafening silence. Few were eager to run against him in handicaps, *with* a weight concession. At level weights, even fewer. Winter's Tale, a top handicapper, was originally scheduled for the Woodward but injured himself and was scratched. One or two others, who also signified an intention to run, changed plans. Thus, the Woodward was a walkover, but even with no opposition, Bid did it in style. He went the mile and a quarter in 2:02⅖, while the previous fall, Affirmed, with keen competition, was timed in 2:01⅗. The Woodward brought Bid's record for the season to a sparkling nine-for-nine.

He had done it all and was an overwhelming choice of the voters as America's Horse of the Year.

In retrospect, the decade of the 1970s was perhaps the most remarkable in American racing history for having produced Secretariat, Ruffian, Forego, John Henry, and those superb boys of all seasons: Seattle Slew, Affirmed and Spectacular Bid.

The entire Secretariat family gathered in Kentucky when "Big Red" went to stud. Groom Eddie Sweat held the champion, while trainer Lucien Laurin, jockey Ron Turcotte and owner Penny Chenery looked on.

Man o' War was easily the greatest American racehorse of the first half of the 20th Century and Secretariat just as clearly deserved that distinction during the second half. Both these magnificent chestnut colts went by the nickname of Big Red, and both were outstanding physical specimens. Both compiled superior records. Man o' War won 20 of 21 starts, with one second. Secretariat won 16 of 21, with three seconds and a third. But beyond statistics, both had a commanding presence that stamped them as special among their species.

The Secretariat story really began in the summer of 1969 at Belmont Park, where a group of prominent racing people gathered in the office of Alfred G. Vanderbilt, chairman of the New York Racing Association, for lunch and the toss of a coin. There was Ogden Phipps, chairman of The Jockey Club, accompanied by his trainer, Eddie Neloy. Penny Chenery Tweedy, daughter of the great sportsman, Christopher T. Chenery, attended in place of her father, who was seriously ill. Mrs. Tweedy was accompanied by farm manager Howard Gentry. And there was A.B. "Bull" Hancock of Claiborne Farm. Everyone wanted to breed to Bold Ruler so the Phippses called the tune and, undoubtedly on the recommendation of Bull Hancock, it was foal-sharing. Selected breeders were invited to send two mares to Bold Ruler, and by the toss of a coin, one foal would go to the owner of the mares and the other to the Phipps family.

The Chenery family had sent mares to Bold Ruler in 1967 and 1968, with somewhat disappointing results, and arranged another two-year deal for 1969 and 1970. The mares chosen for 1969 were stakes-winning Hasty Matelda, who had a Bold Ruler colt, and Somethingroyal, dam of Sir Gaylord, who had a Bold Ruler filly. For the 1970 foals, the Chenerys chose Somethingroyal and their champion racemare, Cicada.

Bull Hancock tossed the coin, and while it was in the air, Phipps called "heads." It was a toss he was hoping to lose because it was known that Cicada was barren. Thus, the loser of the coin toss for the 1969 breeding would get the first and only foal of the 1970 foals, if Somethingroyal produced a live foal. Hancock permitted the coin to fall on the carpet and it came up heads. Phipps chose Somethingroyal's filly, who raced as The Bride while the Chenery family now owned Hasty Matelda's colt, named Rising River, plus the foal Somethingroyal was carrying.

The events of the next two years were curiously intertwined.

Chris Chenery, who played such an instrumental role in the formation of the New York Racing Association and the building of Aqueduct and Belmont Park, never recovered, and his daughter, Penny, helped direct the family stable and stud, with input from Chenery's long-time secretary, Elizabeth Ham. Chenery's trainer of many years, Casey Hayes, who developed such good ones as Prince Hill, Hill Prince, Third Brother, Cicada and Sir Gaylord, retired and was succeeded by young Roger Laurin, son of the veteran horseman, Lucien Laurin.

Lucien Laurin (left) and Ron Turcotte formed a winning team with the Meadow Stable stars Riva Ridge and Secretariat.

his physical talents. The trainer proceeded conservatively, but everything Secretariat did was meaningful. There was also tremendous interest in the big red colt by the media, because of his breeding, and reporters began dropping by the barn to monitor his progress.

Secretariat came to the races on July 4, 1972, about a month after Riva Ridge won the Belmont Stakes. Riva Ridge had won the Kentucky Derby easily, by almost four lengths, to give C.T. Chenery his first victory in the Run for the Roses. But he slipped and slid on a sloppy track at Pimlico to finish fourth

Somethingroyal foaled a big, muscular colt by Bold Ruler named Secretariat. In the spring of 1971, Eddie Neloy died of a heart attack at Belmont Park. The Phippses invited Roger Laurin to succeed Neloy, and Laurin recommended his father to succeed him as trainer of the Chenerys' Meadow Stable.

Lucien Laurin, in his first season on the job, developed the 2-year-old champion Riva Ridge for the Chenerys, while his son, Roger, developed the 2-year-old filly champion, Numbered Account, for the Phippses. The two champions met that fall in the Garden State Stakes, one of the biggest races of the era, and the colt beat the filly soundly.

That winter at Hialeah, Lucien Laurin received the Bold Ruler colt from the farm, and he was impressed with his appearance and

in the Preakness. There had been no Triple Crown winner since Citation in 1948, and people wondered if there would ever be another.

Secretariat was the 3-2 favorite in his debut and ran well for apprentice Paul Feliciano but was impeded at a crucial point. Finishing strongly to be fourth, he was beaten a length and a quarter for all the money in a field of 12, and many thought he was best. There was no question who was best 11 days later when Secretariat won a maiden race by six lengths, again coming from well off the pace with Feliciano up.

From that point on, the season was a steady parade of firsts for Secretariat. He was forced to give one back after the Champagne when he was disqualified for bearing in through the stretch run but he was best that day, too, and in all the others. Ron Turcotte got on him for his third start, at Saratoga on July 31, and Secretariat lagged early but finished full of run to register by a length and a half, apparently with something left as befits a 2-5 favorite. The Sanford and Hopeful stakes at the Spa resulted in easy victories, and Secretariat also made light work of the Futurity Stakes at Belmont on September 16, for which he was favored at 1-5.

The Champagne was a shame because he was best. He finished first by two lengths after racing a mile in 1:35 but came in on horses, and the stewards had no alternative but a disqualification, but two weeks later, on October 28 in the Laurel Futurity, Secretariat won by eight lengths in a manner befitting a 1-10 choice. He missed the track record for a mile and a sixteenth by a fifth of a second.

Secretariat brought his 2-year-old campaign to an end on November 18 in the Garden State. Part of an entry with Angle Light, owned by Canadian industrialist Edwin Whittaker, whose horses were trained by Lucien Laurin, Secretariat was reserved off the early pace. Ron Turcote moved him toward the leaders on the turn and Secretariat took command in mid-stretch, cruising away to win by three and a half lengths. He won rather easily, as he'd done in all of his victories, and he impressed everyone with his immense talent.

At season's end the voters in the recently organized Eclipse Awards balloting did something they hadn't done before or since. They chose a 2-year-old as Horse of the Year. Inspired by the trenchant prose and unabashed adulation of *Daily Racing Form*'s senior columnist Charles Hatton, they dismissed the achievements of the best older horse, Cougar II, the best older mare, Typecast, the champion 3-year-old colt, Key to the Mint, the champion 3-year-old filly, Susan's Girl, and all the others in favor of Secretariat.

It was a final honor for Christopher T. Chenery, who died in the waning hours of the Old Year, leaving a sizeable estate and a crushing inheritance tax burden of about $12 million. The Chenery children had few options except the sale of all the horses. That wouldn't have been a hardship for Penny Chenery Tweedy's sister or brothers but it was unthinkable for her. She phoned Claiborne Farm.

In early August of 1972, Bull Hancock flew to Ireland for a golfing and shooting holiday. He didn't feel well upon arrival, however, and went to see a doctor. The diagnosis was grim: cancer. He flew home and was dead in six weeks. The trustees of the farm and the estate were headed by Odgen Phipps. He selected 23-year-old Seth Hancock to succeed his father, bypassing the eldest son, Arthur Hancock 3rd.

Arthur Hancock eventually sold his interests in Claiborne Farm, founded his own Stone Farm on property adjacent to Claiborne, and became a successful breeder, winning Kentucky Derbys with homebreds Gato Del Sol and Sunday Silence. Seth Hancock, with little formal preparation for the exacting responsibility of directing the huge Clairborne Farm operation, studied intensely and was on an even keel when, a few months later, the call came from Penny Chenery Tweedy. He considered her problem and recommended syndication of Secretariat and Riva Ridge. Secretariat, who was getting ready for his 3-year-old debut, was obviously the priority consideration. After playing with figures and making a few calls, he phoned to say he thought he could syndicate Secretariat for racing and breeding at a world-record figure of $6 million. The actual price was $190,000 a share for 32 shares or $6.08 million, Claiborne receiving four breeding rights for its efforts.

The price was staggering at the time; racing's equivalent of Sonny Werblin signing Joe Namath to a $400,000 three-year contract in an era when top quarterbacks averaged less than $50,000 a year. Namath came through to sell out Shea Stadium, lead the New York Jets to a Super Bowl victory, and make his price seem like a bargain. Secretariat came through, too, though all concerned had a few anxious moments that spring.

Going into the first turn at Churchill Downs, Secretariat could see them all in the 1973 Kentucky Derby, but by the finish he was two and a half-lengths in front and on his way to a track record.

and a half lengths. It was a good start, but not sensational, and some of the new syndicate members must have wondered what they'd bought until Secretariat came out for his second race, the Gotham Mile on April 7. Sent off at 1-10 in a field of six, he led all the way to win by three lengths, the eight furlongs in an eye-catching 1:33⅖. It was the fastest mile ever run in New York by a 3-year-old, and the Gotham results electrified the racing world.

Sham, owned by Sigmund Sommer and trained by Frank Martin, won the Santa Anita Derby of 1973, equaling Lucky Debonair's stakes record of 1:47

Seth Hancock, on the telephone around the clock, was able to complete the syndication in a matter of days. Later that season, he syndicated the 4-year-old Riva Ridge for $5.4 million and the Chenery family was able to meet the tax bill on the estate. Once Secretariat was sold, the first order of business was making plans for his return to the races. There was some thought about trying to get him ready for the Flamingo in early March, but Lucien Laurin quickly shot down that proposal. He refused to rush his horse, who began to train forwardly about the time he was to leave for New York.

Secretariat made his long-awaited 3-year-old debut at Aqueduct on St. Patrick's Day, 1973, in the seven-furlong Bay Shore. Favored at 1-5 in a field of six, he came off the pace nicely to win by four

for the nine furlongs. He returned to New York for the Wood Memorial, adding great interest to that traditional feature because of the confrontation with Secretariat. Here was a worthy adversary for the big red colt and there was quite a build-up in the press.

The result of the Wood was shocking. Secretariat, never really in the hunt, made a move around the final turn but then hung and finished third as part of an entry favored at 3-10. It was the other part of the entry, Angle Light, who saved the day, beating Sham by a head in a relatively undistinguished 1:49⅘ for nine furlongs. Lucien Laurin, watching the race from his box, couldn't believe his eyes and sat comatose until someone nudged him and reminded him that he also trained the winner. He went downstairs with a heavy heart to join Ed Whittaker in accepting the trophy.

"Looking back at the whole affair," Ron Turcotte recalled, "Secretariat was trying to tell me something. During the running of the Wood, he threw his head in the air several times and was simply not the same horse he was in the Gotham Mile two weeks earlier. There was another sign, even before the race. An assistant starter touched his mouth and he went through the gate. But I wasn't looking for signs. He'd been running well and training well, and no one told me anything was wrong. I took stock mentally, galloping back to unsaddle. His legs were okay. His breathing was okay. But something wasn't right."

The second-guessing began after the Wood, and it was heated. Some said Secretariat was not worth what had been paid for him. Others expressed doubt he could get the Derby trip of a mile and a quarter. And those were the favorable comments. Laurin shipped his two colts to Louisville, still in a trance, and the situation didn't improve the next Friday morning when the big, red colt drilled six furlongs at Churchill Downs in 1:12 ⅗ on a sloppy track.

"It wasn't a good work," Turcotte said. "I flew down from New York to get on him, and he just wasn't the Secretariat I knew. I was beginning to get concerned. But when I went down there to work him again on the Wednesday before the Derby, it was a different story. The track was sloppy again, just as it was for his first work, but this time he flew. He went five furlongs in :58⅗ and I felt he was the real Secretariat. After the work, his groom, Eddie Sweat, told me the abscess had finally broken.

"I didn't know what he was talking about because no one had mentioned an abscess to me," Turcotte continued. "But I flew back to New York after the work and I ran into Dr. (Manuel) Gilman at the track. He was the chief examining veterinarian of the New York Racing Association in those days and he checked all the horses before they ran. He told me Secretariat had an abscess under one lip prior to the Wood. All of a sudden, the pieces began to fit together."

Turcotte said that Secretariat's excellent work and the news about the abscess gave him renewed confidence in the colt. He went into the Derby confident about the outcome, but trainer Laurin didn't really breath easily until after the race. On the Friday morning before the Derby, the trainer went to the barn as usual, galloped Secretariat, watched him cool out nicely and returned to his hotel. He had barely returned to his room when the phone rang. Someone called to say that a radio report had Secretariat lame in one knee.

Laurin rushed back to the track, found Secretariat resting comfortably after his mid-morning meal. Shaking his head, Laurin returned to the hotel, his heart and stomach doing the tango together.

Secretariat and Turcotte did their own tango the next day. Coming out of the gate, Secretariat relaxed as Turcotte directed, and raced toward the rear of the 13-horse field. Racing on the outside, Secretariat moved up along the backstretch. Turcotte roused him at the three-eighths pole and he picked up horses quickly.

Meanwhile, Sham, the second choice, was reserved within striking distance of the pace, moved around rivals with no urging, and drew clear entering the stretch as the huge crowd roared, sensing an upset. But Secretariat was now in gear and the two colts were almost abreast as they passed the furlong pole. From the eighth pole home, Secretariat drew out, won by two and a half convincing lengths, and set a track record of 1:59 ⅖ for the mile and a quarter of the 99th Derby, a mark that was still standing after the 120th Derby in 1994. Sham was second, eight lengths ahead of Our Native.

In a twinkling, the red horse had answered all the questions and the press, sensing the first sweep of the Triple Crown since Citation, 25 year earlier in 1948, descended in huge numbers on Lucien Laurin and Penny Tweedy. Both, feeling much better about the situation, were equal to the occasion, and the classic circus adjourned to Baltimore for Act II.

Preakness Week was a party, and Secretariat was the guest of honor. Countless stories were written about every detail of his training and countless features on his life and times appeared on television. A Baltimore station asked me to interview Laurin while Secretariat grazed nearby. As writer and trainer shared a microphone and chatted about the Derby, Red, curious to see what was happening, walked over at the end of Ed Sweat's shank and thrust his head between the two of us. It looked as though he was joining in at the microphone, and it made a lovely scene for television.

There was another lovely scene on the telecast of the Preakness on May 19. Favored at 3-10 in a field of six, Secretariat was eased back at the start, as in the Kentucky Derby, and relaxed immediately for the confident Turcotte. Then Secretariat electrified the crowd by accelerating to the lead entering the backstretch. It was obvious to Turcotte, after a first quarter in :25, that his handful of opponents were going to try to slow the pace to a crawl. Turcotte had an option and chose to exercise it. Never threatened in front, Secretariat raced to a two and a half-length victory and appeared to win with something left.

As the Preakness ended, the board showed a disappointing winning time of 1:55 for the mile and three-sixteenths, against the track record of 1:54. As I was sending the story of the Preakness to *Daily Racing Form*, Gene Schwartz, the paper's chief of clockers, stopped by my desk to show me his watch, which read: 1:53 ⅖. Moments

Turcotte had a lot of kind words for Secretariat as Penny Chenery led the horse to the Belmont winner's circle.

later, Frank Robinson, *DRF*'s chief clocker in Maryland, also came to my desk to report he had the same time as Schwartz.

Daily Racing Form's story reported the difference, and subsequent investigation the next day uncovered the fact that the track's official timer had been assigned additional duties for Preakness Day, which may have compromised his concentration. A hearing into the incident was held by the Maryland Racing Commission, and the official time was later changed to 1:54⅖. However, Secretariat was denied the track record many thought he deserved, and since he also set a record in the Belmont, the apparent miscue at Pimlico was historically unfortunate.

Secretariat returned to New York in triumph, and many racing people, who despaired of ever seeing another sweep of the Triple Crown, were now predicting the red colt's margin of victory in the Belmont Stakes. No one came close. Belmont Week was a media circus and Laurin was interviewed almost around the clock, while Secretariat's photo appeared on the front cover of *Time, Newsweek*, and many other national magazines.

He was the hero of the hour, and if he had won the Belmont by two or three lengths to become the first Triple Crown winner in 25 years, he'd have been hailed as a great champion. But he didn" win by two or three lengths. He won in amazing fashion, befitting a 1-10 choice in a field of five.

In a classic tour de force, Secretariat drew off to a 31-length victory in the 1973 Belmont Stakes to become America's first Triple Crown winner in 25 years.

crowd was on its feet, jumping and cheering and roaring approval. Turcotte kept him going and he won by 31 lengths, setting a track record of 2:24 for the mile and a half as total strangers pounded each other on the back, aware they had witnessed one of the greatest moments in American racing history.

It is the custom to freshen horses who participate in the demanding classics. Some horses are so fatigued that they may not return to their best form until the fall, but Secretariat was a powerhouse on four sturdy legs. He was frisky within days of the Belmont, and Penny Tweedy, anxious to give Midwesterners a chance to see the celebrated colt, agreed to ship him to Chicago for the special Arlington Invitational at nine

Breaking alertly, he raced on the lead with Sham alongside through a quarter in :23⅖, a half-mile in :46⅕, six furlongs in 1:09⅘. At that point, Sham had enough and began falling back while Secretariat picked up momentum. He swept around the turn, drawing away from the others, and the crowd was quick to sense Turcotte's intention to let the red horse run a little instead of conserving him as in the past.

At the end of a mile in 1:34⅕, Secretariat led by 20 lengths. After a mile and a quarter in 1:59, he led by 28 lengths, and now the

furlongs on June 30, three weeks after the Belmont. Secretariat won by nine lengths after leading all the way, timed in a crisp 1:47. Favored at 1-20 in a field of four, he missed the track record by a fifth of a second.

He had a breather in July, then shipped to Saratoga to prepare for his first venture against older horses, the Whitney Handicap on August 4. He drew only four opponents, none particularly distinguished, and was topweight on the scale at 119 pounds. He broke nicely, was well-placed behind the pace-setting Onion, but could never get to that horse, who won by a length in an ordinary 1:49⅘.

"Going to the post that day," Turcotte recalls, "Secretariat seemed dull and not his usual healthy self. He weakened in the stretch run of the Whitney, confirming my suspicions. I learned later that he had a bit of fever that week and wasn't at his best, but they thought he would win on his class. That defeat got to me and I found myself crying on the way home that evening; not for myself but for him. He never should have lost a race. That's how great he was."

The Marlboro cigarette people wanted to sponsor a big race in New York that fall, and initially there was consideration of a match race between Secretariat and his 4-year-old stablemate, Riva Ridge. In time this proposal gave way to an invitational format. Bids went out to top horses across the country, and a field of seven was assembled with the Secretariat-Riva Ridge entry favored at 2-5. Both were sharp, and Secretariat gained considerable stature by beating Riva Ridge by more than three lengths while conceding weight on the scale, 124 to 127. Secretariat also set a record with nine furlongs in 1:45.

Two weeks after the Marlboro Cup, Secretariat was entered in the Woodward Stakes at a mile and a half. It was something of a late decision, for the stable had been considering Riva Ridge for the

A legion of fans were saddened when "Big Red" was retired as a 3-year-old.

Woodward while Secretariat was to make his grass debut in the Man o' War. His preparation was meager for the Woodward, and Turcotte feels that was the difference. Prove Out, who like Onion, the Whitney winner, was trained by Allen Jerkens, won by four and a half lengths, timed in a lively 2:25⅕. Secretariat, second, had 11 lengths on Cougar II, who was third.

With two defeats in three races, some of those participating in the Secretariat syndicate began to get nervous again. But, as in the past, the red horse raced to the rescue. In his first start on Turf, in the Man o' War on October 8, he led all the way, won by five lengths from the United Nations Handicap winner, Tentam, and ran a mile and a half in a record 2:24⅘.

Secretariat brought his brilliant career to a conclusion in Canada. With Eddie Maple replacing the suspended Ron Turcotte, Secretariat went off a 1-5 favorite in the Canadian International at Woodbine, which drew a field of 12. A large crowd was on hand despite furious rains which fell most of the day. Always in contention, Secretariat went to the front with half a mile remaining and brought the fans to their feet with the authority of his acceleration. In a twinkling, he led by five and was 12 lengths in front at the furlong pole. Maple, aware of his responsibility as a substitute rider, took hold of the red horse as he cruised home to score by six and a half lengths.

Had Turcotte been in the irons, Secretariat might have won by 20 lengths.

But he needed no last hurrah to set the seal on his greatness. He was shipped to Claiborne Farm, his place in racing history assured. Horses of his caliber come along once in a century. American racing was fortunate to have two, and they will race down the corridors of time to perpetual glory.

∞∞∞∞∞∞∞∞

In the mid-1950s, Rachel Carpenter of Shelter Island, New York, a member of the duPont family, enjoyed the Gulfstream Park meeting each winter from a clubhouse box adjacent to one occupied by trainer Warren "Jimmy" Croll. They often chatted about horses and Mrs. Carpenter suggested that Croll buy a horse or two for her and train them.

That was the start of a successful relationship that lasted 37 years, until Mrs. Carpenter's death on August 14, 1993. Croll made a number of fortuitous purchases for Mrs. Carpenter's Pelican Stable, but none better than his claim of Parka as a 3-year-old for $10,000. Parka won the United Nations Handicap (now the Caesars International) at Atlantic City Race Course in 1965 and at season's end the spirited 7-year-old was chosen America's grass course champion.

Mrs. Carpenter began breeding on a modest scale, and among her homebred fillies was Sharon Brown, a daughter of Al Hattab, who won the Monmouth Invitational (now the Haskell Invitational) of 1969 for the Pelican Stable. Sharon Brown, never a star, was tough as sandpaper. She made 32 starts in three seasons, winning three times. When her racing career concluded, she was sent to the court of Great Above, and the union produced a gray colt of formidable proportions.

When Mrs. Carpenter died, on the morning of August 14, 1993, her executors confirmed to Croll that she left her entire rac-

ing stable to her trainer. Included in the package was the gray colt out of Sharon Brown, whom Mrs. Carpenter named Holy Bull. Then a 2-year-old, Holy Bull was a promising development and was scheduled to make his debut at Monmouth that afternoon. Croll decided to go ahead with the race as a tribute to Mrs. Carpenter, and Holy Bull, ridden by Luis Rivera Jr., won by more than two lengths after leading all the way.

That was the start of an exceptional career, and before his premature retirement in February 1995, due to injury, Holy Bull was recognized as one of the best horse to race in the U.S. since the retirement of Spectacular Bid.

After a 2-year-old campaign that saw him win all four of his starts, Holy Bull made his eagerl -awaited 3-year-old debut in Gulfstream's Hutcheson Stakes on January 30, 1994. An exceedingly quick colt, Patton, posed a threat, but the 1-2 Holy Bull ran with him and beat him by almost a length, the seven furlongs in 1:21⅕. His fifth consecutive victory earned Holy Bull the favorite's role for the Fountain of Youth on February 1, despite the presence of Dehere and Go For Gin. Holy Bull rolled to the lead as usual, but stopped badly through the stretch, finishing a shocking sixth in his first defeat.

Holy Bull's many fans were dazed by the unexpected result but owner-trainer Croll, after examining his colt at the barn and comparing notes with jockey Smith, felt relieved. He explained that Holy Bull hadn't been getting his normal wind during the running of the Fountain of Youth and that the relatively inexperienced colt panicked. Croll promised the incident would not be a recurring problem, and he proved correct. Three weeks later, Holy Bull galloped to victory in the Florida Derby, winning by almost six lengths after equaling a track record with nine furlongs in 1:47⅖.

Back on schedule as the future-book favorite for the Kentucky Derby, Holy Bull shipped to Lexington, Kentucky, for a final sharpener in Keeneland's Blue Grass Stakes on April 16. Bet down to 3-5 in a field of seven, the charcoal gray colt led all the way to beat moderate opponents by three and a half lengths.

All of this success made his Kentucky Derby experience that much more disappointing. On a sloppy track of the sort he always loved, he was never in the hunt and finished 12th of 14. Jockey Smith could offer no excuse, and trainer Croll was mystified. Holy Bull had only lost once in his career and had a legitimate excuse for that misadventure.

Croll made an excellent decision following the Kentucky Derby. Instead of continuing on the Triple Crown trail, he gave his horse a few days off and then pointed him for the Metropolitan Mile at Belmont Park on May 30. Competing against older horses for the first time, Holy Bull led all the way, conceding weight on the scale to all, and won by five and a half lengths, the mile in 1:33⅕.

Holy Bull's summer campaign was another exercise in superiority. He won Belmont's Dwyer by almost seven lengths, had an easy time of it in capturing Monmouth's Haskell, and answered questions about his stamina in Saratoga's Travers Stakes at a mile and a quarter.

If any doubt about his quality still existed, he settled the issue with a tremendous display in the Woodward at Belmont on September 17. Favored at 9-10 against older horses, he skipped to

Jimmy Croll had a special relationship with Holy Bull.

an early lead, then drew out through the final furlong. To the appreciative applause of the crowd, he tallied by five lengths, sealing his lock on Horse of the Year honors.

Holy Bull had a well-deserved holiday, trained beautifully in Florida for Croll, and drew large crowds of horsemen at Gulfstream Park every time he went to the track. The gray horse made his 4-year-old debut on January 22 in the seven-furlong Olympia Handicap. Holy Bull shifted into overdrive at the head of the stretch, and he went on to score by two and a half lengths, the seven panels in a crisp 1:22.

A crowd of 19,000 was on hand at Gulfstream Park on February 11 for the $300,000 Donn Handicap. Holy Bull was the solid 3-10 favorite, though he was topweight under 127 pounds and was trying to give 12 pounds to as good a horse as Cigar. Cigar, second choice at 4-1, went to the lead out of the gate and showed the way down the backstretch, with Holy Bull on his flank. Holy Bull appeared to draw abreast for an instant and then Mike Smith heard a "popping" sound and was seen reaching forward to hold him together as the gray horse angled to the outside, gradually pulling up.

Horsemen and veterinarians began jumping the fence and running toward Holy Bull across the track. An emergency cast was applied. He was removed by horse ambulance and taken back to his barn with the crowd looking on in shocked silence. Almost unnoticed, Cigar went on to post a five and a half-length victory.

Holy Bull suffered a severe strain of the superficial flexor tendon in the left foreleg. Croll, so civil and even-tempered at the barn throughout the crisis, announced that Holy Bull was retired to stud duty in Lexington and his stud fee was set at $25,000, live foal. He went home with a record of 13 wins from 16 starts, earnings of $2,481,760, and the affection of an ever-increasing segment of the public.

∞∞∞∞∞∞

One of the most remarkable horsemen of any era is Harry Allen Jerkens, who took out a trainer's license in 1950, was leading trainer in New York in five years, was elected to the Hall of Fame in 1975, and still ranked among the national leaders in 1995. After 45 years of almost continual success in a highly competitive field, it is virtually impossible to find someone with a critical comment about the sensitive and gentlemanly Jerkens, who is held in the highest personal and professional regard.

Among the Jerkens souvenirs are such "giant killers" as Beau Purple, Choker, Mac's Sparkler, Handsome Boy, Never Bow, Blessing Angelica, Tunex, Step Nicely, Onion, Prove Out, Poker Night, and Group Plan.

Joseph Jerkens, an Austrian cavalryman, came to the U.S. in 1908, settled in East Islip, Long Island, and opened a riding academy. He also trained polo ponies and hunters for some of his wealthy patrons, and he purchased the occasional thoroughbred racehorse who had broken down. He'd give them time and good care, and

Allen Jerkens gained a reputation as a "giant killer."

often brought them back to the races successfully.

His son, Harry Allen Jerkens, was 5 when he began to come to the barn. He learned to clean stalls and equipment, and he learned how to ride. He took horses into the nearby bay for traditional cold-water therapy on legs. By the time he was 7, young Jerkens was getting on racehorses. By 12 he was an accomplished horseman, and by 15 he bought his first horse, a 3-year-old named Crack Time, for whom he paid $400. The horse had raced once at 2 and been sidelined ever since. Jerkens worked on him throughout the winter, and when the 1946 New York racing season opened April 1, Crack Time was ready. Campaigning in the name of Joseph Jerkens, he earned some $12,000 during the season and that fall was claimed for $10,000.

Briefly, young Jerkens became a steeplechase rider but did not distinguish himself. A spill and a constant battle with weight persuaded him to resume training, and when he turned 21 in 1950, he was able to obtain a license. On July 4 of that year, he saddled his first official winner, Populace, who won at Aqueduct. He concluded the season with 20 winners and began to make a name for himself.

Jerkens performed miracle work with claiming horses. He became nationally known through the success of Edward Seinfeld's Admiral Vee, a son of War Admiral haltered for $7,500 who went on to earn more than $250,000, winning the mile and five-furlong

Gallant Fox Handicap at the end of the 1958 season that began with a victory in the Paumonok Handicap at six furlongs.

Jerkens moved from claiming horses to stakes horses in 1962 when financier Jack Dreyfus, at the recommendation of turf writer Pat Lynch, hired Jerkens to train his Hobeau Farm Stable. The star of the stable was the talented Beau Purple, who had great natural speed. Employing works alone and rejecting the need for a prep race, Jerkens got Beau Purple to the Suburban Handicap on July 4 in a mood to drill a hole in the wind. Stepping the 10 furlongs in 2:00⅗, he upset Horse of the Year Kelso. Then, just to show it wasn't a fluke, Beau Purple upset Kelso a second time, In Belmont Park's Man o' War Stakes on the grass course that fall.

The following winter, Kelso trained for Hialeah's important Widener Handicap, for which he was topweight at 131 pounds. When Beau Purple, under 125 pounds, upset Kelso a third time, Jerkens began to acquire the nickname of "The Giant-Killer." He enhanced that role in 1967 by sending out Dreyfus' Handsome Boy to turn back the 3-5 Buckpasser in the Brooklyn Handicap with the aid of a 20-pound pull in the weights. Jerkens fashioned an even more unexpected victory in 1973 when the little-known Onion defeated the Triple Crown winner, Secretariat, in Saratoga's Whitney Handicap.

A month after the Whitney, Jerkens was repeatedly hailed and applauded by New Yorkers when he appeared in the winner's circle at Belmont Park to greet Prove Out after that horse upset Secretariat in the Woodward Stakes at weight for age.

In 1975, Jerkens, at 45, became the youngest trainer ever elected to racing's Hall of Fame at Saratoga. Twenty years later, that remains a distinction he still holds.

The great trainers are known for their vision, an extraordinary ability to see in horses what other may have missed. Jerkens' vision is legendary in the industry, fueled by stories invariably told with a disbelieving shake of the head.

Angel Cordero Jr. was shepherding a small set of horses trained by his wife a few years ago when he passed Jerkens on the horse path leading to Belmont Park's main track. He called to Jerkens, asking the trainer what he thought of the filly he had in tow.

"She'll be all right when she gets over that curb," Jerkens said. When the Corderos examined the filly's hock back at the barn, they found the curb everyone had missed . . . except Jerkens, who spotted it with a quick look from the back of his pony.

Don Ball, a Kentucky developer with headquarters in the Lexington area, has raced a stable of horses based at Keeneland for

Beau Purple, one of Jerkens' many talented runners, proved a thorn in the side of five-time Horse of the Year Kelso.

a number of years with his son, Mike, as trainer. One spring afternoon, when Jerkens was at Keeneland with a rare Kentucky Derby prospect, he was watching the races from a vantage point on the outer rail near the gap to the stable area. Young Ball, standing nearby, had a horse in the race and was following his progress intently as he made his way around the turn and into the backstretch.

"Mike, your horse just stumbled," Jerkens said. Ball, who had been focusing on his horse, had seen nothing, but when he got to the barn after the race, he found the fracture of the coffin bone only Jerkens had noted . . . at a distance of 100 or more yards.

A perfectionist with high standards in every aspect of the business, Jerkens often sounds off when he comes across a job done with less than 100 percent efficiency, and vents frustrations by tossing feed tubs. But he is quick to forget and forgive, and most of his devoted staff have been with him for many years.

He spends more time with his horses than most of his contemporaries, and he loves to get them out of their stalls in the afternoons for a bit of grazing to relieve a generally monotonous existence. He also places great emphasis on feeding. He personally doles out the various feeds and supplements, varying the amounts with his perception of circumstances. He has considerable empathy with the thoroughbred racehorse and seems able to understand their emotions.

He's had few patrons over the years who attended the sales regularly and bought high-priced individuals. Most of his owners have raced homebreds with all the restrictions implied by the term. Yet Jerkens has consistently done well, his managerial skills as effective as his training skills. He had his most successful season ever in 1994 when he turned 65, just missing the $5 million mark in purses won, thanks to the exploits of such good ones as Devil His Due, a handicap star with earnings of almost $4 million, and the champion handicap racemare, Sky Beauty, who ran off a string of five consec-

utive stakes triumphs during the campaign.

There have been many great horsemen in the history of American racing. There have been many notable promoters. There have been many outstanding judges of conformation. There have been many trainers expert in media relations. Some have shown a penchant for stable management, some have displayed a flair for ambiance and stable decor, some have a natural talent as commentators or inspirational speakers. But until Darrell Wayne Lukas came down the pike in 1978, no one individual touched all of these bases with such spectacular panache.

One set of statistics tells the Lukas story succinctly. He was the nation's leading money-winning trainer for the first time in 1983, five years after completing his switch from the training of quarterhorses to the training of thoroughbreds. He then ran off an unparalleled streak of 10 consecutive money titles, during which period his stable sent out 2,438 winners, an average of 244 per year. During that reign, Lukas' horses earned a total of $125,309,546, an average of $12.5 million per year.

Lukas had an "off" season in 1993, during which his horses won 135 races and earned $4,122,153. He regained the money title in 1994 with earnings of $9,250,591, and was credited with 147 winners. Once again he was the nonpariel.

He has been a collector of achievements. He's won the Kentucky Derby twice, the Preakness four times, the Belmont twice. He had 12 victories in Breeders' Cup competition through 1994, a record. He's trained 13 horses who were champions of their respective divisions, a record, and these 13 won 17 championships in all, including two Horse of the Year titles. He's won the Eclipse Award as trainer of the year four times, equaling a record.

Lukas was raised in Antigo, Wisconsin, a small farming community some 150 miles northwest of Milwaukee, and his work ethic developed early. By the time he was 7 he was delivering newspapers from the back of his white pony. At 9 he leased two acres from his uncle and planted string beans. He hired friends to harvest the crop and sold it to a local cannery at a profit.

At 12 he raced his pony at the county fair grounds. At 14, he competed in neighboring county fair meetings, and a few that were distant. At 16, he and a high school buddy, Clyde Rice, traveled through Iowa and Nebraska, buying, selling and trading horses. They honed their eye for a horse and their sense of value in the toughest practical school, acquiring skills that, on another day and in another setting, would pay rich dividends.

Always keen on athletics and particularly basketball, he attended the University of Wisconsin at Madison with a major in physical education. On weekends he traveled to horse sales in the Midwest, buying and selling all breeds and all types.

He got his first job as a basketball coach, following graduation, at Blair (Wisc.) High School. He also doubled as a history teacher in the tiny community of 1,000, and in his free time raced a small stable at the many bush-league tracks in the area. Two years later, in 1959, he left Blair and returned to the University of Wisconsin for a master's degree. While in Madison, he served as assistant to Johnny Orr, then coach of the Wisconsin freshman team. Lukas also raced a few horses at bush tracks in the area.

In 1961, his tour at the university completed, he landed a job at Logan HIgh School in La Crosse as head basketball coach and part-time teacher. He also trained a stable of quarterhorses at Rochester, Minnesota, 60 miles away, rising at 4 a.m. He drove the 60 miles, trained the horses, and drove back in time to shower and change for

D. Wayne Lukas brought a style all his own to thoroughbred racing.

his teaching duties.

During the summer, he raced his stable at Park Jefferson, Atokad Park and Sunland Park, adding a few cheap thoroughbreds from time to time. In 1963, his success with his horses and the attractive style in which he maintained his barn attracted the attention of George Bunn, a manufacturer of coffee machines from Des Moines, and Herb Alves, a contractor from Minneapolis. They gave him financial backing, enabling him to expand and upgrade his stable.

In the late 1960s, Lukas quit his job in La Crosse to concentrate on racing and developed some of the top quarterhorses of the day. He trained 23 champions, including the celebrated Dash for Cash. He began racing in northern California, where his stable always included a few thoroughbreds. Still primarily active in quarterhorses, he moved the stable to Hollywood Park in 1974, raced the quarterhorses at Los Alamitos and his handful of thoroughbreds in the Los Angeles area.

By 1977 he was deeply involved with thoroughbreds, a number of them the property of Oklahoma developer Mel Hatley and Texas oilman Bob French, who raced quarterhorses with him and were ready to make the switch when Lukas did. Lukas' schedule during this period boggled the imagination. He was at his Hollywood Park barn by 4 a.m. daily, and trained the thoroughbreds all morning. If he had a horse entered that day he'd return to Hollywood after washing up and changing. If he wasn't racing that day, he'd spend the afternoon and evening with the quarterhorses at Los Alamitos, getting home about midnight for a few hours of sleep.

After he converted his stable completely to thoroughbreds for the 1978 season, Lukas won 37 races from 194 starts and had purses of $942,786. It didn't take him long to make a splash. He saddled Effervescing to win the $100,000 American Handicap on the Hollywood Turf course on July 4 for the owner, bloodstock agent Albert Yank. Then, to everyone's surprise, including Yank, Lukas ran Effervescing back five days later to win the $100,000 Citation Handicap on the dirt.

Later that month, Lukas made the whole country sit up and take notice by winning the Hollywood Juvenile Championship with a filly, Terlingua (by Secretariat).

Lukas' stable progressed in 1979 to win 63 races and $1,360,772 and took on a significant new patron in Tartan Farm. Owned by the family of W.L. McKnight of the Minnesota Mining and Manufacturing Company, the stable was managed by Hall of Fame horseman Johnny Nerud, who admired the work ethic of the swashbuckling young Lukas and sent him some nice horses. One was Codex, winner of the Santa Anita Derby of 1980, the Hollywood Derby and Lukas' first classic, the Preakness.

He made his first Kentucky Derby appearance in 1981 with a colt named Partez, owned by Mr. and Mrs. Henry Greene, who had done little to distinguish himself before arriving in Louisville. The Churchill Downs linemaker had little hesitancy in placing the Quack colt in the mutuel field, but Partez, under Sandy Hawley, ran

Lady's Secret delivered the first Horse of the Year title in 1986 to Wayne Lukas.

the race of his career. Coming from far back in a field of 21, he finished strongly to earn third money of $27,500.

Lukas returned to the Kentucky Derby the following year with Tartan Stable's Muttering to finish fifth and has not missed a single Derby in the interim. He won his first Derby with the filly Winning Colors in 1988 and had his second with Thunder Gulch in 1995, the year he passed Derby Dick Thompson as the trainer with the most Kentucky Derby starters.

In 1983, Gene Klein came into racing. Klein paid a record $10 million for the San Diego Chargers football team when he and a group of friends bought it in the mid-1960s from hotelman Barron Hilton. When Klein sold the team, early in the 1980s, the price was $80 million, and two-thirds of that money was his.

Friends of Klein's owned horses and invited him and his wife to the track, Santa Anita, one morning during training hours. Walking through the stable area, the Kleins encountered the great pro football linebacker, Dick Butkus. It turned out that Butkus owned a horse, and he introduced the Kleins to his trainer, Wayne Lukas. The Kleins liked the personable Lukas, and as they left, Klein said: "If you ever find a horse you think we might like, give me a ring."

Six years later, when Klein sold his thoroughbred holdings because of an illness that proved fatal, he estimated he spent almost

$60 million on horses with Lukas. The horses earned over $25 million, and proceeds of the sale put him in the black.

One of Klein's first stars was Life's Magic, winner of over $2.25 million. She won the Mother Goose, the Alabama and the Beldame of 1984, and the Breeders' Cup Distaff of 1985. Klein also raced Lady's Secret, Horse of the Year 1986 and a winner of more than $3 million. Perhaps his favorite was Winning Colors, who beat the colts in the Kentucky Derby of 1988 and earnedmorfe than $1.5 million.

Lukas struck up an association with a retired business executive from Lexington, Kentucky, who had been a racing fan for years and now had the time and wherewithal to become involved in the sport on a substantial scale. William T. Young Jr. made his mark in the business world as chief executive officer of Royal Crown Cola, Big Top Peanut Butter, and other corporations. In 1980, Young purchased Overbrook Farm in Lexington and began to develop the property. Thus, by the late 1980s, when Young began to limit his business activities, the farm was ready to support a racing stable with homebred stock.

One of Young's first major successes came with Corporate Report in the Travers at Saratoga in 1991, the same season his 2-year-old colt, Salt Lake, won the Hopeful at Saratoga and Cowdin at Belmont Park. All three events are of Grade 1 quality. In subsequent years his green and white Overbrook colors grew increasingly prominent

The Lukas family knew both the heights and the depths with the talented Tabasco Cat.

under Lukas' direction. In 1994 he won the Eclipse Award as America's greatest breeder, having bred 12 stakes winners. They included Tabasco Cat – whom he owned in partnership with his college roommate, David Reynolds – winner of the Preakness and Belmont stakes; the brilliant 2-year-old filly champion, Flanders, and the crack sprinter, Harlan, winner of the Grade 1 Vosburgh Stakes.

Tabasco Cat, a homebred son of Storm Cat, had an episodic career which impacted significantly on Lukas and his family. A stakes-winning 2-year-old who finished third in the Breeders' Cup Juvenile, Tabasco Cat spooked at the barn one morning in mid-December of 1993. As the colt galloped down the shedrow, Lukas' son, Jeff, stepped in front of him. Instead of grinding to a stop, Tabasco Cat continued on, knocking young Lukas to the ground. His head was struck hard and he was rushed to a nearby hospital by helicopter.

He was in a coma for two weeks, his life in the balance. Wayne Lukas spent hours at his son's bedside while continuing to train the colt who put him there. By the end of the 1994 season, Jeff Lukas, having recovered his health and most of his motor skills, was back on the job, while Tabasco Cat's earnings had soared to almost $2.35 million. Sidelined for the first half of his 4-year-old campaign by a tendon condition, he was retired to stud.

❧❧❧❧❧❧❧❧

The outstanding riders of the period 1966 to 1994 were the three number-crunchers: Angel Cordero Jr., Chris McCarron and Laffit Pincay Jr. Among them they had won 21,345 races and $526,187,794 through 1994. Those are stunning numbers, but only a small part of the big picture. There was so much talent among the three as to tax credulity, and their memorable moments, on videotape, would surpass "Gone With The Wind" for sweep, drama and length.

Cordero, who rode for 31 seasons, was known for his fierce desire, for winning at almost any cost, for determination that produced many storied victories in a career that extended 31 seasons. When an accident forced him to the sidelines early in the 1992 campaign, he left with a marvelous record that included 7,057 victories, $164,526,217 in purses, and triumphs in all the major U.S. stakes including three Kentucky Derbys, four Breeders' Cup events, five Suburban Handicaps, six Woodward Stakes, etc. Perhaps his greatest achievement was his 13 jockey championships at the highly competitive Saratoga meeting between 1976 and 1989.

His brilliant rides will never be forgotten. He nursed a sore-heeled miler named Bold Forbes to go a mile and a half in the Belmont Stakes of 1976. He was on the second-best part of an entry in the 1974 Kentucky Derby and guided Cannonade to victory with authentic genius in the largest field (23) ever to contest the Run for the Roses. He was at his best in the 1985 Kentucky Derby. Riding the 4-1 Spend a Buck from post 10, he got his mount off to a flying start and had the race won by the first turn. Opening a six-length lead, he nursed Spend a Buck's reserves so skillfully it wasn't even close.

But some of his other rides will never be forgotten, either — principally the Preakness of 1980, when he led into the stretch with Codex, then turned in the saddle to spot the filly who won the Kentucky Derby, Genuine Risk, and proceeded to carry her wide.

Angel Cordero Jr. was always known for his brilliant enthusiasm as one of the century's top riders.

Codex won by almost five lengths, but Cordero's tactics touched off a nationwide furor, and he was pilloried for his sportsmanship.

He provoked considerable rebuke for his role in the Travers Stakes of 1978, which was essentially a match race between Affirmed and Alydar, who had finished in that order in the Triple Crown races. Cordero's mount was a complete outsider, Shake Shake Shake. Down the backstretch, Cordero permitted his mount to drift, carrying Affirmed wide and opening a hole on the rail for Alydar and his rider, Jorge Velasquez, one of Cordero's best friends. Laffit Pincay Jr., riding Affirmed, reacted impulsively, bouncing his mount into Alydar, then speeding away to win. However, Affirmed was disqualified by the stewards, and the Travers was awarded to Alydar.

Cordero, at the time in the midst of a feud with Laz Barrera, trainer of Affirmed, was charged in the press with using the Travers to get even and trying to ride horses other than his own.

Then there was the Belmont of 1979 when he was feuding with the youthful and inexperienced rider of Kentucky Derby and Preakness winner Spectacular Bid, Ronnie Franklin. The two had come to blows in the jocks' room earlier in Belmont Week, and bumped each other in a race. Cordero, riding General Assembly in the Belmont, stalked Spectacular Bid and Ron Franklin much of the

Laffit Pincay Jr.'s career is a testimonial to dedication.

way, then got in front of him and drifted out, impeding his progress. Spectacular Bid finished third, General Assembly seventh.

Before he retired, Cordero compiled more than 200 rulings against him involving fines and/or suspensions, and there must have been another 200 cases where some action was justified.

Angel Tomas Cordero Jr., the son of a jockey, grew up on the grounds of the Las Monjas track in San Juan, Puerto Rico. Even before he turned 18, young Cordero began riding at the El Commandante track and, three days later, on June 15, 1960, had his first winner, Celador. He had a good season in Puerto Rico in 1961 and came to New York in 1962. But he spoke no English, was homesick and broke. He returned to the island, and developed into a good rider– good enough to give him confidence to try the States again. He flew here in 1966 and had his first stakes victory later in the season at Delaware Park when Hermogenes won the Christiana. He won his first riding title at Saratoga in 1967 and was on his way.

Cordero was inducted into the Hall of Fame in the National Museum of Racing at Saratoga in 1988. He charmed the large crowd, frequently flashing the expansive smile that is his trademark. He reviewed his career highlights, then cited regrets: "Perhaps a few, but then again, too few to mention." He had, in fact, done it his way.

There are no statistics for dedication to one's profession, but if there were, the name of Laffit Pincay Jr. would, by consensus, lead all the rest. Virtually throughout his career, covering three decades, he battled weight. He battled it fiercely, to the point of depression. He battled it through physical injury and intense pain. He battled it through periods of bitter personal tragedy.

He never stopped his pursuit. Since he began riding in his native Panama in the spring of 1964, he's ridden steadily, with little time off. His great physical strength and his dogged determination are the keys to his impressive statistics. Even at 48, his age as of December 29, 1994, he remains a powerful physical specimen, one of the strongest jockeys to ride in this country, and one of the great finishers. He has 8,213 winners from 39,902 mounts and record purses won of $183,910,301, a world record.

He is closing in on Shoemaker's record of 8,833 winners, a mark compiled in 41 seasons. The last few hundred winners will be the hardest, but barring serious injury, where age can be a factor, his determination should carry him to his goal..

The son of a well-known jockey, Laffit Pincay Sr., who left his family and went to Venezuela in the mid-1950s, Laffit Jr. was born and raised in Panama City. He was a young tough and a member of a street gang but apprenticed himself to a trainer at Presidente Ramon Race Track and became serious about his work. He rode his first winner, Huelen, in his fifth attempt at Presidente Ramon on May 19, 1964. He was leading apprentice in Panama that season when Jorge Velasquez was leading jockey.

Several years earlier, Fred Hooper, one of Florida's leading horsemen, came to Panama and signed the country's top jockey, Braulio Baeza, to a contract in the U.S. Hooper returned in 1965 and flew back to Miami with Velasquez. That left Pincay as leading jockey in Panama, but when Hooper approached him the following year, 1966, Pincay, too, became a *Yanqui*. He rode his first winner in

this country on July 1, 1966 aboard Hooper's Teacher's Art in the fifth race at Arlington Park.

He rode his 4,000th winner November 18, 1979, at Aqueduct, his 5,000th winner less than two years later, on September 30, 1981, at Santa Anita. His 6,000th winner came on Feb. 17, 1985, at Santa Anita. His 7,000th came on November 9, 1988, at Santa Anita and his 8,000th on August 29, 1993, at Del Mar.

Pincay was America's leading money-winning jockey seven times, posted seven victories in Breeders' Cup competition, rode seven winners on one program at Santa Anita (March 14, 1987), and was elected to racing's Hall of Fame in 1975. He rode six winners of the Santa Anita Handicap, six winners of the Santa Anita Derby and six winners of the Hollywood Gold Cup. Along with the triumphs and the glory there was the rest of the story: seven fractured collarbones, two spinal fractures, collapsed lungs, fractured ribs, twisted ankles, cracked tibias, fibias, radii and ulnas. But these were mixed blessings as Pincay saw them.

"I wish, every time I ride, I'll have something wrong with me," Pincay said a few years ago. "It makes me better. It's like someone saying to me 'You can't do it.' It makes me want to go out and do it."

Physical pain is one thing. Mental anguish is another. Pincay has known his share of both. Through the 1970s, a variety of diets and weight-reduction plans had his emotions on a roller coaster. He was a vegetarian for some six years during that period and recalls he never felt good when meat was not on his menu.

Yet, he has always had tremendous willpower when it came to denying himself food. Once, flying across the country with a prominent trainer, he lunched on a cup of broth and a single peanut.

Pincay's first wife, Linda, mother of his children, Lisa and Laffit 3rd, fasted to even more dangerous lengths, out of sympathy with her husband. In 1984, there were complications stemming from a ruptured appendix, post-operative complications and questionable medical care. She became dependent on barbiturates and, in a fit of despondency, shot herself to death in their home on January 18, 1985.

The years immediately following that tragedy were hard on Pincay and the children, despite the kindness of the racing community, which reached out to assist and comfort the family in every way possible. Gradually, Pincay came out of his shell, remarried and rejoined his circle of friends. He resumed his pursuit of winners, and Shoemaker's record, with

Chris McCarron's winning habits started as an apprentice in 1974, when he set a record with 546 victories. Brother Gregg (right) was both a rival and a booster in Maryland.

enthusiasm. He still watches his weight carefully, but sensibly, and much of the old abrasiveness is gone. The determination to ride and win remains.

Chris McCarron's riding career is a study in milestones. He rode his first winner, Erezev, at Bowie in February 1974, when he was almost 19. In August 1988 when he was 33, he rode Precisionist to victory in the Cabrillo Handicap at Del Mar and passed the $100 million mark in purses won. He was the youngest of five jockeys to reach that figure. In June 1994, when he was 39, he notched his 6,000th winner when Ardestine won the Milady Handicap.

Six thousand winners in about 20 years. That's 300 winners a year, a remarkable average. One hundred million dollars in about 14

years. That is an average of about $7.14 million a year, another striking figure.

It's not all quantity, either. McCarron's work aboard John Henry in 1984, when that incredible gelding was Horse of the Year at age 9, was exemplary. In 1987 he was hailed as a hero when he skillfully held Alysheba together after the Alydar colt stumbled on entering the stretch in the Kentucky Derby. Only deft work by McCarron averted the worst accident in classics history and enabled Alysheba to win the Run for the Roses.

They weren't all near misses. In October of 1986, during the Oak Tree meeting at Santa Anita, five horses went down in domino fashion, and one of them was ridden by Pincay. In a freakish fall, he landed on McCarron's left leg, breaking it in five places. A metal brace was installed to stabilize the fractures, and McCarron needed almost six months of recuperation before he returned to the saddle. He made some good use of his down time by doing color commentary and analysis for NBC's telecast of the Breeders' Cup and acquitted himself well.

In June 1990, there was another spill, this one at Hollywood Park. McCarron fractured the same left leg, and also fractured bones in an arm and knee. A metal rod was inserted in the leg to help speed healing, and, with a determined effort, McCarron was back on a horse two months later.

McCarron and horses: They've been together since 1971, when he landed a summer job with a stable based at Rockingham Park. The stable was trained by O.D. "Odie" Clelland, a knowledgeable and successful horseman who was instrumental in the formative years of many well-known jockeys. Eddie Arcaro was one of these, circa 1930, and Gregg McCarron, who began riding in 1969, was another. Gregg McCarron mentioned Clelland to his younger brother, Chris, and in 1971, when he was 16, Chris McCarron left home in Dorchester, Massachusetts, to work at Rockingham for the summer as a hotwalker for Clelland.

"From the first day, I loved everything about the work," McCarron recalls. "I graduated from Christopher Columbus High School in Dorchester in 1972 and went to work full-time on the racetrack for Odie Clelland as a groom. I was exercising horses in 1973 and began riding in January of 1974 at Bowie. I finished last in that first race and didn't have a clue as to what was happening, but I picked it up quickly and had my first winner in my 10th ride."

McCarron was a quick study. In that first season of 1974, he led all jockeys with a record 546 winners.

The eventful ride on Alysheba to land his first Kentucky Derby victory in 1987 remains one of the McCarron career highlights.

∞∞∞∞∞∞∞∞

In retrospect, the period covered by this book (1894-1994) was the golden era of American racing. Brilliant horses, skilled trainers and daring riders gave us a particularly large slice of racing history.

And we have only glimpsed a fraction of the greatness in this volume. It would take a dozen such books to detail the exploits and courage of the hundreds of thousands of horses and people who have left their mark on the thoroughbred sport through the course of 100 years.

For every Man o' War and Secretariat mentioned in these pages, there was also an Arazi and a Silky Sullivan. For every Regret, there was a Ruffian. For every Max Hirsch and Sam Hildreth and Ben Jones, there was also a Mack Miller and a Preston Burch and an Angel Penna. For every Bill Shoemaker and Eddie Arcaro, a Pat Day and an Avelino Gomez.

A book can but barely scratch the surface of a century's more than 36,000 days of racing. For the whole story, race-by-race and card-by-card, only one source will suffice – *Daily Racing Form*.

Photo Credits

CHAPTER 1

P. 1	*Daily Racing Form*
P. 2	*Daily Racing Form*
P. 3	Chicago Historical Society
P. 6	NYRA Photo
	Keeneland-Cook
P. 7	Keeneland-Cook
P. 8	Keeneland-Cook
P. 9	National Museum of Racing
P. 10	Keeneland-Cook
P. 11	Keeneland-Cook
P. 12	Keeneland-Cook
P. 13	Keeneland-Cook
P. 14	Keeneland-Cook
P. 15	Keeneland-Cook
P. 17	National Museum of Racing
P. 18	Keeneland-Cook
P. 19	Keeneland-Cook
P. 20	National Museum of Racing
P. 21	Keeneland-Cook
P. 22	National Museum of Racing
P. 23	*Daily Racing Form*
P. 25	Keeneland-Cook
P. 27	Keeneland-Cook
P. 28	Keeneland-Cook
P. 29	National Museum of Racing
P. 30	Keeneland Library
P. 31	*Daily Racing Form*
P. 32	Keeneland-Cook

CHAPTER 2

P. 33	*Daily Racing Form*
P. 34	*Daily Racing Form*
P. 35	Keeneland-Cook
P. 36	Keeneland-Triangle
P. 37	Santa Anita Park Photos
P. 38	Keeneland-Meadors
P. 39	Del Mar Photos

P. 40	Jim Raftery-Turfotos
	Keeneland-Triangle
P. 41	Keeneland-Triangle
	Keeneland-Cook
P. 42	Keeneland-Cook
P. 43	Keeneland-Cook
	Keeneland-Cook
P. 44	Keeneland-Cook
	The Courier-Journal-Lowry
P. 45	Daily Racing Form
P. 46	Keeneland-Cook
P. 47	NYRA Photo
P. 48	Keeneland-Cook
P. 49	Keeneland-Cook
P. 51	Del Mar
P. 53	Keeneland-Cook
P. 54	Keeneland-Cook
P. 55	Daily Racing Form
P. 57	Keeneland-Morgan
P. 58	Keeneland-Cook
P. 59	Churchill Downs
P. 61	Keeneland-Morgan
P. 62	Keeneland-Morgan
P. 63	Keeneland-Meadors
P. 64	Keeneland-Morgan
P. 65	J. Noye
P. 67	Keeneland-Morgan
P. 68	Keeneland-Cook
P. 69	Bert Morgan
P. 71	Keeneland-Morgan
P. 72	Keeneland-Morgan
P. 73	NYRA Photo
P. 74	*Daily Racing Form*
P. 75	NYRA Photo
P. 76	*Bay News*
P. 77	Keeneland-Cook
P. 79	Keeneland-Cook
P. 80	Keeneland-Morgan
P. 81	NYRA Photo
P. 82	King Ranch Archives
P. 83	King Ranch Archives

P. 84	King Ranch Archives
P. 85	NYRA Photo
P. 86	NYRA Photo
P. 87	National Museum of Racing
P. 88	NYRA Photo
P. 89	NYRA Photo
P. 90	Turfotos
P. 91	Keeneland-Cook
P. 93	Keeneland-Cook
P. 94	*Daily Racing Form*
P. 95	Keeneland-Morgan
P. 97	Keeneland-Cook

CHAPTER 3

P 99	*Daily Racing Form*
P.100	*The Morning Telegraph*
P. 101	Michael Burns
P. 102	Michael J. Marten
	Monmouth Park
P. 103	Jim Raftery-Turfotos
P. 104	Jim Raftery-Turfotos
	Bert & Richard Morgan Studio
P. 105	Jim Raftery-Turfotos
P. 106	NYRA Photo
	Turfotos
P. 107	NYRA Photo
P. 109	Keeneland Association
P. 110	Michael Burns
P. 111	Gulfstream Park
P. 112	Keeneland
P. 113	Belmont Park
P.114	Belmont Park
P. 115	Bob Coglianese
P. 116	Keeneland-Morgan
P. 117	Hialeah Park
P. 118	Keeneland-Meadors
P. 119	Keeneland-Morgan
P. 121	NYRA Photo
P. 122	NYRA Photo
P. 125	NYRA Photo-Schafer

P. 127	New York *Daily News*
P. 128	NYRA Photo
P. 129	*Daily Racing Form*-Woolfe
P. 130	NYRA Photo
P. 131	Bob Coglianese
P. 133	NYRA Photo
P. 135	NYRA Photo
P. 136	NYRA Photo
P. 137	Santa Anita Park
P. 138	Paul Schafer
P. 139	Hollywood Park
P. 140	NYRA Photo
P. 141	Santa Anita Park
P. 142	Churchill Downs
P. 143	Michael J. Marten
P. 144	Jim Raftery-Turfotos
P. 145	Hollywood Park
P. 147	Churchill Downs
P. 149	Keeneland-Meadors
P. 150	Arlington International
P. 151	Paul Schafer
P. 153	Pimlico-Frutkoff
P. 155	Turfotos
P. 157	Churchill Downs

P. 187	NYRA-Coglianese
P. 188	NYRA Photo
P. 189	NYRA Photo
P. 191	*Daily Racing Form*-Woolfe
P. 193	New York *Daily News*
P. 194	NYRA-Coglianese
P. 195	*Daily Racing Form*-Woolfe
P. 197	Bill Denver/Equi-Photo
P. 198	*Daily Racing Form*
P. 199	*Thoroughbred Times*
P. 201	Santa Anita Park
P. 202	NYRA-Coglianese
P. 203	Michael J. Marten
P. 204	Jim Raftery-Turfotos
P. 205	Santa Anita Park
P. 207	Pimlico

CHAPTER 4

P. 160	*Daily Racing Form*
P. 163	K-III Communications
P. 164	Pierre (Peb) Bellocq
P. 165	Daniel Watson
P. 167	Hollywood Park
P. 168	Jim Raftery-Turfotos
P. 169	New York Off-Track Betting
P. 170	NYRA-Schafer
P. 171	NYRA Photo
P. 173	*Daily Racing Form*-Woolfe
P. 174	William J. Stravitz
P. 175	NYRA Photo
P. 177	Santa Anita Park
P. 179	NYRA Photo
	Daily Racing Form-Woolfe
P. 180	Kevin Ellsworth
P. 181	NYRA-Coglianese
P. 183	NYRA Photo
P. 185	Benoit & Associates

Index

-A-
Abe's Hope, 172
Ack Ack, 140
Adams, Johnny, 146
Admiral Vee, 198
Admiration, 26
Admiring, 88
Affectionately, 45,88
Affirmed, 141,180
Affliction, 25
Aga Khan, 67
Agnes D., 66
Agua Cal;iente, 96
Aile d'Or, 45
Ajax, 46
Alexander, George, 109
Alger, Fred, 37
Al Hattab, 196
Allez France, 88
Althea, 133
Alydar, 180
Ambiorix, 108
Ambrose, Eddie, 16
Anderson, Pete, 156
Andrew M., 22
Aneroid, 51
Angerola, Robert, 66
Angle Light, 190
Annenberg, Moses, 33
Annenberg, Walter, 33
Annette K., 47
Aqueduct, 67,94,106
Arcaro, Eddie, 58,94

Arlington Park, 36
Armed, 61
Artful, 12
Arts and Letters, 149
A.P. Indy, 4
Assault, 77
Atkinson, Ted, 70
Atlantic City, 104
Au Point, 132
Azucar, 37

-B-
Bad News, 42
Bahr, John, 40
Bailey, Bud, 146
Bailey, Jerry, 135
Baird, Robert Lee, 153
Baker, Col. Charles, 112
Bald Eagle, 123
Baldwin, Anita, 36
Baldwin, Elias, 25,37
Ball, Don, 199
Ball, Mike, 199
Ballot, 11,25
Bally Ache, 156
Bancroft, Edith, 172
Bane, Bill 111
Bannon, Joe, 34
Barbizon, 74, 154
Bardstown, 154
Barrera, Laz, 180
Bassett, Ted, 38
Bateau, 92

Bathing Girl, 47
Batter Up, 45
Beam Rider, 74
Beard, Maj. Louie, 37
Beatrice, 67
Beauclare, 78
Beaucoup, 18
Beau Genius, 145
Beau Purple, 199
Beech, John, 96
Behave Yourself, 42
Bel Bush, 149
Beldame, 9
Believe It, 182
Bellocq, Pierre, 164
Bellocq, Remi, 165
Belmont, August, 6
Belmont, August 2d,
6,8,27
Belmont, August 4th, 131
Belmont Park, 6,7,106
Bennington, Newton, 9
Bernet, George, 162
Bewitch, 62,115
Bieber, isidor, 85
Billy Kelly, 43,91
Bimelech, 43
Bishop, W.T., 38
Black Gold, 11
Black Helen, 43
Black Servant, 42
Black Toney, 11,42
Blackwell, George, 110

Blazes, 15
Blind Cowboy, 94
Blind, Eddie, 104
Block, Ben, 79
Block, John, 122
Blue Larkspur, 43
Blue Man, 127
Blue Swords, 113
Blum, Walter, 122
Boland, Bill, 82
Bold Bidder, 129,166
Bold Forbes, 180
Bold Ruler, 73
Bold Venture, 77
Bonnie Pennant, 25
Bonsal, Frank, 70
Boojum, 25
Booker, Alvin, 95
Boots, 23
Borrow, 23
Bowie, 7
Bounding Home, 62
Bourke, Tom, 35
Boyd-Rochefort, Cecil, 69
Bradley, Col. E.R., 11,40
Brady, Diamond Jim, 13
Brady, James Cox, 65
Brady, Nicholas, 171
Brandt, Herman, 26
Breezing Home, 97
Brennan, Bill, 95
Brevity, 79
Brigade, 42

Bright, James, 35
Brokers Tip, 11,43
Brooks, Richard 4
Brooks, Steve, 64,115,122
Broomstick, 8,22
Brosemer, Lao, 165
Brown, H.D., 36
Brunell, Frank, 1-5,33
Brunetti, John, 35
Bruno, Sandy, 134
Brushup, 48
Bubbling Over, 43
Buckpasser, 45,171
Buffle, 84
Bull Lea, 61
Bunting, 25
Burgoo King, 43
Busanda, 69
Busher, 44,50
Butkus, Dick, 202
Butwell, Jimmy, 27
But Why Not, 45,77
Byrnes, Matt, 48

-C-
Cameron, Don, 113
Campbell, J.B., 113,116
Canadiana, 110
Candy Spots, 129,148
Cannonade, 130,204
Cap and Bells, 11
Capt. Hancock, 45
Captain Seth, 57

Careless John, 122
Carey, Thomas, 7
Carpenter, Rachel, 196
Carruthers, Roy, 112
Carry Back, 88
Carry Over, 68
Caruso, 54
Cassidy, Mars, 14
Cassidy, Marshall, 47
Castle,. Vernon, 67
Catrone, Frank, 148
Cauthen, Steve, 181
Cavan, 156
Caveat, 132
Celt, 11,25
Charemma, 45
Chateaugay, 129
Chell, Beverly, 163
Chenery, C.T.,
82,106,190
Chenery, Penny, 188
Childs, Frank, 65
Churchill Downs, 1,22
Cigar, 197
Citation, 61,64,112
Clawson, Dick, 26
Claypool, Bill, 11
Clelland, Odie, 95,207
Clyde Van Dusen, 43
Coaltown, 64
Coastal, 186
Cochran, Gifford, 92
Codex, 202

Cohoes, 45
Cole, A.T., 106
Colin, 11,18
Colloway, J.E., 174
Coltilletti, Frank, 96
Combs, Leslie 2d, 72,107
Commando, 11,18,24
Concordian, 63
Conquistador Cielo, 130
Conway, George, 48
Cook, Neil, 163
Corbin, Junie, 152
Cordero, Angel Jr.,130,204
Corn Husker, 138
Corproate report, 203
Correlation, 84
Corrigan, Ed, 4,7
Cosman, 166
Cougar II, 140
Counterpoint, 114
Count Fleet, 112
Crack Brigade, 55
Crack Time, 198
Creme Fraiche, 135
Creech, Bennie, 56
Croll, Jimmy, 173,196
Cromwell, Thomas, 4
Crosby, Bing, 38
Cruguet, Jean, 135,178
Crusader, 47
Culmone, Joe, 146
Curtis, Charles, 25
Cyrano, 124

-D-
Daisy F., 22
Daly, Marcus, 12,18
Damascus, 149,172

Dancer's Image, 120
Danzig, 4, 130
Danzig Connection, 135
Dark Secret, 68
Dark Star, 117
Darling, Sam, 19
Daryl's Joy, 140
Davis, J.E., 67
Davison, Clarence, 96
Dawn Play, 80
Day, Pat, 136
Decidedly, 110, 156
Dedicate, 73
DeKwiatkowski, Henryk, 130
Deliberator, 126
Delhi, 11
Del Mar, 37
Delp, Bud, 185
Devil's Bag, 132
Devil Diver, 62,97
Devil His Due, 200
Diavolo, 68
Dickey, Robert Livingston, 3
Dice, 68
Dike, 109
Directly, 126
Dispose, 60
Divine Comedy, 141
Dodson, Doug, 81
Dolly Spanker, 25
Dominant, 25
Domino, 10
Dominique,15
Donato, Bob, 175
Donn, Doug, 39
Donn, James. Jr., 39
Donn, James Sr., 39

Donnacona, 14,78
Donoghue, Steve, 30
Don Poggio, 123
Dow, Bill, 163
Downing, C. Gibson, 168
Dr. Carter, 132
Dr. Fager, 172
Dr. Patches, 179
Dreyfus, Jack, 171,198
Drin, 139
Drone, 109
Duchossois, Richard, 36
Dunstan, Nelson, 99
DuPont, Allaire, 121

-E-
Eagle Bird, 96
Easy Goer, 143
Effervescing, 201
Ellsworth, Rex, 70
Enchantment, 29
Endeavour II, 138
Engelhard, Charles, 89
Equipoise, 37
Erb, Dave, 153
Exceller, 141,179
Exodus, 25
Exterminator, 18
Everett, Marj, 36,38
Everett, Mrs. Kelso, 121

-F-
Fabius, 65,116,153
Fairbairn, R.A., 46
Fair Empress, 20
Faireno, 37,46
Fair Grounds, 41,58
Fair Play, 13,18
Fairy Hill, 48

Fairy Wand, 15
Farnsworth, Jack, 163
Fator, Laverne, 93
Faultless, 61
Federal Hill, 74
Feliciano, Paul, 189
Fenian, 9
Fenelon, 68
Ferdinand, 141
Ferraro, Jimmy, 175
Ferrero, Charlie, 86
Fervent, 62
Feustel, Louis, 13
Field, Marshall, 46
Fighting Fox, 58
Find, 73
Fink, Jule, 105,127
Fiore, Frank, 104
Firenze, 11
Firestone, Bert, 39
Firestone, Diana, 39
First Landing, 148
Fisher, Herb
Fisherman, 84
Fitz Herbert, 16,26
Fitzsimmons, James, 31,46,65
Flanders, 203
Flares, 55
Fleming, Don, 161
Flying Ebony, 92
Fogelson, Buddy, 140
Fontaine, Hugh, 153
Forego, 150,173
Forli, 139
Fort Erie, 110
Fowler, Gene, 35
Franklin, Ron, 185
Free America, 115

French, Bob, 201
Friar John, 42
Friede, Ken, 101
Frizette, 11

-G-
Gaillard, Dr. Ernest, 142
Gaines, John, 139,165
Galbreath, J. W., 35,69,106
Gallahadion, 44
Gallant Bloom, 77,84
Gallant Fox, 46,53,92
Gallant Knight, 55
Gallant Man, 74, 148
Gallorette, 82
Garden State Park, 103
Garner, Mack, 43
Garrison, Edward, 31
Garson, Greer, 140
Gautama, 77
Geisha, 116
Gen. Duke, 61, 74, 154
General Assembly, 186
Gerry, Martha F., 173
Gilbert, John, 116
Gilman, Dr. Manuel, 192
Glade, 92
Golden Broom, 14
Gonzalez, Bernie, 180
Gonzalez, Mike, 156
Goodbye Halo, 142
Goodman, Joe, 91
Goshawk, 25
Goyamo, 127
Granville, 46,55
Great Circle, 146
Greek Game, 74
Greek Money, 183

Greeley, Bill, 38
Greenwood, 110
Grey Lag, 21,28,78
Griffin, Mike, 133
Grossman, Fred, 102,162
Guerin, Eric, 84,117
Guggenheim, Harry, 106,128
Gulfstream Park, 37
Gun Bow, 124

-H-
Haggin, James B.A., 11
Haggin, Louis L., 38
Hague, Frank, 103
Hail to Reason, 88
Hal's Play, 152
Ham, Elizabeth, 189
Hammond, Cliff, 42
Hampton, 81
Hancock, A.B., 46
Hancock, A.B. Jr., 107
Hancock, Arthur 3d, 190
Hancock, Seth, 130,190
Handsome Boy, 199
Hanes, Hope, 107
Hanes, John, 106
Hanford, Babe, 122
Hanford, Buddy, 122
Hanford, Carl, 122
Hanford, ira, 79
Happy Go Lucky, 25
Harlan, 203
Harper, Joe, 38
Harry of Hereford, 47
Hartack, Bill, 74,111,122,150
Harthill, Dr. Alex, 134,144
Haskell, Amory, 104

Haskin, Steve, 161
Hastings, 9
Hasty Matelda, 188
Hatley, Mel, 201
Hatton, Charles, 99,190
Havre de Grace, 7,21
Hawley, Sandy, 202
Hawthorne, 1,7
Hayes, Casey, 189
Haynes, Everett, 27
Headley, Hal Price, 38
Head Play, 37
Heartland, 77
He is a Great Deal, 133
Hemingway, Ernest, 100
Henry of Navarre, 9
Hermis, 34
Hertz, Fanny, 113
Hertz, John D., 36,112
Hervey, John, 2
Hialeah, 35,58
Hibbert, Bob, 139
Higdon, Ross, 127
High Bid, 69
High Echelon, 90
High Gun, 77
High Honors, 132
Higley, Jess, 69
Hilarious, 25
Hildebrand, Earl, 31
Hildreth, Sam, 23
Hill, Dr. Jim, 178
Hill Gail, 61,64
Hill Prince, 82
Hill Rise, 111,148
Hindoo, 22
Hirsch, Buddy, 79
Hirsch, Mary, 79
Hirsch, Max, 77

Hitchcock, Thomas,6
Hitting Away, 45
Hollywood Park, 37
Holy Bull, 196
Honest Pleasure, 150
Honeymoon, 63
Hooker, Stewart, 161
Hooper, Fred, 64
Hoop Jr, 98
Hoover, Herbert, 25
Horning, Jack, 39
Hourless, 27
Howard, Charles S., 50
Howard, Lin, 52
Howard, Maxwell, 92
Hubbard, R.D., 39
Hunt, N.B., 167
Hurley, Bill, 44
Hypnotic, 69

-I-
Igual, 80
Inchcape, 28
In Memorium, 30
Insco, 58
Iron Liege, 61,74,155
Iron Mask, 25
Iron Peg, 124
Iselin, Phil, 104
Iverson, Lou, 102

-J-
Jack Atkin, 26
Jack Snipe, 19
Jacola, 52
Jacobs, Hirsch, 85
Jacobs, John, 89
Jacobs, Patrice, 89
James, Basil, 82

James, Frank, 26
Jamie K., 119
Jarvis, Basil, 29
Jeffords, Walter, 47
Jerkens, H. Allen, 195,198
Jerkens, Joseph, 198
Jerome Park, 6,9
Jersey Lightning, 22
Jim Dandy, 46,55
Jockey Club, The, 5
Joe Madden, 26
John Henry, 150,173
John P. Grier, 15
Johnson, James F., 67
Johnstown, 46
Johren, 25
Jones, B.A., 55
Jones, H.A., 57
Jones, Horace, 56
J.O. Tobin, 179
Joyner, A.J., 7,29
Judge, Steve, 126
Judger, 130

-K-
Kauai King, 120
Kayak II, 53
Kearns, Frank, 58,61
Keck, Howard, 109,139
Keene, Foxhall, 10
Keene, James R., 6,10
Keene, John O., 38
Keeneland, 37
Keller, Steve, 37
Kelley, Robert F., 120
Kelly, Grace, 104
Kelly, John B., 104
Kelly, Tom J., 152

Kelso, 98,112
Kenilworth Park, 17
Kennedy Road, 140
Kennelot, 130
Keough, Frank, 91
Kerr, Travis, 74
Kilmer, Willis S., 20,112
King Hairan, 73
King James, 26
King of the Castle, 45
Kirkham, Bob, 132
Kleberg, Bob, 45,78
Klein, Gene, 202
Knapp, Willie, 15,20
Knight, F.D., 20
Kohler, Charles, 26
Kummer, Clarfence, 15
Kurtsinger, Charles, 48

-L-
Ladysman, 37
Lady Violet, 9
Lady's Secret, 203
La Flambe, 46
Lahore, 8
Lang, C. (Chick), 152
Lang, Chick, 92,113
Lardner, Ring, 34
Laskowski, Joe, 102
Latonia, 20,95
La Troienne, 44
Laurel, 7,27
Laurin Lucien, 129,189
Laurin, Roger, 129,189
Lawrin, 58,96
Leach, Dr. M.M., 42
Lee, Dr. John, 121
Lehman, Otto, 36
Leigh, Eugene, 42

Lemon Joe, 57
LeRoy, Mervyn, 38
Letis, Mike, 168
Levy, Dr. Leon, 104
Lewis, William, 34
Life's Magic, 133,202
Ligaroti, 52
Lilly, Marshall, 11,25
Lindheimer, B.E., 36,71
Lion d'Or, 45
Little Current, 130
Loft, George, 78
Loftus, Johnny, 13,31
Longden, Johnny, 82,113,157
Lord Boswell, 81
Loser Weeper, 83
Lowe, Ralph, 148
Lucky Debonair, 148
Lukas, D. Wayne, 133,200
Lukas, Jeff, 203
Luke Blackburn, 24
Luro, Horatio, 110, 137
Lynch, Pat, 199
Lyons, Dan, 101

-M-
McAnally, Ron, 176
McCarron, Chris, 136,206
McCarron, Gregg, 207
McChesney, 26
McCreary, Conn, 62,86
McCulloch, Charles, 36
McCurdy, Charles, 163
McDaniel, Col. David, 24
McDaniel, Henry, 20
McEvoy, John, 161
McGee, 20

McGraw, John, 31
McKnight, W. L., 172
McLaughlin, Jimmy, 31
McLaughlin, Col. R.S., 110
McMurray, William, 34
McVarish, Mrs. A., 175
Mabee, John, 38
Madden, John 28,78
Madere, Colleen, 175
Mad Hatter, 28
Mad Play, 92
Maedic, 48
Maid of Flight, 121
Majestic Prince, 120,157
Make Sail, 128
Malicious, 45
Man o' War, 10,12
Maple, Eddie, 131,195
Markey, Adm. Gene, 182
Markey, Lucille, 59,182
Mark-Ye-Well, 61
Martingale, 29
Martin, Frank, 191
Martin, Royce, 126
Maskette, 11
Masterson, Bat, 34
Match II, 124
Mate, 37
Maxwell, Robert, 163
Mayer, Louis B., 44
May Hempstead, 26
Meade, Don, 43
Mehrtens, Warren, 81
Melton, 12
Menow, 50
Meridian, 8
Middleground, 77,82
Milam, J. Cal, 20

Miller, Clay, 9
Miller, Harvey, 163
Miller, Walter, 18,31
Millerick, Buster, 51
Minger, Mandy, 164
Miss Woodford, 24
Mister Gus, 138
Mitchell, Ben, 112
Moccasin, 109
Modesty, 1,22
Molter, Willie, 74
Money Broker, 117
Mongo, 124
Monmouth Park, 7,103
Mooers, Clifford, 93
Moore, William, 34
Moran, Betty, 135
Mori, Gene, 35
Morrell, Col. Edward, 66
Morgan, J.J., 66
Morgan, James P., 6
Mori, Gene, 103
Morris Park, 6
Morvich, 78
Moseley, Maj. C.C., 139
Mr. Trouble, 83
Murdoch, Rupert, 162
Murphy, Isaac, 31
Muray, Dan, 2
Murray, Hugh, 34
Mustard Plaster, 124
Muttering, 202
My Request, 83

-N-
Nashua, 46,69
Nashville, 73, 138
Nasrullah, 69,108
Nassak, 92

Natalma, 110
Nathenson, Martin 4
Native Dancer, 112
Native Diver, 139
Nearctic, 110
Needles, 153
Nellie Flag, 96
Neloy, Eddie, 171
Nerud, John, 74,168
Never Bend, 128
Neves, Ralph, 139
Newman, Neil, 14
Nickerson, V. J., 176
Nickleby, 152
Nicol, Dave, 31
Nodarse, Vincent, 97
Noor, 116
No Robbery, 129
Norse King, 78
Northern Dancer, 109,148
Nothirdchance, 88
Notter, Joe, 7,19,22
Novelty, 27,32
Numbered Account, 189

-O-
O'Brien, Jerry, 99
O'Brien, Pat, 38
Occupation, 97
Oil Royalty, 166
Oiseau, 13
Old Rosebud, 23
Olin, John, 129
Omaha, 46,55
Omar Khayyam, 23,27
One Eyed King, 128
Onion, 194,199
Optime, 12

Osmand, 92
Otis, Oscar, 99
Our Boots, 126

-P-
Paley, William, 104
Papp, 78
Papyrus, 29
Partez, 202
Pastorella, 18
Pauline Crowley, 93
Paul Jones, 15
Pebbles, 22
Pennant, 25
Pensive, 61
Perlman, J.S., 101,160
Permayne, Bobby, 82
Perrault, 141
Perry, W.H., 109
Personality, 89
Pet Bully, 152
Petee-Wrack, 92
Peterson, Doug, 179
Peter Pan, 11
Pettingill, C.H., 14
Phillips, William C., 162
Philpot, Hurst, 146
Phipps, Mrs. H.C., 50,65
Phipps, Ogden, 44,170
Phipps, Ogden M.,171
Picketer, 29
Pierce, Don, 140
Pincay, Laffit Jr., 131,205
Pincay, laffit Sr., 205
Pincus, Jacob, 9
Platter, 62
Plaut, Lincoln, 102
Playfellow, 67
Polk, Stuart, 93

Pollard, Red, 51
Polly Ann, 21
Polygamous, 54
Polynesian, 63,116
Pompoon, 48,49
Ponder, 64
Pope, George, 110
Porterhouse, 138
Porter's Cap, 60
Potomac, 9
Pratt, Herbert, 67
Pretense, 139
Priceless Gem, 45,88
Prime, William, 42
Princequillo, 108
Prince S., 91
Prince Simon, 108
Princess Turia, 153
Priscilla Ruley, 67
Prove Out, 195,199
Prudery, 25,42
Purchase, 28

-Q-
Quadrangle, 125
Quickly, 113

-R-
Race King, 7,12
Redden, Dr. Ric, 144
Reed, Dr. W.O., 106
Reeves, George, 146
Regret, 18
Reigh Count, 92,112
Reilly, William F., 163
Restigouche, 25
Reveillon, 86
Rialto, 29

Rice, Ada, 152
Rice, Clyde, 201
Rice, Dan, 152
Richardson, Dr. David, 133
Richardson, Noel, 52
Ridan, 183
Riddle, Sam, 10
Ridley, C.C., 15
Riley, 22
Riley, Clinton 4
Riva Ridge, 189
Rivera, Louis Jr., 196
Roach, Hal, 37
Roamer, 23,27
Roberto, 88
Robinson, Jockey Frank, 23,27
Robinson, Clocker Frank, 160,193
Roman Brother, 125
Rosemont, 51
Rosen, Sol, 101,160
Ross, J.K.L., 43,91
Rothstein, Arnold, 79
Rotz, John L., 183
Round Table, 74
Rowe, James. Jr, 25
Rowe, James Sr., 8,12,23
Rubin, Dorothy , 175
Rubin, Sam, 175
Runyon, Damon, 85,90
Ruthless, 9
Ryan, Jim, 132

-S-
Sabin, 130
Saguaro, 127
Sailor, 73
Salt Lake, 203

Salvator, 11
Sande, Earl, 16,29,54,90
Sandler, Michael, 102,161
Santa Anita Park, 37
Saratoga, 69,112
Sarazen, 77
Sceneshifter, 93
Schreier, Mel, 161
Schultz, Dave, 161
Schuttinger, Andy, 16
Schwartz, Frenchy, 160,193
Schwartz, Morton L., 79
Scott, Burr, 91
Scott, Marion duPont, 69
Seabiscuit, 47,50
Searching, 88
Seattle Slew, 141,174,178
Secretariat, 173,188
Segula, 69
Sensitive Prince, 182
Seth, 57
Shafter V., 145
Shake Shake Shake, 204
Sham, 173,191
Sharon Brown, 196
Sheepshead Bay, 9
Sheridan, Gen. Phil, 1
Shoemaker, Bill, 71, 145
Shilling, Carrol, 31
Shipman, Evan, 99
Shulman, Stan, 162
Shut Out, 97
Sideral, 78
Silbert, Harry, 146
Silver Spoon, 116
Sinclair, Harry 25,28
Singerman, Martin, 162
Sir Barton, 17,43,91

Sir Gallahad III, 46
Sir Modred, 4
Sky Beauty, 200
Slew o'Gold, 132
Smathers, E.E., 26
Smith, Ace, 93
Smith, Frank, 43
Smith, Mike, 196
Smith, Tom, 50
Snowden, Hal, 174
Snyder, Albert, 98
Social Outcast, 73
Somethingroyal, 188
Sommer, Sigmund, 191
Sovinski, Vic, 156
Spectacular Bid, 150,185
Spencer, Henry, 24
Spend A Buck, 135,204
Spendthrift, 10
Spy Song, 81
Stagehand, 51,92
Star de Naskra, 181
Star Fancy, 47
Star Gaze, 67
Stephan's Odyssey, 135
Stephens, Lucille, 129
Stephens, Woody, 105,126
Stewart, Jimmy, 38
Straight Deal, 45
Straight Face, 120
Stokes, Albert, 66
Stromboli, 23,27
Strub, Dr. Charles, 37
Strub, Robert, 37
Stymie, 82,86
Summer Tan, 69
Sun Briar, 20
Sunday Silence, 142

Superman, 25
Swale, 132
Swaps, 46,70,147
Sweat, Eddie, 192
Sweep, 11,48
Sweitzer, Robert, 35
Sword Dancer, 148
Sysonby, 7,11,12

-T-
Tabasco Cat, 203
Talon, 138
Tannenbaum, Harold, 162
Taral, Fred, 10
Tappan, George, 66
Taylor, E.P., 109
Taylor, Karen, 178
Taylor, Mickey, 178
Taylor, Frank, 10
Taylor, Matt, 161
Tenney, Mesh, 70
Terlingua. 202
Tevis, Lloyd, 11
The Bart, 150,176
The Finn, 23
The Parader, 24
Thistledown, 95
Thomas, E.R., 34
Thomas, Lucy C., 34
Thompson, Charlie, 91
Thompson, H.J., 42
Thread o'Gold, 62
Thunderer, 25
Thunder Gulch, 202
Time Supply, 37
Tim Tam, 156
Tolleson, Roi, 34
Tom Fool, 8,120

Tompion, 122,148
Tompkins, Gwynne, 48
Tomy Lee, 148
Top Row, 37
Tradition, 12
Traffic Judge, 70,128
Trager, Mike, 168
Trojan, 67
Trotsek, Harry, 173
Tropical Park, 60
Tryster, 25,42
Tufano, Sam, 76
Tumble Wind, 139
Turcotte, Ron, 189
Turkish Trousers, 140
Turner, Billy Jr., 178
Turner, Nash, 26
Twenty Grand, 37
Twilight Tear, 61
Two Lea, 61,116
Twosy, 62
Tyrant, 11

-U-
Upset, 14

-V-
Vagrancy, 69
Valenzuela, Ismael, 123
Valenzuela, Pat, 142
Vanderbilt, A.G., 52,116
Veitch, John, 181
Velasquez, Jorge, 181,206
Vexatious, 25
Venetian Way, 156
Vienna, 62
Villa, Pancho, 57
Vosburgh, Walter, 8,13

-W-
Waldman, Leo, 161
War Admiral, 47
War Glory, 47
War Minstrel, 51
Ward, Sherrill, 126, 173
Warner, Harry, 38
Warner, Jack, 38
Washington Park, 1,36,71
Werblin, David, 36,168
Westrope, Jack, 115
Whichone, 25,55
Whirlaway, 59,97
Whisk Broom, 7
Whiskery, 92
Whiteley, Frank, 149,172
Whitney, Helen, 98
Whitney, H.P., 6,18,25,67
Whitney, J.H, 45
Whitney, Liz, 138
Whitney, William C., 22,26
Whittaker, Edwin, 190
Whittingham, Charlie, 73,126, 136
Whittingham, Joe, 136
Widener, George D., 62
Widener, Joseph E. 10,35,92
Wildair, 25
Wilkins, Katherine, 163
Williams, Bert, 58
Williams, William H., 162
Wilson, A.G., 37
Windsor, 20,27
Winfrey, Bill, 117
Winn, Col. Matt, 22
Winning Colors, 202
Wise Margin, 76

Wolfe, John, 1-3
Wolfson, Lou, 180
Woodbine, 110
Woodward, William Jr.,46,69
Woodward, William Sr., 40,67
Woolf, George, 37,50
Woolf, Herbert, 58
Workman, Sonny, 55
Wright, Lucille, 58
Wright, Wayne, 49
Wright, Warren, 58,96

-Y-
Yank, Albert, 202
Ycaza, Manuel, 128,172,183
Yellow Hand, 15
Young, William T., 203
Your Host, 82,121

-Z-
Zev, 28
Zeveley, William, 29
Ziegler, William Jr., 62